Voluntary Death in Japan

Voluntary Death in Japan

Maurice Pinguet

Translated by Rosemary Morris

POLITY PRESS

This English translation copyright © Polity Press 1993
First published in French as *La mort volontaire au Japon*
© Éditions Gallimard 1984
First published 1993 by Polity Press in association with Blackwell Publishers and with the assistance of the French Ministry of Culture.

Editorial office:
Polity Press
65 Bridge Street
Cambridge CB2 1UR, UK

Marketing and production:
Blackwell Publishers
108 Cowley Road
Oxford OX4 1JF, UK

238 Main Street
Suite 501
Cambridge, MA 02142, USA

All rights reserved. Except for the quotation of short passages for the purposes of criticism and review, no part of this publication may be reproduced, stored in a retrieval system, or transmitted, in any form or by any means, electronic, mechanical, photocopying, recording or otherwise, without the prior permission of the publisher.

Except in the United States of America, this book is sold subject to the condition that it shall not, by way of trade or otherwise, be lent, re-sold, hired out, or otherwise circulated without the publisher's prior consent in any form of binding or cover other than that in which it is published and without a similar condition including this condition being imposed on the subsequent purchaser.

ISBN 0 7456 0870 1

A CIP catalogue record for this book is available from the British Library and the Library of Congress.

Typeset in 10 on 12 pt Sabon
by Graphicraft Typesetters Ltd., Hong Kong
Printed in Great Britain by T.J. Press Ltd., Padstow, Cornwall.

This book is printed on acid-free paper.

In memory of Roland Barthes

La mort si difficile et si facile

(Death, so difficult and so easy)
                                   Paul Éluard

Contents

Translator's Note		viii
1	CATO'S HARAKIRI	1
2	THE ARITHMETIC OF SUICIDE	14
3	TOWARDS A THEORY OF SUICIDE	21
4	SUICIDE AS SYMPTOM	30
5	THE DAWN OF HISTORY	51
6	VIOLENCE AT A DISTANCE	65
7	THE MARTIAL ART OF DYING WELL	77
8	GIVING UP THE BODY	97
9	THE THEATRE OF CRUELTY	122
10	LOVE AND DEATH	153
11	THE TRADITION OF SACRIFICE	188
12	INTO THE ABYSS	210
13	SOME NIHILIST VIGNETTES	243
14	MISHIMA: THE LAST ACT	263
Notes		286
Glossary of Japanese Terms		310
Index		350

Translator's Note

Translations of works not published in French were made for the original edition of this book by Jacqueline Pigeot, Professor of Japanese Literature, University of Paris VII. Where English translations of the works involved exist, I have referred to them. However, if no English translation exists, or if the English translation is unsatisfactory, I have translated directly from the French.

1
Cato's Harakiri

'Never could Jupiter have seen a fairer thing upon earth than Cato's suicide.' So said Seneca. And yet, if we read Plutarch's account of this voluntary death, the most glorious in Western history, it becomes a maze of confusions and contradictions. Cato's relatives, friends and sons realize that he intends to kill himself, and during the evening meal they take away the sword which he keeps hanging by his bed. Cato wonders whether it would be better to demand the sword, thus perhaps making his intentions plain, or to feign indifference and so deceive those around him by pretending that his decision to die is not yet final. Although his secret resolve is firm and clear, and there is no hesitation in him over the deed which must be done and over what that deed will mean, he must still resort to cunning and violence: to the very last, he must continue the exhausting struggle against those who seek to save him from his own decision. He is reduced to striking his servants, scolding his sons, arguing with his friends. Eventually his sword is restored to him. 'Now I am my own man again!' he says. He then reclines on his bed and resumes his reading of the *Phaedo*, looking to Plato to provide a subject for his last thoughts. He falls asleep, reawakens, takes up the book, sleeps again:

> The litle birdes began to chirpe, and Cato fel againe in a litle slumber. But thereuppon Butas returned, and brought him word that all was quiet in the haven, and there was no sturre. Then Cato bad him goe his way, and

shut to the dore after him, and layed him downe in his bed, as though he had ment to have slept out all the rest of the night. Butas backe was no sooner turned, but Cato taking his naked sword in his hand, thrust it into his breast: howbeit the sweling of his hand made the blowe so weak, that it killed him not presently, but drawing on to his latter ende, he fell downe upon his bedde, and made such a noyse with his fall (overthrowing a litle table of geometry hard by his bedde) that his servaunts hearing the noyse, gave a great shreeke for feare. Thereuppon his sonne and his friendes ranne into the chamber, and found him all of a gore bloud, and the most part of his bowels comming out of his bodye, him selfe being yet alive, and seeing them. They were all striken with such sorow to behold it, that at the first they were so amazed, as they could not tel what to say to it. His Phisitian comming to him, he went about to put in his bowels againe which were not perished, and to sow up his wound. But Cato comming to him selfe, thrust backe the Phisitian, and tare his bowells with his owne handes, and made his wound very great, and immediatly gave up the ghost.[1]

THE CODE OF SUICIDE

Such was Cato's harakiri. The opposition of his nearest and dearest only made it all the more terrible. Now let us try to imagine a suicide under broadly similar circumstances, the evening after a terrible defeat: that of a Japanese warrior of a few centuries ago. There is the same unswerving resolve, the same sharp sword, the blood spurting from the pierced trunk[2] – but those closest to him show their devotion only through silence and respect. Indeed, his dearest friend offers to cut off his head with a sword-stroke so as to shorten his last moments. The whole scene is orderly, and becomes a ceremonial. The sad necessity to dissemble with those he loves, the fresh surge of violence when he reopens a wound which overzealous hands have sought to close, the effort of arguing up to the last moment so as to give the prop of reason to the hard choice of death: none of this is inflicted on that Japanese warrior who refuses to acknowledge the supremacy of his vanquisher.

There is a tradition of voluntary death, going back to the time of Kamakura, which suggests what decisions might be taken, and codifies the ritual acts to be performed and the sentiments to be exhibited. It may well be that this tradition, which is confined to the warrior class (*bushi*, samurai), and is in any case fairly recent (it was not established until the twelfth century), has not governed every case of voluntary death known in Japanese history. Alongside those suicides which were done in due form there were many others which rejected such models and were improvised as circumstances might dictate. But the essential point is that in Japan, there was never any objection in principle to the free choice of death – a question on which Western ideology has always found it difficult to pronounce.[3]

In the beginning, opinion was divided among the various schools of antiquity: while Cynics and Stoics accepted suicide as legitimate, Platonists and Peripatetics were against it, using already some of the arguments which St Augustine was to take up again when he constructed the root-and-branch prohibition which Christianity has maintained from century to century ever since. The great philosophers continue their disputes in Cato's mind as he seeks to make his suicide into a rational act: 'Goe your way therefore hardily unto my sonne, and tell him, that he must not thinke to compell his father unto that, which he can not prove good unto him by reason.' Cato, a true citizen of the *polis*, philosopher and warrior combined, desires to die lucidly and with deliberation. Now or never is the time when his acts must mirror his thoughts. During his last days at Utica he frequents Apollonides, a Stoic, and Demetrius, a Peripatetic; perhaps the latter, following his master Aristotle, maintained that to kill oneself is to wrong the community to which one belongs.

It is precisely in order to keep faith with his community that Cato desires to die: to serve his city, its liberties and laws, up to the supreme sacrifice. He has fought to defend the liberties of the people, but Caesar is victorious, and the liberties will perish – or at least, those of the senatorial aristocracy. No force of arms can break the power of this new master; in this Rome on the threshold of empire nothing, even tyrannicide, can block the new form of power that is Caesarism. Cato knows perfectly well that his vanquisher would willingly pardon him and grant him his life – if only he would ask for it. But it is that admission of defeat which he rejects: 'For if I would save my life by Caesars grace, I could do it, if I would but go unto him: howbeit I will not be bound to a tyran for injustice. For it is an injustice in him to take upon him, as a Lord and soveraine to save a mans life, when him selfe hath no authority to command.'

RENUNCIATION AND REVOLT

Thus Cato kills himself in token of his rejection of that sovereign power: in a republic, only the law has power over life and death. Mercy is an abuse of the law. But the republic is passing and with it the liberties safeguarded by the law; Cato chooses to pass away with them, and thus grant them some chance of rebirth. His act acknowledges irremediable defeat; but by taking the failure to its uttermost extreme, it becomes also an appeal to the future. Cato's suicide, like all suicides, is ambiguous: it is both renunciation and revolt, silence and outcry, despair and protest. Like Janus, it looks both towards the past, making it unalterable, and towards the future, making it possible. For the appeal of that death has continued to echo through the Western consciousness: Montaigne, Machiavelli, Rousseau... We can now say that Cato was justified in wagering upon a future which seemed so improbable at the time: he did indeed help to revive the principles which were dying with him. His life was the price which showed up their true worth, and the privileges of his class became the liberties of the future. Death by chance – from an accident or an illness – may be easier, but it is all the more harrowing because it is meaningless. It is voluntary death which can take on meaning, and even if such meaning is not apparent on the first analysis (and there are some suicides whose motives are crazy and entangled), we can still feel its presence, and we know if we remain patient and attentive the act will at last speak for itself.

Cato's death marks a watershed in the history of antiquity. The Republic of citizens was succeded by the Empire; heads of old families became officials of Caesar; civil liberties gave way to the private rights of individuals in isolation. Clashes between leaders, all equal under the law, are replaced by service to the state. In the beginning, the city-state, founded by tyrannicides and lawgivers, whose emergence finds an echo in the Oedipus tragedies of Aeschylus and Sophocles, had succeeded in halting the expansion of oriental despotism at Marathon and Salamis. But under Philip and Alexander, and later under Julius Caesar and Augustus, the power of the one man arose again, this time from within. The debilitating rivalries of the Greek cities, and later the overextended conquests of the Romans and pressure from the urban masses, made new forms of political organization indispensable. A good many of the liberties which the citizens of the Republic had freely granted to one another were called in question – even, at the last, the most radical of them, the freedom to die.

Up to the second century AD, people accused of high treason could, by committing suicide, at least spare their heirs the confiscation of their property. Then an avid treasury eliminated this advantage. Subjects of the empire did have certain rights, granted them by the legal codes, but little by little they allowed the right to dispose of their own lives to be wrested from them. *Tempestiva mors*: the difficult art of dying at the right moment had long been seen as the best proof of reasoned courage in the face of adverse fortune and failing health. But it was already fading out two centuries before it fell victim to Christian reprobation. For Diocletian's scribes, voluntary death was nothing more than an act of madness: *aliqua furoris rabie constrictus*. And when, 150 years later, the Council of Arles spoke of the suicide as *diabolico persecutus furore*, it was merely repeating the verdict pronounced in the name of Diocletian – the sworn enemy of Christianity.[4]

FREE DEATH OF A MAN ENSLAVED

It would be true to say that the citizens of Athens and Rome had taken on two dissimilar attitudes to suicide, reflecting the bipartite structure of their society. They accepted it as legitimate if the perpetrator was one of themselves, a free man turning on himself the sovereignty implied in his status as such. And if some public affair seemed to justify the act, it was recognized as having the greatest value. But the political arena existed alongside the domestic one: in his own house, the citizen was master over his children, his womenfolk and his slaves. Here public law (Greek *dike*, Latin *ius*) intersected with another, earlier law (*themis, fas*), the law of the family incarnate (or so she hoped) in Antigone. The invention of the city-state had done nothing to abrogate it.

Under the aegis of public law, the citizens' homes had to be ruled by an order based on custom. If one of his domestic subjects killed himself, the master of the house could not accept the legitimacy of the act, for it would often imply censure of his authority, a challenge to his power, and diminution of his capital. He would see it as a rebellion, and perforce condemn it in principle. He might approve of such a gesture in another man's house, and admire it in the political arena, but at home he would try to conceal it, or else to devalue it as the act of a 'bad lot', capable of anything and good for nothing, lunatic, crazy. Thus, the ideology of the city-states of antiquity opposed two types of voluntary death: the master's, legitimate in principle and at times glorious, and the slave's, assumed to be shameful and unworthy. The value of the act was inseparable from the status of its perpetrator, freeborn or slave-born. The universal individual, the homogeneous subject whose rights were to be codified by jurists under Diocletian and Justinian, did not yet exist. The master's uplifting suicide found a silent echo in the deep, dark despair of his oppressed slave.

THE DESPAIR OF THE SLAVE

And yet the suicide of the slave has no less meaning than that of his master. In his despair we find the first stirrings of revolt, and his protest resounds in the silence of death like a reproach. By killing himself the slave cries out against the wrongs he has suffered: he gives his life in order to lay down a supreme value, that of justice, and to claim it as universal, beyond the inequitable duality of social conditions. The slave who (following Hegel's schema) drops out of the moral contest and resigns himself to a painful existence, gaining no other advantage than survival, has understood, at last, that nothingness is preferable to life without justice. Before this moment he would have accepted the loss of all freedoms in order to live. But now, by giving up life, he discovers that he has always had one fundamental, absolute freedom, fearful but inalienable, always on offer but with death as the price. In his last moment, through his voluntary death, he tastes the intoxication of this reborn liberty, blooting out previous defeats, cleaving institutionalized inequalities, sweeping away resignation.

The values of liberty and justice, which the citizen would defend to the death (along with the laws of his city and the privileges of his class), now shine out, in the shadows of the house-place, through the suicide of a slave. His death buys them supremacy and universality, within and beyond the house walls, transcending social conditions. At last they can show themselves pure, unmixed with the lust for power of a city-state which draws strength from its virtues, just as a merchant grows rich from his honesty. Now they are a pure response to a thirst for liberty and justice, an absolute, gratuitous and insatiable thirst experienced to the full – by one about to plunge into the endless indifference of annihilation.

SLAVERY INTO ETHICS

Sometimes it could happen that a slave aroused by injustice began to think, instead of killing himself. He could become a philosopher, like Epictetus. Was not every philosopher, even if freeborn, on the slave's side by reason of his vocation as a thinker? A master neither worked nor thought, and when he spoke, speech led to action. But the servant did think. The city-state might keep him out of politics, but could not stop him looking hard at it from the outside and creating an image which would give him the satisfaction denied him by reality. Thus were ideologies woven: ambiguous as dreams, they allowed society to sleep in peace so long as they themselves were allowed to give a symbolic expression to its haunting tensions, and an imaginary solution to its latent conflicts. If a philosopher set out to see through social divisions to the unity of the human condition, he would end up seeing things from the viewpoint of the slave – the forerunner of the intellectual. The thinking mind considers those privileges of the master, denied to so many, and finds them unworthy of consideration. Sweet consolation, to despise what you cannot have – and do not want, if so may others are without it!

Nietzsche said that resentament was a necessary fuel for the thinking mind when forging its ideals. The citizen's freedom is now to be described as a freedom in appearance only. True freedom cannot depend on an accident of birth; it must dwell purely in the will of each and every man. You always have as much of it as you truly want. Some thinkers were to uphold the favourite Stoic paradox: that every man has complete freedom on the sole condition that he becomes conscious of himself as being absolutely free. On a throne or in fetters, a man is always free in himself: his body may be constrained, fear and desire may confuse a troubled mind, but the self which is self-aware is invulnerable.

THE DIGNITY OF THE SAGE

At his last meal, Cato of Utica expounded and defended the Stoic opinion 'that only the good man is free, and all the evil be slaves'. In which case social inequalities are irrelevant – but the duality of the ancient *polis* has in fact been transposed into this ideal division between the sage and the fool, the good man and the evil. The slave can become a sage and so outdo his light-minded master – but only by accepting, within his very self, another master: the *logos*, whose decrees are to be obeyed. After which he is master, infinitely free, in his own mind – but on condition that that mind must be ready at any moment to sacrifice the body to which it is bound. The freedom of the sage can be absolute only if it is identified with the freedom to die. Cato's intimates rightly concluded, from this exposé of Stoic ideas, that he had already silently resolved to kill himself. He had digested defeat and gained access to the dignity of the sage, which nothing in this world can overcome.

The individual's freedom to die, vaunted later by Seneca, paralleled the death of civil liberties towards the end of the Roman civil wars. Stoicism, then in its closing stages of development, made a great point of proclaiming, as if in consolation, that one of Nero's subjects could be no less free than a senator in times past – if he truly willed to be so. Except that the freedom to die had replaced the freedom to act. The public arena had contracted, and the state had become the private estate of the emperor, who administered it as such through an apparatus of military might, fiscal efficiency and organized spying on political opponents. Citizens had become subjects, forced back into their private lives, their lonely destinies. Already the death of the Stoic had ceased to be the glorious end of the master refusing to accept defeat, and had become the obscure suicide of a servant overcome by the unfairness of his lot: an empty protest which could only exacerbate the despotism of the truly despotic. Disgraced subjecs of Tiberius or Caligula would hasten to obey the power which struck them down, and seemed to be denouncing themselves to their suspicious Prince rather than censuring his conduct. The Prince would proclaim himself deeply hurt by this ungrateful way of pre-empting his clemency. By killing himself, or fleeing, the victim acknowledged his own guilt and condemnation.

But such strangled protests could do nothing to change the order of things; soon they no longer served even to protect inheritances from the avidity of the imperial fisc. In the absence of civil liberties, everything depended on the individuality of the ruler and on pure chance. Deafened by passion to the protests of his pedagogues, the Prince might become a Nero; equally, he might become a paragon of humanity like Titus or Marcus Aurelius. Stoics strove to counter public ills by educating the individual, but this ethical endeavour could do little to modify the imperial power. Their protests, even when pouring out of opened veins, still had the feeble accents of philosophical pedantry.

THE SUPREMACY OF METAPHYSICS

A more effective barrier to the excesses of authority was constituted by the metaphysics of Plato in their coupling with Christianity. But first the consciousness of antiquity had to accept an absolute master, the one God in whose name even the freedom to die – the last trace of republican privilege, the shield of the Stoic attempting to defend his dignity in the face of despotism – had to be renounced. Apparently the King of Heaven demanded that sacrifice in exchange for his protection – for he could indeed curb the arbitrary power of his earthly counterpart to any degree the mind was capable of grasping. Even before the triumph of Christianity, the new morality of submission to a supreme Good had been casting doubt on the art of timely suicide. No doubt God, like the emperor, had reason to complain: any suicide rebelled against his purposes and rebuffed his grace. The interdict even extended eventually to the self-inflicted euthanasia of a sick man escaping from pain, which Plato had found acceptable. Thus the Epicurean weighing-up of pleasures against pains came to seem as outrageous as the Stoical vaunting of the dignity of the sage. Epicurus was condemned with especial venom because he sought to relieve human anxiety by denying divine providence and the immortality of the soul. The courageous 'reasoned departure' commended by hedonists and eudaemonists was now despised as cowardly and insane: almighty God must have sole charge of death.

Thus the denunciation of suicide, which was to be progressively reinforced through the first Christian centuries up to the Council of

Arles (452), had a long prehistory in the speculations of antiquity. Aristotle notes that the sovereignty of the city-state outweighs that of the individual over his own existence; by killing himself, a man does the state an injustice, and the punishment laid down in the ancient laws (his right hand was cut off and buried separately from the rest of him) was just. But this argument, based on civic morality, probably did less to discredit the idea of suicide than the metaphysical view argued in detail by Plato: the sovereignty of the individual must yield to the sovereignty of the Good – that is, of God – and man must leave God to decide the time of his death. Even earlier, Pythagoras had condemned suicide, likening its perpetrators to soldiers deserting the post allotted to them by God.

Plato reinforces this idea of submission with an even more weighty image: 'we men are in some sort of prison, and... One ought not to release oneself from it or run away.' Thus Socrates, in the *Phaedo*, just before drinking the hemlock. In fact he was only repeating a formula used in the celebration of the Mysteries. By 'prison' he presumably means a sort of pen for slaves or farm animals; he adds: 'it is gods who care for us, and for the gods we men are among their belongings'. Thus, in words also used by the mystical salvation cults and the Orphic sects, was established the metaphysical condemnation of suicide which was to endure in the West up to the present day. 'Well, if one of your belongings were to kill itself, without your signifying that you wanted it to die, wouldn't you be vexed with it, and punish it, if you had any punishment to hand?' As a token of punishment, self-murderers should be buried in some remote location: 'they shall be buried in those borders of the twelve districts which are barren and nameless, without note, and with neither headstone or name to indicate the tombs.' Thus Plato, in the *Laws*, spreading the mantle of philosophy over the atavistic horror which the populace attaches to the idea of suicide in any civilization – including, probably to a not much lesser extent, our own.[5]

From then onwards, metaphysics and religion saw all suicides as approximating to that of a faithless and trouble-making slave, despairing of his master and destroying part of the latter's capital assets. God's rights over the human race were seen in the image of the master's proprietorial rights over his domestic slave in the society which Plato knew. The world described in his ideology must be like a vast household, subject to the will of the head of the family. All slaves? It could be put more tactfully: all sons, therefore all brothers. One Lord? Better to say one father, whose will is Love, whose law is Justice. But Socrates makes no bones about the subjection which is demanded: 'it is the gods who care for us, and for the gods we men are among their belongings.' Stalin could have found, in Plato, a ready-made formula instead of his famous, and naively revealing, description of his fellow men as 'the most valuable capital asset'. Varying styles of domination, real and imagined, may be opposed to one another and restrict one another, but the formulae by which they are expressed show a strong family likeness.

THE SUFFERING CONSCIOUSNESS

It was a hard condition which a nascent metaphysics sought to lay upon mankind: it was slavery itself, and men must resign themselves to it if they wished to attain the ideal of universality promised by speculative thinkers. Social divisions counted for nothing beside the division of metaphysics: masters and servants, men and women, fathers and sons, all were alike prisoners in the cave. Thus, differences among living *beings* were both reflected and deflected by ontological difference, which pointed to the unity of the Immutable Being beyond all divers *states* of being. '*Re*flected' back on themselves, and *de*flected in that, while ideology did indeed echo the contradictions within society, it also played tricks with them by finding in them an imaginary solution. With Plato begins the odyssey of the suffering consciousness and its inexhaustible duality: eternity against time, truth against seeming, immortal soul against perishable body, essence against existence, the other world against this world. Only the Good can lay claim to sovereignty. God, we are told, is perfect, wholly innocent of the evils which dwell in us. The old Homeric deities, who knew hatred, love, laughter and weeping, and who breathed the unbridled passions of life into mortal hearts, were now to yield to the serene perfection of the Absolute.

Now in the name of the eternal God, the idea of 'becoming' could be put to scorn. A sort of resentment was now felt towards anything born to die: it nourished and perpetuated the idea of transcendence. Once, poetry had exalted the uncertainties of reality, and men were uplifted by the pride of fulfilling their destiny upon earth; now everything subject to time was to be belittled. Socrates would have no poets in his ideal city. He marks a decline, as Nietzsche observed. It is quite hard to reconstruct, from the disjointed fragments of pre-Socratic texts, that early time when philosophers had not yet yielded to the temptation of despising earthly things. Thus passes, in Plato, the world of which Pindar sang: 'Oh my soul, long not for eternal life, but till to exhaustion the field of the possible.' That Pindaric soul was not yet immortal; its nobility consisted in not wishing to be so. It turned down an unending future out of loyalty to the world of the present moment. Such is the natural bent of the Japanese soul also. It does not seek to thwart death or blunt its cutting edge. Whereas the Western soul since Plato has measured itself along eternity and so become its slave, in comparison with the soul's salvation, the deeds poets sing have seemed futile, and speculation has driven poetry away.

Speculation, specularity; anxiety for the future provokes speculation on the Beyond, while speculative thought reflects reality inverted in idealism. Thus did the ancient city-state dissolve into the universal Empire, in which single individuals could no longer unite in mortal action, but only in the dream which consoles us for its absence. Philosophers did try to curb that new form of power which their universalism had nurtured. When the Empire threatened to slide into despotism, men looked to Stoicism and Platonism to restrain it. The hortatory power of Stoicism was not to outlast the death-throes of the *polis* within the Empire. Metaphysical resistance was to prove more durable, because it was to amalgamate with the world of Christian thought. At that point deep feelings were to shake the theoretical edifice of Platonism. And the monopoly of power would be broken once and for all once the Church had the strength to rise up against the state and grapple with it through centuries of dialectic, a dialectic which was to form the warp and woof of Western history down to modern times.

IMMANENT JAPAN

Cato's suicide was a judgement not only on Caesar but also on metaphysics – on that very Plato whom he had read in his final hour. And equally, it was metaphysics which weighted his hesitation and stirred up the resistance which he had to overcome before that horrible gesture, the two-handed disembowelling. If Japanese culture does indeed have an originality worthy of our sustained attention, it must ultimately be sought in an *absence* of metaphysics and idealism.

No doubt medieval Japan, like the Christian West, had culled from Buddhism some notion of salvation and even (among the 'Pure Land' sects) some upsurges of intense fideism, of hope in another world. But such religious sensibilities never imposed a single metaphysical perspective, and never could the absolutism of eternity become a guiding principle in life. Against the universalizing tendency of the Platonist or Christian West we can set the pluralism of Japan; against our doctrines of transcendence, an instinctive and primordial phenomenalism which acknowledges no absolute beyond the perceptible. From the beginnings of their history we see in the Japanese an attachment to the here and now, in this world. It seems that as one goes eastward, there comes a point where metaphysics loses its fascination: it is all-powerful in India, but holds no interest – or at least no dominating interest – for the Chinese mind. And its last traces fade out in the soil of Japan.[6]

Even the arrival of Buddhism was unable to alter this native attitude of mind. Any reasonable man has enough cares in this world: to the Japanese mind, it is rather spineless to worry about another life when all our pleasures and all our duties are to be found in this one. The stern law of transmigration, so distressing to the Indian soul, can be smilingly dismissed:

> This life of ours, let me enjoy;
> In the other life I do not care,
> An insect or a bird,
> Or whatever I become.

This little eighth-century poem by Otomo no Tabito gives us the measure of the transformation wrought in Buddhism: if it conquered Japan, it was then to be taken over by Japanese phenomenalism and swallowed up in the notion of immanence. Did men still aim to escape becoming (*samsara*) and leave a world in which all living was pain? The Japanese Buddhist masters have less to say about deliverance from all life and more to say about freedom in this present life. The Tendai sect seek to make themselves into living Buddhas in the human body. Towards the end of the ninth century the monk Annen said trenchantly that 'Existence in this world is none other than Nirvana.'

According to Kukai, the illustrious founder of the Shingon sect, men and Buddhas have the same essence. Even the Amidists, who do hope in another world, stress rather this present life and the duties it implies. As for Zen – so well suited to the Japanese mind – there is no current of religious thought more resolutely centred and concentrated on this world, this present life, this body, things as they are, what is happening here and now, at the ever-present moment. Illumination (*satori*) is a unifying intuition which annihilates all dualism, all discrimination inscribed in words themselves. Dogen (1200–53), the great exponent of the Soto school, bends opposites back on each other: 'Impermanence is the nature of the Buddha.' Thus all the imported explanations of Buddhism are explained anew, in the direction of an immediate apprehension of reality: 'The Buddha Shakyamuni taught us that appearance was reality. The opening of flowers, the falling of leaves, *that* is reality. And yet fools think that in the world of Truth there could be no opening of flowers nor falling of leaves.'

BEING IS TIME

Dogen puts it succinctly: 'time is nothing other than being, and every being is time.' Surely no one has ever conceived a more radical rejection of metaphysical difference. Many and various are the traditions – Zoroastrianism, Vedantism, Judaism, Platonism, Christianity, Islam, Manicheism – which through the centuries have sought being beyond time; all their very foundations collapse under the formula 'all being is time', *Sein ist Zeit*. Dogen seems to be taking us back to the very dawn of Greek thought, towards Heraclitus and Pindar, before eternity cast its shadow over life. Through him the modern West can rediscover, after a lengthy navigation, some hints of a forgotten origin. Twenty-five centuries of metaphysics separate Heraclitus from Nietzsche: it is a long journey. At this point in our history we are ready to attend to the reflections which Zen – for example – can induce in us. Perhaps, as our understanding of things and writings Japanese, and the works which express them, deepens, we shall be able to advance further along paths of thought which are opening up beyond the old notions of transcendence. Can we escape from a metaphysics opposed to right limits? dispel that accursed consciousness which misrepresents every 'better' in the name of the Good? block the spring of nihilism which annihilates not death but all that dies? Perhaps Japan can indeed emerge from the depths of its own history and encourage us in our arduous hope.

Death in Japan bears few signs of the horrors which fear of another world casts over our decision to die – that spirit of Hamlet which broods over the West: 'To die, to sleep, / To sleep, perchance to dream. / – Aye, there's the rub . . .' The decision to die, and the death-stroke, belong still to this world: it is from this world that they gain meaning, and death itself, as Epicurus would have it, is reduced to a nothingness which is not yet, which is never 'here'. Killing oneself? a rare event, no doubt, and a fearful one for a people so full of vitality: a fierce excess, but one which is accepted and respected; an austere necessity, but one which Japan resolved never to surrender on principle, as if she understood how much of the essence of grandeur and serenity vanishes from a civilization when its people let slip their freedom to die.

2

The Arithmetic of Suicide

Despite what has just been said, people are no more inclined to kill themselves in Japan than they are in the West: rather more than in France, maybe, but less than in Germany.

However, Japan is often seen by us, and possibly by the Japanese themselves, as the 'suicide nation'. Such was, in any case, the title chosen by Okazaki, a demographer, for a book published in Tokyo in 1960. But it is an illusion, as the statistics show.

Let us compare a few recent figures. Table 1 shows the suicide rate per 100,000 of the population in France and in Japan. The Japanese rate, in the 1960s at least, remained quite low on the scale of industrialized nations.[1] Japan has never been subject to the Christian or Islamic prohibition on suicide, but it is still not the 'suicide nation', whatever people may think. The rate is much higher in Hungary, Denmark and Austria.

It is true that the statistics noted by Okasaki in 1960 were much more disturbing (see table 2).

A WAVE OF SUICIDES

During the same period in France, the suicide rate hovered around 16 per thousand. Thus the Japanese figure for the 1950s was among the highest in the world. Okazaki was not wholly mistaken when he dubbed

Table 1   Suicides per 100,000 of population

	1965	1966	1967
Japan	14.7	15.2	12.9
France	15	15.5	15.5

Table 2   Suicides per 100,000 of population

	1954	1955	1956	1957
Japan	23.4	25.2	24.5	23.9

Japan the 'suicide nation', but he was wrong to suggest that this phenomenon, in fact temporary, was a permanent feature of Japanese society. It was merely a wave of suicides which swept across Japan over about ten years, shortly after the end of the war – rather like a tidal wave following upon an earthquake, the earthquake being the War in the Pacific. One can see why the statisticians were excited: if the number of suicides in 1947 is set at 100, then in 1955 the rate in Japan rose to 160, while in France it rose only to 125, and in America, dropped to 88. A 60 per cent increase in eight years: but it was only a secondary effect, which was soon to fade out. After 1960 the Japanese rate returned to 21.1 per 100,000, before dropping to 12.9 in 1967.

In 1964 the sociologist René Duchac published an article in which he succeeded in localizing the effects of the devastating suicide wave – which was in fact retreating (though he was not to know this) just at the time when he was studying it.[2] He showed clearly that the rise was due to a large number of suicides by young men: taking only males into account, the Japanese rate in 1954 (32.5) was the second highest in the world. But a few years later (1960) it dropped to fifth (24.6), then (1964) to thirteenth (17.5), behind France, which was tenth in 1964 with a rate of 22.4 suicides per 100,000 males in the population.

CONSEQUENCES OF THE HECATOMB

How are we to explain the suicide wave we have detected in the 1950s? Can we make out what the statistics are saying, in their elliptical way?

What is society, as a body, trying to tell us through the strangled cries of those who choose death? Was it some sort of trauma provoked by the tensions of the Cold War and the recent onset of war in Korea? It was not: for in 1955 international anxiety was, broadly speaking, on the ebb. In any case, suicides tend to decline in wartime. At the height of the Second World War, the Japanese rate remained very moderate: 12.5 in 1942, 11.5 in 1943. The rise started after the end of the war, and becomes really noticeable only after 1952, culminating in 1955, just when the Japanese economy was getting back on its feet. Good sociologists will tell us that the beginning of what was to become the Japanese economic miracle ought to have brought down the number of suicides, since one of Durkheim's laws states that suicide rates are inversely proportional to economic activity.

Perhaps, if we want to make sense of the figures, we should fall back on psychology. Not some imagined, unvarying psychology of an eternal Japan, but the historical psychology of a particular period which endowed the life of one particular generation with shades and colours that will never be seen again. It was, in fact, the young who were affected: young women, aged about twenty or twenty-five in 1954, who despaired of finding a husband because of the ravages of war, and young men who had been adolescent before Japan's defeat. If we compare the 1955 statistics with those for 1920, a generation back, we can see that adults aged over thirty-five were less likely to commit suicide, while the young, from fifteen to thirty, were much more likely to do so. Irresistibly we are reminded of the confusion in the minds of Dazai's heroes, and of that other novelist, very young at the time: Ishihara Shintaro, whose cynicism seems a mere cloak for despair. The Japanese candidate for suicide would have been born between 1930 and 1935, conceived at a time of population growth fostered by the state, aged about ten at the time of the defeat; he would have responded, as any child would, to the prevailing tone of nationalism, accompanied his father – in imagination – on the Pacific adventure and seen him return into reality, defeated – if not dead.

Ten years later, as he was growing up and looking for a niche in a competitive society, meeting with his first difficulties and failures, it would be hard indeed for him to overcome the distaste he was likely to feel for the dawning prosperity of a new Japan all out for petty profit. How persuasive, at that moment, would be the call of the past, of tragic heroism and dreams! How hard to elude, in the desert of a society where everything was for sale, the nostalgic self-identification with an ideal father, dying so far away, so young, for the glory of a vain service; or with an elder brother who perished at the age you have just reached! Thus, all through the fifties, just as the economy was taking off, several

Table 3 Suicides per 100,000 of population

	1884	1895	1896	1900	1903	1913
Japan	14.4	17.2	17.5	18.1	20.6	20.2

thousand young Japanese were to die for lack of the sorry courage to forget: they were to perish as if in posthumous tribute to the defunct Minotaur of military self-sacrifice. They died in the same spirit of consequential obedience as the warriors of Japan who, following the precepts of *junshi*, followed their leader even into death. They died not *in* war, but *of* war, of the upheaval it had created in their childhood and the moral disruption it had inflicted. Mishima was a tardy addition to their number.

THE FIGURES DROP

Except for this tidal wave of suicide in the 1950s, the Japanese statistics (as far back as the state has been keeping them, i.e. since 1882) have been on more or less the same level as the Western ones. In 1913, for example, Japan, with a rate of 20.2, was a long way behind the leaders in the suicide stakes – behind France (26), Germany (23.2) and Austria (20.9). From 1890 to 1894 the Japanese rate remained below 20, while in China it rose as far as 50, a figure which gives some measure of the acute crisis then being endured by the old civilization of the Middle Kingdom, now open to the joint imperialism of the West and of Japan. That was the fearful and romantic China of anarchy and opium, corruption and confusion, in which Japan was pleased to discern the image of a destiny which she herself had evaded – by dying to herself, via the metamorphosis under Meiji, so as to be reborn to an unknown future.[3]

CHANGES IN THE FIGURES

All in all, the pattern of the Japanese suicide statistics, seen as a whole, is curiously similar to that of the European ones. Reliable figures are available for the Western nations from the beginning of the nineteenth century. Two generations passed before the Japanese began to make the same grim reckoning. But in both places we do see a vast and steady increase in the rate, like a breaker rising towards the shore (see table 3). The 1913 rate (20.2) is significant: Japan reached the 20 level ten years later than France, and in both countries it constituted a plateau

Table 4 Suicides per 100,000 of population

	1955	1962	1964	1965	1970
Japan	25.2	24.7	15.1	14.7	15.3

Table 5 Suicides per 100,000 of population

	1970	1971	1972	1973	1974	1975	1976	1977	1978	1979	1980	1981
Japan	15.2	15.5	16.8	17.4	17.6	18.0	17.8	17.9	17.6	18.0	17.7	17.1

which remained stable for some time. Then, in 1930, the Japanese rate dropped back to 19, and in 1940 to 13.7. Was the straining of national energies keeping suicide at bay? The war forced the level down yet lower, as it did everywhere: 12.5 in 1942. That is the general shape of the Japanese suicide curve: it took twelve years of steady increase to achieve a plateau at the turn of the century, then decreased with the onset of imperialism and war, only to take off again in the 1950s. There was a total of 8,784 suicides in 1943; 22,477 in 1955. With the 1960s the tide ebbed again, doubtless in harmony with economic prosperity and the complacency of the new Japan, which saw itself as a sort of Far Eastern Switzerland, calm, industrious and neutral (see table 4).

In the 1970s, the curve turned up again. The euphoria of the preceding ten years seems to have faded; firms went through more difficult times, jobs were harder to get and to keep, environmental problems (pollution and energy shortages) arose, economic crisis was averted year by year but never dropped from view, and in spite of the prodigies of foreign trade, the means of production seemed to be suffering, not much less in Japan than elsewhere, from the fear of inflation and the terror of unemployment. Japan avoided repeating the 1930s' stampede into nationalism – which had certainly managed to halve the suicide rate, but at the cost of that final bloodbath in the Pacific. Was it a passing malaise or the crisis of a civilization? We are still (1987) living through that historical process; no one can yet pronounce on its meaning, and it is not only Japan which is living through it, in an anguish of self-questioning.

In any case, the suicide rate of recent years seems close to regaining the fateful plateau of 20 per 100,000 on which Japan remained from 1903 to 1930 (see table 5).

THE HEART OF THE WILL

In 1970, 21,535 people were killed on Japan's roads: a far larger total than the 15,728 who committed suicide. The next five years saw a twofold development: the ravages of the motor car were brought under control – it killed a mere 14,206 people in 1975 – while suicides rose to 20,000. The two curves crossed over. Death by motor car – absurd, meaningless, follow-my-leader death – belonged to the 1960s. People got themselves killed without even thinking about it. Then, perhaps, it was time for another death, just as pointless but offering some vision of awareness, lucid or self-deceiving: the old voluntary death, a wakeful, ever-busy phenonenon.

Death is steadily getting rarer in modern Japan. In 1950 the death rate was still over 1,000 per 100,000; thirty years later it was down to 600. There are fewer births as well. The cruelty and wonder of renewed life is slowing down. In a safe, peace-loving, long-lived society, people are better protected against death. But it can still find its way to the heart of the will. It is the value of *life* which seems to be supreme: institutions defend it, everyday thinking is based on it. And yet the choice of death is stubbornly there. In 1930, out of 1,161,509 deaths, 13,919 (1.19 per cent) were suicides. Twenty years later the percentage was 1.80. And in 1980, there were 20,542 suicides out of a total of 722,801 deaths: the percentage had gone up to 2.84. The problem had become graver in the course of that half-century, and nothing has succeeded in checking the threat, so intimate, yet so hard to pin down.

Will this suicide-inducing malaise become the very stamp of modernity? Things were no different in France: the suicide rate hovered between 15 and 16 per 100,000 from 1949 to 1977, but then began to rise steadily, and in 1980 neared the 20 threshold (19.7). But the arithmetic of suicide is powerless to foretell the future. History is a gaping hole of uncertainty which no sociological law can fill in. Shall we eventually reach the 50 mark which China saw in the depths of its confusion? Or shall we rather see what we saw at the turn of the century, a permanent hovering around the 20 per 100,000 plateau? Suicide is a symptom of latent nihilism, a symptom which can be transcribed in figures. It is linked to historical changes, once within nations, now on a worldwide scale.

If we want a meaning for this unpredictable history to counter the siren call of the void, then we shall have to invent one. It may suffice for Japan to readjust its powerful economic machinery by a process of servomechanism; in which case the busy-ness which claims to fill lives can continue its tireless increase, just so long as it endlessly readjusts its modes of production, exchange and consumption to the needs of the moment. No need for radical or essential transformation – only new products, new techniques. Perhaps we ought to be wishing for just that – if we think that it is the reward which *homo japonicus* deserves for his thirty-year-old resolve to become the most efficient of economic animals. But he may have to break out of the economic circle, stop sleepwalking. The gulf may widen between that sort of culture and the too-long-forgotten force of Nature; ecological constraints may check the upward economic spiral. Then there will be no point in technological tinkering. Japan would have to tear down her very way of life, with all its values, and start again from the beginning, as in the time of Meiji. In such a crisis, even if the issue may be a happy one, it is hard to live with the anguish of possible choices. Will Japan have to pass through a crisis of nihilism, symptomatized and revealed by the suicide rate? Do the most recent statistics mark the onset of such a breakdown? Whatever happens, at least Japan will not have to go through it alone. It this world, whose nations are increasingly being drawn together by other things than trade links, each of them has its share of the agony and the hope.

3
Towards a Theory of Suicide

The steady rise in the suicide rate was felt in Europe before Japan. The two graphs show a parallel rise, a generation apart. Durkheim, writing on suicide in 1897, was not to know that the 20 per 100,000 rate just reached in France was to remain unsurpassed for a century. His figures for France are shown in table 6. It looks like an inescapable groundswell – just at a time when general mortality rate was falling from 30 to 20 per thousand. Life was getting longer in the countries which had found a way to modernize; prosperity was spreading, hygiene improving, disease diminishing. The Western bourgeoisie had every hope of winning its fight against death – at least, against its own death. It was a pity that the whiplash of suicide, aimed particularly at that bourgeoisie, had to demonstrate the shallowness of its victory.

In truth the actual number of suicides was not great: of a hundred deaths, scarcely one was self-inflicted. But qualitatively speaking, the paradox of voluntary death was so disturbing, especially now that the evasive but irrefutable language of figures had shown it to be on the increase, that it seemed to hang an invisible but urgent threat over the head of every individual. The figures might give some support to the (sometimes exaggerated) anxieties of the earliest demographers and of many city doctors. The body social was sick, and there were figures to prove it. Modern society has grown up under the oft-repeated accusation of fostering suicide.[1]

Table 6 Suicides per 100,000 of population

	1827	1841–6	1849–55	1856–60	1866–70	1871–5	1876–8	1894
France	4.8	8.5	10.1	11.2	13.5	15	16	20

THE PIOUS AND THE GOOD

Nineteenth-century Europe supplied a twofold commentary on these early statistics. Still redolent of Christianity, it came from the pious and the good. The pious fulminated against the decline in moral standards and the ravages of atheism. The good blamed poverty, loneliness, and the cruelty of man to man. The pious soul addressed the suicide as a criminal, a coward, or at best a madman. The humanist retorted that he was a victim: at worst, unhappy, which is to say unfortunate. The religious viewpoint always dominated: suicide was an evil. So whose fault was it?

All acts, however solitary, singular and silent, trigger echoes in the speech of others: it is they, even more than the intentions of the perpetrator, which endow it with meaning. Our thoughts about one particular suicide, or suicide in general, have their place in a web of discourse which has its own lines of development, conditions of emergence and method of use. Before an impartial study of suicide as a phenomenon could be embarked on, the problematical concept of 'fault' had to be shaken off: this took the whole of the nineteenth century. A time did come when indignation began to seem useless, cruel, hypocritical. Was suicide an evil? It must be – some people were now saying – but to be more precise, it was an evil in society or the individual. No longer was it a murder for which guilt must be assigned; rather it was a symptom which must be understood before it could be treated. The harsh judgements of the pious sometimes lay behind the mental specialists' discussions of 'suicidal mania'; the kind hearts found their echo in the conclusions which sociologists drew from the statistics. But the view of suicide as a symptom which nineteenth-century Europe established was to become axiomatic, and all present discourse on suicide, from newspaper reports to theories of suicidology, remains subject to it.

Every spring, Tokyo sees the publication by the National Police Service of the suicide statistics for the preceding year. They are ritually commented on by the press as more or less worrying symptoms in the body social. Japanese psychologists and sociologists do their best to maintain an impartial tone when speaking of suicide, based on the objectivizing nature of statistics and nourished by the thematics of contemporary suicidology. In this they are the distant heirs of the old mental specialists and statisticians who arose among the nineteenth-ceuntry Western bourgeoisie, intent on making man the centre of its universe of knowledge. Even impartiality – like other virtues – has its history.

INDEX OF MEDICAL IDIOCIES

As they researched further into the origins of self-murder, nineteenth-century doctors and statisticians found that sin was soluble in science. Mental specialists eventually began to see suicide as an aberration – as madness. Esquirol's conviction is unshakeable: 'I think I have proved that no man takes his own life unless he is in delirium, and that all suicides are deranged.' The idiocies of nineteenth-century medicine, whose imperturbable determination is a source of unending diversion, begin to sound like a pronouncements from that fatuous pair, Flaubert's Bouvard and Pécuchet: 'The phrenologist Gall emphasized the density and thickness of the cranial bones, without otherwise singling out the suicide bump. Esquirol contradicted this, and even insisted on the rarity of cerebral lesions, but thought it necessary to point out the lesions of the digestive tract.'[2]

As a corrective to Christianity's age-old condemnation, it was doubtless necessary for the suicidal urge to assume the preposterous form of a hypothetical 'suicide bump' which could actually be felt by a clinically objective hand. Observant reason, which reduced every reality to an object and every object to a thing, even went as far as to maintain, with Hegel, that 'the mind is a bone.'[3] Scientism, that inverse manifestation of a tormented consciousness, imprisoned the impulses of the will in the chemistry of hormones: the suicidal brain was deficient in serotonin. This separation of thought (illusory) from the body (real) reduced the living individual, with his claim to will-power, to an organism without inner life. Not until Freud would the mind renew its alliance with the Word, and the individual be reconstituted – if not in his thinking, then at least on the reverse side of what he says.

FROM INDIVIDUALISM TO NIHILISM

Before the sociologists there were the moral statisticians. The growing precision of the statistics showed them that suicide was a permanent, universal, regular phenonenon: still a symptom, but symptomatic now of a tension permeating the whole social body. In 1841 Claude-Joseph Tissot published a study, entitled *De la manie du suicide et de l'esprit de révolte*, in which he condemns the spirit of the age as subversive and suicidal. Some kill themselves, he says, and others would like to kill society: the aberration is the same. Suicide has been classed as a mental illness; but surely all such mental illnesses ought to be connected first and foremost with the malaise which gripped our civilization when we lost the structures which once protected men against themselves. In 1905 the novelist Natsume Soseki, in his critique of individualism, noted the same sort of loss.

A CURE FOR NIHILISM

Whence came this malaise? Ideological disarray or economic barbarism? On this point the dawning science of sociology divided along two lines of research. In 1881 Thomas Masaryk saw in suicide the 'sad consequence of a progressive loss of religious feeling among the masses' – a mass phenomenon linked to the decline of Christianity.[4] Heaven is empty and the death of God is death to man. Masaryk's arguments subsume the destiny of Dostoevsky's nihilist heroes, driven by a terrible lucidity into killing themselves or others, and like Dostoevsky, he seeks a renewal of religion. Neither art nor science can fulfil a man – certainly not the mere satisfaction of his needs. This renewal would be rooted not in Christian dogma but in Christian values: charity, renunciation, hope. Christ was not the son of God, but he was none the less admirable for that.

Only by rekindling the values of that dead tradition could one bridle the will to power which Masaryk saw unleashed in both individual egos and state imperialism – with the inevitable backlash leading from frustrated megalomania to suicidal despair. Only values are transcendental, and only a religion of values can counter the evil of nihilism, which strikes first at post-Christian societies but spares none, including that of Japan in the process of modernization. Here Masaryk meets Nietzsche – but on the other side of the road, the former revolting against suicide just as the latter is inviting it back within the gates. Nietzsche suggests overturning all religious values, while Masaryk looks to their renaissance. Masaryk breathes new life into the metaphysics of morality, while Nietzsche seeks to dispel every last trace of it, calling man to self-transcendence, beyond good and evil. The two agree only in their diagnosis of the nihilistic malaise, and in casting doubt on socialism's capacity to deal with it.

THE PROMISE OF SOCIALISM

Indeed, at that time socialists were confident of relegating suicide, along with other scourges such as prostitution and drunkenness, to the dustbin of history. In a society based on fresh economic relationships which gave a real purpose to life, no one would want to end it, because it would at long last be happy – or at least, meaningful. Such axioms led self-styled socialist countries into re-establishing forms of repression (starting with silence) not unlike those of the old Christian taboo. It is true that in 1911 the socialist Paul Lafargue, having resolved to limit his life to seventy years, killed himself quite calmly, along with his wife Laura, Karl Marx's daughter. None the less, the so-called Marxist mentality often merely restored the cruelty of the old religion towards the individual in isolation. Makarenko's acerbic comments on the suicide of a young Soviet pioneer (in 'Pedagogical poem', 1933) make embarrassing reading today. The USSR divulged no statistics on suicide rates, and the *Great Soviet Encyclopedia* chose simply to ignore the problem, which was assumed to be solved in the Soviet Union and insoluble everywhere else. When a suicide was undeniable, it was most expedient to see it as a pathological case. This shows the deep identity of the two nineteenth-century theories of man: a gesture which can on longer be accepted as denouncing a sick society must be reduced to insignificance – private insanity.

Thus nineteenth-century efforts to create a purely human science of man created two apparently antagonistic, but in truth profoundly compatible, viewpoints. Mental specialists and psychiatrists on the one hand, demographers and sociologists on the other, all saw the suicidal act as a symptom. The molar and the molecular: the duality is neatly expressed by tle Leninist metaphor of the weakest link. If the chain breaks it may be due to the intrinsic weakness of that link, and/or to the tension in the whole chain. Suicidology steered between the two explanations, always careful to think of suicide as a passive act. As I take my life into my own hands, I am (according to this theory), being taken in by latent forces; never can I be less free than when I believe I am eliminating my enslavement to existence.

THE DIGNITY OF VOLUNTARY DEATH

Nowadays this theory of suicide as symptom is just as solidly rooted in Japanese psychiatric and statistical circles as it is in the West. But can we not ask history to exempt us from a viewpoint which history has created? By hearkening to the voices of far-off centuries in an alien culture, can we lend an ear to a discourse other than our own, which can perhaps restore to suicide the dignity of a voluntary death? Recent statistics tell us much the same thing about Japan as about everywhere else, because they make exactly the same assumptions. But evidence from Japan's past will help us to grasp not the illusion which may foster the act, but the truth that it institutes. If we cease to view voluntary death as either a sin or a symptom, we shall cease to see it as a passive yielding to temptations and impulses, and start to see it as the deliberate choosing of one solution among many, or an ethical gesture linked to principles and values. This detour through the Japanese past will bring us up to a viewpoint from which we may discern the assumptions on which our 'knowledge' is based. For knowledge is the fruit of experience, and the experience is made possible through ethical choices. A different ethic will help us comprehend truths which will remain for ever beyond the range of the suicide theory bequeathed to us by the nineteenth century.

FREUD AND DURKHEIM

I am not suggesting, however, that that 'knowlege' and those theories should be rejected altogether, for they allow us to ask questions without which history would remain dumb. The perspectives of history are unlocked by the same truth values which lie at the foundations of science. It is no use accusing psychopathology and sociology of being partial and reductive, and sending them off into separate corners: better to contemplate their uneasy alliance and ponder the chances of striking truth from their discords. Durkheim and Freud still have a great deal to teach us about voluntary death: their theories never coincide, but they meet at times and finally link, though without quitting their respective spheres. Between them they restore suicide, so often banished into insignificance and aberration, to its proper place. Freud, admittedly, made no direct study of it, but his whole *oeuvre* helps remove it from under the umbrella of insanity hoisted by mental specialists.

Under the death-wish hypothesis suicide becomes the tip of an iceberg of primary masochism: suicide is only one of a series of behaviour types tending to self-destruction, the only difference being that the impulse is a conscious one. Halfway down the slippery slope to desired death, we can situate acts of gratuitous imprudence, fascination with danger – runaway machinery or Russian roulette – pointless revolts and hopeless causes which nourish the failure neurosis. To the same area belong self-immolating austerities, self-privation, self-mutilation, and the severities and stubbornness of the superego. And finally all forms of slow or disguised suicide: alcoholism, drug addiction, compulsive self-neglect, mental anorexia, catatonic trance. It can scarcely be mad to desire death when death seems somehow to be the reason for so much human behaviour – transgression, punishment, regression . . .

True, if I desire death, I desire what I do not know, because I can have no knowledge of death. But for precisely that reason I must, across that void of death, discern other goals which give their own meaning to the gesture of dying. Because it is nothing which I can know about, death can be the scene of many an intention. Revolt or renunciation, aggression or sacrifice, cry for attention or flight from it, exaltation or despair? No act is more ambiguous than suicide, a riddle cast in the teeth of those who live on. Dying by accident, or of disease, is just dying – but by killing himself a man can make the very silence of death into an echo from a labyrinth.

TYPOLOGY

This complexity of implicit meaning impels all writers on suicide towards an attempt at classification: a taxonomy, a typology with four, five, ten or perhaps eleven different categories. The simplest classification is always the best. Imagine a six-pointed star. Its vertical axis will go from melancholy up to maniacal excitement, opposing two possible suicides: the enthusiast and the depressive. To the right of this axis we will put attitudes towards other people: to the north-east, self-sacrificial suicides, to the south-east aggressive suicides expressing protest or resentment. To the left we will put behaviour inspired by the subject's personal anxieties: to the south-west, defensive and escapist suicide, to the north-west suicides for honour or reputation demanded by the narcissism of the idealized self. Finally, in the middle of our star, beyond any of these motives, we will put a seventh type, the gratuitous suicide, the degree zero of intentionality, a tossing of death's coin without a care for how it falls. Whatever the intentions of an act, it will always somehow leap beyond meaning, submit to the hazards of fate and the vain sovereignty of chance. The gesture of suicide is sometimes a challenge to destiny to give some sort of reply. We must bear in mind that several such intentions may help to compose and overdetermine a single act. And that, underneath intentions which the subject is aware of, there may be unconscious impulses, going darker and deeper until they merge with that inertia which Freud terms *thanatos*, which exists in every living man as a relic of the immobility which he has escaped.

Let us recall here the four-square opposing modalities of classical logic: necessity, impossibility, possibility, contingency. We might say that death, in existence, is a paradoxical convergence of the impossible and the necessary. Freud was contemplating a relationship which would see suicide as a radical possibility of the human condition, as against the no less radical impossibility of knowing anything about death except its inevitability. It is a chasm of unknowing in the mind. What Durkheim was exploring was the diagonal which goes from contingency to necessity: the freedom of a singular act becomes meaningful by being fitted into an overall statistical constraint. His careful calculations, based on a century of suicide, led Durkheim, in 1897, to a more or less surprising conclusion: from year to year the number of suicides remains pretty constant in a determined human group, it is a less variable parameter even than the number of deaths. Every nation has its characteristic suicide rate, and so does every region (not counting town and country), each sex, every age group, every generation within the family, every religious and ideological category and every socio-professional milieu.

Every individual belongs to an asssortment of social groups; where their conditions intersect we find the individual's own condition. On this basis, the a priori suicide risk to each of us can be calculated. It is possible to draw up a table, based on statistical correlations, showing the risk and safeguard factors. We are all well aware that chance – car accidents, for example – has its own laws, the basis for the calculation of probabilities. But we must admit at this point that the human will, which thinks itself free to choose, is more like a throw of the dice against the faceless destiny which stirs up our thoughts and disposes our acts. Every area of society is thus traversed by what Durkheim calls a 'suicidogenic current' of determined intensity. The desire to die comes no longer from the centre, but from the outside, from the space within which we relate to, and separate ourselves from, other people. Human beings are centred outside themselves, in their relationship with others; Freud thought the same. Thus every suicide is, as Antonin Artaud said of Van Gogh, a 'suicide of society'.[5] Ever since Rousseau, Western individuals have been suffering from a kind of outraged innocence, sometimes verging on paranoia, which urges them to denounce those evils in society for which they fear they may be responsible. 'Social suicide' is the natural outcome of that feeling. The dawning science of suicide, armed with statistics, was more grist to the mill of the individual in revolt against the all-embracing *fatum* which hung over him. Science reveals the alienation of the individual, the object of its study, and thus makes it infinitely worse.

DURKHEIM'S DOUBTS

The suicide rates are constant only over a short period. If studied diachronically over a century they show variations answering to a deeper historical process than mere events. What chiefly struck Durkheim was a generalized increase all over Europe from beginning to end of the nineteenth century. In France, for example, the rate quadrupled from 5 to 20. This may have been partly due to a steady improvement in the gathering of statistics and a greater readiness to acknowledge a suicide. But Durkheim thought the rate in his time 'pathological'. He was not to know that it was a ceiling beyond which the following century would tend to regress. Following so many other doctors at work in society, therefore, he diagnosed a correlation between suicide and modern life. In his typology, altruistic suicide was contrasted with egoistic suicide, fatalistic suicide with anomic suicide. *Anomie*, a word invented by Durkheim in imitation of the 'anarchy' which overshadowed the closing years of the century, meant the degenerative tendency of modern life.

Traditional societies allowed only the altruistic suicide of devotion and oblation, i.e. voluntary sacrifice, which is at the very heart of Christianity. Those societies were rigid; they knew, but condemned, fatalistic suicides by powerless individuals chained to unalterable rules of life. Modern society claimed to have given the individual his freedom, but in fact it had condemned him to solitude and insecurity. Social groups were falling apart, selfish escapist suicides were becoming more and more common, and so were 'anomic' suicides triggered by the disappearance of obligations. Things were precarious, work had become fragmented and meaningless. The allegiances which had contained and sustained the individual were breaking down, the taboos which had contained his vain inspirations were fading away. Everything was allowed: it was a competitive society in which everyone was condemned to succeed, a desert of contingency where man could no longer find solace in a stable condition and a lasting duty.

To combat these oft-described evils, Durkheim had no confidence in the remedies suggested by Masaryk or Marx. He advocated neither moral renaissance nor proletarian revolution, but a reform aimed at a sharing society which would reforge links between the state and the individual and associate the latter with the unanimity of community living. But what community? First and foremost, the workplace, the professional milieu. The taste for living would return along with the satisfaction of co-operating for a common purpose, the joy of creation which would be born of that sociological ideal, freedom of work at long last. Work was the answer: the cure for *anomie* was ergotherapy.

4

Suicide as Symptom

Do Durkheim's theories have a place in Japan? Japanese society, so dominated by the work ethic, does indeed seem to obey his sociological precepts without need of hearing them. True, when Durkheim spoke of professional groups he was thinking of contemporary trade unions, whereas the essential unit in Japan is the company. Solidarity is 'vertical', from top to bottom of the same firm; horizontal professional links among workers on the same level have little importance. Corporate and class (or caste) consciousness counts for nothing beside consciousness of the clan. Solidarity, based on the company, does exist and it does have a job to do: in particular, in preventing suicide.

The statistics show that Japanese wage-earners are well protected against the suicide risk throughout their working lives. The firm guarantees job security: when it is in difficulties, wages are cut, but there are no redundancies. Job security, recognition for long service, a system of rewards, company accommodation, social backup: under Japanese capitalism the firm neglects no measure which can further the integration of its employees, and assumes a large part of the welfare role which in the West was once played by the Church, and now devolves on the state. Employer and employee are bound not by a precise and dissoluble contract for the sale of working capacity, but by a personal commitment involving total participation in the life of the company.

CLASS STRUGGLE AND CLAN STRUGGLE

Western capitalism has been associated from birth with the hazards of commercial and maritime ventures, i.e. with companies formed to profit from the goods in which they traded. The model for Japanese business practice is a land-based one: domestic production, the extended family organized for the growing of rice on the same, narrowly defined piece of land. In the Western model, relationships were mercantile, contractual, precarious, distant and, in the abstract, egalitarian; in the Japanese, they were family relationships, customary, narrow, permanent and asymmetrical: a sharp contrast. The ideology of Japanese capitalism is heavily familial – some would prefer to say feudal, since feudalism was merely an extension into the military clan system of the dependence, protection and obligation which initially characterized relationships within the family. Such a way of organizing work, originating in a flexible and open-ended family structure, was first adapted to domestic production and then ennobled as part of the feudal ethic – but today it is showing itself well adapted to industrial production. The class struggle, which hampers production, gives way to the clan struggle, which stimulates it. Hence the paradox: the modernization of Japan depends on circumstances etched in her traditions. It is wrong to speak of 'americanization': what Japan *was* has determined what Japan *is*. Management schools go to Tokyo for lessons in work organization and group dynamics, but there is no simple formula for success.

I am not trying to paint a rosy picture of Japanese society: like all others, it has its cruel side, and day by day it is paying the price of its industrial might.[1] It is true that the individual is closely integrated with his working community, but this does nothing to reduce competition. When a company fails the consternation of its employees is all the greater because of their intimate association with their own work and the firm.[2] Wage-earners are well protected from suicide if they belong to firms too powerful to come under threat. But Japan's industrial system is dualist and heterogeneous. The top firms get wonderful results, but underneath there is a host of tiny subcontractors, small businesses and journeymen. At that level the statistics show a much greater suicide risk. Though it may not take the classic form of class struggle seen by Marx in nineteenth-century Europe, economic life can still at times be a struggle to the death.

According to Durkheim 'poverty is a protection.' It may be, if it is accepted from birth as an immutable condition. But when it strikes a ruined petty bourgeois, or a wage-earner unable to pay his debts, then it is a killer. In 1979, more than a tenth of male suicides were due to money troubles. In the last few years a permissive Japan has allowed a proliferation, alongside the traditional lenders against security, of petty usurers who will lend to students and wage-earners on simple proof of identity: at the last count there were a hundred and sixty-two thousand of them. Their numerous advertisements and prosepectuses promise an interest rate of 5 per cent – that is, of course, per month. A few tricks can quickly push it up to 100 per cent a year. Overdue debts are collected by force, and often by hired thugs. The most common form of harassment is a threat of scandal in the workplace. Many victims prefer to disappear, some into death. One is reminded of Flaubert's Madame Bovary, stuffing herself with arsenic to escape her creditor.[3]

CONCRETE AND FOREST

Japan has escaped none of the evils of industrial society, from the invasion of concrete to traffic congestion to the anguish of suburbia; only delinquency remains – perhaps – within bearable limits. Some fifteen years after the French perpetrated the grim housing estates of Sarcelles, in 1972, a big estate of sixty-four unmercifully uniform tower blocks was completed at Takashimadaira, near Tokyo. It now houses 40,000 people. Even in the first year a few despairing souls jumped from the flat roofs, down fourteen floors to the cement of the forecourt. Television and the newspapers exacerbated the problem by publicizing it. Takashimadaira acquired the idiot nickname of the 'suicides' Mecca', and now attracts, year by year, twenty or so clients from all over Tokyo. The roofs have been surrounded by safety barriers and barbed wire, and are patrolled; the inhabitants are asked to give warning if someone seems to be looking a little wildly up at the rooftops – and mothers tell their children to beware of falling bodies. But all these measures seem in vain: the fashion is in. This sort of contagion, by which suicides favour a certain place for a few years, has often been observed.

Great overcrowded concrete blocks are well suited to despair, but for those for whom death is a fantasy of returning to nature there exists, in that country of contrasts, a place free from all human interference. It is a great and trackless forest beneath Mount Fuji, 60 miles from Tokyo: Jukai, the Sea of Trees. It was made famous by a novel published in 1960, in which a young wife finally achieves her dream of leaving her odious husband. Just as she is about to join her lover, she has a compulsion to take the train to Fuji, climb its slopes and drown herself in the forest. Novels may claim to imitate life, but life imitates novels – both good and bad. Since that time people have been coming, alone or in couples, to hang or poison themselves or die of cold in the same forest.

Every October, before the snows, a patrol struggles through the impenetrable undergrowth, and finds some thirty skeletons cleaned of their now superfluous flesh by foxes, crows and wild dogs. Romantic suicides, mostly young women. Clothes give some help to the police in their attempts to put a name to the corpses by matching with the list of missing persons. True, the list is a long one: in 1978 there were 95,000 recorded requests to search for people missing from home, gone in search of a new life – or of death.

Most suicides, however (about 20,000 every year), choose neither Takashimadaira concrete nor the forests of Fuji, nor any other particularly fascinating place. In Japan, as elsewhere, most people kill themselves at home, under a train, in a hotel room, or on a journey. The methods are the usual ones – drowning, hanging, jumping, poison, asphyxia, fire, gun, knife – in the usual proportions. Disembowelling, which under the name of *seppuku* was traditional in the warrior class from the thirteenth to the nineteenth centry, has become very rare indeed, despite the recent example of Mishima. As for motives, those listed by the police in their annual statistics (fear of illness, family disputes, unhappy love affairs, money worries, professional failure, bereavement, depression etc.) are on such a superficial level that they cannot supply much meaningful information. Only a detailed case-by-case investigation could disentangle the complex motivations, which were not always clear in the subjects' own minds.

OVERLEAPING OLD AGE

Analysing the statistics by age groups is more revealing: it shows that the young and the old are the most vulnerable. The suicide graph, age group by age group, is U-shaped. Adults are well protected, undoubtedly because they are closely integrated with a working community. But this protection has to be paid for, at the entrance and at the exit. Retirement brings a crushing feeling of uselessness, commensurate with the centrality of the work ethic to people's thinking. Only add the fear of illness and poverty, and the cup runs over.

Until recently it was customary for the eldest son to live with his wife and children in his parents' house: often a household consisted of three generations under the same roof. But today, in their city flats, children often live apart from their parents from university onwards, or after marriage at the latest. As in the West, family life is tending to restrict itself to the married couple: they risk loneliness for the sake of independence. For example, in 1965 the average number of persons in a household was still 4.51 in the countryside, but only 3.9 in the towns. Thus, ageing parents tend more and more to live alone. If we are to believe the opinion polls, it is then that television becomes their reason for living, sometimes the only reason, certainly the main one. One statistic will show the extent of the problem: in 1979 the suicide rate was 18.5 for the whole population, but rose to 50 for people aged over 65. Moreover, Japan has a rapidly ageing population, with a very low birth-rate and a lengthening life-span. The proportion of old people, currently 9 per cent, will be 15 per cent in about twenty years' time. This is happening in all modernized societies.

The lot of retired people in Japan is an unenviable one: they are not benefiting from economic growth. Unlike their European counterparts, they have no guaranteed and index-linked pension at the end of their active life. The firm gives them a lump sum which some use to buy a house or small business. But most of them have to look for a new job, and can do no better than to put their retirement gratuity at the mercy of commerce by investing it in some bank, where it will soon be eaten away by the inflation which goes hand in hand with growth.

Thus old people kill themselves out of loneliness, out of a depressing feeling of uselessness which robs the discomforts of age and poverty of all meaning, and so makes them intolerable. Why go on suffering? Add to that sometimes what one might call a sacrificial motive, especially in the countryside, among old people still living amongst their children, who suffer no material solitude but feel they cannot be useful and begin to see themselves as a dead weight to be taken off the family's back. Such suicides, especially by widows, are common in the poorer areas, such as the snowy prefecture of Niigata, and in Iwate, Kochi and Shimane. There we find peasant families, no longer at risk of indigence but clinging to the customs of bygone, much harsher days.[4] In those days, in time of famine, it was customary for sons to carry their helpless mothers on their backs to some mountain shrine, where they would pray in the snow and the darkness until the cold stopped their hearts. Even today, amongst those aged over sixty-five, women are more likely to kill themselves than men: 2,578 in 1978, as against 2,277 men. Japanese tradition has always laid heavy stress on resignation, self-effacement and self-sacrifice as feminine traits.

Economic necessity impelled these rural communities to keep their population in balance, by the half-voluntary sacrifice of superfluous widows and by abortion and infanticide (especially of girls) at birth. For several centuries Christianity has been preaching not respect for life (that is a Buddhist virtue) but respect for the individual, from conception to death. More exactly, it has preached respect for the sovereignty of God. Since Abraham, God has been visualized as absolute master over life and death, jealous of any human sovereignty which might attempt to usurp the divine prerogative by interfering with the moment of conception or expiry. But we may be sure that the Japanese peasant, carrying his ailing mother up the mountain on a winter's evening, had in his grief-torn heart an anguish of piety and virtue just as strong as that of any (conscious or unconscious) heir of Abraham, at the bedside of a dying relative, painfully abjuring the temptation to abbreviate his sufferings.

SUICIDE AMONG THE YOUNG

Sadder still are suicides of very young people, adolescents and even children. And the plunge is deeper: they reject not just a few last bitter moments, but life, all of it and at once, with all its myriad possibilities, as if they had the sombre courage to hearken to Silenus' oracle to king Midas: 'What is the greatest good for a man?' 'Never to have been born. Or failing that, to die at once.'

Suicide is a symptom, that is, a surface result of factors uncontrolled by the subject. This is especially true of suicide by the young. But it is not only a symptom: it is also an act, however confused and ill-advised the part played by the will. It is a rejection: firstly of a given situation, but beyond that, a blanket judgement on the value of life. Now this judgement seems to demand an answer. Suicide in the young is always an appeal. Through the bold affirmation sounds a question: 'This life – my life – isn't worth living, so how can Life be worth living?' It is easy to see that a featherweight would change the balance: that is what makes the appeal so disturbing. The act is flung like a cry into the void: it is gratuitous, like throwing a dice. 'Let's see if death will have me!' It can be an expiation, but also a revenge. 'Who am I in this life? Feeble, unloved – and yet, child as I am, capable of blotting everything out at a stroke.' The last vestige of infant omnipotence, the first sovereign adult act. 'At least I'll show them that I have a will: then they'll have to take me seriously.'

You can let yourself die at any age, like the suckling orphans observed in hospitals by René Spitz, who rejected the food which supplied their material need but gave them no love. But actually to kill yourself demands strength, courage, audacity – and a metaphysical maturity which can precede the physical one: the ability to stand alone before the wholeness of being. Every year the Japanese newspapers print stories of children dying by their own hand at the age of ten, or nine, or eight. And, more worrying still, these children did not seem unhappy. Obedient at home and at school, no quieter than the others, they were playing with their little friends only that morning. No warning signs: what family can think itself safe? Sometimes they suggest a pretext, pointless, derisory, the last straw which broke the camel's inexplicably overloaded back: I was scared of the exam, daddy wouldn't buy me some skis, teacher punished me. But most often, silence – leaving families full of doubt, and remorse, and stupefied astonishment.

THE MOST WORRYING SYMPTOM

Between 1965 and 1975, the number of under-fourteen suicides in Japan doubled from forty-six a year to ninety-five. In the same period there was a tenfold increase in the number of stomach ulcers among schoolchildren in the same age bracket. For a long time the suicide figure for minors (under twenty) stayed around the 700-a-year mark: then in 1977 it went to 784, and suddenly, in 1978, to 866: a serious rise, all the more so in that the numbers remained steady that year for other age groups. It alarmed the whole country: there could be scarcely be a more alarming sociological symptom than juvenile suicides. Through the early months of 1979, when the figures were published, the question was discussed endlessly on the radio, on television and in the press. The Prime Minister called a committee of inquiry: twelve experts, psychiatrists, educationalists and sociologists, were asked to identify the problem and suggest a remedy. A manual on suicide prevention was circulated round all the schools in the country by the Ministry of Education. Parents were kept informed through conferences, brochures and discussions. The 1979 figures showed another increase: 919 Japanese people under twenty killed themselves that year. But in 1980 the trend was brought under control: 678 under-age suicides, the lowest figure since the end of the Second World War. Had the preventive methods proved effective? Was it a momentary fluctuation or a continuing trend? All developed countries with high levels of competition and education are more or less affected by this problem of under-age suicide, of which drug abuse is simply a slow-motion derivative. We can only hope that greater awareness will help reduce the unending and elusive massacre.

THE BURDEN OF THE FUTURE

In a competitive society where conditions are no longer immutable, families want their children to 'succeed'. Japanese society has many tensions, springing firstly from competition among firms, but also from the get-ahead ambition within families. The adolescent is expected to be both child and adult, taking charge of his own future – and thereby bending to other people's wishes for him. But are the parents' wishes really their own desires, or do they conform to a preconception of what is desirable? It can be a twisted kind of suggestion: 'Get for us what we want for you.' The Japanese teenager's emotional dependence on his family, and especially his mother, makes him very vulnerable to such a demand: he may never forgive himself if he fails to meet it.

So-called primitive societies sometimes horrify us by the cruelty of the rites of passage to which their adolescents are subjected: symbolic mutilation, trials of courage and endurance. But the absence of such rites in modern societies, both in the West and in Japan, does not make them any the less cruel: it condemns their young to uncertainty, as does the disappearance of the framework which assigned every individual a status, a role, a job to do. It condemns him to fumble after his own desire, his own vocation, duty, truth and future. Under-age suicide expresses a refusal or inability to give a dialectic, progressive, positive reply to the problem of identity which torments individuals awakened by social anomia to the uncertainties of their existence. Who are you? What you can manage to become – nothing else. Young inheritors of a traditional civilization, with a place in the symbolical ordering of their community, are spared this great anxiety. Not a few suicides seem to be in obedience to that most banal and terrifying condemnation, 'You have no future.'

In such circumstances, school studies and rigorous selection procedures become a crushing burden. Six hours in class are followed by two hours' homework, and often a few extra hours of night school. A child can be asked to work eleven or twelve hours a day for the sake of his future. No wonder if such a burden makes life unbearable. Those who resist are given special treatment. In the university hospital at Fukuoka there is a group psychotherapy service for pupils who dislike school. At the end of April 1979, a boy of eighteen and a girl of seventeen elected to die together by jumping out of one of the windows there.[5]

One thing follows another: to get into a good firm you need a degree from a good university; to take the entrance examination for a good university you have to be from a good school; to get into a good school you have to come from a good primary school. In short, competition starts in the kindergarten; the sooner you get on the conveyor belt the better. The child is caught up in the machinery which connects the family to the means of production via the school. His destiny, happy or unhappy, is pronounced by a modern oracle called the examination. Every institution in society is part of the plot: the job-for-life, which seems such a good arrangement to us, demands a rigorous application of selection by the school and university system. The employee whose diplomas have landed him a job in a good company is safe until he retires – and the price is paid by all those who have failed and dropped out at some stage along the line.

THE PRICE OF FAILURE

Truth to tell, such failures, the terror of which can lead to suicide, would not be enough to motivate such an act if they were not given a catastrophic turn by the family background and the vulnerability of the subject. Recall the image of the chain whose weakest link snaps under the tension of the whole. Under-age suicides show, more clearly than any others, the interaction between the sociological and psychological sides of the suicide symptom. It is the psychic frailty of the victim that makes a failure inflicted by an institution seem so important; and that frailty comes from the family background. And the family background is oriented on the social discourse – received opinions and dominant values – which underlies practices and institutions.

Suicide may be a show of revolt against the demands of parents or an escape from the straitjacket of school. Or it can be the reverse, an act of self-punishment, when a fragile psyche turns a failure into a feeling of guilt. Japanese tradition has always stressed the individual's responsibility to his immediate social group – his family or business. This solidarity is a two-edged sword: it can be a protection against suicide, but it can also lead to it. If a young Japanese wants to be successful, it is not for the sake of self-fulfilment, freedom and self-realization: there is no cult of individualism to spur him on. The will to succeed is based on one's duty to show parents the gratitude to which they are entitled. The individual is supposed to owe an endless debt to those who gave him life, for it is the supreme gift. Or so says a still vigorous ideology, nurtured in Confucianism and perpetuated through the educational system. Here again modernization – the desire to get ahead – uses maxims firmly rooted in tradition.

In the last couple of generations the Japanese family has imploded into a married couple practising birth control, producing a sealed unit which has redoubled the intensity of the ambivalent relationship between parents and children. In a large extended family, responsibility could be shared out. Now it is concentrated in a few over-protected children, who carry too great a weight of anxiety, too large an investment. This means that academic failure can be like the ruin of a family's hopes, a waste of the sacrifices they have made – for higher education is expensive in Japan and many mothers do indeed make sacrifices. They have the courage to make them, but not to hide them: they are well aware that a vague feeling of guilt over their self-sacrifice will effectively spur their sons to work harder. Sometimes they underestimate the self-punishment which may ensue from that guilt if the child is unsuccessful. The failure can feel like an unforgivable sin.[6]

Now the Japanese have always been strongly inclined to proclaim their faults. It can go from a mere automatic gesture of politeness to the most drastic acts of expiation. Looking at life in the West, what astonishes them is our reluctance to admit responsibility in public, our propensity to excuse ourselves by alleging outside circumstances or good intentions. It is true that seven centuries of auricular confession may have made Christian consciences somewhat flexible in dealing with responsibility. We have been keeping our admissions of guilt for the confessional ever since the thirteenth century: we have become rather good at speeches for the defence. And we have given up to the right to make moral judgements: what Christian would dare assume such authority and presume to avenge – on himself if necessary – the flouting of the law? The Japanese do not approve of arguing to justify one's faults or of excusing oneself. They esteem nothing so highly as the courage to admit guilt. Their inclination to self-punishment, which we see as morbid and unsound, has always been greeted there with sympathy and admiration as sufficient redemption for errors, failures and faults. 'We Japanese can scarcely understand the different treatment meted out by the Church to St Peter and Judas. Both betrayed Christ: Judas is damned, Peter is the head of the Church – and yet Judas killed himself!'[7]

This traditional attitude can aggravate a depressive state to the point of actual suicide. In Christendom the Church governed feelings of guilt, often encouraging them, sometimes tempering them, but always in control. Our modern individualism, which sees life as an inalienable right, can also be a splendid protection against the severity of the superego. The Japanese are more vulnerable to feelings of responsibility, made up of equal parts of shame and guilt. Here we find fresh traces of traditional virtues (save face but admit the fault), which their education makes both lasting and perpetually relevant.

THE AWAKENING OF THE SUPEREGO

Children in their first years of life are treated with an indulgence which seems to us excessive: the father is distant, often absent, but the mother's duty is to serve her baby day and night. It creates a very close dependence, a veritable symbiosis. In controlling the ever more mobile child, punishments and threats to withdraw love are avoided. Instead of forbidding something directly, which would bring her up against the child's desires, the mother tries to distract him with a sweet, or to warn him: 'You can't do that sort of thing – it's dangerous!' Or most of all: 'What will people say? Everyone will laugh at you!' By bringing in this sort of exterior risk, the outsider's eye, the mother is implicitly emphasizing her solidarity with the child: it is not mother's wrath he has to fear, it is not she who will put him to shame but everybody else, and in particular his father. If there are excuses to be made, she will be the first to make them, though not without pointing out to him that she will be ashamed and embarrassed because she has to take on the responsibility for his little peccadilloes. The deterrent effect of shame is thus increased tenfold by adding a more serious feeling: 'You're making them laugh – and you're making me cry!' Shame and fault are linked in this arousal of the Japanese superego. The heirs of Cain can never escape the eyes of God, even less in the next world than in this. But in Japan you can hide in death, disappear into it entirely and mend the fault as you go.

Even in the West there are suicidal depressives obsessed with self-castigating fantasies. But Japanese culture seems resolved to give the guilt feeling a new turn of the screw by linking it with shame. Any projective test which you try on a Japanese (completing an unfinished sentence, making up a story based on a picture) goes to show that their aggressiveness, curbed at an early stage by the fact that they have *not* been subjected to their mother's wrath, has few outlets, and so is bottled up and turned inwards (the Freudian *Wendung*) in the form of anxiety and responsibility. Modern Japan is not without its criminals, but statistics show that the number of suicides is three times the number of murders – whereas in Mexico (for example) there is only one suicide for every ten violent deaths. Newspaper reports sometimes mention that the crime was completed and compensated by the suicide of the aggressor. The 'taste for violence', which journalists who have spent a couple of weeks in Tokyo believe they have detected in the Japanese mind, is indubitably less characteristic and prevalent than the moral masochism which finds expression in the 'domestic drama' and the tearful confessions heard on television.

The Japanese child comes up against this guilt feeling without having to leave the two-way relationship which makes him so dependent on his mother. He is usually spared any Oedipal jealousies. Japanese children are weaned late and pot-trained without tears as their muscle control improves. Their parents do not impose a strict timetable for the biological functions of nutrition, excretion and sleep. When the child gets tired, the mother customarily lies down beside him, at least for a moment or two, to encourage him to sleep. She sleeps with him, usually in the same bed. The parents' room is the child's terrain; the very notion of a separate room, private territory, is inconceivable in Japanese architecture.

There are no ordeals of solitude and separation such as are imposed so soon on European and American children. Rather does conjugal intercourse give way to family intimacy.[8]

VARIATIONS ON OEDIPUS

In contrast, the normal Western upbringing, of which the world is all the more sharply aware thanks to psychoanalysis, demands the relegation of the child to his own cot, if possible in his own room, by himself, at a fixed time. A sound upbringing, it is thought, should impose discipline, separation and punishment at an early stage. The child must see himself as a distinct individual before the law, authority and his father's 'No'. Freedom? He has to earn it. The Japanese child begins with unlimited licence, and gradually comes to feel the bonds around him. Thus the Oedipal stage has a very different rhythm: in Japan it is dodged, put off, drowned in the symbiosis of mother and child. With us it is tending more and more towards the uncompromising precision, for example, of the childcare classics of Françoise Dolto: 'Listen here: before she is your mother she is my wife. She is going to be sleeping with me. You can have a wife to yourself when you grow up.'

Such plain speaking, which if it is true is true only because our culture made certain primordial choices, may certainly provoke a sort of individuation – but it would look quite crazy in Japan. We are afraid of giving any rein to Oedipal feelings: any symbiosis with the mother, we think, may strengthen alienating links which we, with our cult of individualism, look on with dread. Our rules for parents frown on dependency (captation of wills, castration), and lay the blame on possessive mothers and abusive fathers. The Japanese inclination is to let a close intimacy develop and frown on independence (ingratitude, disloyalty), laying the blame on the faithless and frivolous child.

Thus in Japan, individuation comes later and is more fragile. Lodged in the Japanese psyche is that paradise of oneness from earliest childhood, idealized in memory into a time of purest harmony, when there was no school-age discipline, no obligations, punishments or competition such as came later. This core of nostalgia feeds attempts to regress. The least harmful is simply drunkenness, the bottle of sake turning people of whatever age back into little innocents whose babblings and stumblings meet with unlimited indulgence. Thus addictions, which are in fact severely punishable in Japanese law, can also stand in for a refuge deep in the bosom of the mother, bringer of all blessings – or the bosom of death. But at last, when things are too bad, when the return to reality becomes intolerable, people are tempted to take their search for things past into the realms of death. All in all, Heraclitus' – or Nietzsche's – hypothesis of the eternal return is not the wisest or most plausible. A strange enthusiasm is mingled with the depression. Fantasy at least, if not reason, sees the decision to die as a hope of rebirth.

However indulgent their upbringing in the first few months, it inevitably has its moments of frustration and anger. Father is out of reach: he reigns but does not rule, the child could not dream of attacking him. But mother is there, and there just so as to put up with her baby's tantrums. She is expected to soothe cryings and stampings with soft words. She is careful to make a show of her patience, her resignation, her pain. She will not break down, curb or despise her baby's wrath: she will do her sacrificial best to endure it. That is the strategy imposed by a traditional upbringing: non-resistance. She knows that in time the child will be horrified at having attacked the love-object and smashed links which he cannot do without. Suddenly he will see that his anger is bad and dangerous and will recoil from it; the reaction will turn his hatred to pity, and whatever aggression remains will turn on him: he will identify himself with the victim of his own aggression, whom he loves and depends on. The mother's culturally programmed masochism will have achieved its goal by awakening the superego and the feeling of responsibility.

THE BOND WITH THE MOTHER

Here again we have a contrast with the West, where the superego is formed predominantly by the introjection of paternal authority – in this case, the rival to Oedipus, bearer of the taboo and the punishment. The child's hatred for the father retreats before the castration phobia and condenses into a superego in the subject, in Freud's classic description. Certainly the death of the father, fantasized in the Oedipus complex, is laden with guilt and anxiety, but it will never amount to the sort of absolute catastrophe implied by the fantasy of the mother dying because of a spoilt child. If *he* dies, I can live on, but if *she* comes to a sad end, and it is my fault, then I have no choice but to follow her straight away into death. The Japanese father functions as a shame-provoking Eye, but it is in the relationship with the mother that the anguish of guilt becomes really searing. Thus the superego becomes lodged much earlier, being aroused not by rivalry fantasies but in the generation of the death-wish, which Melanie Klein has observed long before the appearance of speech. The strategy for child-rearing which Japanese tradition inspires in these devoted mothers is quick to produce its ethical effects: the indulgence is not gratuitous and the dependence has its price.

Thus every culture takes up the Oedipal archetype and gives it a particular turn through its rituals and fables, customs and virtues. The Greeks recorded the revolt of the Son, supported by the Mother, in the legendary rivalries of Uranus, Cronus and Zeus. The Jews exalted the wrath of the Father, expelling the rebels from Paradise, drowning them in the Flood and scattering them at Babel; and they celebrated the sacrifice of the Son, Isaac prefiguring Jesus whose will, even unto death, is one with the will of the Father. Japanese theogony speaks of childish violence and maternal sacrifice: the goddess Izanami gives birth to the fire god and dies of the burns he inflicts on her. The feminine principle, nourishing, light-beaming, is under constant threat of disappearance. Amaterasu, the light-goddess of heaven, ancestress of the imperial family, is wounded through the misconduct of her younger brother Susanoo, the *enfant terrible* of the divine race, a perverse and grubby shapeshifter, sniveller and scamp. She withdraws into a cave – and the world is sunk in night, threatened with death. Then another goddess, Ama no Uzume, begins to laugh and dance; Amaterasu is appeased and reappears, light returns, everything is reborn, everything is forgiven.

The bond with the mother, initially biological and affective, takes on a moral significance. Knowing what the mother has suffered, remembering her self-sacrifice, her kindness, her forgiveness, gives deep roots to the Japanese feeling of obligation, which later will be transferred to other connections and will nourish every relationship in life. Obligations: always concrete, particular, specific, a network binding the subject round about. In a word, the Japanese superego is an awareness of bonds, the Western superego an awareness of laws. Ours are faults of transgression, theirs of defection. The law, universal and transcendent, applies equally to all as an inviolable limit, whether it be religious law, the will of God forbidding enjoyment of a desirable and dangerous fruit; or secular, modern law, the order of nature and society guaranteeing the inherent rights of every human being. The Japanese bond is a state of being, produced by common life, welded by a living interlace of silent adherences. It merges with the very conditions of group survival, mingles invisibly with the matter of reality – whereas our laws and values are formulated into principles and commands, and are set apart from life so that they may master and correct it.

TRANSCENDENCE AND IMMANENCE OF GOOD

In the West, authority is transcendent, in Japan it is immanent: it is exercised as a pressure of people as a whole against people individually, as imperceptible, silent and invincible as the air around them. The

Western individual has long been trained to resistance: not just since the eighteenth-century declaration of his inalienable rights, but since long before that, thanks to the conviction (readily suggested by Christianity) that he has a personal relationship with God, beyond and against the world. Plato proclaimed the transcendence of Good, beyond even Being.

This moral metaphysics, enlivened and dramatized through Christianity, soon began to separate the Western soul from the social universe within which the body was bound to exist. At any moment that universe might be condemned in the name of transcendence and idealism: *fiat justitia pereat mundus*, let justice be done though the world perish! Plato joins hands with the Savonarolas of yesteryear and the insurgent Utopians of our own day. It is a moral condemnation of reality, the ancient source of moral nihilism as Nietzsche would have it. To the Japanese way of thinking, on the other hand, justice is merely a euphoria of reality, the balance of the diverging forces of which that reality is composed. This automatically discourages individual presumption: be a manager, or an entrepreneur, by all means, but not a visionary! How can anyone be right and the whole world wrong? For rightness is the implicit harmony of the world. Resentment of reality, unconstrained by idealism and universality, cannot rise to revolt and dissolves straightway into melancholy: renunciation, silence, fading, expiation. From ancient fervour to modern indignation, Western pronouncements have a paranoid note; but the tone in Japanese culture is manic-depressive, veering from the expansive to the withdrawn.

All in all, the Westerner is inclined to believe that his duty is to be vigilant in this world for the sake of the Good. The Japanese is too closely involved with his world, which is all the good he has: his duty is perforce to be vigilant against himself, for the sake of the good(s) of this world. Not that the Japanese superego is stricter: its world is always felt to be close, familiar, enclosed, nourishing, surrounding, protecting. If it gets attentive service it can be relied on to be indulgent. In two domains, those of ideas and those of the senses, Japanese culture has shown itself tolerant, a twofold free space, beyond good and evil, in the very areas where Christianity nurtured those dual terrors, sin of pride and sin of the flesh, where moderns do their best to shed such guilt.

THE NARCISSISTIC ROLE

Thus the Japanese superego, with its links to near and positive responsibilities, was less open to invisible and distant pleadings: it could turn simple, this-worldly duty into its supreme and inexorable obligation. Whereas the Western soul, once bound to think of eternity and the

Everlasting God, now thinks of humanity and the universe. Infinite longings let the ego rise above responsibilities which, if they weigh heavy, are considered too cramping. There was no such counterweight in Japan; social obligations reigned supreme. Westerners like to keep a Brechtian distance between themselves and the gestures which show them forth: don't forget that *I* am here, behind the mask, and that my personality is infinitely beyond the character I have to play!

In Japan people identify themselves closely with their function, merge with it. No virtue is higher esteemed than this total commitment to one's role. It is no militant, Sartrean commitment to a great cause played out on the stage of history, but a simple, silent absorption which binds the person fast to his daily routine. And what better way to conjure the boredom of an ungrateful task than by giving onself to it wholeheartedly? Playing one's part well, however small the part may be, is calming and consoling: the man is none other than the perfected sum of his acts. This is the path to an aesthetic driven to its obsessional limit in the tea ceremony: ten or fifteen years' study before you finally master the art of holding a teacup with all the ennobled perfection attainable in a human action!

Alongside the narcissism binding the individual to his body, there is the narcissistic role, which George De Vos sees as one element in the Japanese psyche. No doubt it is one fundamental reason for Japan's recent economic success. You can explain the dynamism of advanced sectors of Japanese industry in terms of increased productivity (9.3 per cent per annum since 1975!), you can point out the savings and investments which are making firms ever better equipped; but you must eventually fall back on the essential factor, the high quality of work in Japan, which is to say the feeling of responsibility – and you must try to understand its psycho-sociological motivation. This identification of the individual with his task is as dangerous as it is protective: any realization of incapacity is a horrendous assault on his narcissism, destroying the ego's carefully nurtured idea of itself, causing intolerable confusion; and this can upset every corner of a man's life.

RESPONSIBILITY STRATEGIES

Potentially catastrophic can be any criticism bearing on the highly sensitive area of an individual's professional competence, whether from an outsider or from the individual himself in the silence of his own conscience. The Japanese term for a suicide following a reprimand is *shikarare jisatsu*. The individual's social persona is injured: he expiates the fault, or merely the negligence, he has been acccused of, firmly asserts his responsibility and thus recoups his threatened honour – but at the same time, if he selects a resounding self-punishment, it is often a retort to the author of the reprimand which transfers to the latter the responsibility for the act: self-punishment is also vengeance. Guilt is like a fluid which can be accumulated, freed, diverted or exchanged. Such manipulations, shrewdly monopolized by a Christian clergy which drew part of its income therefrom, were freely practised in Japan until the modern tendency to eliminate guilt feelings began to moderate them even there. Suicide (or sometimes an attempt at it, or a mere threat of it) was the keystone of this responsibility-fixing strategy, the unanswerable argument in a struggle to the death which, though it could be clandestine, was a ritual which turned on guilt and shame.

The traditional family, which still largely governs social relations, was often the scene of such manoeuvrings, particularly between mothers- and daughters-in-law.[9] The suicide rate for Japanese women is still high, seventy for every hundred men, whereas in Poland (where Catholic belief protects them) there are only twenty or so, twenty-five in the United States, fifty in Denmark, Switzerland and Germany. Is there a single traditional culture which, having sought to mould female masochism, has not actually increased it? Japanese women were presented with an ideal of abnegation and self-effacement which attracted many of them even towards the virtues of a voluntary death. They were called upon to sacrifice everything, starting with their past: cut off from their own families, they came to depend exclusively on their adopted family, those will became their law. Next to go was their dream of love: marriage being an arrangement between two families, following negotiating procedures which are still in frequent use, they might hope for love to crown their marriage, but could never hope for the reverse. If a woman did fall in love with her husband she would have to renounce jealousy for the sake of peace in society, which always looked with a tolerant eye upon masculine sensuality and fostered its escapades – from mere prostitution to concubinage – while denying any to the wife.

She lived under the same roof as her mother-in-law, who could be counted on to watch her like a hawk and criticize her unsparingly: suicide could be a very tempting rejoinder! She might even be blamed for her husband's infidelities: whose fault is it if you can't keep him? By strengthening the bond between mother and son, Japanese culture set mother- and daughter-in-law at endless Oedipal odds over their son and husband. The best way out was indeed to identify with the rival, to follow her in giving birth to a boy on whom to lavish all her unsatisfied love. The same culturally programmed feelings were reproduced in the cycle that reproduced the species itself. If the young wife was not blessed with a son, the situation could become intolerable: she was reminded that marriage laid on her the supreme responsibility of carrying on the family name which had become hers. Her inability to produce what was expected of her would force her into the background: samurai families had a high rate of repudiated wives. So she might well prefer death, if she had any hope that her demise would stir up some well-deserved remorse. Meanwhile, the threat of suicide, the mere possibility of it (which was hallowed by custom) could be a way of standing up to pressure, and a brake on others' ill-will.

AWARENESS OF DESTINY

It is evident that in this very wide-ranging concept of destiny, individual intentions are left out of account. We are not casting doubt on a woman's desire for a son, or the willingness of an incompetent worker: we are looking only at the facts, and asking the individual to judge them, and herself along with them. A moment of incapacity, clumsiness, carelessness, or simple bad luck, so long as it causes harm or damage to a third party, can cause the perpetrator a sort of embarrassment which her milieu may then set out to render intolerable – unless she elects to remedy or expiate the consequences, at whatever cost to herself, as Oedipus did when he put out his eyes, assuming all the responsibility for a situation which he had not sought in the very least. That distant ancestor of ours may still strike us with awe, but we have moved on since: when we seek to assign responsibility we look behind the act to the intention.

Confessors, acting in all fairness, have taught us to make the blame and the punishment fit the crime of the will – the evil thought – and that alone. The Christian, it is true, assumes that that evil is inexhaustible: 'My will', said Luther, 'will never be content *not* to wish to sit in the seat of God!' Thus we want the sinner to tell us how much he really knew about his act and to what extent he really willed it. At the very end of this psychological regression, first embarked on when in the twelfth century Abelard constructed his morality of intentions, we came with Freud to the discovery of the unconscious. Intention becomes a mere symptom. If the will is ultimately not responsible, then the punishments which society persists in dealing out lose all their moral legitimacy. If the criminal did not will to do what he did, if he did not even know what he willed, how can he be punished?

Japanese thinking went in the opposite direction, away from the unfathomable source of the act. To gauge responsibility they went downstream, towards the results. The individual was made to feel bound by an outcome which he did not intend, fused with his own act even to its most unexpected consequences. He was discouraged from offering excuses. This ethical choice could be justified by the Buddhist doctrine of karma: what happens to me now is a just retribution for my past lives; I can't even blame bad luck, because there is no such thing as chance any more. If I plead innocence I may lose courage and shame myself. It is better to assume, moment by moment, the unfathomable wholeness of my destiny. It can crush me, but not change what I am, what I must be. Beyond all failure I am promised that nobility. I may be a miserable creature, but like Oedipus I can make my misery more admirable than my happier days. I can tacitly despise all those who claim innocence and unawareness, and so try to elude their fate and prolong their petty lives.

These choices, by a whole civilization, give an ethical value and meaning, not symptomatic but clearly expressible, to suicides which, in a different historical context, would be set down as aberrant, and at worst incomprehensible. When Vatel, majordomo to the Prince de Condé, fearing lest he be unable to accomplish all his duties, ran himself through, he was thought to have acted from sheer tiredness, since he had gone for twelve nights without sleep while preparing festivities for a visit by Louis XIV. We can scarcely avoid thinking oddly, almost despisingly, of the honour which bound him even unto death to the burden of his office. We would diagnose melancholia, or overwork. Vatel ought to have been born Japanese. At the court of a shogun his act would not have looked extravagant, abnormal or ambiguous, as it did at Chantilly. What looked like an acute symptom of depression would have attained the full dignity of a suicide of responsibility, *sekinin jisatsu*, a recognized part of the social code. The individual alone cannot give meaning to his acts: he must act with his feet on the ground of his times, just as he relies on words to think and speak with.

OYAKO SHINJU

The same could be said of sympathy suicides, which also have a long history in Japan. The commonest and most grievous form is family suicide (*ikka shinju, oyako shinju*): parents, unknowingly or by persuasion, dragging their children after them into death. The recent tendency of the Japanese family towards the nuclear unit has only intensified an already traditional concept of close family solidarity. Most often we find a mother poisoning or drowning herself along with her baby, a catastrophic manifestation of their symbiosis, for better and for worse, in Japanese culture. Abandoned by a seducer, crushed by poverty, she no longer wishes to live; or is it illness she fears?

Often she is in conflict with her husband. Or is she still in doubt of her capacity to be a real mother? But she loves her child too well to condemn him to the loneliness her death would mean to him. She thinks death would be better for him than separation. She has no doubt that he would ratify her choice if he were already able to voice his own opinion. And she knows that in death she can count on a sympathetic public opinion: they may not approve of her deed, but they will understand it. It will never occur to her that the child might have a separate existence, under God's sovereignty from birth (or from conception), and enjoying the rights which, in the West, the law has guaranteed every citizen since the eighteenth century. Every year more than 200 Japanese mothers perform that twofold sacrifice. An expert in *oyako shinju* counted 494 cases in 1975 alone. Such twofold suicides are not unknown in the West, indeed they are scarcely less frequent – but they are classsed as symptoms of acute melancholia, untamed patterns of action which we are aware of but do not find mirrored in ourselves. Whereas in Japanese culture they have acquired a rationality which fits them in with educational practice, Oedipal structures, ideals of solidarity, and, by degrees, with the decisive choices which become part of the history of a particular society.

BEYOND THE SYMPTOM

We can therefore conclude that interpreting suicide as a symptom, as the humane sciences prompt us to do, is not fundamentally correct, since the symptom manifests itself only along the lines already drawn by a culture. Such an interpretation, conceived in nineteenth-century Europe in answer to the needs of the time, is not enough to make sense of acts which relate to the guiding principles of a different society. Trying to understand the suicides which are even now taking place in Japan, we may first hear the united voices of psychology and sociology, but we soon have to fall back on institutions, values and maxims developed through the history of Japan itself, which constitute the truth horizon against which any particular act must show its meaning. There is no reason to think that those institutions, values and maxims are mere survivals doomed to retreat and gradual elimination. We would be bold indeed to assume *that* – to imagine that the current state of affairs in the West is one through which all of humanity must needs pass. There is more than one road to the future, and Japanese society is remarkable in that it seems able to use yesterday's customs as a short cut to tomorrow's world.

If there were such a thing as human nature, we might be able to ask the humane sciences for an explanation. Psychologists and sociologists could present us with an 'essential' suicide: variable and complex perhaps, but also immutable, like the 'essential' family, art, punishment, work, insanity, power, or any other key element in the make-up of mankind. This would be possible if human beings were separable from time, the old dream chased by metaphysical idealists which scientists have sought to revive. But is there any way of fixing limits, in the name of divine or natural law, which mankind might be unwilling to pass?

We can describe, we can understand, but we can neither define nor determine. What is man? We can only answer, 'Ask it of history', for even to himself man is an enigma dispersed through time. He is no more than the fragmented sum of his potential, of everything of which he is, was and will be capable. What he is is none other than what he can become, and what he can become can only be revealed to us by history, still to come or already accomplished: stored in his memory, or in the strength of his resolve and his hopes. The unity of man is under no threat from any freedom for self-invention which he may assume, because any way of acting which history can encompass can be understood, and if examined, will reveal its hidden logic – which, as Nietzsche tells us, will gradually become intelligible through 'the long, painfully decipherable, hieroglyphic text of past human morality'.[10]

Suicide cannot be defined on psycho-sociological principles alone. It escapes through the open mesh of history, through the threads of meaning given it over centuries of invention: meanings superimposed, entangled, some now superseded, but many still persistent, and indeed more vigorous than ever.[11]

Thus, if we want to grasp the meaning of suicide in modern Japan, we must go back over the whole history of the country, for the meaning of what has once been is fated to recur, right back to the dawn whose light is shown to us by the earliest available documents. In this mirror of history, imperfect and shadowy in its beginning, the images we glimpse will talk to us, question us, as if through us they were even now questioning themselves.

5

The Dawn of History

What we in fact find in the earliest texts composed at the imperial behest (*Kojiki*, 712; *Fudoki*, 713; *Nihongi*, 720), and in the ancient Shinto myths and rituals, is a love of life and a naïve and simple dread of death. The god Izanagi weeps for his wife-sister Izanami, who has died while giving birth to Fire. He goes down into the darkness of the underworld to rescue her. Orpheus did not more than glimpse the immaterial wraith of Eurydice; but what Izanagi sees in the torchlight is Izanami's decaying corpse, already crawling with worms. Overcome with horror, he runs away, rolls a rock over the entrance to the realm of the dead and proceeds to hasty ablutions.[1]

DEATH AND SHINTO

Shinto priests felt the same repulsion: dead bodies, blood, filth, stench and decay, all were taboo (*imi*). They kept well away from the corpse and concentrated on cleansing the relatives who might have been contaminated by contact with the dead. No religion is less interested in death! They left it to Buddhism to give meaning to death and seek some sort of salvation. They were dedicated to this life, its protection, embellishment, and ordering. They were not interested in the next world and had no ideas about it: it was night, and probably nothingness. Why worry? Our world is enough for us, with its duties and rewards. It was a non-ascetic religion with no aversion to sensuality. The Japanese have never blamed pleasure for being what it is, attractive but ephemeral; they have faithfully made room for it in their lives, and here again they seem to be ahead of us on the road we have chosen to follow.

A dead man no longer belonged to this world: whatever his vices and crimes during life, there would be no settling up for them afterwards. A few Buddhist sects were to bring in the idea of retribution and hell, but according to Shinto death would make the deceased into one of the gods, *kami* – a powerful stranger who must be respected, humoured and kept at a distance. Some singing and dancing rituals sought to entertain the dead man's spirit and soothe his annoyance, lest he return from the other world to vent his spleen at being dead! Japanese animism kept a watch on the boundary which protected mankind from the innumerable forces which might be lurking in the universe. These rituals recall the dance of Ama no Uzume before the eighty myriad gods after the disappearance of the Celestial Light, Amaterasu. An odd reaction, one of rejoicing rather than tears: the idea being that at the winter solstice the death of the sun must be overcome by festive prodigality which would restore her failing energy and bring her back to joy. The Aztecs used human sacrifice to the same end: the sun, whom they held to have been born of a voluntary self-sacrifice on his own account, must be upheld in his shining by other sacrifices, no less willing, and it was to this life-giving, self-consuming star that the priests held on high the smoking hearts of their victims.[2]

OFFERINGS AND SACRIFICES

Shinto has a horror of blood. It will have no sacrifices, only offerings. To spirits and gods they offer rice, sake, the fruits of the earth or of human craftsmanship, paper, fabrics, dancing and music. An agricultural society, with little meat, has no need to hedge the slaughter of domestic animals with religious ritual in the belief, held by the Greeks, that their flesh must be shared with the immortals upon the altar. But has there ever been a society which has dispensed with death ritually administered to men or animals for the common good? Has one single civilization ever done without sacrifice, be it real or symbolical? In Japan, where so many traditions endure, the violence of primitive festivals proper to a prehistoric hunting culture has not yet quite disappeared: in the province of Mikawa live animals are torn to pieces at the annual festival of *Kaza matsuri*.

Even pure agriculture had its savageries: according to certain rituals, newly transplanted rice seedlings had to be scattered with the entrails of a deer. The ethnologist Yanagita Kunio notes that in several districts it is still customary to push the girls transplanting the rice over into the mud of the paddy-fields: no doubt this is a distant echo of a rite by which a young girl was sacrificed to the water gods whose co-operation was essential if the irrigated crop was to thrive. So numerous are the legends recounting the (allegedly voluntary) death of a woman devout to the point of self-sacrifice that we might wonder if some provinces did not once have fertility rites involving the glorification and death of the chosen woman, as in the *Rite of Spring*. Certainly some virgins, the *miko*, were, if not sacrificed, at least consecrated to the service of a god, tied to his sanctuary, forbidden to marry. Their sensitivity, heightened by chastity, could make of them mediums or shamans: they could see and speak to the dead, and would dance before them. This institution, less cruel than infanticide at birth or selling small daughters in time of famine, gave rural communities a means of controlling female fertility, which must, according to the immemorial doctrine described by Malthus, be subordinated to the fertility of the earth.

After some great calamity, a famine or epidemic, ancient human instincts will resurface. The gods must be appeased, and ordinary offerings are no longer sufficient. People seek a perpetrator and find a scapegoat. Thus after the great earthquake which devastated Tokyo and Yokohama in 1923, the mob lynched some Korean immigrants – and certain notorious free-thinkers. At one time, people in an area just hit by some calamity might even sacrifice a substitute emperor. In primitive times, the ruler was there to sacrifice his own person if the people suffered misfortune, as Oedipus expiated the plague of Thebes. But before very long the emperor was deemed innocent in all things; his sovereignty carried no real power. He was seen as a cherished child who had to be helped and served, not as a stern master whose responsibility was commensurate with his might.

Japanese culture did not travel far along the paths of political revolt opened up by such a sacrifice, which counted Louis XVI among its many victims. Ancient Japan turned rather to the professionals: there were specialists in responsibility who constituted the hereditary corporation of the *Imibe* – a guild for taboos. According to third-century Chinese sources, people seeking to ensure success in a perilous enterprise, such as a sea voyage or a crossing from the archipelago on to the continent, would take on a man who voluntarily subjected himself to the harshest deprivations and spent his time fasting in the dark. If the undertaking was successful he was rewarded; if not, he was held responsible and killed. As an insurance policy it was somewhat less reliable than Lloyd's. In historical times these professional paid scapegoats dwindled and finally disappeared.

VICTIMS, FROM THE FORCED TO THE FREE

The sacrificial instinct prefers an innocent victim to a supposedly guilty one: he stirs deeper emotions. A legend of the Akita district tells how a girl was offered to the dragon-god of rain in order to stop a flood. This recalls the sacrifice of Iphigenia, the thirst of the gods for human lives. The propitiatory custom of the *hitobashira* or human pillar was a persistent one: it meant burying one or more victims alive (to avoid shedding blood) in the foundations of bridges, dikes or fortresses in order to propitiate the resident gods and confer vital forces. Not long ago some skeletons were found under the vast walls of the fortress at Edo, which was built by the Tokugawa shoguns in the seventeenth century and which since the Meiji period has been the imperial palace. Even now, the first blow for the foundations of a new house is always preceded by a little ceremony: it may be no more than a couple of bottles of sake and a few ritual phrases, but this at least must be done to secure the favour of the powers of earth. The whole of Japanese life is thus adorned with little pagan rituals, which may once have been fearsome, but are now purely ornamental.

In this second type of sacrifice, some violence is still perceptible, and can even shock if the victims are sufficiently innocent. The blinding of Oedipus strikes us with horror, but our pity for the slaughter of Iphigenia makes us dubious about the gods and their priests. A way was found to elude this: there must be a victim, but he or she could be a volunteer, self-immolating, plunging willingly into death's abyss. Jewish culture, from Isaac to Jesus, shows the same evolution towards this third type as does the Japanese. Isaac, like Iphigenia, is still the unwitting and passive victim demanded by the divine will. Jesus *acts*, sacrifices himself and dedicates himself, even unto death, to the salvation of mankind. The story is more moving, even sublime, and heaven is 'not guilty'. Japanese history and legend tell of no comparable sacrifice: they are concerned rather with family honour, successful expeditions, at most the peace of the empire – but the drift is in the same direction. Finally, the sacrifice is internalized and refined into voluntary death. The decision to die absorbs all the violence, and the victim, dying willingly, arouses not only pity, but also gratitude and admiration.

SUICIDE AS OBLATION

Since the dawn of Japanese history, this theme, this mingling of sacrifice and suicide, has been continually heard. One of Japan's legendary heroes, Yamato Takeru no Mikoto, a great traveller, warrior and monster-slayer, was once making ready to cross the narrow straits which connect what is now Tokyo Bay with the ocean. 'This sea', said he, 'is so little that one could jump from one shore to the other!' The god of the straits was annoyed and raised a storm. Yamato Takeru's ship was doomed to perish through this divine wrath:

> Now in the prince's suite there was a woman called Princess Ototachibana. She was the daughter of the Lord Oshiyama, of the Hozumi clan. She spoke to the prince in these words: 'See! The wind has risen, the waves grow mighty. Your ship is sinking. All this is the work of the sea-god. I beg you, let your unworthy servant enter into the sea as a ransom for Your Highness's noble existence!' Scarcely had she spoken than she dived into the waves. Upon the instant the storm died down, and the ship was able to reach the shore.[3]

Is the legend of the Lady Ototachibana an echo of a customary ritual by which people were sacrificed to the gods of lakes and seas? Stories tend to link the death of women with deep water.

All through the Japanese tradition acts of self-immolation and abnegation have been exalted as a high ideal, all the higher in that reality often belied them. A self-effacing suicide was recommended as the simplest and most direct way to restore harmony after conflict. From the twelfth century to the seventeenth – before and after Heian – Japanese society again and again fell prey to civil war and was rent by quarrels over the succession. Its early enthusiasm for renunciation seems almost like an attempt to forearm itself against such things.

One of the greatest emperors of Japanese protohistory, Nintoku Tenno, who was traditionally believed to have reigned from 313 to 399, spent three years in a trial of modesty against his brother. Since each held himself less worthy to reign than the other, the throne remained vacant. One day, a fisherman wishing to present the emperor with a basket of fish was sent bouncing like a ball from one palace to the other, from Naniwa to Uji and back again, so often and for so long (says the *Nihongi*) that the fish went off en route! There is a vaguely comic feeling about this which is still perceptible today in Japanese life, in the protestations and counter-protestations of modesty, in the interminable salutations and identical bows which politeness demands. This competition in reverse can be as empty and deceptive as any other game of mirrors, embroiling the Japanese individual in a kind of self-effacing narcissism which strikes him rigid – unless some decisive stroke cuts across the self-perpetuating confrontation. This was understood by the imperial prince, younger brother of the emperor-to-be Nintoku:[4] 'The prince of the blood said to himself, "I realize that no one could overcome the will of the prince my elder brother. Shall I then cause trouble to the empire by prolonging my life?" Upon which he slew himself.'

He kills himself. But how – by falling on his sword, or by hanging himself? The story does not tell us; the bare indication is sufficient. Euphemism, allusion and ellipsis are preferred to detailed description. Similarly, Lady Ototachibana spoke not of drowning herself but of 'entering into the sea'. To speak too precisely about death would be to conjure it up. And death, even when voluntary, loses none of its power to disturb. Suicides in Japanese stories are often discreet, almost furtive. The motives are described at length, dispassionately and lucidly. The dramatic nature of the act, and its exalted nobility, are emphasized. But the reader is generally spared the gruesome details. The Christian inspiration of a Villon, a Holbein or a Grünewald may choose to dwell on the horror of the death-agony, the decaying flesh. The Japanese never found anything instructive in such spectacles; they were acutely aware of the precariousness of existence, but were not fond of depicting the misery of the fleshly creation.

ON THE THIRD DAY HE ROSE AGAIN

When Prince Osazaki heard that the prince of the blood had perished, he was appalled; he left Naniwa in all haste and went to the palace of Uji. This was three days after the prince of the blood had expired. Then Prince Osazaki beat his noble breast, cried and wept, and was overcome with grief. He unbound his hair, sat across the body, and three times called on the dead man thus: 'O prince, my brother!' Suddenly the prince returned to life. He arose. Then Prince Osazaki said to him, 'Ah, what sorrow! What grief! Why did you go away thus of your own choice? If the dead have any consciousness, what must the late emperor my father think of me?' Then the prince of the blood replied in these words to his elder brother: 'Such is my fate. Who could hold me back? If I come to the dwelling place of our father, I shall tell him frankly that my brother is a wise man, and has several times sought to yield me the throne. But the news of my death has brought Your Highness on a long and hasty journey; how could I not be infinitely grateful to you?' With these words he offered him his younger sister, the princess Yata, born of the same mother, saying, 'Surely she is not worthy to be your wife, but be pleased to number her among the ladies of the court.' Then he laid himself back in the coffin and died.

A most refined courtesy on the part of a man three days dead, to come to life for a moment to dispel his brother's anxiety and commiserate with his fatigue! Under the narrative embellishments the reality is perceptible: in such circumstances, the saving suicide might have had little that was voluntary about it. Often the victim had been put in an intolerable position and had been pressured into removing himself; it was only natural to feel rather bad about this afterwards. Thus the tale of resurrection acts like a dream, perhaps representing (and fulfilling) the Emperor Nintoku's desire to be exonerated from all responsibility for his younger brother's death. These legends and the wonders in them show us the early fantasies of a society seeking in an ideal world for escape from its dawning contradictions.

If shining examples had been sufficient, the empire would never have suffered from fratricidal hatreds or insatiable rivalries. In reality they seen to have been commoner in Japan than elsewhere: such clashes run right through its history. The emperorship, which ought to have settled such rivalries and moderated (and so governed) such passions, often declined to nothing more than a bone of clan contention. At crucial moments, when there was a crisis over the succession, interest groups would form, with each faction supporting one prince or other from the imperial family as its candidate for the throne. Violence made the choice, and that choice was often the outcome of intrigue and sometimes of murder.

DYING FOR LOVE

In private life, rival passions could again flare up in the absence of an arbitrator. Suicide could sometimes seem the best way out, less costly than a duel to the death but just as decisive. Instead of resolving the confrontation by eliminating one rival, someone might suggest removing the object of their passion, without which the quarrel would lapse and peace be restored. Several poems in the *Man'yoshu* describe such conflicts between men enamoured of one women, which could (as Hegel remarked) very quickly degenerate into a struggle to the death over nothing more than prestige. The poem's suggested solution is suicide:[5]

    Poem on seeing the tomb of the maiden of Unahi

    The maiden of Unahi
      In the town of Ashiya,
    From her earliest childhood
      And even at the age to bind her hair
    Never showed herself abroad,
      But stayed at home.
    Then some were driven mad
      By their desire to see her:

Her suitors hastened
> To hedge her all about.
A young man of Chinu
> And a young man of Unahi
Declared themselves rivals
> And together asked for her hand.
Their bows of light wood
> They took, and their quivers,
Ready to plunge into the waves
> Or to leap into flames.
Wrathful
> They fought.
Then the sweet maiden said to her mother,
'When I see
Two such men
> Rivals for my worthless self,
How could I live
> And cleave to one of them?
To the Kingdom of the Dead
> I go to await them' . . .
Saying these few words,
> Weeping,
The girl went away.
The youth of Chinu
> Saw her that same night in a dream:
Following her lead
> He went to join her.
Then the youth of Unahi
> Whom he had left behind
Turned up his face towards heaven
> And cried out in despair,
Stamped his foot,
> Ground his teeth, foamed at the mouth:
'I shall not be outdone
> By my rival',
He said, and girding on
> The short sword a man carries at his side,
He went after the other.
Then their parents
> Came together,
And to keep their memory fresh
> For many years,
So that their story would be told
> Far in the future,
They built the maiden's tomb
> In the middle,

> They built
> > On one side and on the other
> > The tombs of the two young men.
> > When I heard their story told,
> > > Though I knew them not,
> > It was like a new bereavement.
> > > And I wept for it.

Note that the object fascinates by hiding from view. The maiden in the shadows is all the more desirable because she is invisible: her modesty and virtuous self-effacement are enough to arouse the most passionate love. Therefore she cannot possibly make the choice which a Western cultural background would expect of her, the solution which we should find most natural – make up her mind! That would be too cruel to the one not favoured. She cannot decide, no more than a good mother can declare a preference among her jealous offspring. Nor can she promise herself to the victor, for that would be to stir up the conflict for which – for all her innocent intentions – she already feels too heavy a responsibility. But she does possess the initiative for a single act through which she hopes to restore the peace that follows upon sacrifice. The feminine ideal of self-effacement leads logically and irresistibly to a voluntary death. Her example is infectious: the suitor who dreams of her, probably the one who loved her most truly, understands that death is the measure of love – for what would love be if he feared death, and recoiled from the reunion promised in its void? The second suitor, liking the image projected by the first, is then trapped as in a mirror, unwillingly dragged into the machinery of competitive suicide: he has to prove to himself that he is equal to his own ideal – his rival – and so kills himself too.

Hegel has a similar quadrilateral of death, completing the triangle of the two rivals and their object. It is death which presides over the contest, since it is death which each fears from the other, and it is the agony of death which, by eternalizing the difference between slave and master, puts an end to their rivalry. But in the *Man'yoshu* poem, this seems to be transcended immediately, as in the best romantic tradition. Death is the dream of a refuge in which perfect harmony reigns, an equality without conflict: there, the union of separate existences is consummated at last. A dream of fusion in unanimity. All hatreds can be cancelled by a sacrifice. A voluntary death is needed as a warrant of peace. The chief actors disappear in turn, their tombs are together – and the calm of the village, which is their silent spectator, can be restored. Life goes on for a community which might have suffered from their dissensions: it will readily shed tears of approval on the noble behaviour which it has prompted.

The maiden who commits suicide when too thoroughly run after is a theme which recurs several times in the *Man'yoshu*. Some Japanese critics see this as a echo of suicides by *miko*, priestesses dedicated to a god and vowed to chastity. When they fell victim to a seducer, the only possible expiation was a more or less compulsory suicide. It is quite likely, however, that the tale of the maiden of Unahi refers to much more commonplace happenings, prompted by repressed desires within the narrow confines of a rural community. Such love-entanglements were bad for work, stirred up quarrels and could deepen into vendettas if families decided their honour was involved. The peace of the whole village could thus be threatened at close quarters by a giddy girl. Rice-growing is an activity requiring intricate co-operation: nothing is more vital than a good understanding among the divers households which share a given piece of land.

Primitive societies (so-called) counter these dangers by accepting the very strict marriage laws examined by Claude Lévi-Strauss. Japanese society got round them by an exchange of women decided upon jointly by the families; therefore individual desire and its aberrations had to be restrained. Girls were brought up with this idea in mind, and taught self-effacement for fear lest their fancy, backed up by their attractiveness, should inflame desire, arouse rivalry and bring to naught the matrimonial designs of their parents. They were brought up against as high ideal to which their dreams might aspire, which could inspire them if necessary, and which meanwhile would keep them on their guard against the unhappy fate of being too much beloved. Suicide was both an inspiration and a deterrent: it became the only allowable form of romance.

THE AGE OF THE ANCIENT TOMBS

In this warrior-and-peasant society, rural communities needed peace if they were to work, and the peace was founded on the kind of renunciations we have been examining. Meanwhile the warrior clans buttressed their power with similarly austere forms of solidarity. The golden age of agriculture was the Yayoi period, which lasted for five centuries up to 250 AD. After that the introduction of Chinese methods of irrigation allowed a great increase in the food supply. The population grew in proportion, probably reaching crisis point within a few generations. This rice-growing culture, which originated on Kyushu (the island nearest the mainland), now had to take up arms in search of new land for clearance: it advanced towards the Inland Sea and the plain of Yamato, where a centre of power struck root which was to become Imperial Japan. As the centuries passed, the thrust towards the east continued until the entire archipelago had been colonized; the former, barbarian inhabitants, the alien tribes of hunters and fishers, were expelled or assimilated.

During this period of expansion they even managed to establish a bridgehead in south Korea, the colony of Mimana, which lasted for two centuries, up to 562. The warrior bands soaked up the surplus population, spreading as the paddy-fields extended, each clan raising taxes from the lands it protected against the clan next door. Weaponry improved, thanks to steel-making techniques imported from the continent. The iron age had replaced the age of gold – as it always does, for never in human history has this fatal progress been avoided. The power-hunger of the clan chieftains needed an outward sign: it made a covenant with death. This was the age of the ancient tombs, *kofun jidai*. Funeral ceremonies which, from the frugal, rural viewpoint of Shinto, might have been no more than a series of ablutions for the benefit of the living and celebrations for the sake of the dead, took on an unprecedented solemnity. Thus through the third, fourth and fifth centuries, the narrow plain of Yamoto, where the imperial power was rooted, saw the erection of ever more imposing tombs. The virtuous Emperor Nintoku is buried near Osaka under a vast tumulus more than a mile in circumference. Such erections required thousands of slaves and workmen and spectacular expenditure: power was to be exhibited in the pomp of the tomb. Dying was a ruinously expensive business.

But perhaps the most striking expense was always that of human life in sacrifice. Clan chieftains did not like to lie alone in the cold ground; their pride demanded company. When a great man died his household was sacrificed – strangled and buried to attend on him. Human sacrifice, demanded only in exceptional circumstances by the gods of sea, earth, rivers and rain, had become normal practice on the death of a noble lord. Such customs existed in many ancient civilizations: to serve and honour the illustrious dead in the other world, you killed his servants. Five thousand years ago, in Ur of the Chaldees, the victims went down into the royal tomb and there drank poison. Herodotus reports that the Scythians used to bury a king's concubines along with him. In India, the custom called suttee, which required a widow to share her husband's funeral pyre, disappeared only under pressure from the British authorities. Among the Manchus, sacrifices at the death of a prince are attested down to the seventeenth century; yet Confucius had expressed his disapproval of them long before.

THE INVENTION OF SUBSTITUTES

Sacrifices to the dead eventually came to be considered as cruel, and living servants were replaced by substitutes. In the twenty-second year of the reign of the Emperor Suinin, on the fifth day of the tenth month, the emperor's younger brother died. One month later, his coffin was laid in the earth. His servants were buried alive (probably waist-deep) around the tomb. They did not (says the *Nihongi*) perish immediately, and for several days and nights they wept and moaned incessantly. At last they died and rotted away. Dogs and crows came to devour them:

> The emperor, hearing these cries and groans, was touched to the heart. To the great officials he spoke these august words: 'For the dead to be followed by those whom they cherished in life is a most cruel thing. Although it may be an ancient custom, why should we bow to it, if it be not good? From this day onwards, take thought for it that the dead may no longer be thus accompanied!' ...
>
> In the thirty-second year of his reign, in the autumn, on the sixth day of the seventh month, Her Highness the Empress Hibasu passed away. Several days were to pass before her burial, and to the great officials the emperor spoke these august words: 'I know from experience that it is not good for the dead to be accompanied. What shall we do for this funeral?' Then the lord Nomi came forward and said: 'It would be ill to bury living men on their feet, alive, in Her Highness's tomb. How could such a custom be passed down to posterity? I beg you, let me think of a way and suggest it to you!' Thereupon he sent messengers to seek some hundred men belonging to the guild of potters of Izumo. He had them model figures of clay, men, horses, and all kinds of objects, and he presented them to the emperor, saying, 'Let this be a rule for the centuries to come, to substitute these clay figures for living beings and set them up in the tombs!' The emperor rejoiced exceedingly, and addressed to the lord Nomi these august words: 'In truth, the plan you have conceived is pleasing to my heart!' Thus for the first time, clay statuettes were placed in the tomb of Her Highness the Empress Hibasu. These clay (*hani*) objects were called *haniwa*.[6]

COMPANY IN DEATH

From then on, the princely dead were escorted into the earth by an array of clay figures – a clay more lasting than the human body, so that they are often found almost intact in museum display cases. People were still accompanied into death, but henceforth the sacrifice was voluntary. The spirit of sacrifice which leads from Isaac to Jesus, from the forced to the willing victim, can be followed just as clearly in this suicide of companionship as it is in suicides of devotion or self-effacement. The feeling between master and servants, sovereign and vassals, leader and followers, emperor and officials, was so intense that existence could seem hollow and unbearable once he was gone. They had only one life, and in it could serve only one master. A bond between man and man, often forged in battle, could be closer than the marriage bond: the Japanese sanctioned the suicide of companionship (*junshi*) between warriors, but never expected a wife to rejoin her husband immediately, as did Indian advocates of suttee. Julius Caesar remarked on a similar pact binding Gaulish warriors to their chieftain even in death: they swore not to survive him.[7]

Such allegiances were both hierarchical and intimate: due deference did not preclude intense feeling. Differences of status could not be violated, but they could be encompassed by a warmth of feeling which it is hard for us to conceive of. We in the West have tended rather to see solidarity as a horizontal relationship binding brothers of one condition, who felt equal to one another, close because united under one father, patron, prince or principle: obeying divine law, or later rebelling against it, but then all the more united for having outlived even their god. Islam sought to make this levelling irrevocable by deducing it from the grandeur of the Everlasting, but it is just as inextricably bound up with our slogans of revolt: equality, fraternity ... From the dawn of their history, the Japanese have maintained a vertical solidarity which remains operative today, under new guises, in their industrial firms.

Chinese observers were noting this fondness for hierarchy as far back as the third century. The Japanese find equality disquieting: it can so easily lead to contests of prestige, which their polite formulae are constantly seeking to exorcize by negation. Equality must be overwritten by differences of rank or age. The Japanese can experience solidarity only if they feel protected by a complete symbolical apparatus of signs and insignia, by which every individual has his place within a differentiated distribution of tasks and honours, with an overall equilibrium of rights and duties. Japanese mothers are complaisant, seldom deterred by a father's interdicts: a Japanese child, faced with a little brother as a rival for his mother's affections, would be unable to control his jealousy if people did not take great care to establish the hierarchical difference between siblings, and explain to the elder how his age and superior wisdom confer superiority upon him. The real loss he must sustain – his symbiosis with the mother – is compensated by symbolic superiority. Whatever we may think, this approach may be the most humane one: it is some consolation for advancing age!

The strength of the clan depended on these vertical links whose intensity of feeling mounted every step of the hierarchy. The power of a noble house was directly proportionate to the devotion it inspired. Such feelings were assumed, amplified and exemplified in ideology. Kant, summing up several centuries of rationalism, advised us to govern our affections through the healthy apathy of pure reason. Confucius, too, was a leading apostle of moderation. But the Japanese knights of the iron age, and, seven centuries later, of the Kamakura period, were wholly and indeed exaggeratedly given over to emotions immediately apprehended as ethical. They made no distinction between passion and virtue. At the death of their master they sought to offer up their mourning as an exemplary excess. If grief and desolation were not enough to send them after him – by hanging or, seven centuries later, disembowelling – they still felt impelled by noble maxims and illustrious precedents.

Sometimes they killed themselves less out of love for their chief than to show off their courage and loyalty. They yielded to the stirring and glorious idea of themselves which they wished to leave behind. At a blow, they reached the height of grief and heroism and gave irrefutable testimony of the purity of their feelings. They had been taught to despise those who talked about love instead of loving, described their emotions instead of translating them into action. They believed that a single act could be more eloquent than the longest of speeches, for speeches can lie, but actions never. They believed in the absolute sincerity of the ultimate act, after which no other act is possible. That was their faith. Illusory it may have been, for we know that suicide can be complicated, with a suspect pathological element in it: it can say a lot more than its perpetrator intended. But still, it was their faith: they thought that men did not lie in the fact of death, and (like all those with a will to believe) they had to maintain the illusion, and pay its price.[8]

6

Violence at a Distance

The emperor could not give his unreserved approval to such impassioned displays of clan loyalty. His own power rested first and foremost on the imperial clan itself, the most powerful of all, the best-endowed with lands, men and devotion. But the empire was another thing: an ideal of unity, a principle of fair dealing, an authority capable of imposing peace and order on the whole archipelago. Therefore the emperor, being both unable and unwilling to eliminate private allegiance, undertook to contain it: family prestige was an important thing indeed, but how much more so the good health of the empire! And personal feelings had to be controlled for a yet wider reason, the reason of state. Japan was not to be a mere confederation of warring tribes: it had already embarked on the dialectic which was to impel the nation throughout its history. The ideal of harmony within the state was set up against the narrow intensity of personal loyalties.

'SUICIDE OF COMPANIONSHIP' PROHIBITED

This meant downgrading, and subsequently prohibiting, *junshi*, even when the suicide was following his lord voluntarily. It was done in the name of humanity, as when the *haniwa* had been invented six centuries before, but the real reasons were political.

Such shows of despair or exaltation were not to the taste of a state resolved on moderation. Devoted self-sacrifice, which could serve a cause, might still be tolerated; but death in pursuit of the dead was nothing but vainglory. Such sacrifices could hardly fit into any rationalist scheme for relating profit to expenditure: it was the waste of a life which could have been used in another master's service, it was buried treasure which, if left in circulation, might have increased the prosperity of the living. The year 645 saw the Great Reform of the Taika era, whose inspiration came from China. It included sumptuary laws intended to lighten the burden of death upon life, and included condemnation of suicide and any other sacrificial gesture – from expenditure to self-mutilation – intended to mark the passing of a great man.[1]

> The emperor of China has ordained ... that henceforward no precious stones are to be placed in dead men's mouths, and no jewel-encrusted garments or caskets are to be placed in tombs, on the grounds that it was no more than evidence of base stupidity. He added that if the dead were buried, it was in order to hide them, in a desire not to see them. The present poverty and indigence of our people are due solely to the construction of tombs ...
> Normally, when a man dies, certain people follow him into death by hanging themselves; or else people are forced to follow him by being strangled, or he is accompanied by his horse; or treasures are laid in his tomb; or else during the funeral ceremony people cut off their hair or slash their thighs. These old customs must now, without exception, come to an end. Whoever shall violate this present decree by engaging in forbidden practices, the punishment shall fall upon his whole house.

Already the great grave-mounds were growing rarer; soon they would disappear from the landscape altogether. In the spirit of Confucian utilitarianism, certain designated grave-grounds would even be returned to agriculture. Later, in the eighth century, the Buddhist custom of cremating the dead became established. The money spent on the dead was no longer buried with them: it was used for prayers and ceremonies. The ashes were laid in Buddhist temples, which drew a great part of their revenue from the help which their chants were supposed to bring to rest-seeking souls.

THE DIMINUTION OF VIOLENCE

When writing came over from the mainland, a few centuries later than rice-growing and metal-working, it consummated the supremacy of the State. Letters could now be sent, tax returns computed, registers compiled. The first scribes able to handle the ideograms so ill-suited to Japanese were immigrant Koreans and Chinese. But a few generations later, many Japanese had learned to read and write. In calligraphy and in erudition the imperial court of seventh-century Japan was scarcely inferior to the Tang. Some centuries before the European Renaissance, Japan offered the admirable spectacle of an entire society whose elite was devoted to learning and open to a transforming enlightenment. The imperial court and government were the fountainhead not only of power and profit, but also of wisdom and learning.

Not only the art of writing came in, but also written texts: Chinese political philosophy, Indian Buddhist speculation, and much more. Confucian texts proclaimed that the emperor ruled by reason of his virtue: his rage was a sign of weakness. The source of state power was the wisdom of the prince; its end was the happiness of the people. This ideal was supported by Buddhism: the sovereign owed it to himself to be merciful, serene and compassionate. The combined influence of these great springs of Indian and Chinese wisdom began a movement towards peace as the new ideas became part of everyday life. Violence began a slow retreat.

As late as the sixth century the head of the Soga family, though he had encouraged the coming of Buddhism, made no bones about murdering a ruling emperor. In 643, members of the same Soga family, who had spent the whole century manipulating the emperorship for their own ends, took prisoner Yamashiro, the prince imperial, and all his family: all of them, even the women and children, were forced to kill themselves. A year later, Soga Iruka himself fell victim to a conspiracy, and was struck down before the very eyes of the empress during a state ceremony.

Such political proceedings are nothing new to us, but the example of seventh-century Japan shows that they are not irremediable: a few generations later the imperial court was free of them. By the eighth century murders and forced suicides were getting rarer, and eventually they disappeared. In 768, for example, the real power was in the hands of a monk, Dokyo, the empress being under his influence. A certain Kiyomaro opposed his designs, but was not murdered, or condemned to death or to suicide: Dokyo exiled him to a distant province (having taken the precaution of hamstringing him). A year later, when the empress died, the odious Dokyo's punishment fell due; the new emperor did no more than exile him. In 810, the ex-emperor Heizei regretted his own abdication and made a plot which failed; his only punishment was to have his head shaved and to be sent to enforced retirement in a monastery, where he lived very peacefully for another fourteen years. *The Tale of Genji* tells of an imperial prince, Hachi no Miya, who tried to seize the throne: with his two daughters, he went on living in peace, not far from the capital, in a pleasant retirement enlivened by music and pious study.

Thus Buddhism tamed custom – in the long run. Moreover the state, following the Chinese example, had equipped itself with a stable structure and a constitution which introduced some rules into the game of politics. Ambitious men, instead of plotting, could exercise themselves in climbing the degrees of the court hierarchy. The barons had become officials, endowed with a skilfully designed, sixteen-rung career ladder. Instead of defending their clan prestige with fire and sword, they concentrated on the colour of the cap which might crown their heads if their merits gained due recognition. Intrigue was endemic at the court of Nara or Heian: nothing can prevent the centre of power, any centre of power, being the source of unceasing struggle. But the struggle can be regulated. For a few centuries which must stand to the credit of humanity, the death penalty fell out of use, even in the indirect shape of enforced suicide. Exile was enough. What had once been a flight into death became a mere flight into the cloister.

SPELLS, EXORCISMS, SUPERSTITIONS

Buddhism put a brake on violence, but also allowed the struggle to continue by indirect means: the deities of the Mahayana pantheon could be invoked for protection. Potent rites were available. Hatred could be translated into prayers, less often into action. There was a whole Buddhist school, the *Shingon* (an offshoot of Indian tantrism), devoted to charms, spells and incantations. There were monk-healers and exorcists to call upon. The exorcist might even be required to turn sorcerer! In 995, Fujiwara no Korechika, angry at being supplanted as regent by his uncle Michikane, had such powerful spells said against the latter that he died. History adds that the title of regent passed not to Korechika, but to Fujiwara no Michinaga. A few years later, another Fujiwara, surnamed Akimitsu, clashed with Michinaga over whose daughter was to be first in the emperor's bed. The Fujiwara clan had assured its supremacy by supplying the imperial harem, and its monopoly was by then uncontested; the rivalry was confined to cousins within the clan. Akimitsu asked the monk Doman to cast a spell on Michinaga, but it did not work. All he got out of it was the nickname 'Minister for Evil Spirits', a mocking reward for his ill-will.

These skills of prayer and white or black magic had fascinated the Japanese from the first: what they initially saw in Buddhism was a collection of rites effective against diseases, bad spells and evil spirits. The ideal of non-violence was, of course, present as well, woven into the texts, and gradually becoming effective – but the first offshoot of Buddhism was a rich flowering of sly and pusillanimous pseudo-piety, mingled with taboos deriving from Chinese geomancy and astrology. Few societies were ever so superstitious. Japan had always feared the dead, all the more so when it was thought possible to shelter from them in an abundance of ritual. If even a little suspicion attached to the cause of death, lengthy ceremonies were needed as a safeguard against posthumous acrimony. This supersition had an effect on everyday behaviour. An enemy could be more dangerous dead than alive; he might persecute his persecutors. So it was better to get rid of him by exile rather than by murder or forced suicide. In this ever more peaceful society, violent death was becoming less commonplace – and seemed all the more dreadful because of it.

From earliest times, the Japanese had feared the *tatari* of the dead, that is, the vengeance of people who had been killed, or killed themselves, after being falsely accused or unfairly treated. The vengeful soul could persecute its enemies, strike at the innocent in passing, and unleash all manner of scourges. In such cases there was a need for very elaborate rites of appeasement (*chinkon*). Even today, the site of a suicide is often an uneasy place, subject to ritual precautions. Under a tree where some unknown victim has hanged himself, a little altar will be erected, with some flowers, a bottle of sake, or a little rice. Several of the poems in the *Man'yoshu*, such as the tale of the maiden of Unahi, are *banka*, laments addressed to victims dying by violence, and especially suicides. When a victim showed exceptional vindictiveness, expressing his resentment in disasters and epidemics, he was given posthumous honours and hasty promotion: a cult was founded in his memory. If he turned out to be sufficiently powerful and ill-disposed he was given a temple in his honour: he became a god.

THE VENGEANCE OF THE DEAD

That is what happened to the celebrated Sugawara no Michizane.[2] A high dignitary, a talented poet, an obedient subject, a zealous minister, he was a nosegay of all the virtues which a moral state could demand of its servants. He had a brilliant, perhaps too brilliant, career: he offended the Fujiwara clan by trying to loosen their grip on the empire. In 899 he was appointed *udaijin*, minister of the right. Abrupt disgrace came in 901: he was accused of plotting the downfall of the Emperor Daigo. Two or three centuries earlier or later, he might have been murdered, or more likely ordered to kill himself. But court customs in the Heian age were gentler, and he was sent away to Kyushu equipped with the title of supernumerary governor. It was a terrible indignity for one of the highest officers of state, and Michizane survived it only by a few months. He had time to write several elegies on his misfortune: tearful they are, but without a word of resentment against the emperor who had exiled him. His consolation in that distant place was to climb Mount Tempai, and there, turning his face towards the capital, pay his loyal and devout respects. He carried obedience to the point of a prompt and discreet death – just what was wanted. He was even polite enough not to commit suicide; he just faded away.

But afterwards! His enemy, Fujiwara no Tokihira, died soon after, at the height of his glory, and later his twenty-year-old grandson and his four-year-old great-grandson. Michizane's friends (and his enemies' enemies) said that it must be Michizane's revenge; so did his traducers, though it was rather late to feel guilty. Their interpretation was adopted at once by a supersitious public, always inclined to attribute chance disasters to some occult and malign intention. Between 909 and 911 there was a spate of epidemics and floods: Michizane again. In 930 the imperial palace was struck by lightning: another triumph for Michizane! He had been dead for some thirty years, but all sorts of vengeful acts were still imputed to him. Once the most obedient of subjects, as an ex-subject he was among the most rebellious. A contradiction, but it made sense: beneath the morality of the state, which imposed implicit obedience to imperial authority, there subsisted the morality of the clan, which saw vendetta as a virtue.

A compromise solution: one could take vengeance, but on one condition: one must be ready to die, to pay with one's life for rivalries which menaced the peace of the empire. A man who would risk *that* had to feel himself deeply injured indeed. Michizane had paid the price in advance: his submissiveness, his silent disappearance – an acquiescent if not a voluntary death – gave him a right to persecute his enemies. The maiden of Unahi had paid with her life for the freedom to love her lovers and be united with them in death. Many an embittered suicide sought in death the freedom to hate and do harm. The empire needed peace: submission was enjoined on all, submission even to death. But such death could raise a protesting, a threatening echo. Would peace without justice have any meaning? The proud had to be reminded that the dead were slow to forget an insult. According to Judaism, vengeance was the Lord's. The Christian *Pater noster* abjures vengeance and exhorts forgiveness. Japan spread over the state a veil of peace, woven of Chinese and Indian wisdom, and put its hope in the balance of mutual deterrence: don't push your enemy to the end of his tether; he might suddenly consent to die, nothing further will restrain him, and you will then find that he has a very good memory for your offences.

So Michizane's posthumous wrath had to be appeased. Solemn reparations were decreed; he was rehabilitated and his honours were restored, with interest: he was appointed Chief Minister. At last, in 947, he was declared a god. The sanctuary of Kitano was built for him to the north of the capital; many others followed it, all over the country. His lot was so exemplary, vengeance taking over from obedience at the crossroads of two moral systems in perpetual dialectic, that he became one of Japan's favourite divinities.

Michizane's rehabilitation went to the point of apotheosis without any questions whatsoever being asked about the responsibility of the emperor for his exile. The blame was put on his traducers; the emperor had been deceived, His Majesty could not but be innocent. In fact, the emperor often did no more than set his seal on decisions made by the dominant faction. Minorities, malcontents, the oppressed and the insulted could thus revolt in the name of the emperor, against his ministers. The idea of empire could play the ambiguous part played by the idea of God in monotheistic cultures: God sanctions the powers that be, he loves peace and order – but he loves justice no less. Thus rebellion could be crushed in his name just as kings could be censured, revolt stirred up, or revolution directed. Indeed, what revolution has not at some point felt the need to combat its own rebels?

In Japan it was not the eye of God which tempered imperial absolutism, but the principles of Confucius: to rule was to steer through the conflicting currents, seeking always the middle way. The Buddhist ideal of power was a mild one. Finally, animist traditions of belief in the supernatural power of the dead encouraged the taking of precautions. The circumspect Japanese eventually set up a preventive ceremony which took place for the first time in 863, under the aegis of the emperor Seiwa: *goryo-e*, the Assembly in Honour of Souls. It was addressed to the great personages who had fallen victim to court intrigue: they were exhorted to renounce all bitterness in the next world and to spare the people and their governors the calamities which they might have unleashed in their wrath. Just so, for many centuries, on the dais of every tiny village temple, had the *miko* danced to distract the dead from their much dreaded grudge against the living.

A DECLINE IN VOLUNTARY DEATH

Once the emperor had forbidden *junshi* and customs had become gentler, but posthumous vengeance was still feared, it is easy to see why self-murder and enforced suicide became less frequent in the two or three centuries around the year 1000. In the whole of the *Tale of Genji* there is (with the sole exception of Ukifune) no allusion to the practice of suicide, or to the vaguest impulse towards it. It was not anathematized, as it is in monotheist cultures; it was always open to the devoted or the desperate, but it was very much the exception. Rules which, at other periods of Japanese history, demanded self-murder in certain circumstances had ceased, or had yet, to exist. *Pax Nipponica*: the empire was enjoying a quiet life. Prince Genji accomplished none of the exploits attributed by legend to his ancestors, and by epic to his descendants. He concentrated on his career, his love affairs, his pleasures and his children's future. If he thought of death, it was to give a melancholy tinge to his happiness or exhort himself to patient endurance of suffering: in this fleeting world, neither pain nor joy could last. Suicide? A delusion, pitching one into another life with, no doubt, yet more torments. True peace was the reward not of death but of renunciation.

The Buddhist condemnation, not so much of suicide as of violence in general, would not have had such force if it had not offered an alternative solution: the cloister, in which one could die to the world without actually killing oneself: you shaved your head, took the necessary vows, and retired into some mountain temple. There was no such route to freedom in Shinto. While Shinto ruled alone, death was the only escape. But in the Heian era, communities which had renounced the world were open everywhere as refuges from the tribulations of life. In the same way, the Christian taboo on suicide seems less harsh when we see it, from St Augustine to Benedict, alongside the development of monasticism.

The story of Ukifune in the *Genji* sets the two escape routes, suicide and the cloister, side by side. Like the maiden of Unahi, the fair Ukifune was a good girl: gentle, shy, fearful, reserved, naïve, modest, timid, secretive – a paragon of feminine virtue, in fact. Prince Kaoru had a quiet love for her. He was already married, to one of the emperor's daughters, but custom allowed him to set up as many additional wives as he wished and could afford. Ukifune's future was assured so long as she did not fall victim to another prince charming, the handsome Niou, who was after her with all the cunning and energy of passion. Girls who have learned the lesson of obedience too well are incapable of saying no to anybody.

Ukifune realized, rather too late, the impasse she was in. She had to choose between a quiet and lasting affection and a true, but probably inconstant love. And she had to choose quickly: two houses were even now being made ready for her in the capital. Moreover the two princes might collide by her bedside on one of their nocturnal visits. They were, in fact, great friends, but the situation would be so scandalous that Ukifune's reputation would never survive it. How could she make up her mind? She loved one, but she could not break the ties of gratitude which bound her to the other. It was already too late. The truth was about to break, and confound her. It was Unahi all over again, but while the *Man'yoshu* poem sketches the situation in a few bold strokes, the *Tale of Genji* develops an analysis so subtle, so minute that its 200-page account of the episode is one unending fascination. How could Unahi escape her shame? How could she expiate the unintentional crime of betraying her every obligation? Suddenly it came to her:[3]

> 'Ah, indeed I wish I were already dead! For some terrible thing will happen, and scandalous rumours will arise.' She was reflecting incessantly on these disturbing thoughts when her lady mother, hearing the fearful noise of the river, cried, 'And yet there are rivers which are not like this! Surely the prince must be sorry for you for having to spend your life in such a desolate place, which scarcely seems to belong to this world.' And she began to speak in a meaning way.
> Ukifune's serving women took up her words: 'Always people have called this river fearful and tumultuous. The other day, the ferryman's grandson made a mistake with his pole and was swept away. Indeed, you cannot count those who have died there!'
> 'Ah!' thought the maiden, 'if I perished in the same way, they would all feel alarmed and unhappy for a while. But if I lived on, and something dreadful happened to make me into a laughing stock, I would never get over it.' All things considered, nothing seemed to stand in her way, and she considered her design calmly and in the minutest detail. And yet, at the same time, how miserable she felt!

Poor Ukifune! It was not easy to end her young life at a blow. She loved her mother so dearly! She could not forget that the Confucian virtue of filial piety forbade children to abandon their parents by dying before them. But indeed, she loved her mother too dearly not to spare her the shame into which her daughter's shame would draw her. Let there be an end! At any moment the two princes might meet. They were too refined to fight over it, and duelling was forbidden at the Heian court – but their less well-brought-up followers might come to blows, somebody might be killed. So she had to keep the peace, she had to die to prevent others from suffering and dying for her. The ideal of sacrifice, more even than the hope of escape or the need of expiation, finally gave her the courage she needed:

> Whatever I do, whatever way I take, some evil thing will probably happen. Only if I die can there be peace. The past has seen many examples of girls who cast themselves into the water just because they could not bear to see two men equally devoted to them. This life, which will only bring grief if I prolong it, can I not destroy it without regret? Certainly it will cause some grief to my mother, but her care for her other children will distract her,

and she will naturally forget in the end. Surely it would be worse for her if she saw me live on, from failure to failure, tossed by the tempest of life, a laughing-stock for all.

A FAILED SUICIDE, A LITERARY SUCCESS

In the middle of a windy, rainy night, Ukifune set out for the river in spate. But she did not drown herself. Not that the courage failed her: she could scarcely disappoint her readers with a last-minute weakness. But the author, imitating Indian legend, indulges in a touch of Buddhist fairy tale. Ukifune becomes the prize of a supernatural duel. A wandering spirit which haunts the spot (ironically it is the ghost of an exorcist) and is nursing some grievance which prevents it from resting in death, manages to enter into her. Fortunately, the bodhisattva Kannon is on the look-out and seizes this chance of rewarding the girl's piety: she is wafted away into the garden of an old, ruined palace. There, at dawn, some passing pilgrims find her, prostrate and unconscious. They care for her and exorcize her exorcist, and after many trials, she is restored to life.

So a failed suicide. Evidently Murasaki Shikibu, author of this episode in the *Genji*, wanted to make the most of the emotional appeal of suicides. Ukifune's tormented hesitation between her two princely lovers is recounted in leisurely detail; her motivation is lucidly described. The mental logic is so evident that the actual consummation of the act could not add to it, and the author resists inflicting it on us. Drowning is the least violent of violent deaths, but a real drowning would introduce too harsh and sensational a note. And above all, Ukifune has to be spared for further adventures: her attempted suicide has made her so interesting that we cannot bear to lose her. Perhaps many suicides feel that paradox in the secrecy of their last moments; the courage of the final act alters their idea of themselves, and they prove to themselves – by dying – how fit they are to live.

Ukifune survives her decision to die, but the glamour remains upon her. She succeeds in escaping, her weaknesses are expiated, her sacrifice spares her the worst: she gains all the benefits of suicide without the considerable drawback of not being there to enjoy them. She is in a most romantic situation, hovering between two worlds, accepting death and viewing life with consequent serenity. But her trials are not yet over. In the mountain convent where she is received, a young colonel of the imperial guard happens to glimpse her face despite the screens, curtains and blinds behind which she normally hides.[4] She is truly unlucky to be so lovable! She dumbly repels the poems the young man fires at her; but beauty is fated to sacrifice, and must expiate its unintended troubling of hearts. Indecency apart, Ukifune's troubles are sometimes rather like those of Sade's Justine. Persecuted by the desires she arouses, she despairs of reaching the peace which her virtue deserves. There seems no refuge. She needs a sacrificial act to deliver her from the ever-recurring dangers of love. She cuts off her abundant hair, so admired of princes, and takes the necessary vows to make her, at long last, a nun. After suicide, the cloister.

THE SORROWS OF HAPPINESS

Did her renunciation grant her the peace she vainly sought in death? The story breaks off without telling us, but we may suppose that in the epilogue Ukifune would have been forgiven by Kaoru and would have led a devout life in her cloister, alongside his: a good Buddhist conclusion in keeping with the spirit of the age. For the elite of a few thousands to which the author and readers of the *Genji* belonged, life was as sweet, fair and sad as Ukifune herself. There was no more work, no more struggle: it was what Hegel would have called the Sunday of life, when the stirrings of history had ceased and men floated on clouds. Year in, year out, taxes were paid and the court lived in luxury. If the emperor caught cold it was an event; if a prince was born it was an affair of state. The slight boredom which is always the price of happiness was conjured by ceremonies and diversions: contests of refinement, games of intrigue without deadly consequences, light-hearted music, inconsequential painting. Never was a civilization more refined, more bound up in ritual. Futile but not frivolous: under all its gracious appearance, never was there a civilization more melancholy. Unhappy people can always hope, but happy people, if they are not stupid, know their happiness is fragile as a dream, unquiet, under threat. The Buddhist message was inscribed on their hearts: all is precarious, nothing lasts... they knew it all too well.

They had spent a few patient generations in eliminating violence from court life. It had been not abolished but kept at a distance. All was quiet in Heiz-kyo, Capital of Peace, but even a few leagues away things were not so well regulated. Further still, especially towards the east and the plains of the Kanto, life was still wild and rough. The further away from the centre, the more the grip of the state relaxed; the emperor's prefects played only a nominal role, and power belonged to local magnates, leaders of war bands, powerful families – often founded by some offshoot of the imperial harem who had been encouraged to seek his fortune on the frontier, where they were still driving back the barbarian tribes and planting the new rice fields.

The Heian state, for all its absolutist principles, had refrained from acquiring the tools of totalitarianism. It would have meant breaking the clans, and before that, choosing high officials by examination. But nepotism ruled all, and it was a clan, the Fujiwara, which ran things at court, in its own private interests. True, in 645 they had proclaimed the Great Age of Reform: by imperial edict, the state had at a stroke become proprietor of all lands, with the exclusive right of raising a tithe on harvests. But dispensations had been granted immediately. The clans had succeeded in defending their patrimonies against prefectorial inspection and fiscal exaction. Religious land holdings were exempt from tax, as was all newly cleared land. Soon the only people who were still paying taxes to the state were those who were too weak to avoid it. Gradually private interests vanquished those of the state. The Great Reform remained a dead letter. A long process of reappropriation of capital followed the much heralded but unsuccessful nationalization.

Cut off from the country at large, the court was left to pursue its dream of peace, refinement and detachment for another three or four centuries. It was like the groups of statuary in certain temples at Nara or Kyoto, where a meditative Buddha sits amidst the twelve Celestial Warrior Kings: they gesticulate, grimace, threaten, brandish their weapons, all to guard the serenity of the Blessed One. In them, Heian society gives an image of its own situation: violence, eliminated from the centre, had retreated to the periphery. The emperor's only army was the army of court officials. When a rebellion broke out in the provinces, such as Masakado's in 935 or Abe no Yoritoki's in 1055, he had to rely on the warrior clans of the east, the war bands bred among the new rice fields of the Kanto. The day was approaching when those clan chieftains would want more than a letter of thanks: soon they would demand the political power to which their real power had entitled them. The state still believed itself their arbiter, but soon it would become the mere object of their rivalries. Violence, distanced from imperial thinking and from the narrow circles of the court, was to return in the pitiless reality of civil war. A new ethic was coming, and voluntary death was to be at its heart and centre.

7

The Martial Art of Dying Well

History affords few spectacles more grievous than the returning violence which tore through the empire's fabric of peace. Such is the fate of peaceable civilizations: they grow rich from the fruits of their labours, loll in comfort, and fall prey to foreign invaders. Between the twelfth century and the seventeenth the Japanese quite capably invaded and massacred each other. The long-dormant germ of violence started an epidemic. In the provinces the clans took up arms. Highwaymen lurked on the outskirts of Heian. Even the Buddhist monasteries set up private armies, so that quarrels between temples could lead to pitched battles. At one time monks had assembled on Mount Hiei to guard the capital by their prayers; now they carried tumult into its streets, and in their ominous processions brandished spears and saints impartially.

Isolation was death; safety lay under the dominion of an important clan, strengthening its strength so as to earn its protection. Ever wider coalitions took shape, and by the twelfth century this coalescence had produced two rival and more or less equal factions, one directed by the house of Taira (alias Heike), the other by that of Minamoto (alias Genji). Total division, total polarization: as in Dante's Florence, every man had to be on one side or the other. The division, shearing through the entire thickness of Japanese society, from the furthest paddy-field to the court itself, made a struggle to the death inevitable. There was no arbitrator: the imperial ministers were always the last to know about troop movements decreed by the clan chieftains, until one fine morning they saw the mounted ranks marching past their precious garden walls.

Suddenly thousands upon thousands of rough fighting men, jabbering in all the dialects of the east, were taking up winter quarters in the City of Peace. The Fujiwara, in the soothing belief that they were witnessing a war of attrition, fell into the complacent error of all neutrals: the delusion that violence will eliminate violence. Far from being able to arbitrate, the court had not even the means to defend its own neutrality. The clash of rival forces swept through it, rocked it, tore it apart. But the new military elite respected the emperor, putting him under close guard. The court aristocracy was not slaughtered but rendered impotent. The values of peace (understanding, wisdom, knowledge) were overlaid by the martial virtues of strength and determination.

NO QUARTER

The duel between the two warrior houses was triggered by a crisis in the imperial succession in 1156. The Taira had the best of it initially, imposing their own candidate. Three years later Yoshitomo, a leader of the Genji clan, made a bid to shake off Taira domination. His attempted *coup d'é*tat was savagely repressed. Day after day, on the banks of the Kamo, the conspirators and their supporters were beheaded – those of them, at least, who had not killed themselves so as to rob the victors of their apology for justice.

Times had changed: exile and the cloister were no longer sufficient. Execution, assassination and suicide had become once again the ultimate arbiters of the struggle for power. A conspiring monk could be put to death, or a temple burned down, without compunction. Prisoners of war were decapitated, or used for weapon practice or to test the sharpness of a blade. There was no acknowledged right to survive a defeat. Few men made any bones about changing sides, bag and baggage, if the occasion offered, but surrender in battle was not an option. After the battle, rewards were dealt out according to the number of heads brought back; so the heads of the wounded were promptly added to the tally at a warrior's waist. Ransom was unknown. Those of the defeated who could not escape begged their best friends to kill them, if they no longer had the strength to do it themselves. Minamoto no Yoshitomo, defeated by the Taira in 1159, had fled the capital to raise fresh troops in the provinces. His son, Tomonaga, begged to be killed by his father's own hand: he had been wounded in a skirmish with the monks of Yokawa and could not continue the fight. Yoshitomo did as he asked, and then gave him honourable burial.

Shortly afterwards, Taira no Munekiyo desecrated his tomb, decapitated the body and sent the head as a trophy to Kiyomori. They would stop at nothing to ensure the death of an enemy chieftain, in the terror of seeing him back another day, as good as new and thirsting for revenge. It was a duel to the death: only a last look at the headless enemy's livid face could give certainty of victory. These identity parades were rigorous: after the *seppuku* to which Yoshitsune had been reduced by his brother's persecution, he was decapitated and his head sent to Yoritomo's palace in Kamakura. The journey – it was the summer of 1189 – took no less than six weeks, during which the horrid relic had to be kept in a jar of sake.

Was Kiyomori, chief of the Taira, too savage in his repression of the first uprisings? Or not savage enough? His harshness kindled the fires of vengeance, which were to smoulder for twenty years. And yet he was too merciful: he was weak enough to leave several of Yoshitomo's, his rival's, children alive. Twenty years later they rose against him at the head of a new coalition. He had grown old, they had grown up. He died charging his children, for the peace of his soul, to lay on his tomb the heads he had once spared. The spirit of vendetta which brooded over these civil wars made it only wise to destroy the rival clan root and branch, to annihilate the enemy *genos* unto the last generation. It was not enough to kill the enemy chiefs; their children and grandchildren, heirs of their vengeance, must perish too.

Such genocide seemed the price of a lasting peace. Thus victories were always followed by tremendous manhunts, as fugitives were tracked down, families exterminated. We can see why parents might take their children with them into death. Yoshitsune, under attack on his brother's orders in the castle of Koromogawa, commanded with his dying breath that his wife was to be killed, and his son – and his daughter, aged seven days. Where could they hide? In a mountain hut? Would that give shelter from spies and informers urged on by the promise of reward? As for a monastery, no place would be searched more thoroughly. Where could a man and his family find refuge, if not in the ever open arms of death?

Through these centuries of civil tumult, the Japanese proved more merciless to themselves than any foreign invader could have been. These were not racial conflicts, or class struggles, or colonial enterprises, or wars of religion: clan fought clan for purely political reasons. It was a sheer struggle for power – and first and foremost, for the possession of land, and the right to levy taxes on the paddy-fields. The losers had to be eliminated, after which their spoils were shared out. The capital value remained the same, circulating within a clan, redistributed with each fresh upheaval: every war was a new deal. Everyone was playing the same bloody game, the adversaries could scarcely be told apart: subjects of the same emperor, followers of the same cult, bred in the same culture, imbued with the same convictions, born into the same class and often cousins within the same clan, or even brothers of one family: there was not a pin to choose between them, but this only made them thirst all the more for each other's blood.

A WELL-REASONED DEATH

As the power struggle ebbed and flowed, suicide seemed not only the proudest, but even the most sensible course for the defeated. A chieftain's suicide robbed his enemy – not, of course, of victory, but of triumph. They escaped the fearful humiliations which would precede inevitable death. And perhaps, turning their own anger against themselves, they found some satisfaction in punishing themselves for their failure. As for their vassals, they considered it their duty to follow their masters into the next world, or rather the next life, where they could continue to serve him. Suicide was the supreme escape for those who could not flee, and no one could rob them of their last moment of glory. But this solution was the most advantageous for the victors as well, sparing them the hateful task of killing an unarmed enemy and putting a stop to the threatened vendetta: dead men may avenge themselves, but not quite as often as live ones do. A voluntary death would reduce the threat to the quietude of the state; for the state was quiet when the victors could sleep sound.

This reasoned suicide, which became a dogma with the *bushi*, emerges clearly, in Japanese chronicles of the civil wars, from repeated calm deliberations whose interlocutors conclude, all things considered, that voluntary death is the least unsatisfactory, if not the least disagreeable, of the available solutions. The Romans felt the same: they saw suicide in defeat as a legitimate, honourable and reasonable option, though by no means an easy one. For centuries, Christian writers, following St Augustine, determinedly decried Cato, an attitude which has still not quite disappeared. Ever since the Council of Arles, in 452, described voluntary death as 'diabolical madness', the rationale of it has been obscured. Suicide has been anathematized so often as a devil's accomplice that we still see it as something close to dementia. And it is an effort for us to think of it not just as a symptom of insanity, but as an act like other acts, more or less rational like other acts, according to the circumstances in which it is considered, and which confer meaning upon it.

GLORY IN DEFEAT

Japanese warriors started by using the simplest methods of suicide, like Cato falling on his sword.[1] Thus, in 1180, died Minamoto no Yorimasa, with the horsemen of Kiyomori at his heels, at the age of seventy-five. He waited long enough to recite a final poem before the dreamlike architecture of the Phoenix Pavilion at Uji. He had already requested his servant Tono to decapitate him:[2]

> In his grief at having to behead his master, yet living, Tono burst into floods of tears and said, 'I cannot! I would not do it unless you first struck yourself a fatal blow.' 'You are right', replied Yorimasa, and turning towards the west, the recited ten times over, in a loud voice, the invocation to Amida; then (ah, the pity of it!) he spoke these last words:
>
>> For the desolate trunk
>> Which never has
>> Borne any flowers,
>> Ah, how sorrowful
>> Is its ending!
>
> Such were his last words. Then he put the point of his sword against his stomach, fell forward, and died transfixed upon it.

At that time, then, late in the twelfth century, men spitted themselves on their swords; they had not yet begun to slash their stomachs across, for the exact flourish of *seppuku* was not fixed until the next century. For these first-generation civil warriors, the method of execution varied according to circumstances and the inspiration of the moment; they improvised. Most often they sought a momentary respite, fell out of the line of battle, and meditated a short while before killing themselves: just a second or two for a last poem, or at least a last prayer; they turned to the east, towards the Pure Land, the paradise into which the Buddha Amida had reputedly vowed to receive all those who called on him in the hour of their death. But some men ended their lives in the thick of the battle. Thus did Imai, a vassal of Minamoto no Yoshinaka, lord of Kiso, at the battle of Awazu (1184) between two cousins of the Minamoto clan. Floundering in a paddy-field, Yoshinaka has just been hit by an arrow.[3]

> Seriously wounded, the lord of Kiso fell forward with his visor against his horse's neck. Then two of Ishida's squires rushed forward, and to make an end, cut off his head. Sticking it on a sword-point, they brandished it on high, shouting, 'The lord of Kiso, who even now filled all Japan with the noise of his exploits, has been slain in combat by the eldest of the Ishida, Tamehisa of the land of Miura!' Hearing this shout, Imai no Shiro, who was still in the thick of the fight, said to himself, 'For whom should I fight now?' Then he cried out: 'Behold, you lords of the lands of the east! Here

is the ideal of suicide given you by the first warrior of Japan!' And putting the point of his sword in his mouth, he leapt head first from his horse, and died stabbed through and through. Thus ended the battle of Awazu.

Through Imai's last words sounds an echo of the pride which he used to lash his courage into the abyss. The self is never so drunk with itself as when it ends itself – if it accepts and wills that ending. Did he die? No, he killed himself: there is a world of difference. He no longer saw himself crushed by dire necessity, but wielding a sovereignty which made him one with his destiny. His life was quenched, but he knew that its last burst of flame would compel attention from those others who knew that they were mortal. For an instant, he was all aflame, in the unending brazier of ephemerality. His past errors, his faults, his weaknesses, all were consumed in the flare of his voluntary death. Beyond pardon, he was dedicated to glory and to forgetfulness. He was at the pinnacle of humanity.

A WIFE FAITHFUL UNTO DEATH

For a contrast to the blazing virility and manic exaltation of this death drunk with the blood and fire of combat, we can look to the silent, fluid, nocturnal melancholy of another, no less harrowing voluntary death, that of the lady Kozaisho, Michimori's wife. She was carrying his child. She took refuge on one of the ships taking the beaten Taira to the south-west, along with the court of the young Emperor Antoku. It was there that she learned that her husband had been killed by the Minamoto in the last battle. Irrationally she waited five, six days for his return. On the evening of the seventh day she confided to her nurse her considered decision:

> Indeed I should like to bear my child in quietness, and bring him up to find again in him the image of the dead; but every time I saw him, I would yearn for my lost husband and my torments would be multiplied without any consolation. There is a road which all must travel in the end. Even if, against all expectations, I continued to live, hidden from the world, things do not happen according to our heart's desires: some unexpected thing would happen... And this thought, too, torments my heart. When I fall asleep, I dream of him; when I awake his image is there before my eyes. Rather than living, and for ever yearning for him, I have decided to plunge into the waters.

The nurse tries to argue against her, and advises another kind of voluntary death, a gentle and salutary retirement to a nunnery:

And then, of all those whose husbands were killed in the battle of Ichi no Tani, is there a single one whose misery is to be despised? You ought not to consider only your own fate. Bear your child in quietness, bring him up, then retire among the rocks and the trees, clothed as a nun, to call upon the holy name of Buddha and work for the salvation of him who has died.

But the nurse speaks in vain; her mistress's resolve is too calm to be alterable. It remains only to put this calmly deliberated resolve into effect. Kozaisho glides into death unspeaking, unmoving. She has chosen not to outlive her love, seeking in the void the reunion it seems to offer. She entrusts herself to the depths of the sea, to that silent, unmoving element of night, abandoning herself to the nameless intimacy into which all things must sink, as if to be reborn:

> Taking advantage of a moment when her nurse had fallen asleep, the lady furtively arose, and climbed on to the gunwale of the ship. As they were far out at sea, she did not know which direction was west, but seeing a mountain behind which the moon was setting, she told herself that the sky of Amida must be that way. Calmly she spoke the invocation to Buddha. Hearing the cry of the plovers on the white sandbanks out to sea, or the noise of the sailors rowing through the straits, her sorrow was surely redoubled! In a low voice she repeated the invocation a hundred times over: 'Hail, Master of the Paradise of the West, Amida Nyorai! According to thy unfailing promise, I beseech thee, guide me to the Pure Land, and be pleased to welcome duly on one lotus a husband and wife who were torn apart against their will!' Weeping, weeping she repeated these words insistently, and with cries of 'Hail!' she plunged into the sea... Since ancient times, many have been the wives whose husbands went before them into death; but the way of this world makes them change their ways; rare are those who have gone so far as to cast themselves into the waters. 'The faithful vassal cannot serve two masters, the virtuous wife cannot know two husbands', so they say; and the saying is borne out by examples such as this.

THE DEATH OF THE CHILD EMPEROR

The Taira ships had to flee further and further, towards Kyushu, until the day when they were forced into the final battle. In 1185 the Minamoto fleet, led by Yoshitsune, destroyed the Taira fleet at Dan no ura. Many were those of the vanquished who drowned themselves. When she saw that all hope was lost, the widow of Kiyomori, mother to the mother of the young emperor Antoku, showed her inflexible constancy of soul: she took her grandson in her arms and sprang into the waves. This twofold suicide (*oyako shinju*), a parent dragging a child into death, has lodged in the Japanese memory as one of the most touching scenes in their history:

> Seeing this, the lady of the Second Rank, following the plan on which she had resolved long ago, drew over her head the double thickness of her sombre mourning garment and hitched her long silken skirts over her girdle; then, clasping the priceless jewel of sovereignty and hanging the imperial sword at her side, she took the emperor in her arms and said, 'Woman as I am, I will not fall into the hands of the enemy. I shall go with His Majesty. Let those who love him make haste to follow us!' With these words she advanced towards the gunwale. The emperor was then only seven years old, but he was most mature for his age. Such was his grace that he seemed to shed light about him. His black, waving hair flowed down below his waist. Taken aback, he asked, 'My lady, whither do you wish to take me?' Then, choking back her tears, she spoke these words to the child, her sovereign: 'Your Majesty, do you still not know? If, as a reward for observing the ten precepts of Good in another existence, you have been born master of the Empire in this life, then because of previous errors your good fortune has already run out. Condescend first to turn eastwards, and bid farewell to the great sanctuary of Ise. Then, to greet the Buddha of the Pure Land of the West who will come to meet you, deign to turn westwards and recite the invocation. This is a land of pain and misery; I shall lead you to a place of felicity, the Paradise of the Pure Land.' Thus she spoke amidst floods of tears. Then the child, in his pale yellow robe, with his hair curled over his ears, his eyes full of tears, put his pretty little hands together and bowed low towards the east, taking his leave of the sanctuary of Ise; then he turned to the west and recited the invocation. At once, the lady of the Second Rank took him in her arms again, and saying (to comfort him), 'Under the waves you will find yourself a capital!' she sank with him into the unfathomable depths. Ah, what sorrow! In one instant does the fleeting breeze of spring scatter the fair flowers! Ah, what cruelty! The savage ebb and flow of death and rebirth swallowed up his precious body! His Palace had been called the Palace of Long Life, that he might live there many a long day; the door was called the Door of Youth, and it was said that it would be closed to Old Age. But see! before reaching his tenth year, he was but wreckage in the depths of the sea.

Observe that these scenes from the civil wars show events exclusively from the losing side. There is none of the triumphalism, so often founded on denigration of the adversary, which gives a vain and hollow ring to so many tales of real or imagined combat in other cultures. In those fearful struggles the enemy was hated, but not despised: that would have been to despise oneself. It was possible to sympathize with his ordeal. The Japanese narrator (and through him the reader) indentifies with the victims and goes with them to the threshold of death, as if the acts and deeds of the victors had nothing to challenge attention. In the history of Minamoto no Yoshitsune (*Gikei-ki*), the young commander whose brilliant strategy won these battles does not figure in the recital of his own exploits. When he finally does appear, it is to find himself proscribed, presecuted by his jealous brother Yoritomo, hounded from one refuge to another – until the day when, hemmed in on all sides, with suicide the only way out, he meets the same fate which so many of his sometime enemies have met before him. In reality, the battle is to the strong – for the time being – but in the poem, our tears never cease to flow over the vanquished. Not that the Japanese scorn success, but they are rightly convinced that it is insufficient in itself. Failure can bring a man low, but it need not be humiliating. On the contrary, it can be a catharsis for those who know how to face up to it. It is an excellent thing to learn victory, but sooner or later in every lifetime, however triumphant we may suppose it to be, comes its last moment: and then is the time to learn defeat.

THE ART OF SPECTACULAR DYING

Thus voluntary death was a reasonable and fitting possible response to one's predicament. But not only was it a worthy final solution, it could also give clear and spectacular utterance to those cardinal virtues which, through the whole length and breadth of the archipelago, bound together all the *bushi*, warriors, samurai and daimyo, from the feeblest to the greatest, beyond hereditary feuds, through the ever-changing fortunes of war. Death had to be a demonstration of the force and will which constituted a man's idea of himself at that time. It was an idea which any man could convey to his friends and enemies by the leaving of them: an idea which he could wring out of himself. In the midst of bloody and universal fatality, the warrior class responded by inventing certain ethical and aesthetic disciplines. Victory was not enough: something must be created by way of an escape from the nihilism against which victory itself was no protection.

Amidst promises and hope in the Pure Land lessened the bitterness of death, and the heroes of our chronicles duly recall them when the time comes. But hope in another world is not enough: one's life in this world must have a fitting shape. The passing centuries saw the gradual unfolding, polishing and refining of a whole panoply of martial arts, of which none was more esteemed than the difficult art of voluntary death: for it is hard to conquer, but harder still to conquer oneself. All the other disciplines, honed by their contact with the horrors of the real world, could do nothing to mitigate its cruelty, but at least they gave form, value and meaning to the cruelties it involved.

The act of killing oneself became more and more stately, precise and ritualistic. A hasty stabbing or throat-cutting would not do: one had to take one's time, open up the abdomen, drag out one's entrails, and not blench. This was the procedure which became generalized under the name of *seppuku*, a Chinese (and therefore learned and refined) reading of the two words 'abdomen' and 'cut', whose vulgar (Japanese) reading *harakiri* has become more familiar to us.

VISCERAL TRUTH

According to the moralized anatomy of the time, the abdomen was the seat of life and will. The face follows the laws of good behaviour, the mouth speaks and may lie, but below is found the real active force, which is truth. Abdomen and face are as different as being and seeming. Numerous idioms based on *hara* (belly) remind us that these notions are still embedded in many very everyday expressions. Zen Buddhism, whose rise coincided with the rise of the warrior class, laid stress on decisiveness, energy, discipline, and its adepts learned, through long hours of seated meditation, to concentrate their whole attention on the *tanden*, an imaginary point a few inches below the navel, along the very path which had to be traced by the steel blade of *seppuku*. The martial arts, such as archery, swordsmanship and *karate*, still teach that all movements of the arms and legs must flash forth from a source located on that same fulcrum. Thus this centre point was thought to be the link between the body and – no, not the soul, which is a Platonic and Christian notion, but the energy to act which, in the very act itself, lays down the truth of every being. For I am not what I say, nor what I think, nor what I think I am, nor only that which I know I am. Theories of the unconscious have cast down the old, idealistic Western notions of self-awareness. Not that they have lost all validity, but they can grasp only the purest form of the self, never the being which I am.

What I am – thought the *bushi* of Kamakura – is what I do, what I am capable of, the perpetually unfinished sum of my acts, which transcends the awareness I have of them. I am karma, which is the act and the trace of the act, the destiny which involves and contains me, but on which my liberty may nevertheless plant its foot. According to this ideology, truth depends not on the advance of discourse towards the meaning of being (in fact Zen tended to suggest that there was no such advance), but on the very act which an individual's decision implied, especially the supreme act after which there could be no other. It was this truth that the steel blade had to demonstrate before witnesses, following what Nitobe's classic study of *bushi* ideology curiously denotes the 'syllogism of *seppuku*': the truth of my being is located in the abdomen, therefore I open my abdomen, leaving you to tell whether I am a true being or the simulacrum of a man. All the virtues implied in the word *makoto* (sincerity, purity, genuineness, loyalty) are grounded in this presumed link of dependence between truth and energy, in a decisive act which can silence vainly repeated words and establish an irreversible fact. It is for me alone to decide, by acting, who I am.

THE INSTITUTION OF EVISCERATION

It was thus that, in 1189, Yoshitsune, unjustly overcome along with his faithful few, surrounded by thousands of enemies, turned to suicide to protest his innocence and crown the brilliant victories of his short life with an exemplary death. But which way to choose? 'Remember', said one of his vassals, 'our friend Tadanobu who slashed open his abdomen: men still admire his courage.' Yoshitsune acknowledged that this was the best, because the hardest, method, and therefore the most glorious, and he decided to select it: 'He placed his sword under his left breast, and violently thrust it in, piercing himself through to the back; he widened the wound on three sides, and fetched out his entrails. He wiped the blade on the sleeve of his robe, drew it back across him, and leaned on his elbow-rest.'

He did not, of course, die immediately: abdominal wounds ensure only a long death agony. It is hard to imagine a more painful, or less effective, means of suicide. Only its symbolic value allowed it to catch on. The bloody demonstration of prowess tickled men's pride, and fostered the masochism which is the dark side of a strong will. The physical agony was the worst possible, but it was accompanied by a moral apotheosis: in his last moments any man could be a hero. His act transformed him, ready for a glorious death. Not for him the tormenting and insoluble question put by Augustine: 'My God, who am I?' This question, sharp as the steel blade, has cut away at the Western soul: in the eyes of God, who alone knows the truth and for all eternity (for he decreed it), am I numbered among the elect or among the damned? Western civilization gravitated around the Supreme Being, that of feudal Japan around the Supreme Act. Men believed that their act could establish and prove their own truth.

As the twelfth century drew to a close, evisceration was still in its very early stages, uncommon and insecurely established. Then it became codified and generalized. The author of the chronicle of Yoshitsune, who wrote more than two centuries after his hero's death, sought to claim him as the precocious advocate of a practice which had since become the norm. The sword, inconveniently long for such an office, was replaced by a dagger about ten inches long, called the *wakizashi*, made of the incomparable steel, purer than any made in Damascus or Toledo, which only Japanese smiths could temper, and which (helped by a wind from the gods) had vanquished the weapons of the invading Mongols in 1274 and 1281: the excellence of Japanese technology is nothing new. The short blade, driven into the left side, had to be pushed through to the right. Certain virtuosi could sometimes manage a supplementary, perpendicular cut from epigastrium to hypogastrium. After which one had to keep some strength in reserve for the actual dying, finishing oneself off with a stab to the heart or a slash at the carotid artery. During the troubled era of Shokyu (1219-22), which sparked off the Emperor Go-Toba's vain attempt to restore the power of the court, assisted *seppuku* or *kaizoebara* came in: behind the subject, squatting on his heels, a second man – vassal, faithful follower, friend or companion – stood with raised sword, ready to deliver the *coup de grâce* by cutting the victim's head clean off.

The authors of warlike chronicles are often very explicit in their descriptions, and obviously relish the detailed embellishment of their heroes' anatomical exploits with a view to leaving us with some horrific and stirring images. Later, routine came in, the forms became fixed and then fossilized: everything had to be done correctly up to the last moment, death could no longer be improvised as it had been during the first century of civil war. Later still, treatises were written, outstanding examples written up, figures of evisceration listed like figures of speech. The grand style, rather archaic and exaggerated, was to take one's entrails in both hands and give them a vigorous throw in the enemy's direction.

A RUSE OF WAR

Thus, in the second month of 1333, died Murakami Yoshiteru, follower of the Prince Morinaga. At that time, in the early fourteenth century, the power of the Hojo clan (descended from the Heike), who had ruled the country for over 100 years after Kamakura, was visibly tottering. The Emperor Go-Daigo was conspiring to fulfil his dream of restoring the absolute power which the court had had in the Heian era, and Prince Morinaga, his son, was engaged in guerrilla warfare to the south of the capital, in the mountains of Yoshino. The Hojo troops had successfully surrounded him and his situation was hopeless; the prince was only postponing his death until the final assault on his castle. It was then that Yoshiteru came to him and exhorted him to flee. 'Give me your breastplate', he said, 'I will borrow your name, and I will give up my life to conceal your flight.' At first the prince rejected this strategy: 'If die we must, whatever happens, let us die together!'[4]

> Then Yoshiteru retorted: 'Ah, what a disappointment lies in your words! When, under the Han, Koso was besieged at Keiyo, and his vassal Kishin begged him to let him pass for Koso so as to deceive the enemy, did not Koso accept? With views as petty as yours, what an ill thing it is to espouse the great cause of the Empire! Come, come, take off your breastplate.'
> And he unloosed the prince's girdle. Then the prince yielded to his reasoning and exchanged breastplates and tunics with him. Said the prince: 'If I live, I shall not fail to pray for your salvation in the other world; and if I, too, fall into enemy hands, I shall not fail to accompany you towards the realms of darkness.' And, weeping, he passed through the sanctuary of Katte no Myojin and fled southwards.

Beyond their differing ranks, and despite a respect for hierarchy which goes as far as self-sacrifice, their comradeship in death means they can speak with complete freedom. Yoshiteru is exalted by his imminent sacrifice. This, rather than his learned ability to cite Chinese examples, confers the authority he wields. All he need do now is carry out his stratagem, and his martyrdom. The chronicler spares us no detail:

> Yoshiteru climed on to a bastion of the second wall and watched the prince ride away; when he saw him vanish over the horizon, he told himself that the moment had come. Thereupon with his sword he cut down the shutters before the arrow-slits and showed himself; then, raising his voice, he proclaimed his identity (*nanori*): 'I, a descendant of the goddess Amaterasu Oomikami, second son of the Emperor Go-Daigo, the ninety-fifth emperor counting from Jimmu, prince of the First Rank, officer of the department of Military Affairs, I have been deposed by a rebellious minister. To satisfy my wrath in hell, I will now kill myself. Watch me: I will give you an example for the moment when, having cast your last throw at the game of war, you have to slash your own stomachs!'
> So saying, he took off his breastplate and threw it down to the bottom of the bastion. Keeping only his wide silken trousers, he took off his tunic. He put the point of his sword against his unblemished skin; from the left side to the right, at a blow, he cut open his abdomen; taking his entrails in his hands, he threw them upon the planks which covered the bastion; then he put his sword in his mouth and fell forward on to it.
> The besiegers, those of the main body as much as those on the wing, all said, 'See! the prince has killed himself; I must be the first to take his head.'

And, breaking ranks, they all together rushed to that place. Meanwhile the prince, who had set off in the opposite direction, had fallen back to the river Tennokawa.

Throwing his entrails towards the enemy was an act of bravura, a challenge, almost a piece of sarcasm. Never was martyr more proud, distant, or self-willed. He dies on the silent laughter apparently provoked by the success of his costly stratagem. Did he already know that he would have his revenge? On the threshold of death he prophesied: the fortunes of war were soon to turn against the Hojo. Then they would have to remember Yoshiteru's example; and a few months later, in summer 1333, when the Kamakura regime collapsed, many of them did indeed commit *seppuku* in their turn.

COLLECTIVE EVISCERATION

The beginning of the end for them came in the last days of April, when Ashikaga Takauji turned his coat for the first time; the Hojos' most powerful vassal betrayed them to join the supporters of the imperial restoration. The shogun's troops, commanded by Hojo Nakatoki, were defeated in the streets of the capital. They attempted a retreat towards Kamakura, with the young puppet emperor as a hostage, as he had once been for the Taira. But very soon Nakatoki realized that there was no escape: the Tokaido road was too long, and the regular troops had been reinforced by gangs of mercenaries who hung on his flanks and brought back heads for reward:

> Nakatoki, the former governor of Echigo, waited for a moment for Tokinobu to arrive; the rendezvous had gone by, time was getting on. 'Come!' he said to himself, 'he, too, must have gone over to the enemy... and now, whether I retreat or whether I flee, where can I go? Better to slash my stomach once and for all.' The decision taken, his face grew calm again. Then he spoke to his men in these words: 'Seeing that the fortunes of war are inclining more and more toward the other side and the house of Hojo is drawing to its end, you now prize only this name of warriors which you have, and without denying those to whom you have by long custom been bound, you have consented to follow me so far. I have no words to tell you what I feel about your devotion. My greatest desire is to express my gratitude to you, but the fortunes of my house have run dry, and I have no means of doing so; thus my intention is now to kill myself for your sake, so as to render to you in another life the debt of gratitude which I owe you in this. Worthless as I am, I am an ornament to our

house: therefore the enemy has decreed that whoever takes my head will become lord of a fief of a thousand households. Make haste, therefore, to take it and put it in the hands of the Minamoto as reparation for your past enmity and gage of your future fidelity.' Before even finishing this speech he took off his breastplate, undid his robe, disembowelled himself and collapsed upon the ground.

Seeing this sight, Kasuya no Saburo Muneaki, choking back the tears which were falling on his sleeve, cried, 'Alas! It was for me to be the first to kill myself, to be your guide in the realm of the dead! How bitter it is to see you go thither before me! In this life, I have been with you to the very end; in the realm of the dead, too, my eyes will always be upon you. Be pleased to wait a moment for me: I shall escort you over the mountains of hell!' With these words, seizing the sword which the governor of Echigo had driven into his stomach to the hilt, he plunged it into his breast, and, embracing the knees of Nakatoki, fell on top of him.

After him, Sasaki, ex-governor of Oki, his son Jiroemon, his relatives Saburo Hyoei and Eijumaru, Takahashi Kurosaemon . . . [150 other names are mentioned] and many others, 432 men in all, disembowelled themselves at the same moment.

The carnage can only be imagined – the floods of blood, the simultaneous death-rattle of hundreds of men, a holocaust of the feudal faithful, an epidemic whirling all before it. For suicide does not have to be an individual, furtive, solitary act: it can also obey collective emotion, and history is strewn with these massed and willing sacrifices. Many years before, in 73 AD, the Jewish zealots who had rebelled against the roman legions killed themselves, to the last man, in the fortress of Masada. At least they had every reason to fear their conquerors; the best they could hope for was enslavement. But we should also recall the strange contagion of suicide in Guyana on 18 November 1978, when 900 followers of The Revd Jim Jones drank death from a cauldron of strawberry syrup laced with Valium and cyanide. Suicide seems less difficult when a whole group can do it together.

THE FEAST OF SUICIDE

On 5 July 1333, fresh scenes of collective *seppuku* marked the fall of the shogun's city of Kamakura. After five days of fighting, the chief of the Hojo clan, the regent Takatoki (called 'the lay monk of Sagami' because of his eccclesiastical pretensions) set fire to the palaces which had witnessed his glory and took refuge, with a few hundred faithful followers, in the temple of Toshoji. In the great hall where the dignitaries of the regime had gathered there began a strange feast:

At this, Takashige began to run higher and thither crying, 'Quick! Quick! Kill yourselves! I, Takashige, will be the first and set you an example.' Scarcely had he spoken than he took of his cuirass, of which only the breastplate remained, and threw it away. Then he seized the cup which was before His Lordship the Regent, had it filled three times over by his younger brother Shin'emon, then set it before the lord of Settsu, an adjutant in the Department of Justice, who had become a monk under the name of Dojun: 'For him who is my friend!' said he. 'And this to go with the drink!' With these words, he drove the sword into his left side, slashed his stomach wide open through to the right side, brought out his entrails with his own hands, and collapsed before Dojun.

Dojun raised the cup, saying, 'There's a good accompaniment for sake! The poorest drinker could not refuse the drink.' With this jest he half-emptied the cup and set it before the monk of Suwa. Then, in his turn, he killed himself by slitting his belly open. Jikisho, the monk of Suwa, calmly emptied the cup three times over, then set it before the Regent, Lord of Sagami, who had become a monk, saying, 'The young men have shown all their skill, but can age be an excuse for not doing likewise? This is what we should all do as an accompaniment to our sake!' With these words, he slit his belly with two strokes in the form of a cross, and pulling out his sword, he set it before his Lordship.

The lord of Nagasaki, who had become a monk under the name of Enki, seemed still to be wondering about the fate of His Lordship of Sagami, and was slow to slit his own belly. Then the young Shin'emon – he was then just into his fifteenth year – bowed down before his grandfather saying, 'It is written that it is our filial duty to do honour to the name of one's fathers: surely the Buddha and the Gods and the Three Treasures will grant me their mercy!' So saying, he pierced the arms of his grandfather, whom age had spared, with two sword-cuts through the elbow, then slit his own belly; laying the old man upon the earth, he fell on top of him. Encouraged in his duty by the example of this boy, His Lordship of Sagami slit his stomach open, closely followed by the monk of Jo. At this sight, all the members of the clan, and the men of other houses who had taken their places in the hall, vied with each other in laying bare their snowy breasts; some slit their stomachs, some cut their throats, each choosing the death he preferred, an admirable sight! . . . In all, 283 men of the clan strove to see who first would accomplish his *seppuku*. As they had set fire to the building, flames burst forth and black smoke blotted out the sky. At this sight, the armed men posted in the courts or before the doors slit their stomachs in their turn and flung themselves into the roaring flames; sometimes father and son, elder brother and younger brother, transfixed each other and fell upon each other's corpses. The earth was flooded with blood, like a river stretching out of sight; the avenues were heaped with corpses like a great battlefield. Though the burned-out bodies could not be recovered, they later attempted to identify the dead: the total of those who perished in that place alone was over 870 men. As for those – relatives and followers, monks and laymen, men and women –

who, hearing this news, resolved to repay their kindness by joining them in the underworld, or, remaining in this world, wasted away in grief, no one knows how many they were in the more distant fiefs, but in Kamakura alone they number over 6,000.

The text makes no attempt to conceal the hesitations of the least enthusiastic and the oldest: the older one is, the less keen one is to die. But the presssure grew, and they had to yield whether they would or no. The sight of blood speeded the contagion; soon a suicidal frenzy broke out which carried all before it, an orgy of voluntary death. Reading the *Taiheiki*'s account of the civil wars of the fourteenth century, we can gauge the frequency of collective evisceration, in small groups or great crowds. The practice had become vast – epidemic. This act of prowess, initially one of pride and individual resolve, became banal, a routine sending of sheep to the slaughter, and voices were raised in criticism of such premature resignation.

CRITICISM OF *SEPPUKU*

In the battle which raged on the beaches of Kamakura, the forces of Sadanao, governor of Mutsu, were decimated: he was left with only 300 horsemen. Surrounded by the enemy, with his back to the sea, cut off from the town though he saw the smoke of its burning, he had no further hope of victory or of life:

> A good thirty of Sadanao's closest vassals (did they think that all was over? Or did they want to encourage their master to kill himself?) took their places on the white sand of the courtyard. They took off their armour and, in serried ranks, disembowelled themselves. Seeing this, Sadanao cried, 'Aha! Behold the goodliest hotheads in Japan! It is by exterminating the enemy, by winning fame for posterity, even if you are one against a thousand, that you really show courage! Come, let us advance boldly into this last battle, and encourage the soldiers to do their duty!'

So *seppuku* was not an infallible remedy. If those eviscerated vassals could still hear it in their agony, Sadanao's criticism must surely have astonished them. Did voluntary death *not* have the value of an absolute in each and every case? Was the supreme act just another act, good or bad depending on circumstance, and subject to judgement? *Seppuku* was the linchpin of the collective morality of the *bushi* caste. But Sadanao had shown that one could hold the terrain of military endeavour against the fatalism of the suicidal impulse, not just to cling to life but for some more demanding ideal which left no room for suicide's implicit defeatism: better to die in battle, ready for anything, and cheerful even in the face of despair.

Moreover, the warriors' very minds held, under the virtues of war, other, more ancient values which also demanded consideration. Filial duty, emphasized by Confucius, fobade dying before one's parents. The great Buddhist examples of meekness and forgiveness were bound up with hopes of salvation which still carried weight. The feudal devotion which beat at the heart of their world demanded exposure to danger, but never licensed the desire of death: the bonds of allegiance forbade the waste of a life which might have value to one's lord. All these were potential curbs to the spread of *seppuku*. They are sometimes expressed in the chronicles of these wars, as in the arguments used by Masashige's widow to deter her son, the youthful Masatsura, from imitating his father's suicide as he was tempted to do. Kusunoki Masashige, a paragon not only of martial virtues but also of implicit obedience to imperial authority, disembowelled himself after the battle of Minatogawa in 1336. The pro-restoration party was crushed, and a new shogunate, that of the Ashikaga, was about to commence. Masashige's severed head was exposed for several days in the capital; then the victor, Asashige Takauji, considerately had it sent to the widow to receive her last farewell.

THE DUTY OF LIVING

When Masashige left for Hyogo, he had given instructions, and left Masatsura saying that he was sure to be killed in the next battle. Thus mother and son were reconciled to the idea that this departure meant a final separation. And yet, when they saw the head, which was indisputably his, but with closed eyes, livid, utterly changed, their hearts were filled with grief and they could not keep back their tears. The child, then in his eleventh year, seeing his father's head so different from what it had been in life, seeing, too, his mother apparently unable to keep from sobbing, wiped on his sleeve the tears streaming down his cheeks, and went to the family chapel. His mother, seized with suspicion, immediately rejoined him through an outside door. In his right hand he was holding the unsheathed sword engraved with their family crest, which his father had left him as an heirloom when he went to Hyogo; and, with his wide silken trousers lowered to his hips, he was ready to disembowel himself. His mother rushed on him, seized his arms and said to him amidst floods of tears, 'They say that the sandalwood tree smells sweet as soon as its buds begin to swell! Young as you are, how, if you are your father's son, can you so misunderstand your duty? You still have the soul of a child, but try to see clearly! When your late father left for Hyogo, if he left you at the staging-post of Sakurai and told you to return home, it was certainly not for you to pray for his salvation in the other world! And it was not for you to slit your stomach open! "Even if my luck has run out and I must lose my life on the battlefield", he said, "if you hear that His Majesty has established himself somewhere, gather up the young surviving warriors of our house, and take up the struggle again! Destroy His Majesty's enemies, and restore your prince to his throne!" Those were the instructions he left for you. You undestood his last words perfectly, you repeated them to me; how could you have forgotten them? By doing thus, you will ruin your father's reputation, and you will be unable to serve His Majesty!' Such were the reproaches she addressed to him, weeping, and so prevented his intent. Then the child, from whom she had seized the sword, prevented from disembowelling himself, staggered weeping from the priest's chair in which he had seated himself, and added his sobs to those of his mother.

These soldiers' children had a terrible precocity: scarcely old enough even to play at war, they already knew all the practical details of that hardest of deaths. In a surge of grief, the son identifies himself with his father to the bitter end. To save him from this blast of despair, his mother speaks not of her love for him – though it has dictated her actions – but of his hereditary vocation to serve, and therefore to live. When the natural clinging to life has passed, there is still a last line of defence against suicide: moral obligation, often seconded by religion and metaphysics. I cannot kill myself unless I own myself. 'But you belong to your City', St said Augustine; or 'to your God', said Plato before him. 'To the emperor', said Masashige's widow, combining the theme of personal feudal allegiance with resurgent state absolutism. For another five centuries, the principle of exclusive devotion to the emperor was to remain obscured under the private loyalties of the clans and the narrower bonds of the feudal system. But with the Meiji Restoration in the nineteenth century, Masashige's heritage was to be laid on the whole of Japan: the bellicose values forged in the civil wars were to be pressed into the service of imperial unity.

In medieval Japan, the cruel, unbending and arrogant rituals of *seppuku* gave suicidal impulses a moral prestige which no other civilization has ever accorded them. But there was no established right to die; there were no established rights of any kind, for morality consisted exclusively of duties. The desire 'not to be' could sometimes satisfy and justify itself through the ethic of service; but in the last instance it was this ethic, and not the individual's private emotions, which proved decisive. In those distracted times, when the longing to end it all was only too easy to explain, criticism of *seppuku*, or rather the abuse of *seppuku*, emphasized that all acts were slaves to duty. This did not mean that *sepppuku* lost its place in the ethics of the warrior class. Its prestige remained unrivalled and its fascination endured – but as the centuries passed, its collective ravages became less spectacular.

Fear of pain and death alone would not have curbed it, for the very horror of it gave it power to attract. But like all institutions, it eventually lost its first vigour, and wore itself out by its very excesses. Then it became a talking point: it was discussed, codified, hedged round with casuistry, adapted to every fashion. And the more it was talked about, the less it was done. This excessive practice had burst forth from a simple heart broken by defeat, a last leap into a glory purer than victory. By the end it was no more than a class privilege, a piece of anachronistic ostentation which served the men of swords for five or six centuries as a justification for their arrogance.[5]

8

Giving up the Body

After the battle of Minatogawa (summer 1336), Kusunoki Masashige, surrounded by Ashikaga troops, admitted defeat and asked his brother Masasue to tell him his last wish before he died. Masasue answered with a laugh: 'I wish to be reborn seven times as a man, so as to exterminate the enemies of the court.' This reply pleased Masashige. 'Killing is a sin, I know, but I too wish to be reborn in my present condition, so as to destroy still more of His Majesty's enemies!' With these words the two brothers disembowelled themselves and gave each other the *coup de grâce*.[1]

This is the apogee of the warrior ethic. At the climax of their bloody destiny, the two men wish only for it to go on exactly as it was before. *Amor fati*: they want their life back again, despite all its cruelty. They laugh at death, which is nothing to them, and return eagerly to their old existence. Even defeat has not defeated them, for it has not taken away their zest for willing, doing and living. Theirs is the last, amazing word of Oedipus: All things shall be well. They can give themselves this dying accolade, that through their acts they have forged the will to repeat endlessly the acts which they have willed – nothing more. They are the incarnation of the Nietzschean morality which stems from the idea of the Eternal Return. So fair an end, without regret or repentance or remorse, cannot express any desire to be done with life: it is the pure love of life up to its last, consummate moment.

MAN OF WAR, MAN OF RELIGION

If a monk could have heard that final dialogue, he would have been horrified. Can a living thing cling so passionately to life that it no longer feels life's bitterness? No thought of salvation, no detachment? Did death mean nothing to such men, though it tore them away from themselves and all they loved? In their blindness and passion they would have reason to fear rebirth as *Ashura*, the dedicated fighters of Buddhist legend, unresting and merciless:

> Once fallen
> In the path of the Ashura,
> Near and far,
> Trees are but enemies,
> The rain, arrow-points,
> The ground, well-honed blades,
> The mountains, citadels of iron,
> The clouds, gonfalons or clashing shields;
> Swords cross in pride,
> Eyes blaze with madness,
> All is passion, desire, envy, anger and blindness.[2]

A warrior gives death and receives it, or, at need, inflicts it upon himself; but he does not think much about it. Death is the long- or short-term object of all his acts, but never of his considered reflections. It is a means to an end, and he need not dwell on it. He fears imminent death as much as anyone else, but, the danger past, he is careful to forget about it. That is what gives him his attractive youthfulness and gaiety. A man of religion cannot be content with so light-hearted an approach. Once awakened to the throught of death, it remains with him always. In primitive cults, men of religion are fascinated by sacrifice and devouring fire. In their profoundest speculations, they return incessantly to it, even if only to deny its supremacy and take comfort (as in Christianity) from the promise of eternal life.

The thought of death lies at the heart of Buddhism. No other doctrine save that of Heraclitus (a contemporary of the Buddha) begins its discourse with a more remorseless description of reality: the world is a house on fire, everything is a 'becoming', a shifting mixture of being and nothingness. The lineaments of a landscape or a face are no less evanescent than those of a flower or a flame. Nothing remains unchanged by time, nothing exists outside time. From the earliest stages, Buddhism was devoid of any principle of eternity, even God or the soul: there is only 'becoming', a journey from nowhere into nowhere. Every being is a temporary aggregate of elements, condemned to eventual dissolution. Living is pain, the pain of tearing loose from from every attachment, ending with life itself. We can escape from the wheel of painful becoming only by the methodical practice of renunciation, detachment and lucidity. This can open a way to salvation: the wise heart bows to the inevitable, the irremediable. Nirvana is awakening to the truth of the *samsara*.

Thus Buddhism has, in principle, no answer to the human desire for permanence: it offers no flattering hope of eternity. But it offers no encouragement, either, to the desire not to be. One cannot 'not be': death is the way into other lives. Any desire to continue to be, or to cease to be, is folly; the only good is the wakeful will which guides us to a true vision of the real, beyond all matching opposites. In the Pali of the Second Noble Truth of the ancient canon, the Buddha condemns impartially '(1) the thirst for sensual pleasure (*kama tanha*), (2) the thirst for existence and becoming (*bhava tanha*), (3) the thirst for non-existence (self-annihilation, *vibhava tanha*)'. There is no support for would-be suicides or melancholics in this doctrine whose aim is to pass beyond the impulses of life and death into the middle way of rationality: life is neither loved nor hated, nothingness is neither feared nor desired. It would be a prejudiced critic who would accuse Buddhism of pessimism or nihilism, as did thinkers as different as Nietzsche and Claudel: they refused to see further than Schopenhauer's interpretation. Is it nihilistic to believe that becoming has no pre-existing goal, since this is the first step to *giving* it a goal of lucidity and deliverance?[3]

THE MIDDLE WAY

Buddhism preaches the middle way in all things, equidistant between two opposites – for example, asceticism and sensual pleasure. Siddhartha Gautama, so the story goes, fled the luxury and soft living of the palace where he was born, and for six years subjected himself to the most rigorous fasting, living on a jujube, a sesame seed and a grain of rice! He was reduced to skin and bone, and would have died of starvation had he not realized that his goal was not death, the accomplice of birth, but awakening. He accepted food, resumed his meditations, and received enlightenment. He had escaped first the temptation of pleasure and desire, secondly that of asceticism and wilfulness. The wisdom of early Buddhism eschewed sacrifice and the savage austerities professed by so many Indian ascetics at the time – especially the Jain, who went to absurd lengths so as not accidentally to crush an insect, but thought there was infinite merit in crushing out one's own life by starvation.

Parsva, the founder of Jainism, went away into the mountains and died after a month of fasting. To kill oneself was to reach perfect freedom.

Later, some members of the *digambara* sect of pious Jains, who went about 'clothed in emptiness', even burned themselves to death. One of the Indian ascetics called by the Greeks 'naked sages' (gymnosophists) had himself burned on a pyre in front of Alexander the Great. Another did the same before Julius Caesar. As masters of themselves they were in no less proud a position than the master of the world. Their death was a triumph of the will, and the triumph was a dramatic performance: Mishima aspired to the same success. Similarly, the philosopher Peregrinus, one-time Christian turned Cynic, solemnly announced that he would deliver himself up to the flames before the crowd assembled for the Olympic Games of AD 165. When the time came he kept his promise. A man dizzy with self-will needs no other executioner than himself. Even bereft of an audience, he can drink deep of a satisfaction for which he thinks life a fair price.[4]

Spiritual endeavour demands, and develops, increased will-power. But to stop there is to stop short of wisdom. A will which seeks only to strengthen itself is as vain as desire. Buddhism warns against the will to self-will hidden in asceticism and against the wallowing in sacrifice which it engenders. Violence, too, is a reprehensible way of passing on from one self to another. Siddhartha Gautama died at the age of eighty without feeling the need to make his death a sensation. He was wiser in this even than Socrates, who could not resist becoming a martyr to his own virtue, and stirred up the wicked against himself. The salvation offered, or rather pointed out, by Buddha had no element of sacrifice, and depended not on his death, but on his teaching and example. For the founder of a religion *not* to die a martyr is rather remarkable. What use is death in that case? It was the most discreet, the most decisive deterrent against self-inflicted, or self-provoked, death that could possibly be imagined.

THE CHRISTIAN ANATHEMA ON SUICIDE

Christianity is at the other extreme: the Crucifixion meant that sacrifice was central to it from the outset. This made it all the more vital to draw a clear dividing-line between sacrifice and suicide, and to distinguish allowable (and glorifiable) forms of voluntary death from those that were forbidden and damnable. The Christian condemnation of suicide, formulated by St Augustine in the fifth century, repeated by innumerable councils (Arles, Orléans, Braga, Toledo, Auxerre, Troyes, Nîmes) and rapidly included in canon and civil law, is based on the notion of a supreme god, a notion absolutely foreign to Buddhism. Such a god must be sole master over life and death. Therefore we must not despair of his justice. All the more reason to condemn Cato in comparison with Job, to see cowardice in the courage to die and compare it unfavourably with the courage to endure. Lucretia was much to blame, and even Pelagia, who jumped off a house to avoid rape, was suspect.

To kill oneself was to usurp a sovereignty which belonged not to man but to God – and by delegation, to those authorities licensed to apply the death penalty. St Augustine allowed suicide only if God induced it by a direct order to the individual conscience, as must surely have happened (he says) in the case of Samson. In such cases one could kill oneself and still be obedient. But such examples were extremely rare; in all other cases, suicide was an outrage against the sovereign, robbing him of his rights over the individual. It was a cardinal sin, the sin of Judas, more fatal and more perverse than the orginal sin itself, for it added despair to defiance, and rejected redemption as if trying to build a barrier which even forgiveness could not cross.[5]

BETWEEN HOPE AND DESPAIR

The interdict was severe because it had to be, so great was the promise. If we can be assured of another life free from death and pain, why should we linger in this one? Doubtless this naïve calculation inspired many a Christian martyr. Later, in the seventh century, Mohammed's promise of paradise was a great stimulus to the courage of the warriors of Islam. But (said St Augustine) the time of martyrs is past. God orders us to live, to endure the trials of the world he has created. Through the centuries of persecution people had deliberately provoked the prefects of the Empire: the prize was one's own salvation and their damnation. Tertullian thought that getting oneself killed by the wicked was an imitation of Christ. 'Go and hang yourselves, drown yourselves if you want to', said a Roman proconsul, 'but leave us magistrates in peace!' The Donatists, later to be adversaries of Augustine, were experts in indirect suicide: they made a great display of profaning pagan idols and forced magistrates into cruel reprisals. It was a gloomy policy, this dying happy in the assurance of another world after having proved the wickedness of this one. Ten centuries later the Cathars often defied their persecutors without a word spoken, by a fast to the death. For them this fallen world, creation of a satanic demiurge, was ruled by the forces of evil. The *endura*, frequent in the Cathar villages of southern France tormented by the Inquisition, raised its perpetrators to the Godhead by way of self-starvation.

The same breath of suicidal heroism blows through stories of the vicious persecution of Christians by the Japanese authorities in the early seventeenth century. Many a fresh convert hastened to his martyrdom with a zeal to equal that of the early Christians. The Jesuits embroidered these bloody themes into edifying tragedies which were acted in their colleges in Europe. Corneille had probably seen them: in *Polyeucte*, his tragedy of early Christian martyrdom, there are elements which may have reminded spectators, aware of the most recent tribulations of the Faith, of the martyrs in far-off Japan.

Even without hatred of this world, and in the complete absence of persecution, love of Christ can be enough to make death easy, even desirable. St Paul freely admitted to the Philippians his 'desire to depart, and to be with Christ'. Many a heart has cherished the 'holy desire of death' in the name of divine love. The soul felt the paradox so unfogettably expressed by St Theresa: 'I die for I cannot die.' But it had to be remembered that that God of love was also a God of justice. We can be sure of God, but can we be sure of ourselves and of our own innocence? That would be a sin of pride. Thus the 'salutary terror' of judgement moderated the impatient desire for death.

In the early fifth century, when St Augustine wrote *The City of God*, Christianity had become the religion of the Empire and any impulse to suicide had become suspect. Killing oneself might be a renunciation, but it was also a challenge; it might mean eternal silence, but often its sole intention was to denounce everything that made life unlivable – oppression in particular. Suicide has always been the last recourse of those who cannot fight back: at the price of accepting death, extreme weakness can still make its mark. Not that the weak can rival the strong, but their lowly struggle with despair can at least find a voice. St Augustine, writing when the Empire had turned Christian but was tottering to its fall, aimed to consolidate all powers by founding them in God.

The idea of a supreme sovereign had two possible political consequences: it could be used to challenge the rulers of this earth, but it could also be a consecration of their majesty. Augustine fixed on this, showing that all powers must come from one source, the supremacy of God and his Church. Yes: all powers can unite, in solidarity rather than rivalry, all from the slightest to the greatest – and twenty years after Augustine's death, at the council of Arles, the bishops did their best to salve the consciences of slave-owners and domestic tyrants: 'If a servant of any condition or either sex goes as far as to kill himself (as if to provoke the patience of the Lord) when under the sway of some diabolical madness, he alone shall be guilty of the blood that is shed, and the odium of another man's crime shall not fall upon the master.' That the evil counsels of the devil were responsible was a very useful excuse for those who really had driven someone to despair. The later invention of 'madness' and the threat of the psychiatric hospital was but an echo, albeit a fast-fading echo, of the torments of hell.

THE UNMOVED CENTRE

Buddhism never inveighed so vigorously against suicide, because in Buddhism it was never seen as a challenge to an omnipotent will. Buddhism is firmly rooted in a world-vision devoid of transcendency and sovereignty, ruled by the unbending decrees of uncreated 'becoming' and above all, by karma: a being is the fruit of the acts he has sown. There is little point in postulating a supreme judge over all acts, if they are judged throughout time by their effect – even from one life to the next. The act of suicide, if prompted by illusion or passion, simply resumes the dialectic of opposites: as an escape it is delusory. If you die, you fall back into another life, which will probably be a good deal worse than the one you wanted to leave. You might lose the rare advantage of knowing the Law of Buddha and the enlightenment it brings. You are on the wheel of conditioned consequences, and a desire for life or for death will take you out into 'becoming' – to the rim of the wheel.

In primitive Buddhism, nothing existed except this becoming, and you could not escape from the wheel into any sort of outside transcendence; but you could, suddenly or little by little, reach the hub and find rest at that central (and therefore immobile) point where opposites are resolved. When you reach this place of perfect equilibrium, all pain ceases and life and death are seen to be equivalent and inseparable, since individual death is the reverse side of the coin of sexual reproduction. What does it matter if you live or die? If you cease to contrast them, you are free from their vain and agonizing duel. You live as one already dead, and that is living indeed: calm contemplation, passionless action, undestined freedom.

Buddhism teaches the supreme generosity of caring for nothing, which implies a readiness to give and renounce all things, and the supreme deliverance of not being held by anythings. One Japanese word for taking holy orders, *shashin*, means 'giving up the body'; it also applies to voluntary death inspired by religion. Free from all attachments, one must still undo the last fastenings which bind the flesh into a body that says *I*. The goal: disdain your body and it will not retain you. It is hard to reach. In the thirteenth century a Japanese monk confessed: 'This life should be a matter of indifference to me, yet I cling to it; the gulf where my body should be thrown is not yet hollowed out in my breast.' Christians believe that at death the body is separated from the immortal soul. Not so the Buddha: he said that nothing is immortal, the soul does not exist, and it is not death but enlightenment which frees us from our shackles. Death is no help if the enlightened will has not first attained to pure detachment from life, by the very process of living. When this central point is reached, death can crown the achievement: a perfect extinction, its serenity marking the consummate renunciation of the body. No more raging fire of becoming, no more birth or death, but an ineffable unity cancelling the dualism of all opposites.

The Buddha's death, as described in the scriptures, has no sacrificial element, no goal, no power of redemption – but it is voluntary. If he wished he could have lived several million more years, this being (they say) the privilege of the Tathagatas; but having conveyed his teaching and founded his community, his task was accomplished, and he decided to pass on. One day he told Mara, god of the dead, 'I shall die in three months.' He could have lived longer, but he preferred to die, and freely chose the moment. When the day came, he comforted his disciples and spoke his last words to them: 'All that exists must perish sooner or later. Be alert, therefore, and vigilant!' Then he concentrated his mind, and through his psychic power attained utter peace and perfect extinction. His disciples were left with the one task of giving his body to the flames; all was over, and there was no need to fear a rebirth.[6]

VOLUNTARY BURIAL

Many Buddhists, in imitation of their founder, attempted to die with perfect deliberation. Thus did the priest Kukai, posthumously named Kobo Daishi, who in the ninth century brought into Japan the esoteric Buddhist sect deriving from the Indian tantra. Traditions concerning Kukai's death repeat elements from a legend which came via China, brought back there from India by two pilgrims, Fa Hsien in the fifth century and Hsuan Tsand in the seventh. This was the story of the last moments of Kaçyapa, a pupil of Buddha. He went deep into a rocky cave in the Cock's Foot Mountain. There he sat motionless in meditation. The cave was sealed. Was he dead? Waiting, rather, with absolute impassibility, for the coming of Maitreya, the Buddha of the future. In a few thousand years' time this sage of the sleeping mountain would awake to share the task of salvation. A tenth-century Japanese text, 'Antecedents of the Foundation and Practices of the Monastery of the Diamond Peak', tells the story of Mount Koya: there, in the forests far to the south of Heian, Kukai, on his return from China, chose to establish his esoteric sect. In 935 he decided his work on earth was complete and put an end to his labours: he also went to await, in perfect immobility, the coming of Miroku – who is Maitreya, the Buddha of the future:

> The Great Master built a place in which to concentrate his mind, and in the year called the second year of Jowa, on the twenty-first day of the third month, at the hour of the Tiger, assuming the crossed-legs position, making the seal of concentration of Dainichi within this place, he began to concentrate his mind. His age was then sixty-two. According to his instructions, his disciples chanted the precious name of Miroku.
> Afterwards, for many years, the Cave of his meditation was opened at regular intervals, and the August hair of the Great Master was shaved, and his August clothing changed; which practice later ceased, and had not happened for a long time when the man called Rector of the Monks, Kanken of the Hannaya Temple, who was then second superior of the Toji (and was a great-grand-disciple of the Great Master), came to this mountain on pilgrimage and opened the Cave of meditation; upon which a mist arose, which made everything like the darkest night, so that he could see nothing; then, after a few moments, he saw the mist sink down, and behold! as the wind came and blew around the cave, the August clothing, which had now rotted, appeared falling into dust, carried away by the wind. When the dust settled, the Great Master appeared.
> As his August hair had grown about a foot long, the Rector of the Monks, having washed himself and dressed in a pure robe, entered in to him and cut his hair with a new razor. As the string of his August crystal rosary had rotted, the Rector of the Monks gathered up the beads which had scattered before his August Person; he put them together and threaded them in the right order on a string and put the rosary back in his August hand. Preparing a robe in the pure manner, he clothed the Great Master in it and went out. When he (the Rector of the Monks) was about to leave the chamber, he wept and was seized with grief as if he was about to accomplish this separation for the first time. After which, filled with awe, there was none who dared open this chamber. Nevertheless, when people came on pilgrimage, the door of the sanctuary, when they had climbed up to it, would open ajar all by itself, and noises would echo round the mountain. At certain moments, there was the noise of a bell being struck; in any case, strange things happened. It is a place deep in the mountains where even the song of birds is rarely heard, and yet no one is ever in the least frightened.
> At the bottom of the slope the two divinities of Niu and Koya have their porticoes side by side. They protect this mountain as they once swore to do. Because the place is extraordinary, the pilgrims now come unceasingly; but no women ever climbs up there.
> This was the man called Kobo Daishi of Koya. Thus is the story told.[7]

Others followed Kukai's example: the practice of voluntary burial is well attested in Japanese Buddhism. This sort of claustration is called *ishikozume*. In 1683 and 1783 the mummified bodies of twenty-four ascetics were found on Mount Yudono. They had been buried alive, two of them quite recently. Aspirants to this death had first to spend 1,000 days under a series of severe restrictions, after which the emaciated body was lowered into a pit ten feet deep, which was then closed. A little air could get in through a bamboo pipe. It has been observed that these monks were mostly anchorites only loosely connected with the Buddhist community. None of the highest dignitaries, save Kukai, ever chose this fate. Asceticism comes more readily to the unfortunate: it affords them a hope of finding in death the success which eluded them in life. According to one theory, known as *shokushin jobutsu* and widespread from the ninth century onward among the Tendai and Shingon sects, it was possible for a human being to become Buddha in his present body, with no need to reach absolute perfection beforehand via innumerable successive existences. Thus these ascetics had themselves buried alive in the hope of speeding up the process of enlightenment. Voluntarism; a short cut, a single deed which would pluck them the slowly ripening fruit of transcendent wisdom.

THE RETURN OF SACRIFICE

Primitive Buddhists had rejected asceticism: the will became violent if it strayed far from the middle way. But afterwards, as the Mahayana treatises unfolded their endless pages, the original doctrine, so similar to Democritus' materialism or the eudaemonism of the Greeks, gradually drifted back to the old religious instincts of sacrificial cruelty. They developed a metaphysics and a richly varied mythology. The Buddha was pictured as a supreme being, absolute, permanent and eternal. Legends purporting to describe his former lives attributed views to him which are not mentioned by the earliest witnesses. The methodical practice of detachment and concentration was no longer enough: Mahayana saints undertook to deliver all beings without exception.

The karma theory of cause and effect holds tht every individual is the sole factor in his own destiny; it faded before the hope of assistance, and prayers and entreaties, unknown in primitive Buddhism, reappeared. It was no longer enough to seek one's own salvation: it had to be given, shared, or received. Or if it must be sought, it would be sought in a swift, decisive act, and not via the long road of thought. Siddhartha Gautama had protested against the sacrificial act; called karma by the Brahmins, it was laden with negative connotations in the founder's mind. Sacrifice is pointless, it gives the illusion that a desired goal can be reached via destruction – but violent means are impure, and the desire for a goal enslaves the will. There is no goal, not even salvation, for the freedom of the Buddhist goes even so far: deny nothing, destroy nothing, desire nothing except the awakening to reality as it really is.

Back crept religious emotion into the originally temperate doctrine; sacrificial gestures reappeared and were attributed to the Buddha himself. In one story of his past lives he appears in the form of Prince Mahasattva, who met a starving tigress with seven cubs. 'Now I must sacrifice myself', thinks Buddha-to-be. 'This vile body which for so long I have nourished, clothed and served, but which one day will betray me and perish, will be used for a sublime action which will speed me across the ocean of becoming.' Does he mean to serve the appetite of the tigress, in his compassion for life in its blindness and cruelty, or his own thirst for perfection in the quest for his own salvation? In either case, he sacrifices himself:

> The friendly prince then threw himself down in front of the tigress. But she did nothing to him. The Bodhisattva noticed that she was too weak to move. As a merciful man he had taken no sword with him. He therfore cut his throat with a sharp piece of bamboo, and fell down near the tigress. She noticed the Bodhisattva's body all covered with blood, and in no time ate up the flesh and blood, leaving only the bones.
>
> It was I, Ananda, who at the time and on that occasion was the Prince Mahasattva.[8]

This most celebrated episode in the Buddhist scriptures is painted in oils on one of the lacquered panels of the 'beetle's-wing reliquary' (*tamamushi zushi*), a delicate seventh-century work of art in the Horyuji temple. Doubtless it inspired many a pious reverie. On the witness of so excellent an example, the more violent an act was, the holier it might seem; so long as it was voluntary, there was no curb on sacrificial prowess.[9] Hatred of the body and the will to master it united with compassion for other beings and the desire to win salvation by prompt ad decisive action rather than meditation. Counsels of moderation began to fall on deaf ears. 'Hate life, hate it only, throughout your life', said one monk. The fourteenth-century *Ichigon Hodan* contains a collection of aphorisms by Japanese monks, whose doctrine boils down to the most determined nihilism: 'Be sure to develop an aversion to your body and hate it constantly, and nurture in your heart the desire for death.' The words sometimes seem to echo the 'I die for I cannot die' which troubled some Christian souls: 'Today, when my sickness is slightly eased, I faint at the notion that I might not die.' But the austerities of a frugal life may be no enemy to health. Might it be, ironically, that those who are least attached to life live longest? 'Since I retired from the world, I have striven in my desire for an early death. I have exercised myself in this for more than thirty years, and now this thought never leaves me for a single instant. In my desire for an early death, the least delay breaks my heart and fills me with sorrow.'

This taste for death, this overt melancholy, are not feelings that the Buddha would have approved; he was quite content for his community to smile and live happily. Ippen Shonin, a wandering monk of the thirteenth century, leader of an Amidist sect, defined the correct attitude: 'Give up your body. But give up also your heart which desired to give up the body. Then you will enter into the serenity of the Buddha.'[10]

THE USES OF ASCETICISM

Those melancholy monks merely waited gloomily for death. Others hastened it, turning on their frail and impure flesh, inflicting pains and ordeals upon it, unable to forgive it for being neither insensible nor immortal. Weariness, privation, austerity, mutilation... They might show their resolution by cutting off an ear, like Myoe Shonin, a reformer of the Kegon school. Often, in support of a vow, they removed a finger, in moderate imitation of the second Zen patriarch Hui-Ko, who cut off his left arm at the elbow so that Bodhidharma would receive him as a pupil. They made it a duty to endure rough weather without flinching, fleeing the warmth of human company to meet the full rigour of nature among the mountains. A very common practice was to endure the most bitter cold by chanting sutras under a waterfall. The essential beliefs of Christianity may produce a mad thirst for expiation such as inspired (for example) the flagellants. In Japan religious masochism made itself felt less in the domain of fault and expiation than in that of privation and endurance. The Christian penitent fears lest the Father punish his desires; the Japanese ascetic wonders if the Mother will fail him in his need. Human beings have many pretexts for yielding to their dark curiosity to know the limits of their own endurance, until they cross the indefinable line beyond which feeling, goaded by will, falls into the abyss of night.

The ascetic seeks to acquire spiritual powers, if only for the sake of the adulation given by ordinary people to any deed which has cost something to the doer. But deeper than any desire for power is the obscure satisfaction he gets from tormenting, and finally destroying, himself. Carried away by the logic of the death-wish, some of them ended by vowing to give up their bodies in homage to the Buddha and for the salvation of all beings. After a period of increasingly harsh devotions, they would drown themselves, starve themselves to death, throw themselves off a mountain or, even more spectacular, 'make their body a lamp'. There is an important text in the Mahayana which was given special attention by the Tendai sect from the ninth century onwards, and was later (in the thirteenth century) venerated by the Nichirens: the sutra of the 'Lotus of the True Life'. The twenty-second chapter tells how the bodihisattva called 'King of medicinal Plants' (Bhaisa-jyaraja), known in Japan as Yakuo-bosatsu, decided in one of his former lives to give up his body to the flames in homage to Enlightenment. It was a prestigious antecedent, and suicides by fire are well attested among Chinese Buddhists. In Japan, one of the laws of the Taiho era, promulgated in 702, strictly forbids priests to indulge in self-cremation.[11]

No authority could tolerate suicidal impulses carried to such extremes: it is all too easy for religious asceticism to turn into protest and stir up political revolt. In 1963, in the streets of Saigon, monks would soak themselves in petrol: about thirty of them sacrificed themselves in this way at the fall of Ngo Dinh Diem. As far back as 800, at the Council of Lhasa, two monks killed themselves – one by stabbing, the other by burning alive – to defend the subitist theories of Zen against the majority who preferred gradualism, a carefully staged route to Nirvana. In the Nara era, then in the Heian period, and right up to the moment when the Tokugawa finally subjected it to rigorous state control, Buddhism was involved in the struggles of the times, and many a monk sought to employ his scorn for a body tuned to austerity in the sevice of whatever cause he deemed good. Failing the salvation of all beings, or some point of doctrine, the good cause for which he threatened suicide might turn out to be the tax privileges of his monastery. Violence was regaining a foothold in Buddhism, in the guise of asceticism and devotion. The founder's rules of moderation were forgotten, and the illusion of sacrifice resumed its former eminence, stipulating pain and death as the means to ensure success or vindicate an idea.

THE AMBIGUITY OF BUDDHISM

Examples of voluntary death within Buddhism are inescapably ambiguous. Have they a definite aim? In that case they are sacrifices, even if the aim is salvation; the later writings of the Mayahana take this direction. But choosing death can also be understood in the spirit of primitive Buddhism as a simple giving up of the body, a pure act with no precise intention, and therefore with no effect on karma, a sign of the supreme detachment achieved through meditation. Such men set no more value on anything, even their bodies; they had no further aims, even salvation; all desire was extinguished, the will no longer sought any object or project, and finally the being drifted away in perfect serenity.

This ambiguity pervades the whole of Buddhism: is it an exercise in impassibility or a compassionate religion? A twofold tradition which in medieval Japan bore the twin flowers of Amidism and Zen.

Zen, with its strong tendency to austerity and elitism, teaches its adepts to rely on their own resources in striving towards the light. Amidists, on the other hand, mistrust themselves and trust in the power of the Other: the thirteenth-century Japanese patriarchs of the Pure Land developed a complete theory of Grace. Honen (1133–1212), like St Paul, said that salvation was by faith. His disciple, Shinran, concluded that the Buddha Amida could grant all things, which of course included grace, and the faith which suffices for grace. Similarly, the god of St Augustine chooses those to whom he will give the grace of belief. The difference is a matter of generosity: the way to the Christian paradise is through the strait gate. How many would pass through? asked the Christian preachers of the Middle Ages. One in a thousand? One in ten thousand? Amida holds wide the door to his own Pure Land: by merely calling on his name one can be saved, whatever one's crimes. This indulgence had a great appeal in the darkest hours of the civil wars, when the *bushi* caste was at its most rampant, and ordinary people needed some such hope in another world to console them for the miseries of this one. Even today, the fideism of Shinran continues to inspire the sect of the True Pure land, which is the most popular among Japanese Buddhists.

Despite all the devotion to the Virgin which was the parallel to contemporary Japanese Amidism in twelfth- and thirteenth-century Erope, the dominant image in Christian thinking from Augustine to Kierkegaard, an image going back to the story of Abraham, was surely that of a stern father. Up to the seventeenth century the whole of Western civilization lived in fear of the wrath of God. But Amidism reveals, under the feminized guise of Kannon, bodhisattva of compassion, the Mother of succour, forgiving and indulgent, whose image is fixed deep in the Oedipal consciousness of the Japanese by their upbringing. Now, the salvation of the one is inseparable from the sacrifice of the Other. But the bodhisattva does not merely sacrifice his life, as Christ did. It would be a poor gift according to the measure of Buddhist compassion: good enough for a hungry tigress, perhaps. To save the human race, or rather all living creatures (for human beings are not unique in their suffering), Kannon sacrificed nothing less than his own salvation. Sublimity indeed – as if Christ were to sacrifice his divinity. But is that perhaps the real meaning of the theology of the dying God?

The bodhisattva, then, on the verge of acquiring omniscience and felicity, deliberately renounced them, or so say the Mahayana texts. He refused the nirvana due to him until such time as all living beings were also delivered; he would not consent to escape from suffering until it had disappeared from the entire universe. Can generosity ever have gone further? The religion which began with the determined solitude of a man sitting under a tree broadened into a surge of limitless fellowship. Christian charity (save that of an Origen or Angela of Foligno, who would extend it even to demons) seems timid by comparison, so timid that it finally cankered in the souls of such as Ivan Karamazov.[12] The salvation of all beings – however gross their intellect, however perverse their will – can alone satisfy the compassion of the Buddhist. The bodhisattva Ksitigarbha, venerated in Japan under the name Jizo, specialized in travelling through hell to bring salvation: he was in hell, but paradise was in him. It is the only possible occupation for a self-respecting saint: the music of the celestial spheres can scarcely be expected to detain a pure heart which has sounded the abyss of desire, evil and pain, and is only too impatient to return there.

THE CONSOLATIONS OF AMIDISM

In the light of this limitless goodness, any theory which purports to justify the burden of suffering by the weight of sin seems cold, dry and hollow. Even the doctrine of retribution through karma yields to this infinite forgiveness. A deeper wisdom reveals at last, beneath the externals of sin and punishment, the terrible innocence of earthly suffering – its ultimate absurdity. We suffer, we inflict suffering on others, and all, alas, for nothing. Suffering is pointless, it has neither meaning nor reason, it is not even justice, or a lesson. The grace of Amida can awaken the soul to its native purity, its essential folly in thinking itself guilty and assuming itself to be wicked. No despair can elude this gift which seeks nothing in return. This is why priests in No plays speak the words which awaken souls from obsessive passion, unquenchable desire and recurring torments which, according to the illusion of sin, outlived even death. Hell is just a bad dream; you would not be in hell if you did not believe in it.

By the eighteenth of his forty-eight vows, Amida promised to receive all the dying who called on his name, and to welcome them, with no further conditions, into his Pure Land. So vast a consolation! At the last moment, the human heart, rent with the wounds of life, will be appeased: all will meet again on high, on the same lotus. A hard death, which means one that is thought on, weighed up, assumed, decided on and finally performed, becomes less bitter and less harsh when surrounded by such promises. Beaten warriors and parted lovers turn east before they die.

Thus did General Taira no Koremori, who drowned himself at the age of twenty-seven, not so much to ensure his own religious salvation as to escape the reprisals of the Minamoto who had vanquished his clan. He had made it a point of honour not to be taken alive; it would (he thought) be an insult to his father's name to be dragged through the streets in chains. But the chains of the heart were no less heavy. He had had to leave his wife and children in the city of Heian and they were never out of his thoughts. How could he hope for salvation while still bound so closely to other people? He went first to Mount Koya, hoping to take refuge in religion, but he felt far from ready for the necessary renunciation. None the less he shaved his head, as did the two companions who were sharing his fate. Then he went down south, along the mountain paths of the Kii peninsula, as far as the sanctuary of Kumano, a celebrated place of pilgrimage. Perhaps it was there that he took his final decision. He realized that he could find salvation only in death: at a stroke he would escape his adversaries and snap the bonds of affection which were hampering his spiritual progress. By sacrificing his life he would be reborn, even as he drowned, in the Pure Land, saved from the loves of this imperfect earth and ready to bend down from above and save those he had loved. With his two companions and a monk friend as escort, he reached the sea near the waterfall of Nachi and took ship, his heart still aching with the thought of those he would never see again:

> He turned eastward, joined his hands, and recited the invocation to Amida. However, he was still saying in his heart, 'I am living the last moments of my life, but how will they know it in the capital? They must be waiting anxiously for the slightest rumour about me. But my fate must be made known in the end: what weeping will be caused by the news of my death!'

IMPASSIBLE COMPASSION

Thus the voluntary death of Taira no Koremori is presented as an ascetic climax: he is to overcome his last weaknesses by a voluntary act which will cut them off at source. The asceticism of the heart is no less severe than that of the body. It is easy to imagine the smile of the Buddha veiled in a halo of invisible tears. For that civilization, impassibility and not love was the ideal. But no motion of the heart was unknown to it and it was inexhaustibly attentive to the intensity of human sorrow. The monk at Koremori's side respects his slow and bitter progress towards a decision. He does not plead, or direct, or forbid. Should he defend life? According to Buddhist principles, a conditional state like life or death cannot be set above the freedom of a conscience in search of truth. In any case there is no pre-set limit or revealed law which can be imposed on the autonomy of progress through thought to a decision.

Therefore the monk lays no blame on Koremori. Neither does he pity him. Was pity ever an adequate answer to pain? Buddhism offers neither pity nor charity, but compassion; and profound compassion dwells nowhere but in the purest serenity. Pity is weakening, humiliating; charity may be degrading. Impassible compassion is the only fit confidant for the secret of pain and weakness. It knows all but judges nothing; understanding all, it flinches from nothing. In the No plays, also inspired by the Amidist ideal, the flute tells of the exhaustion of ineradicable nostalgia; the protagonist's dance to the quickening rhythm of the drums is the ardour and fury which overflow like lava from a long-extinct volcano. A dance of possession, a dance of deliverance. The No often features a wandering monk who happens to wander into the hell of the human heart; but it is enough for him to remain determinedly immutable. Under his imperturbable gaze, with no word of pity or blame, the strongest passions are consumed in their own dying fire.

When the time comes, Koremori's monk companion and witness merely reminds him of the commitments which underlie the hope in the Pure Land:

'It is enough that your faith be deep, without the slightest shadow of a doubt. If so, then if with perfect devotion you call ten times – what am I saying? once only – on His Name, Amida Nyorai, reducing His Body, immeasurable as the sands of the river Heng, to the measure of three cubits and six spans, surrounded by Kannon, Seishi, and all the serried ranks of the innumerable and holy cohorts of the bodhisattvas and Buddhas all made visible to your eyes, to the music of instruments and hymns, will appear on the instant at the eastern portal of Paradise to receive you. Thus, even if you believe yourself to be plunging into the depths of the blue sea, it is certain that you will really be rising above the purple clouds. And if, becoming a Buddha, you attain perfect detachment and achieve Enlightenment, then without a doubt you will be able to return to this vale of tears whence you came, to be the guide of your wife and children, thus accomplishing your return to this sinful world for the salvation of men and angels.'

With these words, he rang the ritual bell to urge him to prayer. Then Koremori, seeing his chance to achieve salvation, immediately cast aside all idea of affection, and in a loud voice spoke a hundred times the invocation to Amida; and, crying 'All hail!' he threw himself into the sea. His companion in holy orders, Shigekage, and Ishidomaru, speaking the August Name in the same way, followed him into the waves.[13]

The death of Koremori and his two companions, in the sea off Kumano, belongs to a long tradition attested from the ninth century to the eighteenth: rebirth in paradise via drowning (*jusui ojo*). According to Mahayana legends, the compassionate bodhisattva resided on Mount Potalaka (in Japanese, Fudaraku) which was in fact a staging-post on the road to the Pure Land of the Buddha Amida. In Japanese Amidist circles it was firmly believed that Kannon's Fudaraku was an island in the ocean off the Kii peninsula. Here we rediscover the archetype of the Fortunate Isles mingled with the belief common to most sea-going peoples, that the dead live beyond the sea. Thus they could take ship for Fudaraku, singly or in a group, after a last pilgrimage to the sanctuaries of Kumano. They would set sail chanting the litanies of Kannon and Amida, repeating the *nembutsu* over and over again. Eventually, at a sufficient distance from the shore, they would step overboard, or stave in the boat with an axe. These pious suicides became more numerous from the thirteenth century onwards, when the spread of Honen's and Shinran's fideism had established hope in the Pure Land and confidence in salvation by the power of the *nembutsu* alone. The Japanese fondness for technical improvements then produced a boat with a detachable bottom specially for this kind of voyage: instant submersion guaranteed.

In the sixteenth century certain Jesuits were witnesses to this custom. They were already only too quick to write off the Buddhist Venerables as 'pure demonic inventions', as Francis Xavier put it. These suicides confirmed their darkest conclusions: not content with exploiting the poor dupes in life, Satan was inveigling them into the last temptation of death:

> Nothing is more common than to see along the sea-shore boats filled with these fanatics, who hurl themselves into the water weighted with stones, or stave in their boats and let themselves sink slowly, singing the praises of the god Kannon, whose paradise is, they say, at the bottom of the sea. A host of people look on, praising their courage to the skies and asking for their blessing before they disappear.[14]

Father Charlevoix was exaggerating. Buddhist drownings are well attested, but to say that nothing was more common is untrue. In any case, when he published his *Histoire et description générale du Japon* in 1736, the fervour was no longer what it had been, either in Japan or elsewhere: belief in Fudaraku, the Pure Land, the vows of Kannon and the promises of the monk had waned, and the last ship which left the shores of Kumano never to return sailed in 1722. In any civilization, however convinced of the existence of a better world, one can count on the natural fear of death to limit the number of early departures. One believes, but does not know; one is sure, but not quite certain. Shinran himself, although he dedicated his life to proclaiming the faith, openly admitted that he was in no hurry to test the hopes whose mouthpiece he had become. Amidism certainly encouraged voluntary death: thus we know that in summer 1176, when Honen's preaching was most active, a few dozen of the faithful threw themselves into the River Katsura, which flows east of the capital: every fashion has its excesses, and a bathe, even a suicidal one, has its attractions in the summertime. The promises of the monks cost the lives of a few enthusiasts every year, eager to taste the delights of which they had heard. Doubtless it was not too dear a price for the ineffable consolation promised to all the dying by the good news of *nembutsu*, like a balm on the smarts of the last moments of life.

An interdict such as Augustine's is too severe and too costly; and is it even a deterrent? For those who really want to die it is just another turn of the screw of their despair. It is a poor kind of justice which imagines that those who have had their reasons – or unreasons – for despairing of life will be damned for ever. If we must have a faith, let us have the faith of consolation in preference to the faith of terror. True, there is a Buddhist hell, and in the Indian imagination it is well furnished with colourful torments. But it is a purgatory rather than a hell, for it too is impermanent, and one can leave it sooner or later for a less painful existence. When Francis Xavier preached the Christian dogma of eternal hell in 1549 and afterwards, it plunged his converts into the profoundest gloom, and they shed silent tears: such a cruel idea would never have occurred to them. Their parents, damned because they were not Christians? It was a heavy price to pay for the 'good news'.

A FAILED SUBMERSION

As if the anguish of death were not enough in itself, the menace of dogma had to intervene as well. Even after its grip had been loosened somewhat by the consolations of Amida, it still had enough power to nullify, at the very last moment, a decision which society had surrounded with flattery and approbation, for example, the painfully comic misadventure of a young priest in the thirteenth century, who had overestimated both his faith and his strength of mind:

> This, too, is now a thing of the past.
> A monk, who had introduced himself as an ascetic intending to jump into the River Katsura, began by entering the temple of Gidarin-ji, where for 100 days he recited the ritual of contrition. People came from far and near to pay homage to him; ladies thronged the road to the temple as their

carriages came and went. What they saw was a monk aged a little over thirty, frail-looking, who tended to avoid people's eyes; sometimes, as if in his sleep, he would call on the name of the Buddha Amida. The rest of the time he seemed, from the way his lips moved, to be reciting the *nembutsu*; sometimes, he sighed and gazed upon the faces surrounding him; then the audience would jostle to meet his eyes, in a fine confusion.

On the appointed day, in the early morning, he entered the sanctuary whither the monks had preceded him, and the long procession set out. He brought up the rear, clad in coarse paper, wearing a stole, sitting in a cart. His lips moved as if to say something; he avoided people's eyes and from time to time heaved a great sigh. The crowds of spectators at the roadside threw a hail of rice over him. And from time to time the ascetic would say, 'It's getting into my eyes and nose! It is intolerable! If they had any finer feeling, they would put it in a paper bag and send it to my home address!' Then, among the ordinary people who came with clasped hands to do him homage, those who had some sense in their heads muttered, 'What does this ascetic mean? Strange that, on the point of flinging himself into the water, he should tell us to take the rice to Gidarin-ji, and that he can't bear to have it in his eyes and nose . . .!'

Thus they came to the end of the Seventh Avenue. The throng of idlers who had come to do honour to the river-bound ascetic had swelled: they were more numerous than the pebbles on the bank.

They took the cart up to the water's edge and stopped there. Then the ascetic asked what time it was. A monk who was with him answered, 'Past four o'clock.' Then he said, 'it is still a bit too early to go and be reborn in the Pure Land. Let us wait until evening.' Tired of waiting, the people who had come long distances began to drift away; the river-bank became empty of people. There remained only those determined to stay until the bitter end. Among them was a monk who said, 'Do you really have to make an appointment to be reborn? I don't quite understand this . . .'

At last our ascetic stripped to his underclothes, and, turning eastward, he flung himself into the water. But his foot caught in a rope which was hanging from the gunwale and he was left floundering on the surface. Then a disciple disentangled him and he went down head-first, blowing enormous bubbles. Seeing this, a man who had come down to the water's edge to get a better view seized his hand and fished him up again. The ascetic wiped his face with both hands, spat out the water he had swallowed, and then, turning to his rescuer, clasped his hands and said, 'You have done me a great service; I shall repay you in paradise.' And he set his foot on dry land. Then the crowds round about and the local urchins picked up pebbles from the bank and threw them at him. Naked as he was, he fled along the riverside; but the crowd went on throwing stones unmercifully, and eventually hit him on the head.

This abortive sacrifice is a comical echo of Koremori's touching hesitations. Even the presence of a sizeable audience, attracted by the perennial fascination of death, fails to provide the stimulus it gave Peregrinus at the Olympic Games. At the last moment, the terror of death proves greater than the terror or ridicule. A man of little faith, doubtless a rapscallion: the text calls him a *hijiri*, an ascetic on the fringe of the religious establishment, living on his wits. Doubtless life was not easy for him, and death, alas, proved harder still. Others at the time showed greater resolution.

OBSTINACY

Once there was a man called Sanuki-no-san-i. The husband of his nurse, who had taken holy orders, had long ago vowed to seek rebirth in the Pure Land. One day he said to himself, 'If all does not go as I wish, and if, after catching some foul disease, I have no prospect of dying as I would wish, I would find it very hard to carry out my vow.' Therefore, covinced that the ony way to die in the right frame of mind was to die before he could fall ill, he resolved to make a lamp of his body. To test his constancy, he had two hoe-blades heated red hot and put them against his buttocks, which were soon in a state that was terrible to see. After a moment, he decided that the thing was not so awful as all that, and made ready to burn himself alive.

But suddenly he changed his mind: certainly it would be easy to make a lamp of his body, but this did not guarantee that he would be reborn in paradise; indeed an ordinary sort of chap like him would be in danger of feeling some doubts at the last moment. On the other hand, Mount Fudaraku... a place here in this world, where you could go whilst still alive... and forthwith he decided to go there.

He bandaged his hurt buttocks, and since there was a place he knew in the province of Tosa, he went there, acquired a brand-new boat, and put in a lot of practice in steering her; then he persuaded a sailor to tell him when a good north wind had got up.

When this came about, he hoisted the sail, and off he went quite alone, and steered for the north.

He did have a wife and children, but with so strong a resolve it was useless to attempt to detain him; so they were left gazing at the empty horizon, weeping, in the direction that the boat had gone. People at the time, seeing how constant was his will, assumed that he must have reached his goal.[15]

Here, religious fervour counts for less than thorough planning. Determinedly he thinks through the past and the future, the advantages and the disadvantages. The imponderable logic of the story seems to be asking us whether all the generous *élan* of Buddhist faith must lead up to this courageous but petty obstinacy. True, the Crucifixion led up to

Pascal's wager! Thirst for salvation can travel a strange road which ends in the reconciliation of ardent faith and cold calculation.

THE RIND AND THE KERNEL

It would be unfair to leave the last word on Japanese Buddhism with this resolute but rather dim suicide, or even with better examples of medieval Amidism. The fideism of the Pure Land was vastly influential, but it was too far from the Buddha's original thinking: rather than pointing to the heart of the doctrine, as did the fideism of St Paul, it traced its outer limits. It was on the brink of fading into simple religiosity. It was the rind, and many people asked for no more. But those who sought the hard and fruitful kernel did better to look to Zen.

Zen teaches us to rely on ourselves: man is alone in a world without transcendence. The Venerables who gather homage upon the altars are only expedients (*hoben*, Sanskrit *upaya*), like the honey which helps the medicine go down. Salvation is beyond faith, and it is a great mistake to rely only on the Scriptures. Another life? No, Enlightenment is to be achieved here and now, for those that can. What we can intuitively understand is that opposites are united, nirvana and samsara are equivalent, and the absolute is identical with uncreated becoming. Being is time. The Pure Land is our own land seen through pure eyes which are capable of loving it as it is. The master Dogen (1200–53) said it was folly to imagine that in the world of essences leaves did not fall and flowers did not bloom. Rebirth was into this world. Death is nothingness which is not. A Zen monk would probably not have disapproved of the last words of Masashige. There is nothing, except this life.

Zen dismisses the Amidist illusion of a helping mother-figure. No more compassion for a wounded heart: the cure is a burst of silent laughter. Zen teaches that to abandon self-pity is the quickest way out of unhappiness. Impulses to suicide feed on longings for another world, the fantasy of life in the womb, the return to the symbiotic fusion which precedes all separation. Zen is a methodical weaning process. Its tone is detached and humorous; it aims to win its freedom by slaying the illusion of maternal unity. Hence its perennial attraction for the Western mind. The tone of the West is one of revolt, for it has to grapple with the disappearance of the paternal image projected on to God by Christianity.

> This world of birth and death is no other than the august life of the Buddha. If you seek to hate or reject the world, you will lose the august

life of Buddha. If you set your heart upon it and remain attached to this world of birth and death, again you will lose the august life of Buddha.[16]

Dogen teaches us to desire neither death nor life: he was returning to the middle way preached by the Buddha. Suicide betrays an excessive attachment to the gifts and promises of life. Without illusions or disappointments you would have no reason to kill yourself. The healthy abrasiveness of Zen is the ideal antidote to suicide, but it does not use the usual deterrents. 'There is no freedom to kill oneself': Aristotle and Plato had brought out that argument long before Augustine and Thomas Aquinas. Is there any other argument? But what if one kills oneself *so as* to be free? Great indeed is the temptation to cut free of the moral, religious, social and metaphysical swaddling bands in which mankind has been pinioned for its own safety. So loudly do the opponents of suicide shout their opposition that they start one thinking that there must be a sort of glorious freedom about it. If one is not allowed to die because life means being of service, being useful, being obedient, it is hardly surprising if voluntary death occasionally seems preferable. Does not this one act bring all the liberty heart could desire? Alas, no: Buddhists saw, long before Freud, that the will is not free if it does not know what it wants. Acting and wanting are not enough: you must also know what you are doing. Zen stands the usual argument on its head: 'If you kill yourself, you are not yet free.' This warning, which owes nothing to moral or religious intimidation, is clear enough to the ears of modern man; it should suffice to take the shine off the halo of defiance which still surrounds voluntary death. What is the only value worthy of life? Liberty. Should life be sacrificed to liberty? No: liberty is a virtue which will flower in life when it has transcended both the fear and the fascination of death.

THE ASCETIC AND THE DRAGON

Japanese culture is steeped in the principles of Zen, but they could not satisfy its more primeval religious needs. Miracles, magic, faith, exorcism, worship, sacrifice, prayer and devotion went on from age to age – up to our own day, in fact. The ascetic young hero of a story written in 1966 by Shinohara Shiro, priest of the sanctuary of Nachi, gives up his body in a way which combines several currents of strong religious feeling. Jitsukaga is a mountain-dweller, one of those *yamabushi* who were believed to have attained to supernatural psychic powers by the practice of self-denial. 'He was tall, with long hair and beard, and had lost an eye.' About 100 years ago, Jitsukaga used to travel the footpaths of the

Kii peninsula between Yoshino and Kumano, leading guided parties of ascetic pilgrims (*sendatsu*). In 1884, at the age of forty-one, he drowned himself in the waterfall of Nachi:

> One day, when they had put some tea out to dry before the door of the Doi house in Owase, a white dragon appeared in the midst of the tea-leaves. Seeing this, the master of the house, terror-struck, tried to beat it to death with a stick, but the serpent disappeared.
>
> The next day, the daughter of the house caught a high fever and was thrown into a state approaching madness. When they enquired by divination the reason for this strange malady, it was decreed that it was because of the white dragon. Although many methods were tried, no cure could be found. Therefore they called the *sendatsu* Jitsukaga, who was then engaged in ascetic practices at the waterfall of Nachi. He was taken to the Dois' house and held a service of invocation, during which the girl's condition improved. But when he went away, the malady suddenly worsened again. The Doi child was then taken to the master of Nachi, who put her through the great secret rite of *hikime*.
>
> Then the girl, becoming possessed, revealed to Jitsukaga: 'I am the nine-headed dragon divinity of Owase. When I appeared to accept the tea-offering of the house of Doi, they tried to kill me. Happily I escaped with my life, but I decided to bring about the extinction of the Doi family. Not knowing the arcana of the secret rite of *hikime*, I have been compelled to submit to the law of Jitsukaga and admit defeat. But from now on I, too, shall engage in the practice of asceticism, and enter into this struggle for power.'
>
> With these words it disappeared; the girl returned to normal and went home safe and sound. Shortly afterwards, Jitsukaga lost the struggle, and in his anxiety, called many people to him. He celebrated the great service of the 108 lamps. Then, taking the place of the girl who had fallen under the curse of the dragon divinity, he flung himself into the waterfall during the night. Even in its very depths, he kept up the position of seated meditation.
>
> The great master Gokido of the Gyoja-bo hermitage in Zenki came and clove the water with the nine and ten secret *mudra* of the sword. Then, guiding a raft to the east of the waterfall, he hoisted Jitsukaga on to it. He buried the body in Jitsukaga's own hermitage. But as this constituted a pollution of the sacred ground, he was later taken to the cemetery of Jo-no-o.
>
> A generous donor from Ichibata paid for the funerary monument. Then, in the seventh month of year 5 of Taisho [1916], on the thirty-third anniversary of Jitsukaga's death, Osawa Masao and his followers donated the wall around it. The priest of the sanctuary of Nachi, Shimano Mori, wrote the text which was graven on the stone. On the fourteenth day of the twelfth month of year 41 of Showa [1966], the eighty-third anniversary of Jitsukaga's death, an oratory was built under the waterfall. In it was

lighted the sacred lamp of the service of the dead. Since then it has been the resting-place of the soul of Jitsukaga and of the forty-eight other souls of those who have returned to the divinity by throwing themselves into the fall.

Written on the last day of the twelfth month of year 41 of Showa [1966].

Written by Shinohara Shiro. [NB: the present account was based on the Memoirs of the great master Osawa Enkaku, also named Osawa Masao.][17]

Wonder-tales die hard. The dragons of Far Eastern legend still haunted outlying fields – and young girls' bodies – right up to the end of the nineteenth century. Here the unquiet depths of popular belief stir again: shamans armed with talismans and spells strive to tame the caprices of theriomorphic deities. But far from trying to uproot this animistic folklore, Buddhism adapted to it, laying down its spiritual values over the old panic terror: self-sacrificing compassion, coupled with impassible detachment. Jitsukaga's motives for suicide remain unclear, the confusion stemming from the syncretism of religious thinking in the story. Is he disgusted at having lost the fight? Is it the logical outcome of his asceticism? A sacrifice in which he takes the young girl's place? His attitude in death – sitting under the waterfall in the lotus position – must certainly indicate that he gave up his body in correct traditional Buddhist fashion, full of serenity and concentration.

The combat of the ascetic and the dragon reminds us of Rimbaud's words: 'Spiritual combat is as ferocious as battles among men.' One must be armed for the fight, and the Buddha is surnamed the Victor; but his victory was not over some terrible god, it was over the terror of religion itself. In this story, Buddhism shows its greatness by crowning the obscure struggles of an exorcist with a perfect serenity: no doubt it set a final smile, a smile of victory and peace, upon the still face of the drowned ascetic.

9

The Theatre of Cruelty

When St Francis Xavier landed at Kyushu, in the middle of the sixteenth century, he found Japan no less turbulent and divided than the continent of Europe. There was nothing comparable to the wars of religion and the great doctrinal quarrels of Christendom. But under a silent and invisible emperor and an impotent shogun, the Japanese state had ceased to exist. The whole country had broken down into petty kingdoms; and every petty king in his castle was at war with every other. It was a time of fragile coalitions, short-lived truces, fleeting victories, inconclusive wars: *sengoku jidai*, the age of warring kingdoms.

These struggles, which for generations turned Japan into a reasonable simulacrum of the hell of the Ashura, seemed all the more terrible for being devoid of ideological motivation. They fought for the sake of fighting. In contemporary Europe, at least the lust for war could be clad in loftier pretexts: the unity of Christendom or freedom of worship, fighting for God. But in Japan, the war-lords were machiavellian without delusions: they wanted power for the sake of power. And usually no holds were barred: intrigue, trickery, perfidy, treachery, violence or destruction. The vassal army had fallen apart, and by now most of the troops were mercenaries, hired thugs. The feudal princes (daimyo) milked their territories dry, taxing the free circulation of goods at every toll barrier. This disruption of market forces meant that a bad harvest in any one part of the country caused instant famine.

What could anyone do? Rovolt against this abuse of power? There were some peasants' revolts, but they, too, were local, and were quickly repressed. The easiest thing to do was to flee the taxes and drudgeries of one's home region and sell oneself to the highest bidder by becoming a mercenary (*ashigaru*). It was a vicious circle, a ring of steel: the victims could be relied on to turn the screw of their own oppression. The atrocities of those centuries of civil war were often committed by hired soldiers, ex-peasants drunk on their new strength. Theft, rape, fire, waste and pillage: that was the tally of the ten-year-long war of the Onin era (1467–77) which devastated the self-styled Capital of Serene Peace with fire and sword.

Thus did Japan become the theatre of cruelty: the cruelty of war. It was enough to make man despair at the sight of his own image. And yet this was the furnace which forged the Samurai as he was to reign for centuries over Japanese society, and as he still reigns in the minds of those of us who see him through the mists of time: a shining paragon, one of the highest types of humanity ever seen on this earth.

FROM VIOLENCE TO WILL-POWER

Despite the social upheavals (*gekokujo*) which had brought down the ancient families, chivalric traditions (*kyuba no michi*) had survived and were assumed by the newcomers. The disciplines of war were developing; aspirations to strength and skill were shaping a new ideal. After all, it is impossible to create anything worthwhile without resistance and rejection. The stage was so crowded with petty treasons that they created the counter-resolve to be loyal even unto death.[1] The sight of greed showed the true value of disinterest, and deliberate austerity exposed the hollowness of ostentation. The moment must eventually come when the desire for power reaches its zenith, and is paid for by a renewal of self-mastery. Freely chosen bondage is the daughter of tyranny. Thus cruelty, purged and sublimated, laid down a stern ethic. 'What', Antonin Artaud once asked, 'is cruelty? To the mind, cruelty means rigour, implacable dedication and decision, irreversible and absolute determination.' Even amidst its worst confusions, man never loses confidence in life, because the confusion gives him the chance to exercise the virtues he has made his own. They were not fighting for a noble cause – the war needed no idea to justify it – but the idea of war as the theatre of the military virtues certainly had its attractions.

Violence turned to will-power, and will-power rose to self-sacrifice. They had to learn to kill, but it was nobler to learn to die, to kill oneself. Military virtue culminated in abrupt and total resignation; if someone has to win, then somebody else has to lose. Even the most dashing attack was not more highly praised than a decision to 'end it all'. Thus voluntary death became the hidden, unchanging, bleeding heart of the warrior ethic. The final sanction of every duty came in the polished form of *seppuku*. The Jesuits, whose missions lasted for some sixty years, did not have enough time to obliterate that four-century-old tradition. Ever solicitous toward the elite, they none the less pushed their advantage with the warrior classes: the purchase of a Portuguese musket probably set many a kinglet of Kyushu on the road to the true faith.

One of the greatest warriors of the time, Konishi Yukinaga, baptized in 1583 under the name Augustine, was Christian enough to refuse the invitation to suicide issued to him after the battle of Sekigahara in 1600. The Tokugawa had to go to the additional trouble of beheading him in public. Similarly, in 1638, the young Amakusa Shiro, who at seventeen, clad in a white kimono, had been the angel of revolt of the Christian peasants of Kyushu, omitted to kill himself in the hour of defeat. But in that same hour, following the old instinct at times of catastrophe, the insurgents' wives and children, Christian as they were, threw themselves into the flames. The fires of that desperate revolt were soon doused: Japanese Christianity, for all its heroism, sank and was lost in the long night of political repression.[2]

The Christian prohibition on voluntary death inevitably slowed the spread of the new religion among the warrior class: for all the 700,000 converts it could muster at best, it was never strong enough to challenge so well-established a custom as *seppuku*. True, the massive collective disembowellings of the fourteenth century were a thing of the past. Suicides were still numerous after great defeats, as in 1615 when the troops of Tokugawa Ieyasu stormed the fortress of Osaka, but orgies of *seppuku* had gone out of fashion: the act now tended to be a sober and rigidly defined one, a ceremonious solo performance exhibiting assimilated virtues. Voluntary death had been built into the ever tidier architecture of class ethics, and was formalistic or moralistic as the spirit of the times dictated. Well-mannered ladies of the warrior class killed themselves by severing the jugular vein with a dagger, the *kaiken*, kept hidden in the thick folds of their brocaded girdles. Men disembowelled themselves according to a meticulous rite whose cruelty, from the Muromachi period onwards, was normally cut short by the *kaishaku*: it was his job to put a quick end to a slow and studiously correct ceremonial.

THE PRIVILEGE OF EVISCERATION

Some examples of lower-class *seppuku* are known from the Edo era, among shopkeepers, for example.[3] But they are the exception which proves the rule, and no doubt contemporaries were shocked at this usurping of a right reserved for a higher class. For a peasant, artisan or merchant there was always the rope or the river. Evisceration was a privilege, like heraldic devices or wearing two swords. An unpleasant privilege, but it was jealously guarded, and inculcated from childhood.[4] The sons and daughters of samurai very soon learned that their acknowledged superiority often also implied the duty of sacrificing themselves to the honour of the family name, that is, to pride of class perceived as an ethical priority. The warrior ethic had a fearful precocity; the age of suicide came all too soon. Once two brothers tried to assassinate Tokugawa Ieyasu. As they were of noble birth, they were granted the privilege of disembowelling. But to prevent a vendetta, the youngest son of the family had to accompany his elders; after watching them carefully, he killed himself in his turn in perfect samurai style. He was just eight years old.

Seppuku was the harshest and most spectacular of the prerogatives which set the warrior class apart from the common people. From the end of the sixteenth century, the rulers of Japan did their best to widen the gulf, in an attempt to strangle social mobility and raise insuperable obstacles between one social condition and another. Christian missionaries were expelled and persecuted. Soon the whole country was to be sealed off, by the decrees of 1633, 1635 and 1639, from all outside influence. Similarly, every segment of society had to be shut in with its own function, customs, rights and duties. Men died in the condition into which they had been born; this immobility was deemed necessary to the social equilibrium and the peace of the realm.

For everything comes to an end, even war: above the warring kinglets one, then two, then three dictators arose in succession: Nobunaga, Hideyoshi, Ieyasu. They brought order out of chaos and established their own supremacy. By one of those ironies so abundant in history, it was a *parvenu* who first insisted on keeping the social classes apart. In 1588, Hideyoshi, who had come from nowhere to be the master of Japan, had all swords not belonging to samurai tracked down and confiscated. Local powers who were capable of raising and commanding a local militia were forced to choose between the career of arms, in the service of a feudal prince, and the cultivation of their own lands. Again Hideyoshi was differentiating social classes, discouraging agrarian revolt, securing the taxes and blocking the vents of dissatisfaction. A fluid and ebullient society slowly took on the chill of rigid absolutism.[5]

THE NEW ORDER

The price of peace was heavy, but Ieyasu was in no mood to bargain. Hideyoshi's son might become a rallying-point for the opposition; he had to be crushed. In 1615, the vast fortress of Osaka fell, and the road to the capital was decorated with 35,000 enemy heads. At the same time, the shogun's henchmen went in search of Hideyoshi's grandson, the last offshoot of the family, a child of six who was murdered for reasons of state. Thus began one of the longest periods of peace in history. But the terror of the army or the police would probably have been insufficient to restrain people for long. Ieyasu proved himself a good lawmaker as well as a victorious soldier: his draconic and meticulous enactments brought the great lords under his heel.

While France was putting her destiny in the hands of the Bourbon monarchy, Japan was inventing her own version of absolutism and laying down the inexorable authority of the restored state over the scattered remains of feudalism. Pax Tokugawa: peace indeed, but an armed peace, a martial-law peace patrolled by the men of war. The Edo government was called the Great General Headquarters (*bakufu*). The supremacy of the warriors (*bushi*, samurai) was emphasized incessantly: the state relied on them to maintain the rigour of the law, less because of their numbers (less than a fifteenth or even a twentieth of the population) than because of their prestige. They were respected, and they had to be: if a commoner fell short, by word or deed, of the required reverence, the offended samurai had the legal right to cut down the offender with complete impunity (*kirisute gomen*).

But if the new order were to be accepted, threats of force and unbending rules had to be complemented by moral rigour. Ieyasu himself was the first to realize this: first a killer, then a lawmaker, finally he became a moralist. He was a fervent Amidist, but he also admired the precepts of Confucius. At the end of his life he told his assembled vassals the secret of his success: 'Answer evil with good.' This seemingly evangelical maxim (in fact it comes from the *Tao-te ching*) sounds strange in the mouth of an elderly despot, veteran of fifty battles or more. But we can be sure that he was not being ironical. Times had changed: the peace of the Tokugawa was to be not only military, but also moral – and rather hypocritical. The swashbuckling samurai were now to rest on their laurels and grow outwardly respectable. Violence congealed into discipline. Imposing gestures, deep voice, composed gait, stately bearing: the samurai's whole body was the theatre of his dignity.

At that time morality was at a premium in Europe, and the prestige of virtue was no less impressive in France than in Japan. Rebellious conviction had yielded to acknowledged norms, the sacred was no more than the foundation of social ethics. The French hereditary nobility, which flaunted the same principles of honour and service as the samurai, failed to impose its own value system, for after the defeat of the Fronde it was the bourgeois idea of Christian charity which prevailed. The nobility took refuge in gibing at the new Pharisees and their dupes, in refined irony and ingenious scepticism. French moralists like La Rochefoucauld went into the attack with their weapons of perspicacity, and found self-interest under every coat of virtuous varnish. In Japan the warrior ethic carried conviction because it laid stress on self-sacrifice. Its Pharisees could strut about without being suspected of hypocrisy. For a very simple reason: physical courage, as Stendhal observed, is the only virtue which cannot be assumed.

A man who will defend his honour to the death can hardly be accused of insincerity: he acts, and that is enough; his act translates a truth which no amount of suspect speech could ever establish. All virtues can be practised for the sake of the good reputation they confer, or for profit in this world or the next, or for health, wealth or salvation. But a morality which will go as far as suicide can scarcely be suspected of seeking an advantage beyond itself. It was because of *seppuku* that the warrior ethic was never subdued to any utilitarian end; *seppuku* confirmed its sovereignty over life and gave it the irrefutable sincerity which was at the root of its prestige. Voluntary death was the key which locks the house and thus makes it safe to live in: it was the supreme sanction authenticating the whole structure of military obligation. Every samurai had it dinned into him from childhood that he might have to commit *seppuku* one day, and while it was the acknowledged privilege of a minority, it also set a seal on the whole of Japanese society: it was the linchpin of the whole structure. Paradoxically this ethic, forged in the tempests of war, came into its own as a keeper of the peace.

HONOUR AND SERVICE

Seppuku, invented in time of war, spread far beyond its origin, following the meandering motivations of moral conscience in response to the twofold demands of honour and service. The glory of the individual reached its apogee just as the individual began to merge with the cause which he acknowledged as his *raison d'être*. Thus a vassal accompanying his master in death (*junshi*) used *seppuku*, which was then known as *oibara*. The spirit of service could go no further, especially as this last service was completely superfluous. But it continued the most ancient traditions of feudal loyalty. It could express a devotion as intense as a lover's, which might or might not have (platonic) homosexual overtones, but was always redolent of that exalted, narcissistic virility which forges the bond among warriors. Many vassals thought their own honour depended on it: they wanted to give proof of their disinterested gratitude. You must, said the author of the *Hagakure*, serve as though you were already dead, never thinking of yourself.

Feudal devotion, when absolute, ceased to the servile. It did not mean blind obedience to the master: he was obeyed only if his order was worthy of himself. A vassal was no flatterer. The young prince Nabeshima Tsunashige, tired out by a long march though he was only twenty years old, asked one of his men to cut him a walking-stick. Just as the vassal was handing it over, another, older man snatched it from him: 'Would you encourage our lord to be a laggard? You must not give him everything he asks. Use a little judgement in future!' Apparently the shift from the 'heroism of silent service' to the 'heroism of flattery', which Hegel saw as characteristic of Versailles, did not afflict the warrior nobility of Japan.[6]

It was acknowledged that the hardest duty of the disciplined serving man was to hold out against errors, idiocies and abuses from above. Confucius, whose influence burgeoned in the Edo era, had always insisted that there was a duty of protest, which had been formalized in China in the form of a college of censors. How did one protest? Not by rebellion. In words? Probably. But better still, by a voluntary death conflating disagreement and submission, a deed which in its silence was more eloquent than any speech. The youthful Oda Nobunaga gave himself up to pleasure and neglected his dominions. One of his vassals sent him a letter of criticism – and sealed it by *seppuku*. Recalled to his senses by this suicide of protest (*kanshi*), Nobunaga amended his conduct so effectively that he became a great man and the master of Japan. A life lost for a lesson which must never be lost. Such was also the intention of Mishima, horrified by the frivolity of the twentieth century.[7]

Between disapproval and indignation, indignation and resentment, the boundaries are unclear. Often any moral intention was lost in simple anger: men killed themselves to heap coals of fire on a rival's head – suicide of resentment (*sunshi*), or of vengeance (*munenbara*). Many conflicts which, in Europe, would have ended in a duel had a suicidal outcome in Japan.[8] You killed yourself, defying your enemy to do the same: a potlatch, brief and stunning, spending all that you had. The authorities encouraged this introverted aggression as being conducive to public order. One suicide, or even two, was preferable to fighting in the streets. Armed quarrelling was punishable by death: survivors of any such bloody affray were likely to be told by their shogun or daimyo to make an example of themselves by committing suicide. If, instead of setting on your opponent, you disembowelled yourself straight away, you were justified and all the shame was his. All your humiliation was wiped out and you would be understood, approved of and mourned for.

Western observers were struck by this custom, and the astonishment of the sixteenth-century Jesuits was echoed long afterwards in one of Paul Valéry's 'disrespectful thoughts': 'An odd sort of vengeance! A

Japanese will go and disembowel himself on his enemy's doorstep to make him do likewise.' By Valéry's time the custom had fallen out of use. Perhaps it had never been very common. But it ought to be understood nevertheless, because it fits perfectly into the web of attitudes inculcated under the Tokugawa, and because even today it has a very attenuated echo in certain polite observances: one man's modesty compels the other to be equally modest, with a plethora of alternating politenesses, a verbal potlatch. Looked at closely, this 'vengeance' is no stranger then some Western customs. The intolerable shame of an enemy's final gesture of suicide has its own logic – like the consciousness of sin driven home to us by the willing sacrifice of Christ.

SELF-PUNISHMENT

Of all the uses of *seppuku*, the commonest and most significant, in that moral age, was as a self-punishment motivated by an exaggerated sense of responsibility. The samurai was taught to make himself the first scapegoat for infringements of law and honour. Without this prompt and final sanction the whole network of obligations might have slackened, the careful discipline faded away – or so it was feared. For the honour of the samurai consisted not merely in serving and doing his duty, but also in supervising himself, mastering himself, answering for himself in every deed he did. The ideal of self-control was a necessary adjunct of the ideal of devotion. Any carelessness was a humiliation which must be blotted out. Samurai might kill themselves to expiate a careless error (*sokotsushi*). Between a punishable fault and an innocent mistake was a vast area of negligence which was deliberately made subject to the extremest sanctions. This disciplinary rigour was written into the law and extended to the common people: in 1742 it was decreed that a carter who had caused a fatal accident must be decapitated! The feeling of responsibility extended to situations in which the victim, on examination, had clearly intended no harm. He did not ask himself what he had *meant* to do: he was judged, and adjured to judge himself, on what he *had* done. It was his duty to be aware and alert to all his actions, at any moment.[9]

In Europe Christian penitence had long since exempted the individual from the task of self-judgement. Capital self-punishment gave Japanese military custom its grim conviction just at the time when the nobility of the West were relaxing under the casuistry of intention so ably manipulated by their Jesuit confessors. For centuries Christian priests had assumed the task of moral governance; in Japan the warriors did it themselves, and very rigorously too. Yamaga Soko, the first theoretician of *bushido*, in the mid-seventeenth century, asked himself what a samurai was actually *for*. He was never asked to work, as the common people had to – and since peace now reigned, he was forbidden to fight! Was he, then, no more than a parasite? No, said Yamaga: he has the essential job of teaching the whole people by his good example. He keeps watch over himself and everyone else: 'If someone in one of the three classes of the common people transgresses a moral principle, the samurai punishes him on the spot, and thus becomes the defender of morality on behalf of the whole country.' Such severity would soon have made him hated if he had not been its first victim. If he was to be a warrior for the good, he had to prove continuously that he would not spare himself. And the crueller he was to himself, the more approval he knew he would get.

CEREMONY

The penal code of the Tokugawa was built on these customs of self-punishment. It decreed suitable punishments for the warrior class: *hissoku, heimon, chikkyo, kaieki*: simple arrest, close arrest, house arrest, removal from the list of samurai and, the fifth and highest decree, capital punishment by *seppuku*. This compulsory disembowelling, called *tsumebara*, was a meticulously organized ceremony. The protagonist washed himself and tied back his hair, and put on a white kimono dyed a very light blue, with no heraldic devices. He could express his last wishes, or, by special permission, write a letter. Then he advanced to the place of execution, which might be a room in a Buddhist temple, or a pavilion set apart in the noble house where he had been under arrest pending sentence; often it was simply a part of the garden closed off by curtains and screens, all white, the colour of mourning. There, turned towards the north, were mats covered with white material, on which he sat down. Red felt carpets, to soak up the blood, were also used. One might have thought that the hosts would be worried lest their house be polluted, a powerful taboo in Shinto; but a treatise tells us that this was not so: blood could not pollute the home of a warrior family, so there was no need to call on the priest and his exorcisms. It was enough to take all the necessary precautions: for example, if the ceremony took place in the garden, the path the condemned man must tread was covered with mats set close together, so that he would not have to wear shoes. In such a situation the blood might rush to his head and his sandals might drop off without his realizing it, which would be very awkward. There was an obsessional attachment to little things which helped fill the void of death: everything had to be settled to the smallest detail.

THEATRE *IN CAMERA*

A handful of motionless witnesses were present: officers representing the shogun or daimyo, the impassive delegated eyes of the sovereign. And there were assistants called *kaishaku* who supervised and seconded the protagonist and speeded his death-agony. Like all punishments, the *tsumebara* was a spectacle, but it was a spectacle *in camera*, for an invited audience only. The general public could see only imitations, which were frequent in the Kabuki theatre. The samurai listened while the condemnation to death was read out. Sometimes he was offered a final cup of sake. Then a dagger nine *sun* and five *bu* (about twelve inches) long was brought to him on a tray with the sharp edge turned towards him. The blade had been wrapped in white paper, with only the point exposed to a length of two *bu* and five *rin* (about half an inch). In some cases, the blade was blunted to make the punishment more severe. The doomed man stripped the upper half of his body and lowered his girdle below the stomach. Then he seized the dagger and plunged it into his left side. At this point, one of the *kaishaku*, who had been silently standing behind him with drawn sword, would decapitate him with a blow on the back of the neck. The *kaishaku* had to keep calm, and strike hard and true. For a time, in the seventeenth century, the height of the art was to leave a flap of flesh which would keep the head attached to the body and stop it rolling about in what was considered an undignified fashion. Oh, the tyranny of fashion!

SKILLED SWORDMANSHIP

The choice of *kaishaku* was generally left to the victim, who would ask his best friends. Many were reluctant to accept: as the *Hagakure* remarks, there was no glory to be won, and if one happened to make a mess of it, it was an indelible shame! You had to be sure of your skill, so it was very useful to get your hand in by practising (for example) on criminals of inferior rank condemned to be beheaded. Normally executioners were from a class of pariahs called *hinin*, 'non-humans'. But a samurai sometimes turned executioner just to test his nerve. Yamamoto Tsunetomo, searching his memories for the *Hagakure*, described the education of his elder brother:

> Yamamoto Kichizaemon was five years old when our father Jin'emon ordered him to kill a dog; fifteen when he had to kill a condemned man. The Lord Katsushige, when still an adolescent, was ordered by his father Naoshige to practise this same skill. It is said that in the process he once

decapitated ten men in swift succession. That is how persons of quality behaved in those days, whereas today even the sons of warriors of lower rank have no idea how to cut off a head: a serious gap in their education! Some might say that you can do without it; that to decapitate a bound man is no great achievement, a fault, a pollution: excuses, excuses! In fact, as I see it, people are neglecting valour and are interested only in making themselves look pretty and polishing their nails. If you examine the real feelings of those who are reluctant to kill, it is because they lack the heart that they fall back on fair speeches, giving all sorts of reasons for not killing. Now, it was certainly because it was necessary that Lord Naoshige gave the order to practise it. I used to go and train at the place of execution at Kase; it gave me an extraordinary feeling. To be disgusted at it is a sign of cowardice.[10]

Often the plebeian corpses thus dispatched became *tameshimono*, exercise fodder for samurai who, in the absence of living flesh, could carve up a few dead limbs. Another custom, *tsujigiri*, was illegal but fairly common: young warriors challenged one another to ambush a passing citizen and cut him down. Peace reigned, solemn and unbending, but the cruelty of warlike habits was never quite forgotten.

In some cases of *tsumebara* the beheading was put off to make the execution more perfect or the punishment more severe. It was up to the *kaishaku* to do things properly:

In the course of his life, Makiguchi Yohei often performed the role of *kaishaku*. When a certain Kanehara had to accomplish *seppuku*, Yohei accepted that office. Now, at the moment when Kanehara had the point of his sword against his stomach and was about to pierce it, he found himself unable to do this. Then Yohei went up to him and shouted, 'Hey!' in his ear, and stamped his foot. Kunemara recoiled and so drove the blade across his stomach. After cutting off his head, Yohei said, 'And yet he was a good friend of mine.' And he wept.

Often the condemned man did not have to do the disembowelling: the *kaishaku* would cut his head off just as he was holding his hand out for the dagger. However, there was nothing in common between the *tsumebara*, even if cut short, and decapitation, which was considered dishonourable because the victim was bound: it was therefore reserved, by special decree, for samurai who were judged to have dishonoured themselves in advance by some shameful crime. The *tsumebara* kept the spirit of voluntary death intact even if the *kaishaku* intervened straight away, because the protagonist, being free to move, had the awesome privilege of choosing his last moment. He could put out his hand a second earlier, or a second later, and that instant of time opened up an abyss of freedom. *Seppuku* may have been part of the penal code, but that made it none the less a voluntary, noble and honourable death.

THE HORROR OF PUNISHMENT

The authorities of the Edo period had a twofold policy on punishment, exploiting both honour and horror. There were two categories of sanction, the sublime and the atrocious. According to the seriousness of the crime, commoners could be put in the pillory, tattooed, whipped, banished and, if the death penalty was required, beheaded, burned or crucified – for the cross, imported along with Christianity, was in common use. (In fact, crucifixion and firearms, along with syphilis, were the first fruits of contact with the West; for two centuries they were the only fruits.) Such executions were in public, whereas *tsumebara* was a silent and private ceremony. There was a place of execution at Asakusa, in the north-east of Edo, and another to the south, in the Shinagawa district beside the busy Tokaido road. Corpses were often left there, exposed as a warning to passers-by. In 1691, at a time when Western eyes were beginning to revolt at the sight of executions, Engelbert Kaempfer, doctor to the Dutch company in Nagasaki, complained about this practice.

The Japanese penal tradition had long been exceptionally indulgent: offenders were banished. Burning at the stake, practised for some years under the emperor Yuryaku (457–79), had been out of use for centuries. But with the persecution of the Christians the theatre of penal cruelty was fully open. 'The Japanese', wrote Montesquieu, 'see punishment as the avenging of an insult to the prince. The joyful songs of our martyrs were regarded as an insult to him.'[11] The sadism of the Bakufu succeeded where Rome had failed: worship of the Crucified sank under the weight of crucifixions. Commodus and Diocletian could have taken lessons in despotism from Ieyasu, Hidetada or Iemitsu. The Tokugawa prescribed the cross as punishment for the most serious crimes against authority: political conspiracy, murdering one's master, father, husband or teacher, and, in that segmented country, smuggling goods past toll barriers. The victim, the rebellious slave bound to the avenging wood, unable to move, raised up before the eyes of the whole people and slowly suffocating under the weight of his own body, was the total opposite of the protagonist of *seppuku*, that brief and energetic act, that sober and shining performance put on by an elite before the impasssible gaze of its sovereign.

The penal code was totally asymmetrical. No society has ever made it more cynically obvious that justice distinguished between the dominant class and its underlings. It was a dualistic, legally heterogeneous and inegalitarian society. Montesquieu, well informed about the persecutions, saw only the despotic side: 'In Japan, man has made an effort and surpassed himself in cruelty.' The ferocious *Edict of a Hundred Articles* is contemporary with Montesquieu's *L'Esprit des lois*, and if he had been able to read it he would have been confirmed in his verdict: 'They are not seeking to punish the offender, but to avenge the prince.' Certainly, where the common people were concerned the sole weapon was fear. But for the warrior class there was an appeal to honour and virtue. To use Montesquieu's categorization, sovereignty was not 'despotic' *vis-à-vis* the samurai, but 'monarchic' – and in some ways even reminiscent of the military republicanism of Sparta. Certainly, the offender was not corrected but annihilated. But he (as it were) annihilated himself, of his own free will, less to assuage the prince's anger than to satisfy the impersonal ideal of martial valour which he bore within himself.

That is not to say that the samurai were more gently treated; on the contrary, they were more closely watched, more often punished than any other class. Rural communities, for example, were free to follow their own customary laws; except in cases of insurrection, the shoguns and daimyos did not intervene. By reserving the *tsumebara* for the warrior, this class-conscious justice was sanctioning the ethic of the class which was the keystone of the social order. If the ruling class behaved well, everything would go well – so Confucius believed. And people behaved well only under the threat of punishment: so the jurists believed. Thus two contradictory Chinese ideologies, Confucian optimism and juristic pessimism, were reconciled when the ancient native tradition of *seppuku* was given its place in the penal code.

MASTERING THE MASTERS

Similarly, in Rome, failed conspirators of senatorial rank used to open their veins, to the relief of the emperor who was thus spared an execution which would have tarnished his reputation for clemency. In gratitude he allowed them to bequeath their fortune to their heirs. In China, at one time, the Son of Heaven used to send his former friends the 'three precious gifts', giving them the choice of a leaf of gold (to choke themselves), a silken cord (to hang themselves) and a flask of opium (to put them to sleep for good).[12] But such despotic expedients lacked the support of a class morality of long standing. In Japan, the *tsumebara* was grounded in such morality. The ethics of voluntary death had allowed the warriors to be recognized, and to recognize themselves, for what they wished to be. The state took them at their word, suiting its chastisements to their virtues.

No penal system was ever so economical – costly, perhaps, in terms of human lives, but so smooth in operation. The fault was punished by eliminating the offender, in a process which ensured both his obedience and his co-operation. Neither victim nor executioner, in the liturgy of punishment he himself executed the law graven in his own body from birth. However harsh the judge, he could count on the co-operation of his victim. Even if he thought the sentence unjust, he would take pride in performing the ceremony without a murmur of protest. Even the most trifling offence would be willingly expiated by so noble a death. Until the last moment he would be treated as a noble and free man; in his turn, he refrained from appealing against the sentence. Without complaint or revolt, he faced up to his destiny, and he went to meet it, great-hearted enough to accept all. The *tsumebara*, freely distributed and untiringly employed, was the cardinal institution which allowed an absolute ruler to rule the ruling class by confirming its own idea of itself.

THE PRINCE'S VENGEANCE

For great crimes, that is for any threat to the state, the state might sometimes dispense with *tsumebara*. In 1651 a conspiracy was discovered among the *ronin*, 'floating men', i.e. unemployed, unpaid and masterless samurai, fighting men out of a job, about a tenth of the warrior class (sometimes more in difficult times), who were a constant headache to the authorities. The plan was to set fire to the town of Edo and seize power in the confusion. One of the leading conspirators, Yui Shosetsu, had time to kill himself, but his accomplice, Marubashi Chuya, was arrrested and put to the torture. Samurai were not exempt from this in criminal investigations. It was not the custom to condemn them unless they had confessed, so the extremest means were used to extract an admission.

It was not until 1873, when Gustave Boissonade heard the shrieks of some victims and complained to the Japanese authorities about their outdated procedures, that torture fell out of use. Chuya's family – wife, children, other relatives – was massacred. He ought to have been condemned to *tsumebara*. Instead he was crucified. The sovereign's vengeance showed the extent of his fear. Perhaps he also thought the people deserved an interesting spectacle: Ishikawa Goemon, a famous brigand, was of the warrior class, but Hideyoshi ordered him to be fried alive in boiling oil. A taste for the unusual? Or was it a learned imitation, knowing that in ancient China transgressors of the law were sometimes boiled alive in cauldrons on which that same law was graven? Such were the grim decisions of the Jurists, whose influence on Japanese absolutism was no less that that of Confucian morality. According to the 1742 Edict of a Hundred Articles, when a great offender escaped justice by suicide his body had to be pickled to allow time for the judges' deliberations, and their sentence applied to the corpse.[13]

Thus the sovereign occasionally set aside the liturgy of samurai law to indulge his ancient instincts of ferocity. But times did become less cruel, though later than in the West. Japan invented no merciful guillotine, but certain torments, still legal but considered too horrible, fell out of use. For example, the saw (*nokogiribiki*): the offender was put in a pit, his head in an iron collar protruding at ground level. Two blood-soaked bamboo saws were laid alongside, and for two days any member of the crowd who felt so inclined could saw away at the miserable victim's neck. In the Edo period they found it necessary to remove the victims from the pit after the two days and behead them, for there was no longer anyone willing to make use of the saw.

GARRISON LIFE

The use of *tsumebara* was dictated principally by the need to curb the endemic restlessness of a war-oriented society. It was disciplinary as well as penal, designed to force the men of war to accept the rules of good behaviour required in peacetime. Attempts had been made to sever them from the land and concentrate them, often with nothing to do, in the cities, below the citadel (*jokamachi*). Edo, with its enormous fortress, was the greatest garrison town the world has ever known. All these fighters were, by definition, restless, impatient, quarrelsome and vengeful. The *Hagakure* is full of tales of vendettas and brawls which regularly ended in *seppuku*. Under the universal peace the instincts of war seethed constantly. Death was duly administered to end such disturbances. Those who followed the logic of fatalism and honour, supremely indifferent to life, could behave in strange ways:

> One evening in Edo, four or five *hatamoto* had gathered to play go. In the middle of the game, one went off to the latrines. During his absence a quarrel arose, and one of the players was killed by a sword-thrust. The lamp went out amidst general confusion. The man in the latrines rushed out: 'Come now, all of you! Calm down! It's nothing. I'll deal with it. Bring a light!' This was done, and calm was restored. Then he cut off the head of the trouble-maker, saying, 'My luck in arms must have run out, since I was not there when the quarrel started. I ought to be condemned to *seppuku* for cowardice. In any case, if people say that I had taken refuge in the latrines, I shall be forced to disembowel myself without a chance to

explain. Rather than dying alone, covered with shame, it is better to die after killing someone else. That is why I did what I have just done.' Such were his words. This affair came to the ears of the shogun, who praised the conduct of that individual.

CONTRADICTIONS OF A WARLIKE PEACE

That paradoxical attitude was quite symptomatic of the contradictory position of the warrior class. They were told to keep themselves in readiness for war, and to die if suspected of cowardice. But at the same time they were told that to draw the sword was death! Gregory Bateson's research has shown that children in such double-bind situations are heading straight for psychosis. In the best Confucian tradition, the shogun and the daimyos, who controlled the samurai, were supposed to rule them in a fatherly kind of way; but their ambiguous injunctions nevertheless opened an irrevocable schism in more perceptive individuals, who were often tempted to escape it by death. Occasionally something happened which exposed the contradiction, and a samurai had to ask the question which expresses the anguish of so many children: 'I am ready to obey, but what do they want me to do?' One day, one of the followers of the lord Matsudaira was told that some of his fellow clansmen had got into a fight. He ran up, found them dead, slaughtered their enemies and went home with a clear conscience. But an officer of the Bakufu summoned him and solemnly read the charge to him:

> The man then answered, 'Now I understand what you meant: you accuse me of breaking the law, going against the rules. But I have not done anything of the sort! Of course all living things, and naturally all men, cling to life; I do so myself, very much. Nevertheless, I though that to be deaf to the news that my comrades were in a fight was to be false to *bushido*, so I rushed to the spot. If, seeing my friend dead, I had gone quietly home, I would certainly have prolonged my life, but I should have flown in the face of *bushido*. If I have observed *bushido* at the cost of my life, which I loved, it was only to observe the warriors' law, so as not to break their rules. I have only one life, and I left it in that place. I beg you to declare your sentence as soon as possible.' It is said that the officer, deeply moved, shelved the affair and sent to the lord of Sagami the following advice: 'You have a good servant there. Guard him as the apple of your eye.'

BUSHIDO IS DEATH

The dominant class paid a heavy price for its domination: death waited on the slightest deviation and was the prompt solution to every conflict.

There were two ways out of the contradictions of the warlike peace: emphasizing the values of subordination, order and discipline, and interpreting the ethic of service to mean useful and fruitful work. Under Confucian influence, the warrior was becoming a conscientious functionary, careful to promote the interests entrusted to him. This bureaucratic viewpoint was supreme in circles nearest the central power. But the further from Edo, the further down the ladder of talented and well-disciplined minds, the further into rougher milieux where the warriors (sometimes mere unemployed *ronin*) had nothing to lose but their lives, the more other feelings came into play: honour was a fiercer thing, men of exaggerated loyalties affected to despise mere useful accomplishements, and the spirit of war reawakened: comradeship, boldness, carelessness, prodigality.

From his far-off provincial enclave, Yamamoto Tsunemoto, author of the *Hakagure*, became the spokesman of all the extremest manifestations of *bushido*. He looks straight through to the extremest conclusions. Death and the warrior are one. Others, peasants or townsmen, may grow rich, work, *do* things; but the warrior lives every day as though it were his last, thinking only of all that he must *be*. He should live as if he were already dead: then he will have nothing more to fear. He will experience a unity of opposites reminiscent of Zen, and so attain to liberty and serenity. His extreme of violence will then gather him the same fruits as Buddhist non-violence. Such a man will never be the slave of his own purposes or his own duties. Nothing he does can fetter him if he always sustains his will to be on equal terms with death:

> I have realized that *bushido* is death. There is no other choice but death. That is all. One goes forward calmly. To say it is foolish to die after a failure is the silly talk of townsmen. When it is urgent to choose between life and death, do not consider the end: everyone would rather live, and no doubt reason also prefers it, but to continue to live without having attained your goal is cowardice. Here we are on unsafe ground. To die on a failure is foolish, it is madness, but it is not dishonourable. That is the solid ground of *bushido*. When you die every morning and every evening, unceasingly; when you are always and everywhere encompassed by death, then perforce you gain liberty in *bushido*, and, safe from all dishonour, you fulfil your vocation.

DEATH, THE WAY OF THE WARRIOR

There could be no simpler and more forceful expression of the relationship which binds the will to death and loosens it from everything else, taking a man beyond any particular task and setting him free in an essential emptiness which alerts him to the impossibility innate in himself. Those sentiments from the early eighteenth century come to us from a universe mightily strange to all our own convictions. Without fear, without reproach, and without hope, the samurai is indifferent to the future, to plans, successes and profits. He despises reason and is content to be intimate with death, the only principle of all virtue:

> The lord Nabeshima Naoshige once said, 'Bushido is the intoxication of death; even if dozens came against him, they could never overcome a man drunk with death.' When we are in our right mind we can do no great deeds; to do them, we only have to lose our reason and plunge into the madness of death. In *bushido*, those with clear minds are soon outstripped. No need for loyalty to your lord or filial respect: all that matters in *bushido* is the intoxication of death. Loyalty and filial respect will come of themselves to dwell in it.

However, under the effects of the long peace and of Confucian teaching, common sense did gain some ground. Accompanying someone in death (*junshi, oibara*) began to seem pointless and barbarous.[14] It was a scandalous waste: why throw lives away and destroy talents which might be useful to a new master? These utilitarian objections were mingled with political considerations: the state was trying to weaken the bonds of loyalty exalted by voluntary death, because it always feared to see them used against itself. *Junshi* was not as pointless as it seemed. It had always had an essential function in the clan. Its losses enhanced prestige and proclaimed the indissoluble unity of the warrior community, which was the guarantee of its strength.[15] An anecdote from the *Hagakure* telling of an incident from about 1580 shows up a potlatch situation, with two princely families vying against each other in the suicide stakes:

> When the daughter of the lord Ryuzoji Takanobu was given in marriage to the lord Hata of Karatsu, the latter sent Yanami, lord of Musashi, to fetch her. At this juncture the maiden fell so ill that they despaired of her life. Then Yanami declared that since he had come to join her suite, he would follow her into death by *oibara* if she did not recover. They made great efforts to dissuade him, but he was quite resolved.
> The council of the house of Ryuzoji debated the matter: 'It would be unseemly if no one from our house committed *oibara*. But we would never find anyone to accept such a commission. Maybe, however, officer Hashino would agree . . .'
> He was called in and they explained matters to him. 'That is the situation. It is very unfortunate for you, but you will have to disembowel yourself.' 'That is a rather unexpected request!' rejoined the officer. 'I am scarcely the right person for an affair on which hangs the reputation of

this noble house. It is rather you, lofty individuals of established reputation, who ought disembowel yourselves.' He added, 'Nevertheless I shall accept the honour.' Upon which he hastened to the hostel where Yanami was staying and told him, 'I have gained from the benevolence of the noble lady. I must discuss the *oibara* with you.'

But the maiden recovered, and they were able to celebrate the marriage.

Here we have a dual mimetic situation: whichever clan failed to equal the expenditure of the other would inevitably be shamed. Therefore they absolutely had to find a volunteer, even if it was a compulsory one – not that that joke would ever have occurred to them. It is always easier to elicit such devotion from those of lower rank than from people of importance, who are always inclined to think that their talents make them indispensable. Officer Hashino is not too enthusiastic, but he goes to his *seppuku* as he would accept a death-or-glory mission in wartime. And indeed it is wartime, war for the reputation of the clan, as required by feudal convention. His reply is a model of restrained irony. His slightly bitter lucidity shows off his perfect loyalty better than blind obedience would have done. After that it is only fair that the maiden should do her duty and recover, i.e. overcome her anxiety or reluctance to be a pawn in the family's matrimonial chess game: she realizes that this marriage has put lives at stake on both sides. If her reluctance (or perhaps some secret love affair) really has made her ill, the sight of others' courage gives her the courage to overcome it.

FOLLOWERS IN DEATH GO OUT OF FASHION

At the time of this marriage, about 1580, such one-to-one relationships were still uncontrolled. Less than a generation later the resurgent state imposed itself as arbitrator: all inter-clan negotiations now had to go via the sovereign.[16] And from then on daimyo marriages, in particular, were tightly controlled because they might encourage coalitions. The Bakufu had suppressed clan warfare, but not the clans themselves. And vassals were still in the habit of killing themselves when their master died. For example, when Matsudaira Hideyasu died in 1607, four of his closest servants disembowelled themselves. But when Tokugawa Ieyasu died in 1616 and became a god, he forbade anyone to follow him (article 76 of his will). From then onwards Confucianism counted as the official ideology, and scholars recalled that Confucius himself had opposed this custom, which had obtained in China in his day.

The last great wave of accompanying suicides followed the death of the third shogun, Tokugawa Iemitsu, in 1651: thirteen of his vassals disembowelled themselves to follow him. But already several of the daimyo houses – Hoshina, Ii, Ikeda, Kuroda – had banished the custom from their dominions. Finally, the Bakufu issued a general prohibition in 1663. And when in 1688 a vassal killed himself after the death of the daimyo Okudaira Tadamasa, they decided to make an example of him: Tadamasa's heir and his whole clan were transferred to an inferior fief, and the two sons of the over-faithful follower were condemned to death. Thus did reason of state put an end to one of the oldest and most glorious of the feudal traditions. It was just at this time that Richelieu successfully put an end to duelling. In Japan, as in Europe, absolutism was the sworn enemy of the more ostentatious displays of honour, and common sense was setting limits to the waste of lives. Yamamoto Tsunekomo's intransigence would doubtless have led him into *junshi* if the practice had not been forbidden both by the Bakufu and by the private rules of the Nabeshima clan to which he belonged. But the cloister was an acceptable substitute: when his master Mitsushige died in 1700, Tsunetomo shaved his head and turned monk. It was in the peace of his hermitage that he set down all those bloodthirsty anecdotes in his *Hagakure*.

THE VENGEANCE OF THE FAITHFUL RETAINERS

There were other feudal traditions which were never abolished, among them the vendetta (*katakiuchi*).[17] The Bakufu's authority could not always prevent confrontations from degenerating into a fight to the death. A good example was the Ako affair (*Ako jiken*), which exploded amidst the brilliant prosperity of the Genroku era. On 21 April 1701 the young Lord Asano Naganori, daimyo of the small estate of Ako, lost patience with the arrogance of a certain official of the shogun's court named Kira Yoshinaka, grand master of ceremonies. He rushed at Kira with drawn sword and wounded him on the forehead, but Kira managed to escape. Asano had drawn sword within the palace walls! The Bakufu moved like lightning: within a few hours Asano received the order to kill himself, and the *tsumebara* took place that same evening. His fief was granted to another family and his 300 vassals, now unemployed, became *ronin*. Kira, who was very well thought of at court, was not even reproved. Five days later the news reached the town of Ako. The vassals were summoned to a general assembly. Should they submit or revolt?

On the advice of Oishi, doyen of the samurai, the obedience party won the day, and the fief was surrendered to the shogun's envoys without resistance. A few days later a second meeting was called on the pretext of planning a protest suicide (*kanshi*) to express the *ronin*'s resentment of the Bakufu's decision. Only a small number of the vassals took part – about fifty: the shadow of voluntary death picked out the most resolute. It was to them that Oishi unveiled his plan for vengeance: Kira was to be murdered. Forty-seven *ronin* formed a blood-brotherhood for the purpose. But such an armed attack was no easy matter in a society so tightly policed. They would have to elude the spies of the Bakufu and the suspicions of Kira. The *ronin* took their time and invented a thousand cunning plots and precautions. Suddenly, on the night of 30 January 1703, the deep silence of upper-class Edo, asleep under the snow, was broken by the sound of the drum, the clash of arms and the shouts of combatants. The forty-seven faithful retainers, armed to the teeth, were assaulting Kira's residence. They slaughtered the guards and burst into the apartments. Kira, hiding in a coal-cellar, was finally discovered and courteously requested to disembowel himself. But he refused, so they had to behead him. The sun rose on a scene of carnage. Then the procession of *ronin*, in perfect military formation, crossed the town to the temple of Sengakuji, where they laid Kira's head on the tomb of the master they had avenged.

The Bakufu debated the matter at length. The *ronin* spent two months under arrest in various important houses, where they were treated with all honour while awaiting the verdict. Had they not simply put into practice the feudal virtues they had been taught? Such was the opinion of the shogun, Tokugawa Tsunayoshi. Could they not allege *bushido* as a defence, as Lord Matsudaira's vassal had done? Confucius himself had fostered the vendetta by acknowledging that a son could not be expected to live under the same sky as his father's murderer. In Japan the head of a clan, to whom his vassals swore allegiance and who fed them, counted for at least as much as the head of a family. But the state could not simply ignore the enterprise, which was suspiciously like a conspiracy, a deliberate affront to public order. It was allowable to avenge the death of a father, elder brother, or master – so long as one sought official permission beforehand. If the *ronin* of Ako were to be punished, it would be for their secretiveness rather than their violence. The solution? *Seppuku*: not so much a punishment as the apotheosis which was the final goal of the Way of the Warrior. Everybody knew that they knew, and had known from the moment they took their first oath, that it would end in that way.

The Bakufu may have been tacitly grateful for their attitude: armed resistance in Ako itself would have been a much more serious matter. A protest suicide would have been a direct affront to the shogun's executive, which had been responsible for Asano's hasty execution, the dismissal of his vassals and the impunity of Kira. By opting for vengeance, Oishi turned the resentment away from the government on to Kira. Kira was vilified as a miserable individual, cowardly, greedy and corrupt, and so became the scapegoat who prevented the *ronin* from looking like rebels and the state from feeling threatened. All in all it was a narrow escape for the Bakufu, which might easily have been compromised. Instead, it turned the vendetta to its own advantage – just as the police gets a fillip when people see rival gangs fighting in the streets. By choosing to kill Kira, Oishi deserved well of his late master, but even better of the state. There were good and bad conspiracies, then, and good and bad *ronin*: the vengeful ones, the loyal retainers of 1702 worthy of *seppuku* and some favourable publicity; and the unworthy rebels of 1651, condemned to crucifixion and never spoken of, because they had made a direct attack on the supremacy of the Tokugawa state.

The theatre took up the event, Chikamatsu being one of the first to dramatize it in 1706. Many other versions followed, the most celebrated being a play by three joint authors, which was produced in 1748 in the puppet theatre, and subsequently on every Kabuki stage: *Kanadehon Chushingura* ('The Treasure of Faithful Vassals'), a permanent success of which audiences never tired. Probably the emotion of the Osaka bourgeois audience was tinged with the anxiety which increases fascination: they knew that the civil peace which guaranteed their well-being was a fragile thing, and they could feel the volcano of clan struggle quivering under their feet. Fortunately, they could tell themselves, the state is stronger and has the last word, because it can enmesh the men of war in the web of their own idealism: *seppuku* closes the scene. This small-scale representation was to the horrors of war what *bonsai* is to a forest: it conjured the threat of war by turning a threatened political saga into a series of scenes from private life: touching devotion, heart-rending situations, punishment of the villain.

Like the tragedy of Antigone, *Chushingura* uncovers an ethical schism: on the one side the authority of the state, on the other the demands of clan loyalty. But Antigone's *pietas* is clearly a challenge to tyranny: in Creon's already totalitarian state, any private act immediately takes on political overtones. The Tokugawa regime was authoritarian, but did not aspire to totalitarianism: it respected clan and family morality so long as vendettas were careful to dispense with any sort of political target. Sophocles emphasizes the conflict which was tearing Greek society apart; his vision is tragic because he shows the law split between two irreconcilable imperatives. The authors of *Chushingura* take an optimistic view: good triumphs over the most disturbing events, and the peace of the state is finally reconciled to the demands of feudal loyalty. Thus the story of the forty-seven vassals became a myth rather than a tragedy, a myth in Lévi-Strauss's sense of a society's preferred image of its own contradictions: contradictions calmed, resolved and overcome.

WE ARE NOT MURDERERS

Such a reconciliation could come about thanks to *seppuku*. Where public order met feudal honour, the 'voluntary' *tsumebara* could be both an expiation and an apotheosis. Death, if accepted in advance, could satisfy both honour and the state. Sugawara no Michizane had long ago furnished an example of total obedience in life, and in death of total vengeance. The forty-seven vassals would escape the accusation of murder if they thought of themselves as being already dead. Vengeance was respected as a virtue on a par with gratitude. Duty (*gi, giri*) tells us to be just and remember our debts, both towards those who do us wrong and towards those who do us good. The duty of vengeance gives proof of its sincerity with a voluntary death. You must be avenged? You can be avenged – if you will die for it. That will show that you have got beyond hatred and are following the dictates of justice. An important lesson in ethics which certain Russian revolutionaries, such as Kaliayev, learn in Camus's play *The Just*: no pretext can justify a killer unless he is willing to die in doing the deed. To these moral effects of *seppuku* could be added certain political advantages: capital punishment, accepted in advance, put a stop to the snowball effect inherent in all vendettas. When the forty-seven vassals went in procession through Edo, they ran the risk of being attacked by men of the house of Uesugi, allies of Kira. They would have been defended in their turn by the house of Matsudaira, of which Asano was a junior member. How far would the contagion have spread? But everyone knew that they were going to die and had accepted it; they had chosen their destiny; their passage was marked with respect even by their enemies. No one attacked them, and the strictly limited vendetta died with them.

CRITICISM OF THE HEROES

The reconciliation of feudal honour and public order in the Ako affair was perhaps less solidly forged than it appeared. Certainly it was contested from both sides. In the successful dramatized versions those discordant critical voices were silenced. The most inflexible advocates of *bushido*, such as Yamamoto Tsunetomo, concluded that the long and tortuous conspiracy of the *ronin*, with its precautions and subtleties, lacked spontaneity, honesty and the noble disregard of consequences which ought to be the height of moral courage. Even as Kabuki audiences were applauding their self-sacrifice, the *bushido* extremists were complaining about their lack of self-sacrifice, their narrow enslavement to a single goal. The champions of voluntary death were accused of living too long:

> Some men have been covered with shame because they did not take vengeance after a quarrel. It is enough to rush ahead and get yourself killed. This spares you the shame. If you worry about the outcome, you miss the opportunity, you make excuses by saying the enemy outnumbered you, and you end up deciding to call a halt. Even if thousands of enemies come against you, you must make up your mind to exterminate them one after the other, and make a start: that is the way to succeed; that is how you may come well out of the affair.
>
> The forty-seven *ronin* who avenged their master, the lord Asano, by attacking their enemy's house by night, were in error because they did not disembowel themselves in Sengakuji, there and then. After their master's death, it was a long time before they struck. If their enemy had died of disease beforehand, it would have been exceedingly unfortunate for them.

But the most insistent criticism came from common-sense voices concerned for public order. They were uneasy about the danger to the state of such violent impulses. Was voluntary death really a sufficient excuse for any kind of conduct? Did dying invariably put you in the right? In an essay on the Ako affair, a Confucianist author close to the shogun's government, Ogyu Sorai, slated the moral irresponsibility of Lord Asano and his vassals. He emphasized the hypocrisy of putting all the blame on Kira. Clan loyalty, when it set out to be unconditional, led to a self-induced blindness which nullified any sort of enlightened moral principle:

> Everybody imagines that the forty-seven vassals sacrificed their lives as a posthumous service to their master, thus exhibiting an utterly disinterested loyalty. Everybody calls them 'warriors of duty'. But it was Asano Naganori who tried to kill Kira Yoshinaka, and not Yoshinaka who had killed Naganori, so you cannot say that he was their master's 'enemy'. Naganori lost his fief of Ako because he tried to kill Yoshinaka; it was not Yoshinaka who destroyed it. How can you say that he was their master's enemy? Naganori, in a burst of anger, forgot his ancestors and acted like a savage. He was wrong to try and kill Yoshinaka. We might say that he failed in his duty. We might very well say that the forty-seven vassals inherited all the bad conduct of their master. But can you call that 'duty'? Unable to save their master from dishonour by remaining alive, they preferred to die so as to carry out his dishonourable design. If we try to imagine their feelings in such a situaton, how can we not pity them?

Ogyu's denunciation of violence and loyalty seems to show anxiety over a peril still far in the future: it was true that extreme right-wing terrorists would eventually bring down the Japanese state, in the early years of the Showa era. The faithful vassals, ferocious in their self-sacrifice, would have acknowledged the methods, if not the aims, of that later wave of political murders. And yet people had really wanted to believe that the reconciliation of martial values and state power was both durable and beneficial: after the fall of the Tokugawa, when in 1868 the emperor Meiji arrived in his new capital (formerly Edo, now Tokyo), one of his first acts was to do homage on the tomb of the forty-seven *ronin* at Sengakuji. It seemed that the myth had not died with the society which gave it birth. Or if it lived on, *was* it only behind the footlights, under the nostalgic eyes of those easily fascinated by the sublime horror of an actor's *seppuku*?

DEATH AND THE THEATRE

The more we think about that savage incident, the more we are struck by its theatrical aspects. Chikamatsu and the other authors did no more than restore to the theatre something which it seemed to have inspired in the first place. The theatre of cruelty was played out in reality before it came on to the Kabuki stage. Oishi and his noble companions set out their destiny like a melodrama, with a stock situation, a hard and simple plot-line, their own interpretation of the facts and their own casting, and they got well into their characters. It was theatre within theatre: like Hamlet feigning madness, they feigned faithlessness, forgetfulness, indifference. Oishi, like Lorenzaccio, even feigned spineless debauchery to deceive prying eyes. Suddenly they appeared, sword in hand, in their true character. But it was still a character they were playing, before the whole city of Edo. Their exploit savoured of a theatrical gesture which left their audience petrified: a supreme gesture, a spectacular gesture, but an empty one. They were avenged on Kira, but it was an ostentatious display of exemplary devotion. Were they inspired by pure duty? Yes, so as to flaunt their chivalrous and solemn self-sacrifice. Their aesthetics dictated the attitude in which posterity would eternally view them: simple, savage and symbolical, colour plates for a textbook of martial morality.

The whole thing was a piece of theatre, except their deaths. When they disembowelled themselves the blood which flowed was real. The warrior class, because of its behaviour, its demeanour and its every gesture, was a theatrical spectacle. But there has never been a ruling class in any society which has not hogged the limelight. What distinguished the samurai was rather their obsessive sincerity. Their solution to the insurmountable dialectic of reality and appearance was *action* –

even to death. Nobody can go on believing it is all an illusion if the actor so identifies with his role that the death he stages becomes real. Voluntary death did not just offer the state an expiation of excessive feudal honour, it also served to authenticate the theatre of war and to conjure the element of dissimulation forced by society on hearts which dreamed of perfect, transparent sincerity. Maybe death is the only way to convince yourself that you really are what you are.

THE SYSTEM WEARS THIN

While the play of the ruling class was played out on the higher stage – the usual human comedy with the occasional dramatic climax – the silence, the labour and the sufferings of every day continued below them. The years of Genroku, so explosively marked by the Asano affair, were the happiest ones of the period: the economy expanded, the population grew, a brilliant cultural life developed in the towns. Later on, while the peace remained unbroken, times got harder. The countryside was overpopulated, but production remained steady. The Tokugawa, for deliberate political reasons, crushed the daimyos under ruinous sumptuary expenses. Lords got into debt and dismissed their vassals, who swelled the ranks of the *ronin*; or else they overtaxed goods in circulation and overexploited their estates, scorning the sane principles of management which the physiocrats were currently teaching to the landowning nobility of Europe. Protest movements multiplied: local (and inevitably scattered) uprisings by peasants unable to pay the tribute demanded, and in the towns, riots by hungry mobs unable to pay high food prices. The only result was implacable oppression: the ringleaders became martyrs, often voluntarily. For example, Sakura Sogoro, crucified along with his wife after seeing his children beheaded. His crime? He had come up to the shogun's litter holding out a petition.[18]

TERMINAL DECLINE OF ABSOLUTISM

Society still lay in fetters of iron. Were they protecting it or killing it? At the top, rigor mortis was setting in. Decisions were formed slowly along a path strewn with surreptitious compromises; suspicion and secretiveness were rife. The shogun's power was vanishing into the labyrinth of his own suspicions; nothing was open, nothing was clear. Sometimes he would announce a Great Reform: a few corrupt functionaries were recalled, all the social classes were lectured, sobriety and diligence were enjoined. All public ills were to be cured by the practice of virtue, a return to the past. A few people, like Oshio Heihachiro defending the hungry masses in Osaka in 1837, went from Confucius to Wang Yang-Ming and took their political convictions to the point of armed revolt. But such commitment always expressed itself in the tired old form of a remonstrance, which was always suicidal from the start; its perpetrator knew that the price of his protest would be failure and death.[19]

The rulers of this society made immutability their religion: laws were fixed and hereditary. Steeped in Buddhism though they were, they wilfully ignored the law of impermanence. They had refused to adopt the Chinese examination system: those who inherited offices knew best how to fulfil them, and the hazards of birth, which gave sons other talents than their fathers', were a threat to social structures. Absolutism issued its decrees in a tone of solemn admonition; but already another, silent reign had begun, the reign of a mobile, impersonal, indifferent element which was deaf to decrees, could creep in anywhere and knew how to bend men's minds: the reign of money. Well into the nineteenth century the father of a certain Fukuzawa Yukichi was complaining that schools were teaching children that shopkeeper's tool, arithmetic. The samurai still took pride in knowing the price of nothing. If he was too poor to have a servant to do his shopping, he went at night, hiding his face so that the local shopkeepers could pretend not to know him. But soon he would have to learn to count – to learn foresight – and to realize at last that quantity, of whatever it might be, is no less important than quality, even the quality of men's hearts.

STEAM POWER AND GUNS

These internal contradictions would not, perhaps, have been enough to transform a society so firmly sealed in, so closely watched, held down by the best-disciplined military caste there has even been. The disruption came from outside, a cargo in foreign ships. It was not now the galleons of former times, which had shown Japan the measure of its backwardness. Japanese society had won control of itself, but that was not enough: it had now to win control of other forces, steam power and gunpowder. In just fifteen years, from 1853 to 1868, the country went through the severest crisis in its history, in depth and acuteness comparable only to the French Revolution. The Bakufu, forced out of its policy of isolationism, gave in to the demands of the gathering pack of Western powers, but so grudgingly that it revealed its own weakness. The opposition resurfaced. To the clans defeated by the Tokugawa at Sekigahara it seemed that their revenge, after two hundred years, might come. But it was less a clan struggle than a factional one, the clans being divided within themselves: almost everywhere, the youngest, least privileged samurai, the fire-eaters, carried the day over the sluggish and impotent conservatives. Japanese society had assumed that all was for the best and for ever, and had bypassed history on that assumption, but morality was no longer enough. They were back in the world of politics, of dog-eat-dog; they had to choose objectives and strategies, know how to want and know what they wanted.

THE CUNNING OF REASON

In the long run they all wanted the same thing: security and independence for their country. But how? To keep the foreigners at arm's length, would they have to discover the secret of their strength and imitate them, on the principle of know your enemy? Or would it be enough to want – really want – to get rid of them? At first the latter illusion prevailed, and Japan went backwards into the future, its eyes fixed on the past. Its aims were resumed in the slogan *sonno joi*, 'Honour the emperor and expel the barbarians!' But that slogan and those aims were themselves a mask over the real desire, a straightforward way of discrediting the Tokugawa: the will of Japan, in the short them, was a will to power. It sought only domination. What was to be done? And more important, who was to do it? Who would have the power to do it? In the upshot of one of the most contorted pieces of historical reasoning the world has ever seen, the victors were eventually reduced to doing what really had to be done, which was *not* what they believed they wanted. Thinking to restore the old, they brought in the new. Those who, like Saigo Takamori, were too high-minded to seek only power, and too intransigent to pretend that they had really willed the unexpected outcome of their actions and reconcile themselves to being the fools of necessity, were soon left with only one choice. And that was death.

The ethical divide was echoed in the factional divide. In the bureaucratic circles closest to the centre of power, they knew they had a long task of compromise and acculturation ahead of them. They were right – eventually, for being right can take a long time. In the short term, the most radical adherents of *bushido* turned into fanatics. The *ronin*, having nothing better to do, set themselves to murder all traitors, that is all men in power – including foreigners where necessary. Secretive and perpetually angry, the terrorists took over the methods of the forty-seven vassals: hidden preparation, lightning attack.

The spirit of self-sacrifice burned brightly in them, but not in the narrow confines of a provincial clan out for private vengeance: now they were fighting to save the entire country. Sorrow overhung them, for the samurai saw it as a duel to the death – death or glory: 'If the foreigners seize the whole country, there will be no point in living any longer and no way out for my whole family except death.' But the duel pitted the samurai only against themselves, and if they won the prize was not survival, but extinction. When they turned to the emperor, as was done enthusiastically by the clans of the south-west (Choshu, Satsuma, Tosa, Hizen), it meant that clan-consciousness was yielding in the face of national peril. The clans once defeated at Sekigahara thought they were avenging themselves on the Tokugawa, but they were really preparing their own elimination. Like the forty-seven vassals before them, they failed to outlive their own vengeance. Immediately after their victory they surrendered their fiefs to the emperor, and in 1871 the 305 feudal clans became imperial prefectures.

THE VOLUNTARY DISAPPEARANCE OF THE SAMURAI

Above all it was a factional fight. Briefly it was a clan struggle, when from 1866 to 1868 the great fiefs of the south-west made a coalition against the house of Tokugawa. A class struggle? Never. All the upheaval was confined to the warrior class, which went alone into the fight and tore itself apart, divided against itself until it eventually disappeared altogether. Peasants, artisans and merchants simply looked on. The bulk of the population never disputed the supremacy of the ruling class: the warriors had never seemed so necessary, in the fact of this new peril. The samurai, unlike the French nobility, never fell under the knife of a rival class: sole architect of their own abolition, they contrived it at first unconsciously, but in the end consentingly – the voluntary death, a destiny accepted.

Victorious less over the Tokugawa than over themselves, the faithful followers of *bushido* lost, in a few short years, all the roots of their selfhood. In 1870 the class system was abolished. In 1873 conscription was brought in: the military life was no longer a family heirloom. In 1871 carrying two swords ceased to be obligatory, and in 1876 it was forbidden. Other privileges, such as heraldic devices, family names, and permission to ride a saddle-horse, were thrown open to everybody. The hereditary salaries paid by the clans were turned into government bonds and then abolished. Finally, in 1873 *tsumebara* was struck off the penal code. Nothing remained but memories and nostalgia. The European nobility persisted in its snobbish illusions; the warrior nobility of Japan despised such pale survivals and preferred to die out entirely.

DEATH OF THE SAMURAI

It is hard to find a name for such a drastic change. Some talk of the Meiji Restoration, but that only takes account of the imperial authority and ignores the novel connotations of the Japanese *ishin*. 'Reform'? Inadequate to so profound a change. 'Revolution'? Maybe, so long as we understand a revolution quite different from anything in Western history, a revolution without revolutionary ideology, without class struggle, without subversion from below. 'The Meiji Renaissance' is better. It was a spring: a bitter, stormy spring full of hopes and anxieties. It was an opening up, a slackening of bonds. But from the sadness of all that was dying sprang the hope of new birth. One aspect of human greatness was disappearing, never to come again. It was all the sadder for being accepted.

All the more poignant was one of the last *tsumebara*, that of Taki Zenzaburo, which took place in early 1868. An officer of the lord of Bizen, he had been harassing the beaten Tokugawa troops, and on 4 February 1868 had given orders to fire on the foreign enclaves at Kobe. Only two or three people were hurt, but the government of the Emperor Meiji pronounced a death sentence. Representatives of the foreign power, one per legation (making seven in all), were invited to see the sentence carried out. A. B. Mitford, secretary to the British ambassador, wrote an account of it. It was the first time that the closed ceremony of *tsumebara* had been revealed to Western eyes. We can guess at the sombre pride inspired by the scene. You who would know what it is to be a samurai, come, and see, and bear witness, for soon it will be no more than memory.[20]

The scene took place at night, by candlelight, before the high altar of the Buddhist temple of Seifukuji in Kobe. On a dais a few inches high, covered with mats, a carpet of red felt had been laid. On the left seven Japanese witnesses were drawn up; opposite them, on the right, were the seven foreign representatives. The condemned man entered, ceremonially dressed: a solidly built man of thirty-two. One of his friends, known for his skill as a swordsman, came with him as his *kaishaku*:

> Slowly, and with great dignity, the condemned man mounted on to the raised floor, prostrated himself before the high altar twice, and seated himself on the felt carpet with his back to the high altar, the *kaishaku* crouching on his left-hand side. One of the three attendant officers then came forward, bearing a stand of the kind used in temples for offerings, on which, wrapped in paper, lay the *wakizashi*, the short sword or dirk of the Japanese, nine inches and a half in length, with a point and an edge as sharp as a razor's. This he handed, prostrating himself, to the condemned

man, who received it reverently, raising it to his head with both hands, and placed it in front of himself.

After another profound obeisance, Taki Zenzaburo, in a voice which betrayed just so much emotion and hesitation as might be expected from a man who is making a painful confession, but with no sign of either in his face or manner, spoke as follows:

'I, and I alone, unwarrantably gave the order to fire on the foreigners at Kobe, and again as they tried to escape. For this crime I disembowel myself, and I beg you who are present to do me the honour of witnessing the act.'

Bowing once more, the speaker allowed his upper garments to slip down to his girdle, and remained naked to the waist. Carefully, according to custom, he tucked his sleeves under his knees to prevent himself from falling backwards; for a noble Japanese gentleman should die falling forwards. Deliberately, with a steady hand, he took the dirk that lay before him; he looked at it wistfully, almost affectionately; for a moment he seemed to collect his thoughts for the last time, and then stabbing himself deeply below the waist on the left-hand side, he drew the dirk slowly across to the right side, and, turning it in the wound, gave a slight cut upwards. During this sickeningly painful operation he never moved a muscle of his face. When he drew out the dirk, he leaned forward and stretched out his neck; an expression of pain for the first time crossed his face, but he uttered no sound. At that moment the *kaishaku*, who, still crouching by his side, had been keenly watching his every movement, sprang to his feet, poised his sword for a second in the air; there was a flash, a heavy, ugly thud, a crashing fall; with one blow the head had been severed from the body.

A dead silence followed, broken only by the hideous noise of the blood throbbing out of the inert heap before us, which but a moment before had been a brave and chivalrous man. It was horrible.

A samurai had died. Soon the samurai would be no more. A double sorrow for those who saw that the civilization capable of forging such men had, like them, had its day. The very presence of the foreign representatives was a sign of the fatal impact from which it was never to recover. In the ears of Taki Zenzaburo, and of all who could see themselves in him, the fleeting universe, whose forms appear only to vanish again, spoke that evening its last words of bitter wisdom: 'Learn to die.'

1 A *haniwa* in the shape of a
  warrior. Tradition says that these
  terracotta models were first made
  on the orders of the Emperor
  Suinin, so as to put an end to the
  human sacrifices which used to
  take place at the funerals of great
  men. (Paris, Musée Guimet.
  Photo: Giraudon.)

3

4

2

2 The naval battle of Dan no Ura (1185), at which the Minamoto overcame the Taira. Above, the widow of Taira no Kiyomori prepares to cast herself into the waves, carrying in her arms the child emperor Antoku, aged seven. (Photo: Tokyo, Idemitsu Museum of Art.)

3–7 A Kabuki actor miming the *seppuku* of Lord Asano Naganori in a scene from *Kanadehon Chushingura*. (Photos: Fred Mayer/Magnum.)

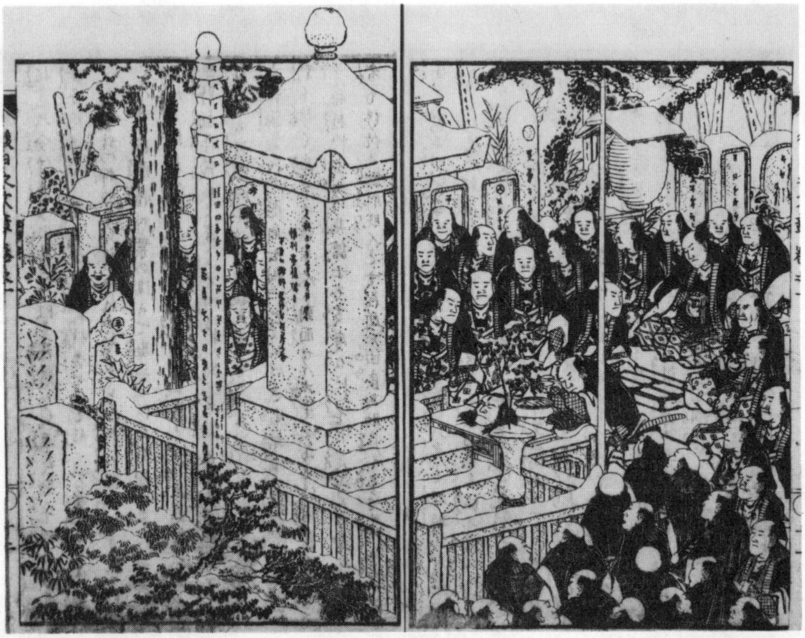

8

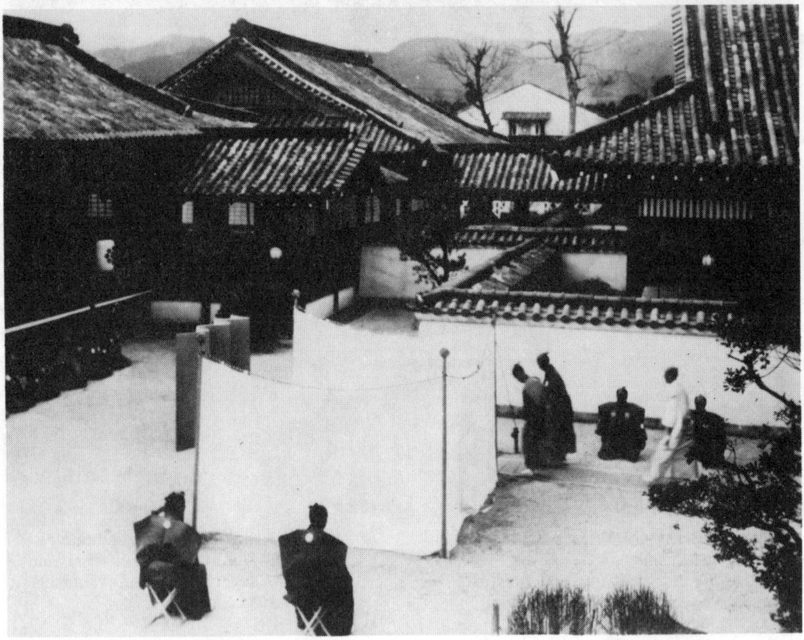

9

8 The forty-seven Faithful Vassals deposit the head of Kira on the tomb of their master Asano, whose mortal enemy he was. (Engraving by Hokusai; Photo: Paris, Bibliothèque Nationale.)

9 The forty-seven vassals are conducted one by one to the place appointed for their *seppuku*, in a film version of *Chushingura* by Mizoguchi (1941). (Photo: Max Tessier Collection.)

10 The hero of *Harakiri*, a film by Kobayashi (1963), reflects for a moment before disembowelling himself. In token of protest he has refused to put on the ritual white robe. (Photo: Max Tessier Collection.)

11 Johei the stationer and the courtesan Koharu after their love-suicide, from Shinoda's film version (1966) of *Shinju Ten no Amijima*. (Photo: Max Tessier Collection.)

12

14

13

12 Saigo Takamori, determined to follow his lord Shimazu Nariakira into death, plunges into the sea along with a monk friend named Gessho (1858). Saigo survived this attempted double suicide, Gessho did not. Twenty years later Saigo, defeated by the Imperial armies, performed *seppuku*. (Photo: Arne Lewis.)

13 A group of kamikaze pilots, volunteer members of the Special Units (*Tokkotai*). (Photo: Hulton-Deutsch Collection.)

14 The writer Akutagawa Ryunosuke, who was to poison himself so as to put an end to the 'vague anxiety' which was tormenting him. (Photo: Chikuma Shobo, publishers.)

15 Mishima Yukio posing as St Sebastian pierced with arrows. (Photo: Tokyo Kishin Shinoyama.)

16 Mishima posing as a *bushi*, his carefully nurtured muscles setting off the long sword. On his forehead he wears the device of Kusunoki Masashige, 'Seven lives to serve my country'. (Photo: Tokyo, Kishin Shinoyama.)

17 Mishima in his film *Yukoku (Rites of Love and Death)* acting out a rehearsal of his own last act. (Photo: Max Tessier Collection.)

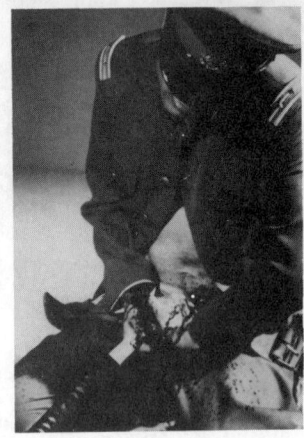

10

Love and Death

Throughout the Edo era, both public and private life were dominated by the principle of subordination to authority implicit in official Confucianism. The household was subject to the same order as the state. Family storms and crises produced their victors and vanquished, rebels and victims; and in this microcosm of the political power struggle, voluntary death again proffered a final solution, sanctioned by custom and always in mind. Requited love often induced it; death for two is half as hard, and banishes the awful loneliness of suicide. The heart that has lived for love and sunk under adversity consummates its love in death: sacrificed to love, it is free to love if not to live. Greater love has no man than this: to die for it.

A DISAGREEABLE MOTHER-IN-LAW

Of all the domestic dramas (*sewamono*) written by Chikamatsu for the puppet theatre in the first twenty years of the eighteenth century, the majority (some fifteen out of twenty-four) end in a twofold lovers' suicide or *shinju*. The last in the series, *Shinju Yoigoshin*, first performed in 1722 when the author was seventy, despicts a family quarrel eventually resolved by the double suicide of the hapless young lovers. The plot is nakedly simple. Hambei, son of an impoverished samurai, is adopted at a fairly advanced age by a childless merchant couple from Osaka. A few years later, his adoptive parents marry him to a very young girl called Ochiyo. The two fall in love and conceive a child. Then comes the dramatic twist: the mother expels her four-months-pregnant daughter-in-law from the house in Hambei's absence. Ochiyo takes refuge in her father's house, fearing at first that Hambei may have connived at the cruel expulsion; but in a few words she is undeceived, her husband's love for her remains constant. He is, alas, totally bound by the debt of gratitude (*giri*) he owes his adoptive parents. When he realizes that his mother's decision is irrevocable, he suggests to the girl that they commit suicide together, and she bitterly agrees. In the last act, Hambei and Ochiyo, clinging to one another, stumble through the night to a nearby temple to offer their tearful distress to the compassionate Buddhas; and there, before the shadowy slope of the temple roofs, he cuts her throat and then stabs himself.

Chikamatsu is out to move his audience to tears: tears which, as he knows, they find a strange pleasure in shedding. Our credulity may be strained by the motives of this double suicide: the young couple's resignation seems a little premature, and the mother-in-law's obstinacy too poorly motivated to be credible. But can we not guess at what remains unsaid? Japanese literature has always excelled at this sort of suggestion. There are a few clues: Hambei joined his new family quite late, at the age of twenty-two. It would scarcely be surprising if the feelings of the lady of the house towards him were something other than maternal. She might have overcome her jealousy if Hambei had not so soon given his wife what she never had from her own husband: the hope of a child. In a final attack of envy, the barren woman curses and banishes the image of contentment and fertility which her daughter-in-law is constantly inflicting on her.

Though it does not come out clearly in the dialogue, the plot resonates profoundly with the typical Oedipus triangle of Japan: mother, wife – and son, the object of their rivalry. In Chikamatsu's play the trouble all stems from the fact that the impassioned mother, armed with the authority of Hambei's debt to her, meets no obstacles: her husband is a shadowy, feeble character, nothing like the ideal Confucian father. The daughter-in-law can scarcely be expected to stand up for herself: until her child is born – especially if he is a son to carry on the family name – she is in a most precarious situation, and must think of herself as a guest, almost a servant, in the house of her parents-in-law.

According to the Chinese customs imported in the Nara era and resumed in the state Confucianism of Edo, a wife who turns out to be (for example) flirtatious, talkative, impertinent, frivolous, jealous or barren can be repudiated and sent back to her parents armed only with a letter saying that her ex-husband has surrendered all his rights in her and intends to restore her dowry. Such a threat was enough to ensure total submission from a young wife; she could always get her own back when she herself was the lady of the house, eager to perpetuate the unjust arrangement by inflicting it on her own daughter-in-law. It is up to the son to defend his wife, but in *Shinju Yoigoshin* the hapless Hambei never even thinks of starting a fight. Not because he dare not; strength he has, but he uses all of it to keep himself within the bounds of *giri*, in blind submission to the duty of gratitude which, according to the morality of the time, was the supreme value in human relationships. As the son of a samurai – albeit the adopted son of merchant – he has made this severity into a point of honour. The measure of freedom he allows himself can stretch only as far as death. The combat that most touches Japanese hearts is a combat of self against self, where all the hero's strength is locked up and turned inwards. Japanese theatre is less interested in the clash of wills than in that silent and motionless suspense, scarcely revealed save by a certain quivering tension.

Hambei is self-contained, self-constrained, straining to fit the image of the perfect son. In his mother's presence he will even go so far as to strike his wife and drive her out! But a moment later he is ready to die with her. He is a sacrifice not to duty, but to love. As long as he lives he will do his best to honour the unpayable filial debt which is incurred at birth, or in his case at the second birth of adoption. There is only one way out: voluntary death will give him unqualified freedom to love. At that price his moral debt of servitude is instantly paid off.

Hambei is thoroughly imbued with Confucian principles, but sees them as a part which he must act. He obeys them meticulously, then casts them off in a trice: dying, he becomes his real self again. This was true of many cultural imports from the mainland: they were parts which people rehearsed devotedly. In the end Hambei does forget one item imported from China: that a good son considers it his duty to keep his body, loaned by his parents and no possession of his, intact in their service. He ought even to avoid unnecessary risks, keep away from cliff edges and steep paths – and if he must go on a boat, he must; but go swimming, never! Confucius allows suicide in defence of honour and virtue, protest suicide for example. But to die for love – what a hopeless folly! There is room for friendship in the Confucian moral order, benevolence is a universal requirement, and sex for reproduction is allowed – but love, that fertile source of trouble, danger and misery, is out of the question. In any case, marriage has nothing to do with the contentment of husband and wife, and everything to do with the perpetuation and prosperity of the family line. Love, for Confucius and his followers, was the worst kind of egoism, a shared selfishness; and to crown all, it was fatal to happiness in any case.

Chikamatsu's characters are torn between duty and sentiment, *giri* and *ninjo*, like some of Corneille's heroes. But in Corneille's *Le Cid*, for example, the dialectic stretches into the future, when the contradiction may be transcended: 'Give it time' is the king's advice to Rodrigue. In the West, love itself has ethical value and can be reconciled to each and any other virtue. There is no such hope in Chikamatsu: the moral order is too rigid, the fight is lost before it starts, and the lovers accept their fate. Without defiance, if not without complaint, they bid farewell to the future. They never blame society for parting them, nor the family for forcing or rejecting them. In their unhappy circumstances, they feel the weight of their own past, the inevitable consequence of faults committed in other lives. A Buddhist analysis *(inga)* of the causes of suffering has long since convinced them that they have only themselves to blame. They hasten into the refuge of death: the only hope they have left lies in another life.

UNHAPPINESS AND COMPASSION

Has love any place in this world? Alas, no, is Chikamatsu's reply. His tragic pessimism seems like a very distant echo of the legend of Tristan and Iseult. His lovers cannot live their love, it is asking too much; but they cannot live without it, it is better not to live at all. An easy conclusion for a tender heart, and it would be a hard-hearted critic who would blame them; we can only pity them, and be silent. Amidist religion, the opposite pole to Confucianism, pins all its hopes on another world and preaches the virtues of compassion and forgiveness, with mercy an ever open door for the unfortunate. Before killing themselves Chikamatsu's lovers turn towards the Paradise in the West, which comforts them in their last moments. This is more than Christianity at its height would ever grant to the despairing – as if despair could be foiled by the threat of punishment. But those without hope are also without fear. As Denis de Rougemont remarked, Tristan's dark passions are better suited to Cathar pessimism than to orthodox Christianity with its excessive attachment to the order of this world. Similarly, in Japan, those who defied the world and loved until death had to turn their backs on Confucianism, on a morality suited only to this life: their hearts cherished the illusion of another world where they would be forgiven and 'reunited on the same lotus'. They sank their passion in the mercy of Amida and the compassion of Kannon. They yielded themselves to death and darkness, trusting to awaken in the dawn of a love unbounded by terrestrial horizons.

The Confucianism of Japan, which was rooted in the morality of *giri*, must have encouraged the excesses of many a family despot. But its conquest was never complete: deep in people's hearts the Buddha reigned on. And deep in their minds they could still find the threshold of voluntary death: acknowledged, recognized, it was a standing challenge to arbitrary injunctions, however heavily cloaked in morality. A master, be he father or overlord, demands obedience, not death: of all the ways of escaping him it is the one he most fears, for such a death is a punishment for him, and he has everything to lose by it, starting with his belief that he is acting for the good of others. 'If he suffers he'll thank me for it later. But if he dies . . .?' Such a thought may loosen the grip of authority just a little. The heart-rending scenes in Chikamatsu's plays stimulated and satisfied the inexplicable need to pity and weep, but they also bore an implicit warning; perhaps they even helped to restrain a few parents too much inclined to stand on their rights.

Everyone knew that the sight of the youthful victims would be enough to turn public opinion their way; their sins and errors would be forgotten, their decision excused. They would not be insulted with the idea that they had died on a mad impulse, as blind Western opinion often suggests when imputing its own blindness to the victims. The silent witness of the deed would be received in respecful silence. This tenuous approbation might be an additional motive, over and above the harshness of their parents and the cruelty of circumstance, for suicide in young people, shy and violent and sorry for themselves, liking to feel that others were sorry too. Vulnerable, defenceless, they would run to meet death without the slightest sign of repugnance, without trying to explain, without a word of rancour or excuse. Death would be sufficient justification. They knew that their prompt resignation would be deplored, but not blamed. Dead, they would receive the compassion which they could no longer hope for in life.

A collection of seventeen short stories by Shohoken, published in 1704 and entitled *Shinju Okagami* ('The Great Mirror of Lovers' Suicide'), has this sympathy for lovers in despair. The stories, based on real events, abound in impossible situations, hopeless disappointments, and abuses of power defied to the death by suicidal lovers. The narrator tells the story without comment: he does not criticize the principles of authority, nor any social or moral constraints – but neither does he ever blame the deed by which they are defied and eluded. From story to story he evokes the catastrophes caused by the vanity of authority and the fascination of the abyss.

PATERNAL ABSOLUTISM

A story only a few pages long, 'The Shamisen of hate', tells of a strange misunderstanding which, thanks to a father's arrogance, has a fatal outcome. Once upon a time, an impoverished samurai decided to abdicate his rank and become a haberdasher in the capital city. Having made his fortune, he retired with his wife to live a few miles out of Kyoto, in the small town of Sumizome. He entrusted his business to his only son Ryushichi, a bachelor of twenty-four likewise endowed with a shrewd business sense. In Sumizome lived the virtuous widow of a warrior, who was striving in extreme poverty to bring up her daughter, Ocho, aged about twelve. In her extremity she sought help from the retired business couple, who soon decided to kill two birds with one stone and buy the girl as a wife for their son. Ocho was sent to Kyoto; the young couple fell in love and eagerly acquiesced in their parents' wishes. Where, then, is the sudden misfortune so useful to good story-tellers? Well, Ryushichi takes it into his head to spend a mint of money on making an accomplished artist of his future wife, apparently with the sole intention of improving his leisure prospects: he makes her learn dancing and singing, and engages the best teachers in the capital to teach her to play the *koto* and the *shamisen*.

Hearing of this expenditure, the father is seized with a sudden, absolute, unshakeable conviction (with the paranoid overtones so common in the Oedipal relationship between father and son): all this money is really being poured out so as to make the girl into a professional flirt! He is really projecting on to his son, whom he envies, his own vague shame (perhaps aroused by the sight of the noble widow) for the greed which started him on his demeaning commercial ventures. The conviction is crazy, but not wholly improbable. The father knows, and the son is well aware, that money rules beneath the surface reign of virtue, and feminine accomplishments, skilfully marketed, can be very profitable. The indignant father has at his disposal all the powers granted by contemporary society to the head of a family. He finds a pretext to bring Ocho back to Sumizome, and the father, to punish the son, does exactly what he thought the son intended to do: he sells the girl for an agreed sum to a brothel-keeper from a western province, who will profit from her youth and accomplishments:

> Ryushichi, knowing nothing of all this, spent his days waiting eagerly at the door for her return. After ten days a letter came from Ocho telling of his parents' plan. She added that he must be very annoyed, and that she could not bear him to suspect her unjustly, but that his parents' orders were so weighty that she would have to leave for the west willy-nilly; however, she begged him to consider the day of her departure as the last of her life, for she had no intention of living any longer; in memory of past happiness she asked him to pray for her salvation in the other world. The ink of the letter was pale, he thought, as if she had shed tears as she wrote.
>
> Mad with grief, Ryushichi left for Sumizome that very evening: the evening bell was ringing... On the way, he made up his mind not to not

go to his parents' house, and asked Ocho's mother to fetch her in secret, saying that she could sleep at her house that night. Then they took a byway back to the capital. His raging parents wrote to tell them that they no longer considered them any children of theirs, and that they would make a beggar of Ocho's mother.

Then, thinking that if they lived they could never be united, but if they died together, calmly, they would have no more to fear, husband and wife made up their minds, and fell to the same sword.[1]

We can see that the narrator is wholly in sympathy with the young couple: from the parents, violence, confusion, even blackmail; from their victims, dignity, calm and resolution. The deed is done with quiet deliberation. The girl takes the lead, first to be faithful to her love, secondly to protect her mother: his parents will be disarmed by their sacrifice, and see reason. The son tries to live and escape the arbitrary decision. Why did he not seek an interview with his father? But he knows that explanations only increase misunderstanding: his silence conveys a distrust for words which is profoundly rooted in Japanese culture. The Western outlook, formed by classical antiquity on the one hand and the Judaeo-Christian tradition on the other, apprehends truth either through logic, dialectic and rhetoric or through promise, scripture and prophecy. In either case it puts its trust in the explicit Word: doctrinal statements, books of law, philosophical dialogues, evidence, confession, discourse or declaration.

Not so in Japan, where truth resides in the deed which the word, a slave to convention, may only obscure. Not that the web of words is powerless to reveal anything – but it will do it by allusion, tacitly, obliquely, unexpectedly. Truth cannot be captured by mere words; it slips between them, beneath their apparent meaning, through the gaps between them. Freud thought this; his intuition might almost have been prepared for him by the long Japanese experience of the implicit. No culture had greater respect for codes, which ruled every aspect of life; but no culture was ever so suspicious of codes, never mistaking them for anything but artefacts, which is what they are. Why try to justify yourself by an utterance which is not susceptible to validation by any other utterance? Only a deed can make known what has been. The son was disinterested, but misunderstood. His death is the proof of this. Voluntary death, then, is a paradox: only by ceasing to be can one be sure of what one *has* been.

THE FRIEND OF PLEASURE

Others wre, happily, less vulnerable, and refused to wilt under the paternal wrath: they loved life enough to elude, or even defy, any number of threats. In 1686 the novelist Ihara Saikaku published his *Five Women who Loved Love* (*Koskoku gonin onna*). In one of the first of these passionate biographies we meet a youthful prodigy by name of Seijuro, a frequent visitor to houses of pleasure, in whom the most beguiling ladies meet their match. Though only nineteen, 'the vows of love written during his affairs might have been bound into a thousand packets, and the fingernails his mistresses had sent as pledges of their devotion were more than a ditty box could hold.' One day his father, outraged at his goings-on, loses patience: Seijuro is shamed, cursed and disinherited. At this news the fair Minagawa, his favourite courtesan, who always knows what is expected of her, decides that the moment has come for a graceful departure:

> But as he rose in tears to leave, Minagawa came back clothed in garments of white, ready now to die, and clung desperately to him. 'How can you live? Where will you go? Oh, now is the time to end it all!' she cried, pulling out a pair of knives. Seijuro was almost speechless with delight to find his lover faithful after all. But the brothel people, seeing what was going on, drew them apart and led Minagawa back to her master.[2]

Seijuro's joy was nothing but vanity at receiving a fresh pledge of love. Saikaku leaves us to guess at his reluctance. Only love could give him the strength to die; pleasure-lovers are not in nearly such a hurry. They might come to it one day, but later – much, much later. As for the fair Minagawa, her enthusiasm is most significant, for surely it conveys the hidden despair of those daughters of joy as Saikaku understood it? Earlier, in 1684, in the eighth chapter of his 'Great Mirror of Seduction' (*Shoen okagami*), he had listed eighteen deceased courtesans from Shimmachi, one of the pleasure districts of Osaka. They were all natives of the poor and mountainous province of Etchu (now the prefecture of Toyama), and they were all supposed to have jumped off Mount Tateyama, in the east of that province. One after another, in fact, they had decided, doubtless on some home visit, never to return to their glittering prison. This bare list throws some light (soon to be confirmed in Chikamatsu's plays) on the sorrows of courtesans, the dark, despairing side (usually well concealed) of that light-headed world where laughter, song, luxury and pleasure were the order of the day.

In his outspoken and amusing tales, Saikaku does nothing to hide the miseries of pleasure or the cruelty of love, but his characters generally have such vitality that they overcome the temptations to suicide which come their way. These light-hearted, elliptical, inventive stories sometimes depict violent passions, but more often they concern light-hearted intrigues, passing encounters, all the bitter-sweet ups and downs of that 'floating world' (*ukiyo*) which is so skilfully captured by the masters of the Japanese print, from Moronobu to Utamaro, as if to capture for all eternity the fugitive instant, the ephemeral charm of a once-glimpsed face. The word *ukiyo* has many Buddhist connotations: it is the impermanent world of illusion denounced in many a priest's sermon. But Saikaku's heroes have no intention of escaping it: they are wise enough to live with it, and ironically lucid enough not to be fooled. They accept in advance whatever it may chance to give them – and chances it gives them in plenty. On reaching the age of fifty-four Yonosuke, hero of *Koshoku ichidai otoko* (1682), a great 'friend of pleasure', reckons that he has made love to three thousand seven hundred and forty-two women and seven hundred and twenty-five boys. As for his female counterpart, the lady of pleasure in *Koshoku ichidai onna* (1686), she calculates her professional haul at over ten thousand men!

These tales, then, are outspoken, cynical and salacious. Licentious they are not: no rape, no treachery, no accents of revolt and defiance such as resound through the shady adventures of Western libertines, from Don Juan to Laclos and Sade. Saikaku's heroes do not need to prove villains, or incapable of love, before they can take their pleasures where they will. The springtime, pagan innocence of their adventures is lit with humour: they are not transgressions but a game, even a sport. No hostile heaven, no outraged society pursues them with vengeance: pleasure has its own, acknowledged place in the scheme of things. The reign of morality is undisputed, for Edo society had its severe and rigoristic side: the powers that be have power, and social bonds are tightly tied. But it was not a totalitarian, or even a puritan, society. Menaces to the social order were dealt with severely, even savagely; virtue was praised, duty and will-power exalted. But such obligations left a measure of free play. Beyond good and evil there was a place for the good-humoured tolerance of mere enjoyment. Merchants worked hard for their money: they had to have something to spend it on. As for samurai, it would indeed be awful if they ruined themselves and had to sell their swords to the highest bidder, and so they were warned – but against love, not pleasure. No one ever ruined himself for a courtesan, unless he happened to fall in love with her.

If marriage was really not enough, if you longed for something more exciting than home comforts, it was less trouble to love a boy. It was tolerated, even encouraged; it encouraged a sort of brotherly rivalry. Rather than risking the proverbial rapacity of the daughters of joy (or their employers) it wsa better to fall for some young fellow soldier, where innocence and simplicity were more likely to be found. On this point the *Hagakure* gives a generous ration of good advice – Mishima Yukio thought it excellent. Tsunetomo was of the opinion that you would only have one true love in your life, and you could not be too careful about it: 'When you love a man older than you, you must test him over about five years; when you know exactly what his feelings are, then you can trust him. If you are to help and assist each other even at the expense of your lives, each of you must know the other's very soul.' Such, to the pure heart of a samurai, were the accents of homosexuality, which Christianity first rejected and then associated with licentiousness, holding it to be at least frivolous if not perverted; for him it was a chaste and serious thing.

THE ORGANIZATION OF PLEASURE

As for those who did need women – aside from their own wives – they had untrammelled access to the houses of pleasure. The best ones were very expensive, but they did free one from the perils of adultery – risk, intrigue, vengeance. In Edo society, naturally, these establishments were very well regulated: the names, doings, sayings, comings and goings of clients were scrupulously recorded. In 1612 a certain shrewd businessman proposed to gather all the scattered brothels of the capital into a single district (the famous Yoshiwara, closed down in 1958): in his application to the Bakufu he stressed the fact that it would make it much easier to keep the clients safe, i.e. keep a close eye on them, and especially on the *ronin*, always a potential threat to the peace of the state. It would help protect families, firstly by giving a safe outlet to restless masculine desire, second by helping to track down the child-stealers whose disgusting trade was to kidnap little girls to sell as unofficial prostitutes: any sale would have to be ratified by the name, address and signature of the parents. Was there ever a more reasoned application? A well-conducted society does have to make sure that free love is properly organized. The Bakufu took the point entirely, and a few months later granted the necessary authority and building land. Safety and freedom, those ambitious ideals of the lawmaker, were reconciled in a uniquely satisfactory way.[3]

By the end of the seventeenth century twenty-five flourishing districts (*kuruwa, yukaku, yuri*) had been set aside in the largest Japanese cities. At this time two thousand girls (*yujo, joro*) were employed at Yoshiwara; in the best days of the nineteenth century it went up to four thousand. In the great liberation movement at the beginning of Meiji it was decided to emancipate them: the imperial decree of 2 October 1872 forbade all trade in human bodies, and all contracts of prostitution were declared null and void. But where could they go, what else could they do? Most of them remained slaves of their own free will, and the houses continued to prosper – and recruit.

Japanese prostitution kept to its special districts and establishments (*joroya, okiya, ageya*). In these establishments tariffs and (as you might say) morality were strictly controlled; they were really more or less expensive hotels equipped with more or less young and pretty girls, all good fun but perfectly respectable, not in the least like the sordid bawdy-houses depicted by such as Toulouse-Lautrec. The unconventional freelance prostitute was an unknown species. Nor did rich Japanese, like their wealthy bourgeois European counterparts, fancy sharing the expense of keeping a famous beauty in the style to which she was accustomed. That sort of clandestine contract, which kept some famous courtesans in unheard-of luxury, developed alongside the limited company. Japanese capitalism then, and long after Meiji, was still at the stage of domestic property and merchants' guilds.

All very open and above board, and it was really time for a touch of hypocrisy. Ordinary folk went about quite openly under the lanterns of Yoshiwara (Edo), Shimabara (Kyoto), Shimmachi and Sonezaki (Osaka), but samurai were expected to hand over a few coins at the entrance in exchange for a straw hat (*amigasa*) whose wide pulled-down brim would hide their faces. It was for the same reasons that the Venetian nobility invented the black mask and the domino. In this world set apart from society, distinctions of rank no longer applied: everyone was equal, money permitting. A busy, artificial little world, the theatre of pleasure, orderly and ardent.

The sword-bearing samurai left his trusty blades in the lobby – to defuse drunken quarrels, certainly, and keep steel out of masculine squabbles, but also (in the gloomy reckoning of the brothel-keepers) to prevent a bedside sword from giving a girl the idea of ending her status as a piece of goods. Poverty had driven them; sold, sometimes at a very early age, by their parents, or even later by their husbands, they were generally bound by a ten-year contract. Many never made the end of it. Escape was unthinkable, for the district was walled and moated, and they were allowed out only once or twice a year, to visit the cherry trees at Ueno, to accomplish a vow at some temple, or on a last visit to sick or dying parents. Where could they hide? They would soon be caught. The bravest fled into death, sometimes fortunate in that their lovers sought to go with them.

Sometimes a girl known as a model of skill and good sense might persuade a client to buy out her remaining years of service: he would settle the price with the brothel-keeper and she would become a rich man's concubine. But most of them were resigned to never leaving the place: once their charms had faded they became chaperones, madams, musicians, make-up artists, dressers, or mere servants or scullery maids. Many, grown indifferent to a body they no longer owned, let it die of disease. The death registers of Yoshiwara girls buried in the temple of Seikan-ji have come down to us from 1743 onwards. The figures are chillingly precise: they died at the average age of twenty-three, or to be completely accurate, 22.7.

And yet, in the best houses, the courtesans whose names we know, whose lovely faces look out of so many prints, their graceful forms decked in poppies and dragons, seem to have all they desire in their enclosed universe: feasting and song, dancing, music and flowers, witty conversation, delicate allusions, delightful little parties, all the subtleties of art, all the lavishness of luxury, all the gaiety of company. It was like a second flowering of court life, as brilliant as that of Heian, and as peacefully absorbed in its games and its joys. Another society, laughing alongside the seriousness of the first, given up entirely to pleasure. You could spend hours there, charmed by the courtly grace of the courtesans, surrounded by a whole busy little court, just as glittering and refined as the palace in all its splendour. If you were light-hearted enough, and rich enough, you could forget (at least for a while) that the true master of that little world, discreetly anonymous, was money: behind the smiling faces, behind the politely bent backs of the brothel-keepers, its chill despotism ruled all.

ILLUSION AND TRUTH

This is *ukiyo*, the world of illusion. Amidst such a plethora of charms, why should anyone need truth – except true love? The client was assiduously flattered, to keep him faithful and amorous – which meant that he spent more. Tender glances, timid avowals, amorous languishings, were all elements in a sometimes successful strategy. But the client who fell for it would find in his beating heart the question, 'Am I loved?', 'Do you love me?' – which is really saying, 'Love me!' Because the beloved must be free; all you can ask her (or him) is to be sincere. Love may deny itself eternity, but it will have truth. But it asks in vain: a hasty avowal is doubtful, a sincere one disappointing. As King Lear learns to his cost, truth lies in Cordelia's 'love, and be silent'. Freud suggests, perhaps rightly, in relation to this moment in Shakespeare that true love can be found only in death, pale, silent and forever faithful. On this point the bellicose *Hagakure* agrees with Cordelia: 'The height of love, I take it, is secret love. To languish in love all your life, to die of love without a word, that indeed is true love.'

A surprising delicacy under the rough exterior of the swashbuckling Tsunetomo, and a surprising wisdom in his evocation of the will![4] For a love which has to talk and ask questions is not pure, and its weakness will kill it some day. An anxious heart, ever demanding words, forgets that love can be divined, or maybe put to the test, but not confessed or argued over. Constant's Adolphe spends hours analysing the impulses of his own heart, but the more he wants to know if he really loves, the less he *does* know. So how can you promise the beloved something which you cannot honestly be sure of yourself?

Only the effects of love are real; you cannot capture the imagined springs of its lasting power, it will only elude and disappoint you. If to love is to 'imagine' that you love, what truth can there be? The rule – to which Japanese culture submits – is that words, so fertile in misunderstandings, must eventually yield to unspoken proofs: bodily passions, a decisive motion of the will. Marivaux's young heiresses, anxious to find true love, are lucky: for them, truth triumphs over appearance without having to leave the theatre of words. The Japanese, more sceptical about words and gestures which cost nothing, refused to grant proof of sincerity to a clever talker. Once again they found a code, not of expression but of action: a whole series of trials capable (perhaps) of eliciting a true verdict. Through voluntary action rather than fine words, the heart might show itself for what it was. The Japanese word for lovers' suicide, *shinju*, in use since the end of the seventeenth century, literally means the centre of the heart, and hence the warrant of a true feeling inexpressible in words, an active proof of love – to the death if need be. Even if it was not a proof of true feeling, it certainly showed that the perpetrator would die to *make* his feelings true.

LOVE AND MEMORY

Fujimoto Kizan (1626–1704), a regular visitor to the houses of pleasure, was so fascinated by them that he decided to write a moralized codification of their customs. The cruel art of war had its own ethic, *bushido*; why should not the delightful art of the courtesan have its own precepts, laws, disciplines and virtues, the *shikido*? In his *Shikido okagami* ('The Great Mirror of the Way of Love', 1678), Kizan prescribed the various tokens (*shinju*) which lovers could give or ask of each other. He sets them out in five stages: you could, in that order, tattoo a part of your body, cut off a lock of hair, deliver a written oath of eternal fidelity, pull off a fingernail, and finally cut off a finger:

> The other four varieties of pledges – fingernails, oaths, locks of hair and tattooing – can be carried out, as part of a calculated scheme, even if the woman is insincere. But unless she really loves a man, it is hard to go through with cutting off a finger. Nails grow back in days, a head of hair

in months, oaths can be hidden away, and tattooing can be erased when a woman no longer sees a man. But giving up a finger makes a woman a cripple for life, and she can never restore things to what they were. The act should therefore be performed only after grave deliberation.[5]

This is entertainingly pragmatic – as if love could be metered on a scale of sacrifices: a fingernail isn't a reliable proof, but a little finger... she loves me! Kizan does not mention voluntary death, for its value as the supreme token was too well known, it was the true *shinju*, and the other procedures were but pale echoes of its sacrificial spirit. Kizan was probably reluctant to introduce too serious a note into a book chiefly devoted to the pleasures of love, but he knew perfectly well that death was the most irrefutable of proofs, the only one to silence every suspicion. Those who died for love, loved truly, but too late for the knowledge to have much meaning. Like the warrior's belly in *seppuku*, the lover's heart is torn open to an empty truth, the everlasting, immutable truth of the void.

All these symbolical injuries, short of the voluntary death which is their culmination, are at once a sacrifice and a notice: you spend a part of yourself, you cut, cleave and dig, so as to leave an indelible mark. It is thus, according to Nietzsche, that human beings forge a memory out of pain, become capable of making promises and answer for the future through the memory of self-inflicted suffering. Is cruelty, then, the only thing which can overcome the forgetfulness of time? Indifferent 'becoming', which dissolves all things continually, is met with a solemn, costly and memorable self-destruction: sacrifice will not rot. That is why, in primitive rituals, signs are branded on adolescent flesh. Psychoses are scored with the marks of trauma, retraced by compulsive repetition. Similarly, the history of nations is graven with their tribulations and torments, their traditions and destinies, first inscribed, then written down when the analytical consciousness finally becomes able to escape the past by describing it in detail.

Ukiyo, the floating world. Buddhists say, 'Remember; everything forgets everything, including itself.' Love swears to forget nothing; Kizan will help it fulfil the oath. And a woman thirty years later asks herself, 'Who *was* that young samurai for whom I so stupidly cut off the tip of my finger?' All living things forget; life is not memory but new beginnings and old endings, round and round the wheel of forgetfulness. Those who die for love refuse to disappear so easily, and cannot be accused of conniving at forgetfulness. Many other things they may be reproached for, but not that. They know quite well that their love cannot be eternal, surrounded as they are by people saying, 'Wait, and you'll feel it less and less.' That they know only too well. But they will run ahead of forgetfulness: of all motives this is the one most likely to hasten them. They will break free and be reunited in another life, defy the power which oppresses and separates them, wipe out insults and justify themselves, prove their hearts are true, all of that: but above all, they will love, if not for ever, then at least until the end.

Better to die straight away than to let love die in the changeable, mortal heart where once it burned. If love cannot be made eternal, voluntary death will at least make sure it is irremediable. In the West there was an eternity of love, as conceived in God. In Japan, despite Amidist sorties in that direction, the heart could not dream of so complete a fulfilment. What lay above all things was the utter void. In Edo society, love remained marginal, hazardous, fleeting and fragile – often humiliating, always only too human, but all the more shattering for that. Denied eternity, it clung to death. You could love flowers, music, fine thoughts, anything you thought would endure (the sky? the sea?) – but to love a mortal creature as it was, with all the desperate disappointments that love might bring, was the bravest kind of love: it was risking your life.

Angela of Foligno and Theresa of Avila loved madly, but their love was too completely purged of the dangers of reality. A poor girl from Sonezaki, clinging to her sad, debt-ridden lover's arm, had ventured no less far than they through the night of doubt towards the frontiers of love. Love of God, so confident, does not regain that utter seriousness until it is set against the horizon of the death of God. The greatness of Christianity lay, from the beginning, in its readiness to ascribe to the Eternal the crazy insight of a God loving enough to endure death. The idea never quite lost its edge, even under the heavy burden of interpretation laid on it by St Paul. There is no point in loving God unless he needs that love to exist, since his own love can only be his death.

Many a courtesan in Edo Japan took her lover with her into death. We may find this surprising, but it is well attested in the real-life incidents which inspired so many plays and novels at the time. It is the last remnants of puritanism in us which provoke the astonishment: we have been so thoroughly taught to distinguish between love and the pleasures of sex! For us the prostitute in love is a soon-to-be-hackneyed invention of the Romantic imagination. But the Japanese did not need to read Victor Hugo, Balzac or the younger Dumas before they believed a prostitute capable of genuine feeling.

Nothing is more alien to the Japanese spirit than that theme of redemption through love, so dear to the pious bourgeois of the nineteenth century. Unless sexual pleasure is thought to be a vice from the outset, there is nothing to redeem. Self-sacrificing love and bacchanalian pleasure can indeed offer a choice between good and evil, as in the first act of *La Traviata*, in which the 'fallen woman' is called upon to choose between them. Or in *Tannhäuser*, when the prisoner in the Venusberg aspires to deliverance through suffering. This shifting Western schism between exalted love and sensual pleasure, which contrasted (for example) religious mysticism with licentious enjoyment, never took a hold in Japan. In Japan love was not idealized or sacred; it remained closer to the flesh, simpler and more real. We may smile at the stuffy compassion of the lover in *La Dame aux camélias*; the ladies of Yoshiwara certainly would have:

> Quite simply, I am sure of one thing: when a woman has not been educated to the knowledge of good, God nearly always offers her two paths leading her back to it. These paths are love and sorrow. They are hard paths, and those who tread them do so with torn hands and crippled feet. But on the thorns along the wayside they also leave behind the ornaments of vice, and they reach the end of the road stripped to a nakedness which before God is no shame.[6]

No such hypocrisy in Edo: it had chosen to give prostitution a task, a status, a domain within its well-ordered society. It did not smell the sulphurous odour of vice in so useful a profession. The prostitute inspired neither disdain nor repulsion. People were sorry for her having had to sell herself, or be sold. They knew that flood, famine and calamity always brought the dealers in human flesh, the pimps (*zegen*), into the countryside like vultures to buy little girls from starving families. The most sympathetic could guess at the misery of life in that profession: it was called *kugai*, a Buddhist term meaning 'world of suffering'. No one would dream of taking offence at it. On feast days whole families often strolled through the streets of Yoshiwara, where the children were thrilled to see the beautiful silk-clad ladies tripping along under their shady parasols, surrounded by their diminutive attendants. When love came, with its accompanying torments, delights and calamities, it was received as a decree of fate, both fortunate and dangerous. It never took on the aspect of a costly redemption sent from Heaven to a persistent sinner.

LOVE AND THE DAUGHTERS OF JOY

These well-educated, well-disciplined girls – so accomplished that they were later to be generally and euphemistically called *geisha*, which means 'artist' – were all very young: they never had time to become as blasé as their profession – and their peace of mind – really required. So often did they feign love that they were sometimes caught in their own snare. Houses of pleasure were frequented by brilliantly dandified young men (*tsu*), in love with love, like Saikaku's Yonosuke: their charm (*iki*), and chic (*sui*) made them real heartbreakers. One might awaken a courtesan to her unhappy state, to full awareness of her enslavement and to the desire to escape it in any way possible, and at any price. What only yesterday had seemed a simple, normal thing to do became suddenly hateful, and she dreamed of refusing every client save the beloved.

The most celebrated girls always had a certain freedom of choice, coquettish deliberation, even capricious refusal: they were on the highest levels of amorous dalliance, *tayu* (leading ladies) or *tenjin* (celestial angels). But if a girl took to despising all clients save one, and maintaining a sulky silence with all the others, the house would be ruined – and what an awful example to the rest! Because with girls living together – in a school, convent or anywhere else – love is contagious, indeed epidemic. A good brothel-keeper would swiftly and ruthlessly put a stop to such exclusive attachments; if the clients fell in love, so much the better, but not the girls: it was against professional etiquette.

In *The Life of an Amorous Man*, Saikaku tells how a brothel-keeper called Gonzaemon punished his most valuable asset, the fair Mikasa, for falling in love with Yonosuke. Not that Gonzaemon was unusually brutal; a little too severe maybe, and inclined to take himself seriously: he had to act in the best interests of his business and assert his authority as head of the household – just like a father whose favourite daughter had fallen foolishly in love and mooned about refusing the most brilliant marriages. Every house – family home, house of pleasure, or business – was subject to the same laws: economy, stability, survival, all were threatened by love. You had to prosper or go under, and ruin would soon follow if the father or manager was weak enough to abdicate his responsibilities.

Love, so ungrateful, so culpable, so prompt to rebellion, had to yield to authority. Mikasa was demoted from *tayu* to scullery maid, and dressed in rags. But she welcomed the humiliations, feeling that she suffered them all for her lover's, or at least for her love's, sake: they were a proof most gladly given. Formerly bought and sold, she felt the need to give herself now, but she could not. A virgin is more fortunate: she has only to give herself to her lover and he will be convinced. But a daughter of joy, what could she give? Her fingernail, her finger ... her life? Mikasa made it a point of honour to offer her sufferings, although Yonosuke knew nothing of them; she wished to serve him, even if he had no need of such devotion. She was serving not so much her lover as love itself. This was not redemption, but a woman's (or girl's) own ethic, as good as any warrior's: honour and service unto death, even if death achieved nothing more than to fix her forever in her present state.

When the first snow fell, Gonzaemon tied her to a willow tree in the courtyard. She remained there, day and night, for over a week, refusing food, determined like an ascetic to deliver herself by starvation. 'Well, let her die then!' thought Gonzaemon, 'though she cost me a good deal: that will make it clear to the whole household that I am the master here.' Eventually Mikasa managed to let Yonosuke know that she was about to die. Not that he was really in love with her, as she, alas, well knew. But his honour was also at stake in this battle of wills:

> An hour later Mikasa, giving up all hope, was about to end it all by biting off her tongue when Yonosuke came rushing up. He was robed in white, the emblem of death, apparently meaning that he had decided, if death must come, then Mikasa should not die alone. This brought the entire household out into the garden ...[7]

Eventually Gonzaemon yields and Yonosuke wins the resolute courtesan. Saikaku, virtuoso of the *haikai*, merely outlines the scene, but we can easily imagine the rest. The news of Yonosuke's arrival runs through the house; courtesans, clients, attendants, servant girls rush in a chattering throng along the corridors to see the satisfyingly spectacular scene which the theatre of life is for once ready to offer them. Mikasa's angry lover is as determined to die as she is, if need be: he knows that everything depends on his resolve. He enters clad in the white kimono which makes his intentions plain. In his hand is the dagger with which he will stab his mistress and then himself. Will he also threaten the virtuous householder with revenge for his own self-inflicted death? No, because a moment's thought will bend Gonzaemon's resolve; perhaps his more flexible and tender-hearted wife will intervene and show him where his real interests lie. There must be a negotiated settlement to this silly quarrel into which his managerial pride has brought him. For even if he is justified in law, and before his own conscience, even if the police inquiry exonerates him, there will be a fearful scandal. The house would never recover from such a pair of suicides.

Tragic happenings are very bad publicity for a house of pleasure. Moreover even the most hard-headed of honest businessmen must wake up sometimes in the stilly watches of the night and think about the dead ... Good riddance to the obstinate little fool, and to her lover too, the spoilsport, upsetting honest girls! But can you be so easily rid of people who have killed themselves under your eyes without your having raised a finger to save them? Hard to sleep on that with a clear conscience: you might see ghosts, phantasms, perhaps conjured up by your inevitable remorse. So it would really be much more sensible to yield the fair rebel – for a consideration – to the man she loves. You might lose money on the deal, but you will save yourself a lot of trouble, and maybe some uncomfortable nights. The public likes excitement, but it prefers a happy ending: it will grant Mikasa that fame her courageous love deserves. And she will have no need to return, a pale and bloodied spectre, to trouble the dreams of her former employer.

GHOSTS AND GUILTY CONSCIENCES

Ghosts were – and still are – no laughing matter in Japan. There is still a regular output of television programmes which discuss the question with an abundance of photographs and eye-witness accounts – slightly humorous, perhaps, at times. Here are the lurking remnants of animist beliefs, long since denounced as superstitious and persecuted by the monotheists. But it was this pagan culture, sleeping under its Buddhist mantle, which provided the fifteenth century with an expression for the darkest terror of death in that purest of art forms, the No. The No theatre is dominated by ghost stories: ghosts seen, ghosts half-seen, ghosts seen in a dream between waking and sleeping.

Later, in the Edo era, stories of ghosts and strange apparitions (*kaidan*) gave readers an agreeable shiver. The masterpiece in this genre is Ueda Akinari's *Ugetsu monogatari* ('Tales of Rain and Moon', 1768). People still feared, scarcely less than in Heian times, the vengeance of the dead (*tatari*), the anger of spirits (*onryo*), and denizens of the other world who still had a score to settle. As Michizane's story goes to show, the best vengeances, easy and risk-free, are those of the dead.[8] Among the many motives for suicide a long-cherished grievance had always had its place; and Edo culture, by discouraging revolt, only encouraged resentment. Even those who died for love could store up a grudge: by saying goodbye to this cruelly indifferent world they could be avenged for many an injustice received and borne in silence.

It was scarcely the best publicity for a house of pleasure to count the odd suicide among its dear departed. And as for ghosts . . .! A drunken client awakes and half-sees a shadow on a wall; he remembers certain stories he has been told, his night of pleasure comes to an abrupt end and he is off home. A brothel-keeper had to avoid that sort of reputation, and girls who contemplated making that last escape from his vigilant eye knew well that the threat of it was some safeguard against injustice.[9] 'Well', thinks a keeper, looking at one of his girls hanging from the girdle of her kimono, 'if we can't prevent it, we must at least keep it quiet!' And quiet the whole household would keep. Every family (and a brothel is a family of a sort) has its secrets, some sad, some silly; and a good many deaths must have been concealed in this way. In

Chikamatsu's plays the lovers will try anything to get out of the locked house: they flee and die in the open air, in the chill of early morning, as if to forestall the lies and the silence.

Happily there were precautions one could take against ghosts. A final solution might be the exorcist, skilled in intimidating and soothing a wandering spirit; but there were simpler things to try first: if people believed a method would work, then it probably would. In fourth-century Athens suicides had their right hands cut off to prevent them working mischief. In Edo Japan, the corpse was sometimes doubled up, with its feet and hands tied together, then tied in a straw mat and thrown nameless into a common grave. That was how dogs were buried, and since nobody had ever heard of a dog having a ghost (this being the lugubrious privilege of human souls), such a burial was thought sufficient to keep undesirable visitors at bay: everyone believed it, from the silliest scullery maid to the boss himself, and since they believed it, there was no ghost.

Some precaution was certainly needed: Japanese religion had nothing to say either for or against voluntary death. Certainly retribution was feared in the next life, and some people would remember certain Buddhist descriptions of hell (though these were not much mentioned in the Edo period); but suicide had never been considered a crime. One's other acts might cause anxiety, but not that one. Suicidal lovers, happy in their Amidist convictions, hoped they *would* be reborn in a better would where they would be reunited. The priests would tell you that killing a living (and therefore suffering) being, or breaking a heart out of wilful cruelty (and therefore adding to the pain of the universe) were serious acts with worrying consequences in the next life: you might be done by as you did, by *becoming* the trembling animal, or the broken heart, and having to feel that suffering which you had refused to understand and respect. But killing *yourself* – why not, if duty demanded, reason advised or destiny required? Buddhism respects not so much life as the pain which is life. Respects it, not in resignation but to be rid of it. Its causes are examined not in order to justify it, but to find a way out of it.

No Western domestic tyrant needed to fear suicide: Christians, holding it to be unpardonable even by God, had done their best to prevent and quell it. If it did happen, a twofold interpretation could immediately be brought in to relieve the tyrant of responsibility: suicide was madness, and satanic madness at that. Those who chose such a death confessed themselves (in the words of the Council of Arles) to be *diabolico persecuti furore*, insane and possessed by the devil. As for the stern father, the greedy pander, their consciences were clear. 'Satan has been at work in my house, and the silly woman was certainly mad if not actually possessed; I always thought so, and now I know so!'

Christians saw suicide as a crisis in man's relationship with the divine will. The deed was seen as one of metaphysical revolt, and so was not subject to the moral responsibility which would have given it meaning within the human world. Initially this worked to the advantage of the survivors – the family, the exonerated powers-that-were – but later perhaps to that of the victims, if they lacked the pride to hold on to their reasons for dying. If they were assumed to be mad then they were excused, and buried in the churchyard with everybody else. God forgive you, we are sorry for you (says the priest), so long as you are mad! In Japan, suicide was never divorced from ethics: it was and remained a voluntary death, a moral act – reasoned, deliberate, part of the here and now. You could understand why it had been done and find out who was really responsible. What you would find would be a lucid and completely human truth; whereas the doctors of the West, right up to the nineteenth century, would find only mania, melancholy and – alienation.

THE LAST RESORT OF THE OPPRESSED

The values of courage and love were not projected on to God; it was the courage to die, and that alone, which revealed them. Voluntary death could reveal them, as a last resort. In another story by Saikaku, a careless young clerk forgets to get a receipt from a shopkeeper for a large sum of money. The lying shopkeeper accuses him, saying, 'He gave me nothing, he wants to keep the money for himself; no doubt he has spent it in gaming and pleasuring.' The clerk kills, and therefore vindicates, himself. That is enough to reveal the truth and bring down retribution on the shopkeeper, who is dishonoured, unmasked and shortly ruined, while his wife dies of shame. Similarly, in *Sonezaki shinju*, the first of Chikamatsu's domestic dramas, Tokubei is cheated, robbed, humiliated and dishonoured by his supposed best friend Tahei. He resolves to die, for how else can the truth come out? He tries to explain, pleads, seeks to establish the truth; but in this world of appearances, all the appearances are against him. The more he talks, the less people listen. Then he thinks, 'Why am I wasting words? Within three days I, Tokubei, shall be vindicated, and the whole city of Osaka shall see how pure are the depths of my heart.'

In the judicial ordeal it was heaven which gave the proof; here the human will must do so by answering for itself in death. Ohatsu, a nineteen-year-old courtesan and Tokubei's beloved, who has never doubted or hesitated for a moment, accompanies him in death – or drags him after her. For love, as much as justice, needs truth in order to triumph, and in this uncertain world justice is no less perilous than love.

But in voluntary death you can be sure of justice. The lovers will not see this twofold victory, but they will sacrifice themselves for it in the certain knowledge that it will be theirs. Just before daybreak, in the little wood of Sonezaki, Ohatsu unfastens her blue girdle and slits it with a razor to make a long silken ribbon. They use it to tie themselves to a tree. 'And now, kill me quickly!' His hand trembles, his eyes are darkened, he strikes twice, thrice, but his blow goes awry. At last he finds her throat, plunges in the blade, feels her shudder and collapse – and with one blow, he cuts his own throat.

The domestic tyrant, left unsupported by religion, might perhaps look to the state. It certainly tried to curb the despair of lovers: in 1722 the Bakufu issued a decree forbidding *shinju* as tantamount to murder, the perpetrator to remain unburied. At long last the authorities were taking notice, after two decades which had seen a wave of lovers' suicides in the great cities of Japan, particularly Osaka (a clear sign of the melancholy which haunted the houses of pleasure). In just two years, 1703 and 1704, there were thrity-six well-documented cases of suicide by courtesans; how many others never came to light?

People were as fascinated by these tales of love and death as they were by the vendetta of the forty-seven faithful vassals of Ako, which happened at just that time. In Edo the samurai slew themselves for justice, in Osaka the courtesans and clerks killed themselves for love. And all such surprising or moving incidents, social upheavals and natural catastrophes were published as they happened in illustrated broadsheets, sold hot off the press by street vendors and called *ezoshi*. Great lovers' suicides were sold on the streets to a shuddering, weeping or thoughtful public, just like sensational newspapers today. The theatre fed on these emotions, and doubtless stimulated them as it did so. As early as 1683 a play about a lovers' suicide was put on, attracting little interest. But in 1695 the death of the merchant Sankatsu and the courtesan Hanshichi was acted in the Kabuki theatre with some success: the play ran for 155 days. What deep well of tears had been broached in the hearts of the busy *chonin*, dwellers in the noisy cities? On the unreal stage they saw and understood, too late, the distress which they might have met, unknowing, in the crowds outside; or, as they now realized, even within themselves.[10]

Did suicides then begin to imitate the theatre which was imitating them? Indeed they did, in a dizzying shift between reality and reflection reminiscent of *Werther*. On 22 May 1703 a young employee, deep in debt, and a courtesan of Sonezaki killed themselves spectacularly; their bodies were scarcely cold when the Takemoto puppet theatre advertised a play on the subject. This was *Sonezaki shinju*, written by Chikamatsu with feverish speed: not only was the commission urgent, but through it, at the age of fifty, he had discovered his true genius. Less than a month later the puppets were sobbing most convincingly to the strain of the *shamisen*. It was an overnight success. The almost bankrupt Takemoto theatre had paid off all its debts within a month. This was the first of the domestic dramas *(sewamono)* which made Chikamatsu's name and are still his chief claim to fame. They ushered in a new emotional tone: familiar, intimate, modern and urban. About fifty years later Diderot, in *Le Fils naturel*, believed he had invented a new genre which he called 'genuine drama'; but his bourgeois characters are too self-assured, like premature Prudhommes. In 1731 John Lillo brought out his *The London Merchant*, but in the West the merchant was generally confined to social comedy. In Osaka he went straight into extreme situations of intense lyricism. After all, people died for love every day; there was no need to cloak the event in far-off history or legend, as in Hugo's *Ruy Blas* or Wagner's *Tristan*.

In Japan it is the samurai of the historical plays *(jidaimono)* who often look hollow and vain: their virtue sustains the social order, they never suffer from self-doubt, but it is all to save face. Chikamatsu wrote both *jidaimono* and *sewamono*, and the contrast runs through the entire Bunraku and Kabuki repertoire. On the one side the *tachiyaku*, strong, resolute, solid characters; on the other, young male lovers *(nimaime)*, hesitant, fragile, indecisive and true to life – for truth, in conduct as in speech, emerges from contradiction. These two heroes and two theatrical styles, one rough and one tender, *aragoto* and *wagoto*, reflected the duality of the contemporary social structure. On top were Edo, the Bakufu, the warrior clans, the ideology of virtue, the austere and unbending façade of the nobility. Underneath were all the get-rich-quick exuberance of Osaka, the ups and downs of commerce, the frenzies of pleasure, the luxury and the sudden ruin, the simple intimacy of family life and the unexpected impulses of an unruly heart, all the fluctuating emotions of getting and spending; and in the spending the great fevered city refreshed itself for the fray.

THE STATIONER'S TRAGEDY

Sonezaki shinju was the first in a long line of plays about lovers' suicides *(shinju sewamono)* which Chikamatsu wrote at the rate of almost one a year during the first twenty years of the eighteenth century, the last of his long life. His mastery of pathos is shown most clearly in *Shinju Ten no Amijima*, based on two real-life suicides which took place at dawn on 13 November 1720. That evening Chikamatsu was dining in a Kyoto restaurant when the puppet theatre sent a breathless messenger to tell him what had happened. He got into his palanquin, returned to Osaka –

a journey of several hours – and immediately seized his brush to begin the fluent writing of his most accomplished play. Six weeks later audiences were weeping over the sad life of Jihei the stationer, Koharu his mistress and Osan his wife. Anyone could see themselves in this trio of very ordinary heroes, heart-rending in their innocence. Ill-will is not tragic, but that good intentions can have catastrophic results is a terrible truth well known since the days of Oedipus and Antigone. All three are trapped in the double bind of duty and love, *giri* and *ninjo*. They seek solutions, but the web of pain strangles them: there can be only one, tragic issue, the death of the lovers.

Osan, out of love for her husband and duty to her two children, asks the young Koharu to give up Jihei. She is not the deceived and jealous wife, for she has never been deceived. In any case the mistress is a courtesan, and in the Japanese society of the time only a wife could be guilty of adultery.[11] Osan overcomes her jealousy; Koharu overcomes, or rather consummates, her love. Love sacrifices all, and at its height, sacrifices itself. Tender-hearted, she has loved to be loved, but when she sees how frail are human beings, how painful is love, she begins to wish she were not loved. The happiness of the beloved is too precious, and the highest proof of love may be to say nothing, to efface herself and be forgotten. Osan realizes that Koharu cannot make such a sacrifice and live, and she gives up her demands, out of compassion and because she thinks that women, even if one is a wife and mother and the other a common prostitute, share the same condition and so have a duty to one another. The wife decides to pawn her clothes, and everything she has of value, to buy back the courtesan who has had to sell herself: economic slavery is clearly described here as a modern form of destiny.

Having once turned away from the old romantic idealism, Chikamatsu brings it back into this tangle of contradictions. Lovers' raptures founder on the two reefs of this prosaic world, moral debt and monetary debt. Can Koharu, now paid for and free, become the acknowledged concubine of Jihei? Alas! Love knows, during its one brief hour, that it cannot but die, if not by self-destruction, then by the slow process of time. The best, certainly the most splendid, thing is to let your love burn, unappeased, to the end. Moreover, Osan is unfortunate in having a father who wants to see her happy: with the authority parents had at that time, he intervenes to take back his daughter, whom he sees being treated with disrespect. Jihei is forced back on Koharu. Cut off together from a society indifferent to love, they find in each other's eyes the courage to give up life.

Without that supreme self-sacrifice, which hastens it towards death and despises even the need to endure, love might well deserve Confucius' accusation that it is no more than a conjunction of egoisms. If you love, you must justify it by giving up your self. Buddhism, with its discipline of deliverance and salvation, was all against that closest of bonds which is love. But, it being also a discipline of self-sacrifice, a Buddhist would find it must easier than a narrow rationalist to understand the dissolution of the self (*muga*) in the effervescence of strong emotion. In which case he could hardly judge and condemn lovers.

Of all pains the pain of love is the most absurd, and therefore the most innocent. Love is a madness, but therein it is pure, like flame, empty and transparent. You might expiate a sin by dying for love, though perhaps only that of having broken with the world or become too attached to a mortal creature – imagined faults which reconcile you to your destiny by making it a retribution. But the most touching truth is the supreme innocence of gratuitous suffering and gratuitous love, which takes fire and burns away unexplained, like life. Into such revelations of emptiness only Amidism had ever deeply ventured, finding there the source of its infinite compassion, beyond all illusions of judgement. Other religions, even orthodox Buddhism, invented guilt structures (original sin, retribution through karma) to make some sort of sense out of the trials of life. But only love, all-giving and forgiving (the insight which Christianity had, but so quickly smothered), can take human beings beyond the desire for justice and fulfil their uttermost potential.

UNIVERSAL FORGIVENESS

It is Amida's pure compassion which awaits Chikamatsu's lovers at the end of their road to death, lighted as it is by the love shining within them. All is forgiven, all grudges and injustices are forgotten. Deliverance is in their dizzying approach to the void, an awakening to a freedom never known or dreamed of. They can even forgive themselves at the last. All creatures shall indeed be saved: this boundless promise is the last word that reaches them from this world. The long tradition of the journey (*michiyuki*), which grew so well in Japanese soil, bears its finest fruits in the conclusion to the *Amijima*. In the night and cold the lovers set out seeking death, triumphing over a thousand hesitations – and now they see that they have journeyed to salvation. They have come to a temple which will soon awaken to prayer. Beside it is a canal, with a weir. In consideration for the wife who sought to let them live, they decide not to die in each other's arms: between their breathless and separate bodies they will leave a clean and empty space of transcended love, love expressing its ultimate truth of self-sacrifice.

> *Narrator*: She holds him in her arms. Their faces meet. Through their hair, wet with tears, blows the icy wind of the plain. Behind them ring the bells of the monastery of Daicho-ji.

Jihei:	Mercy! How short is even this long night, short as our lives...
Narrator:	Already the sky grows pale. The monastery bell is ringing for the morning service.
Jihei:	Now, now we must die, and die well.
Narrator:	He draws Koharu to him.
Jihei:	Leave no tears on this face, so soon to be still in death.
Koharu:	I shall leave none.
Narrator:	Before that pale face, paler than the dawning day, that smiling face, the hand of Jihei begins to tremble. It is not she, but he who first feels his sight grow dim. Where can he strike? Tears spill from his eyes.
Koharu:	Fear not! Quickly, quickly!
Narrator:	Encouraged by her, he takes his dagger. The invocations to Amida, borne on the wind from the monastery, urge him on. 'Hail to the Buddha Amida!' Brandishing his blade of deliverance, he stabs her with his dugger. He holds her tightly, but she falls backwards, writhing in terrible pain. The sword-point has missed her throat, Koharu is suffering the cruellest agony. Jihei plucks up courage, takes her in his arms and plunges in his sword to the hilt. Thus ends her short life, like a dream cut off by the cruel dawn. Tenderly Jihei lays her on her side, her head to the north, her face turned eastward, and covers her with his mantle. He weeps, but the grief of his loss is beyond tears. Taking the sash, he puts it round his neck. From the nearby monastery he hears the last lines of the chant: 'Believers and unbelievers alike, all the creatures of the universe are saved.' Then, crying, 'May we be reborn on the same lotus! Hail to the Buddha Amida!' Jihei leaps from the top of the weir. For an instant, in his death agony, he sways like a colocynth in the wind. Then his breathing is halted, like the water in the sluice. All the bonds of this world are forever broken. Fishermen, going early to work, find them: 'Aha! Two dead bodies! Come quickly, come and see!' The news travels swiftly, the rumour spreads. And all those who hear of the suicide of the two lovers of Amijima, who have attained the salvation which the Buddha promises all living things, weep at the tale.

Did the intensity of Chikamatsu's lyricism really seduce some lovers into death who otherwise would have resigned themselves to a prosaic life? Or did he rather, by purging the emotional tensions of the times and giving them an imaginary release, help to prevent their realization? Is poetry innocent or guilty? The debate is unending. But there *were* a good many suicides in Osaka during those twenty years, and the authorities decided on a crack-down. In 1704 the theatres were forbidden to perform scandalous and disreputable scenes borrowed from real life. Great families had to be protected, and political allusions suppressed. This rule was applied in Edo; but Osaka was of merely commercial importance and so enjoyed a large measure of administrative autonomy. In 1712, to the satisfaction of the influential Confucian scholars (*jusha*) who had the ear of the authorities, the Bakufu passed a decree forbidding the dramatization of lovers' suicides; but since the theatres were reluctant to give up this emotional (and therefore profitable) theme, the government confined itself to forbidding the use of the word *shinju* on theatre posters. The titles of Chikamatsu's plays written in 1720 (*Shinju Ten no Amijima*) and 1722 (*Shinju Yoigoshin*) show that nobody bothered to extend this discipline to the Osaka stage. Negligence? Yes, and social snobbery too: the heartaches of prostitutes and small shopkeepers were really not of much importance.

AVATARS OF ADULTERY

Theft, arson and murder were much more worrying to the authorities; so too were highway robbery, vendetta, anything which might bring on a rebellion. Suicide may be a first sign of refusal and resistance, but it is a voice quickly silenced. Even if it expresses the uneasiness of a society, it does little to disturb its slumbers. Without statistics it is little understood, sometimes ignored and unrecognized, at other times fantastically exaggerated, like the English 'spleen' as perceived in eighteenth-century Europe. Adultery, with its attendant risk of vengeance, seemed much more of a threat to the social order, and Edo law prescribed harsh punishments: decapitation, even crucifixion in certain cases. This, of course, refers to an adulterous wife, since in that inegalitarian and asymmetrical society the husband was allowed his freedom, his access to the houses of pleasure, and one or two resident concubines (*mekake, tsukai onna*) – if he could afford it.

At one time, Japanese woman had enjoyed an enviable degree of freedom: the *Tale of Genji* shows that gentle ladies used to enjoy a little amorous intrigue more than any other courtly entertainment. One of the first caprices of Genji, the Radiant Prince, was to fall in love with the youngest wife of his beloved father the emperor, and even make her pregnant with a son, whom the emperor naturally and joyfully believed to be his own, and who was to succeed him. Romance could go a long way in the eleventh century. Whatever they knew, or suspected, the husbands of that day (and social level) were too refined to take umbrage, and had the wit to understand that they, as lovers, would benefit from their ladies' freedom. Even later on, the warriors of Kamakura professed a lofty indifference to the infidelities of their wives.

It was in the Muromachi era that family structures and social customs became tighter, a change partly due to the dominant Chinese cultural influence. In 1420, for the first time, a man was beheaded for carrying on an adulterous affair within the palace precincts. In 1480 a husband was acquitted after killing his wife and her lover. The judgement was codified, and thereafter, men having been licensed to indulge their vanity and cruelty in the name of honour, any wife who loved outside marriage knew that her life was at stake; often they accepted a freely chosen death to escape the indignity of the official punishment. In the great enclosure of the Edo era, wives became *okusama*, the lady of the interior, the housewife. All her commerce with the outside world was strictly controlled by convention, all social intercourse was forbidden except with children and close relatives. Mothers were as closely confined in the home as prostitutes in the houses of pleasure. The first, in this pair of institutions held in balance thanks to the subjection of women, was no less of a victim than the second.

The suicides of shopkeepers and courtesans commemorated by the elegiac Chikamatsu did not directly affect either the ruling class or the security of the home. Therefore it was a long time before any measures were taken against them. Eventually, in 1723, a laconic – and draconian – edict was promulagated, to the satisfaction of panders and scholars alike:

> When a man and a woman have committed suicide for love, their bodies shall be left unburied. If one of them survives, he shall be treated as a murderer. If both survive, they shall be put in the pillory for three days and reduced to the rank of beggars. It is strictly forbidden to write down and circulate, or act out, accounts of such deeds. Offenders will be prosecuted.

This text sedulously avoids using the word *shinju*: the scholars pointed out that the pictograms placed side by side two symbols (heart-interior) which, in the word *chu* (loyalty), were one on top of the other. They could not allow a graphological coincidence to suggest any sort of resemblance between a cardinal virtue and a deplorable practice. *Was* it a coincidence? It was not. The writing showed something which the scholars refused to see. *Shinju* reveals the depth of the heart; it is the loyal, faithful will which gives the heart strength. *Chu* is honour shown in battle, in the service of the warrior; *shinju* is honour in a love-relationship which exhibits the devotion of a woman. It is there that she shows her courage. To love well is no less perilous, perhaps no less magnificent, than to fight well; lovers can prove themselves by suicide, as warriors can be *seppuku*. Virtues do not always dwell where writing would have them dwell. The scholars invented some colourless pedantries – *joshi* (dying for love), *aitai jini* (shared death) – but they never supplanted *shinju*, which was written on all men's hearts by the tearful poetry of sorrow. No decree could reach it there.

Lovers' suicides probably did become less frequent. The Kyoho era had been famous for them; the Gembun era (1736 onwards) was famous rather for kidnappings and elopements. This gave the brothel-keepers yet another weapon against defiant girls: 'Thinking of killing yourself? It's gone out of fashion. In any case don't bungle it, or you'll be a beggar all your life. That's the law!' These beggars (*hinin*, literally 'non-humans') were pariahs, outcasts of society, most of them beggars, viewed with repulsion. The new decree was contemporary with the French *lettres de cachet*, used to help families discipline their more troublesome offspring. The power of the state and the power of the family can help each other out on occasion. When a person eager for life is threatened with loss of liberty, the threat is a serious one. But what punishment will have any effect on people resolved to die? What will shake their sovereign indifference? The 1723 decree aimed at deterring undecided potential suicides, as did the Christian laws on the treatment of suicide, which were so often mitigated by the excuse of madness. Once the irreparable act had been committed, people lacked the horrid courage to add to its cruelty: it was better to hide the whole thing from the authorities, rather than betray a poor corpse. Most of the Yoshiwara courtesans who killed themselves in the eighteenth and nineteenth centuries were buried at Seikanji, even if their lovers had died with them, and were given a gravestone just the same.

The decree was also aimed against the *ezoshi* and the theatre, whose sad stories and lyric embellishments could amplify the effect of real events. Thus to blame public curiosity was to take the symptom for the cause – which was really more obscure, perhaps buried in the depths of economic crisis. After the rapid expansion of the seventeenth century, which culminated in the Genroku era (1688–1703), production and population both stagnated in the hermetically sealed Japan of the Tokugawa. To combat these difficulties, the Bakufu alternated between rigorous austerity and permissive laxity, both equally unsuccessful.

The system had reached its constitutional limits, and the authorities, unable to rethink the structures of the society they were attempting to govern, could deal only with the surface effects. It was easy enough, for example, to accuse *Sonezaki shinju* of demoralizing the shopkeepers of Osaka. In 1705 they confiscated the fortune of the Yodoya family so as to put the bourgeois in their place. In 1706 they devalued the coinage.

Every time that the daimyo and their vassals got too deeply into debt, moratoria were declared and debts arbitrarily written off, at the expense of commercial lenders.

While the European bourgeoisie was beginning to realize its own strength, that of Japan (which was no less enlightened) was being mercilessly despoiled and thoroughly crushed under the heel of the dominant class. Social constraints, humiliation, money worries, hopelessness, lack of opportunity: any of these can drive people to their deaths. Not just drive them but attract or drag them: the ills of civilization provoke romantic escapism and a longing for another world. Two generations later, in the Germany of *Sturm und Drang*, there was a similar wave of suicides, which were blamed on *Werther* by people who failed to understand the contradictions inherent in the difficult birth of capitalism and the modern world.

The threats in the 1723 decree were never strictly put into effect and were soon forgotten. The regime was authoritarian, not totalitarian; anything which was not a direct threat to the social order (and the *shinju* plays took care to avoid this) could be tolerated. Despite official approval of neo-Confucianism, there was no less freedom of thought than in Enlightenment Europe. Christianity, it is true, was still strictly prohibited, but for political rather than ideological reasons, remembering the revolt of Shimabara. The idea that an idea could be dangerous *per se* had still two centuries to wait, for the imperialism which ushered in the Pacific war.

Confucianism had a leaning toward orthodoxy, but it never had the strength, nor even the will, to police social customs, books, or ideas. A few scholars went on grumbling about the decadence of the modern age. Some ten years after the suppression of *shinju*, Miyakoji Bungonojo gave them something to grumble about by inventing a new kind of ballad (*joruri*), a vividly expressive and emotional (and therefore exceedingly 'dangerous') combination of music and declamation: 'Since these *joruri* have been performed', wrote one sage, 'acts of debauchery have hugely increased.'[12] According to him it was a positive 'epidemic of vice', and even 'high-ranking officials' had been induced to commit adultery! This style of lyrical recitation, called *bungobushi*, and its immediate successor the *sonohachibushi*, eagerly took up the *shinju* theme at its most emotional point, the *michiyuki* or journey into death. No legislation had had any effect on the sensibilities of poets and audiences.

Meanwhile, the Kabuki still got its best effects from *seppuku* scenes exalting the pomp and circumstance of glorious war, while taking occasional and successful account of the harlot's progress and her suicide for love. Chikamatsu's profound simplicity, tenderness and compassion were out of date: even in scenes of lovers' deaths, the theatre now preferred the feverish baroque torments which were harbingers of decline, if not yet of fall: as, for example, in Mokaumi's *Izayoi and Seishin* (1859). In a society still sleeping jealously over the threshold of its contradictions, the dream was in danger of becoming a nightmare.[13]

Those on high never persecuted lover's suicides very severely. The epidemic had had the good taste to spare the military class, and so long as it affected only the common people, the state could afford to ignore it. Among the seventeen suicides recounted by Shohoken in *Shinju okagami* ('The Great Mirror of *Shinju*', 1704) there are eight merchants, seven artisans, a peasant – and only one warrior, an unemployed *ronin* to boot. The same proportions occur in Chikamatsu. If amorous soldiers had been falling right, left and centre then something would have been done about it. When a lovesick grenadier killed himself during Napoleon's Italian campaign, the latter immediately had it proclaimed throughout the army that 'a soldier must overcome the pain and melancholy of love, and there is as much true courage in enduring the anguish of the soul as in standing fast under fire from a battery.'[14]

Saikaku, it is true, wrote several stories about samurai committing murder or suicide out of love for a comrade.[15] There never has been a boarding school or college or prison or even regiment entirely free from the disorders of love; and the chaste patience (for five years) counselled by the *Hagakure* sometimes yielded to the assaults of passion. But Saikaku always presents these amorous and suicidal samurai as models of manly virtue: far from threatening the warrior ethic, they are a credit to it, showing that bravery, honour and devotion are all exalted in love situations. Moralists had nothing to fear: a warrior in love is more warlike than ever, like Epamonidas' invincible homosexual battalion. Love can be midwife to virtue: thus, a thirteen-year-old page dies under torture at the hands of his jealous lord rather than reveal his lover's name. The lover kills the tale-bearer (it was not done in Edo to avenge yourself on your lord, however cruel) and goes to disembowel himself on his beloved's tomb. In another story, a boy of fifteen realizes that his lover is his father's murderer. His mother says, 'Avenge us!' The two friends vie with each other in chivalry: 'Kill me!' 'No, take up your sword and we'll fight it out.' The mother is touched and intervenes: 'You are both men of honour. Be lovers again this one night. Justice is for tomorrow.' And at dawn she finds their corpses in the same bed, transfixed by the same sword. This is nothing like the sombre fascination of Chikamatsu's lovers, the dizzying attraction they feel for ruin and the void, their stumbling steps guided with sleepwalker's certainty into the way of deliverance. Saikaku's warriors kill themselves, if anything, in an excess of vitality.

A TRICK

In the society described in these tales, voluntary death was a familiar and oft-mentioned thing; but Saikaku is not particularly happy about it. His characters tend to avoid, dodge or postpone it; or if they face up to it, like Yonosuke when he saves the fair Mikasa, they come off victorious. Of his 'Five Women who Loved Love', only one kills herself: Osen the cooper's wife. Caught by her husband *in flagrante delicto*, she seizes a convenient carpenter's chisel and stabs herself to the heart, while her lover takes to his heels. It is a simple, thoughtless panic reflex, a world away from the heart-rending hesitations and slow crawls towards death found in Chikamatsu.

Twenty years *before* the perfecting of the drama of lovers' suicides, Saikaku already seems to be parodying it, as when he tells us of a cunning pair of lovers who elope after faking an ingenious suicide scene. Osan, wife of an almanach maker of Kyoto, has just seduced and run off with a prudent and rather unromantic young clerk, Moemon. The lovers, hiding in an inn by Lake Biwa, are well aware of their danger. To ensure (by terror if need be) that all houses are nests of virtue, the new shogun, Tsunayoshi, has just increased the already severe penalties for adultery and seduction, which will be all the worse in this case because it was all 'in the family'. Strangers did not generally have access to Japanese houses at that time, but one could not altogether exclude the husband's apprentices, clerks and workmen – only protect his property (which included his wife and daughter) against theft by the severest penalties. Thus Osan and Moemon can hope for no mercy: capture means crucifixion. Lake Biwa stretches before them like a vast, calm sea; Osan thinks that it would be so easy to drown herself in it along with her beloved:

> 'After all, we may find that longer life only brings greater grief', Osan told him. 'Let us throw ourselves into the lake and consecrate our lives to Buddha in the Eternal Land.'
>
> But Moemon, though he valued his life hardly at all, was not so certain as to what would follow after death. 'I think I have hit upon a way out', he said. 'Let us each send letters to the capital, saying that we shall drown ourselves in the lake. We can then steal away from here, go anywhere you please, and pass the rest of our years together.'
>
> Osan was delighted: 'When I left home, it was with that idea in mind. So I brought along five hundred pieces of gold in my suitcase.'
>
> That, indeed, was something with which to start life anew.[16]

They add some artistic verisimilitude by paying two local fishermen to plunge into the lake at the correct moment, so that, under cover of darkness, the illusion of *shinju* will be totally convincing. Night comes, the inn sleeps:

> When Moemon and Osan had prepared themselves properly, they opened the bamboo door of the inn and roused everyone by shouting, 'For reasons known only to ourselves we are about to end our lives!' They then rushed away, and shortly, from the height of a craggy rock, faint voices were hear saying the *nembutsu*, followed by the sound of two bodies striking the water. Everyone wept and raised a great commotion over it.

The lovers could have lived happily ever after in some distant village. But Moemon gets bored: he longs to see the capital again, and spend an evening in the theatre. He is recognized, the husband is alerted and sends out his thugs. The lovers are handed over to the authorities, tried, condemned and crucified. This cruel tale is quite true: the execution took place in 1683, on the twenty-second day of the ninth month. Did Osan on the cross wish she had chosen a gentler death in Lake Biwa? But at least the trick had brought her a few months' happiness. Living takes just as much courage and honour as dying, when you know whom you love and what you want.

Chikamatsu's characters let themselves sink slowly into the ocean of *ukiyo*; a touch of hope would bring them up again, but there is none, and they hear only the voice from the abyss. Tossing over those same deeps, Saikaku's lovers bob about with cork-like insouciance as long as they possibly can. The end will come, and a bitter one, but it is a destiny they accept. Bodies wear out, nature too: behind all happy and unhappy chances the impassive face of necessity is gradually revealed. They do not want to die, but they have to learn death and accept it; it would be madness to hate it. The smiling resignation which informs the closing pages of these voluptuous tales seems quite close to the spirit of our own times. The exploits of the great Western libertines seem strained and unnatural by contrast. Chikamatsu (like Wagner but with wholly different means) hypnotizes us with his lyric skills – until the time comes to wake up. But lovers in love with love are so gay, so simple, so open, that we can only wish to be their friends.

FROM PLEASURE TO DELIVERANCE

Beginning as a high-class courtesan, a lovely and capricious *tayu*, the friend of pleasure, slid year by year down the long hierarchy of the daughters of joy, like a general stripped of his proud insignia and demoted to a mere subaltern with all the dirtiest jobs to do. At sixty-five, with rouge over her wrinkles and artificial hair, squeezed into a borrowed kimono, she might be seen patrolling the darkest riverside walks of Osaka, far from the fairy lanterns. Then, like Villon's *belle heaumi*è*re*, she found remembered beauty the worst horror of life: 'On rainy nights I would ask the lightning, which most people fear, to take pity on me and strike the house and bring it down on me. I no longer wished to live: I had had enough of this miserable world.'

If only hating life was enough to rid you of it! Would the promise of Buddhism be enough to break the final bond? One evening she went to Daiun-ji, one of the Tendai temples in Kyoto, and suddenly she felt an impulse towards deliverance, like ascetics of older times who took to the water in a burst of Amidist enthusiasm:

> By then I had come to the foot of the moutain where is the source of the river Narutaki. Nothing now lay between me and the mountain of Supreme Enlightenment, and my only desire was to unmoor the boat of Buddhist law, in which we cross the sea of passion, and gain the Further Bank to be instructed in the Way. I began to run at full tilt to throw myself into the lake of Hirosawa which was nearby. At that moment I was prevented by an old friend. He built for me this hut with its bamboo roof; he besought me to die at the hour fixed by destiny and exhorted me, now that I was leaving the false life I had led up till then, to return to fundamental consciousness and enter into the Way of the Buddha. Full of fervour, I am wholly absorbed, morning, noon and night, in repetition of the *nembutsu*.

This old friend is Saikaku himself, trying to save her from drowning – a crude solution. 'You seek salvation by violence', he seems to be saying, like a Zen master, 'but where will you find it, if not in this life? For there is no other. It is not enough to die, you must die without hatred, and with a smile. You can see that death is not a serious thing; the death of a being is nothing; how can you fear the nothingness which is not? Cease this resentment against time; it has but taken back what it once gave. To own nothing: that is perfect freedom. From this hermitage you can look back with a smile over past tribulations: think of them, the better to bid them farewell. And be a nun, if that is what you want.'

Yes: under the Confucian veneer of Edo, the two deeper currents of Japanese feeling flowed on side by side: Zen and Amidism, laughter and tears, no longer adversaries but allies in this task of arousing human awareness to the endless, empty innocence of uncreated becoming.

As for Yonosuke, once the lover of the valiant Mikasa, he has become hard of hearing, walks with a stick, has a wrinkled face. How has it come about? He cannot tell. And all the lovely ladies he once knew are white-haired now: what a curious thing! It is time to build a ship, which he names *Good Pleasure* (*Yoshiiro-maru*). The inside is lined with love-letters, the ropes are spun of ladies' hair once given as love-tokens, and here he is, ready to sail. He invites six of his oldest friends: 'Perhaps we shall never return! So let us drink to our departure. At long last we have lost our taste for pleasure. I shall take you to the Island of Women, and you shall see!' And with this jest they weigh anchor, and on a fine day in the tenth month, the *Good Pleasure* sails away over the tranquil ocean – towards the horizon whence no traveller returns. A parody, then, of the prayerful embarkations of pilgrims from the shores of Kumano in search of salvation on the distant dream-island of Fudaraku, home of Kannon and the compassionate Buddhas. But the parody is perhaps more moving than the grave and holy departures which inspired it. For Yonosuke has no illusions, even now when they might be sweet. He has the courage to joke at a moment when joking is a good deal harder than prayer. He has the dignity neither to regret nor to despise pleasure, now that pleasures past count for nothing and even the appetite for them is gone for ever. To the last he is sincere and true to himself and to life – his life. Smiling, he drinks to his coming death, and advances calmly to meet it.

11

The Tradition of Sacrifice

Many wonderful things have come to a natural end, and vanished by their own choice from the stage of history. It is the final proof of their greatness: they are not defeated, but answer the call of destiny. No guillotine for the warlike nobility of Japan: they faced up to the foreign threat with a revolution whose price was their own disappearance. It was only a national revolution they attempted, a rousing of their country's strength, but it caused the whole social edifice to totter; and those who, like Saigo Takamori, went against the upheaval were swiftly crushed beneath it. Thus the warrior class had to conquer itself and take self-sacrifice to the point of death; but if Buddhism is right, every death is but a change.

From 1868 onwards the privileges of the samurai were abolished one after the other by imperial decree. Many entered the civil service of the new state; many joined the army, giving it the officer class it so much needed. Others went into industry and learned the ways of peace; some even shook off their fine disdain for money and turned shopkeeper. They mixed like a leaven with the rest of the social body. Little by little they lost their exterior distinctiveness, but their inner qualities remained. They were not so much destroyed as disseminated. Their spirit spread but remained active; their virtues of honour, loyalty, devotion, discipline and sacrifice were held up as an official example: the state, through its schools and armies, undertook to inculcate them in all its subjects. The children of Japan, as pupils and (later) conscripts, were all called upon to be samurai in spirit, if not by birth.

Bushido, no longer the code of a vanished caste, became part of the national creed. In *Bushido* (1895), Nitobe's attempt to explain his country's soul to Western readers, he writes:

> We have no religion comparable to Christianity, but the morality of our former warriors is enough. A people can live without believing in the other world, but not without belief in something: it must at least have faith in itself if it is to continue to exist. And since faith is shown in sacrifice, must we not teach our children to die well, if we are to survive?

He who fears death dies defeated, he who defies it lives a conqueror: this paradox had often been heard on the battlefield. In the great transformation of the Meiji era there was one fixed point, the tradition of sacrifice, which continued not so much in homage to the past as in view of future trials. Never had the secrets of invincibility seemed more vital, in this world open to the greed of any power equipped with steam and gunpowder. The rulers of the new Japan knew that other peoples might be richer, better armed: caution was needed. But the battle always goes to those who know best how to die, so boldness too was needed. 'In the struggle between nations our long acquaintance with voluntary death will be our trump card.' If the warrior class vanished it was to make room for a new, rejuvenated militarism which carried on its essential traditions by learning to kill and die for the state.

THE RISE OF NATIONALISM

It is probably true to say that no modern revolution, from 1789 to 1917, has done other than reinforce the power of the state, whatever its original intention. The great changes of the Meiji era were no exception to this rule. The new imperial state, which for several decades was governed by an oligarchy of about twenty wise heads from the southern clans such as Choshu and Satsuma, soon began to wield a power which even the Tokugawa, in their wildest dreams of omnipotence, could not have imagined. After more than 500 years the cause of the Restoration, for which Kusunoki Masashige had laid down his life in 1336, had finally triumphed. All allegiance, which had once been dispersed among some three hundred local feudal lords, was suddenly transferred to the emperor (*Tenno*, the Celestial Sovereign) and concentrated on that one single source of national destiny.

With the Bakufu gone and the clans wiped out, the emperorship, which for eight centuries had been only intermittently important, marginal and most often ornamental, suddenly took on a supreme and unique value. It was the unmoved mover, the incarnation of the (supposedly) absolute unity of the state and the nation; the silent sovereign became the final cause of every political act – and in that society any act with any moral value had some civic virtue: people studied, travelled, looked after themselves so that the emperor's subjects should be well educated, enlightened and healthy. Nothing was done which was not meant to be useful. Death, even without hope of another life, no longer seemed absurd if it could be the final homage of a dedicated life.[1]

It did seem that this remorselessly proclaimed Meiji ideology was infinitely more efficacious than Tokugawa repression; here was the longed-for solution to every dispute. If (thought the oligarchs) every Japanese could be persuaded to serve the emperor with all his might, the whole nation would be devoted to the state. There would still be foreign wars, but internal conflict would vanish in a single-minded devotion to the nation on which every energy would be focused. The indoctrination was performed chiefly by two of the best-disciplined state organs, the schools and the army, which practised the recitation of the Imperial Rescripts and all sorts of patriotic ceremonial. In families the same rules were endlessly repeated, if not out of civic zeal then in prudent conformity. And in the press, whatever the current conviction the same underlying ideas remained. But even the most tightly knit ideology cannot still all the eddies of social life.

In the Japan of Meiji, of Taisho and of Showa, the chanting of slogans of unanimity had to vie with the clash of interests and the machinations of rivalry. Sometimes the whole country spoke with one voice, sometimes opponents clashed implacably. Opponents and rebels did not disappear, but when they revolted it was in the name of the *Tenno*, to rescue his virtuous self from the evil counsellors who were obscuring his glory. Men slaughtered one another in his service. The Christian God, for all his omnipotence, never succeeded in halting strife in the West, so how could devotion to the emperor have put an end to dissension in Japanese society? They exalted him, worshipped him as a god, made sacrifices to him, but it made no difference. The more his transcendence was affirmed, the more it served as a pretext to attack a state which allegedly served him ill, and ministers who had betrayed him.

In 1935, for example, some army officers bent on sedition suddenly discovered *lèse-majesté* in the apparently anodyne theories of a Professor Minobe who (twenty-five years earlier) had defined the emperor as the supreme organ of state. Their indignation was carefully calculated to cover specific objectives in a cloak of deep respect. Before taking the ship by storm they would politely remove the emperor – in a heavenward direction. If it was acknowledged that the state must serve him and could therefore fail in that duty, revolt became a virtue. Those who proclaimed that the sovereign was above all institutions and all politicians considered they had the right to violate the former and assassinate the latter. Within a generation, the imperial ideology which the Meiji oligarchs had fostered (because it bolstered their authority) was being used to justify extremist conspiracies and stir up discord, though not a word of its official expression had been changed. The state claimed obedience on the same grounds as the rebels trumpeted insurrection. Perhaps the Japanese are right to be distrustful of what people say, or even what they think.

But the official doctrine still had a long road to travel, protecting the state, safeguarding peace at home, rousing energies, fostering devotion. As a bible it rather lacked coherence, for it came from disparate sources. Anyone from Bismarck to Confucius could lend a hand to the ancestral mythology, provided he exalted civic devotion to the point of sacrifice. The oligarchy saw liberal and democratic influences from Britain and France as a threat to the state – i.e. to their own power – and leaned rather to the victorious authoritarianism of Prussia, with its doctrine of force and decisive action. But they were by no means cynical about it; their Confucian background reminded them that politics is the art of ruling virtuously and wisely. In fact the Meiji state answered much better than the Tokugawa state to the prescripts of Confucianism, with the enlightened paternalism of its centralized authority, with entry to the schools and the army open to the most talented irrespective of hereditary privilege, and with a bureaucracy more diligent, more impartial than ever before.[2]

FROM THE BIRTH OF THE SUN...

Japanese absolutism was not content with secular doctrines of the state: never would the people be content with the virtue of force or the force of virtue. Civic virtue was underpinned by legend, the immemorial antiquity of the Japanese nation was brandished as a promise for the future. It was exalted in religious terms, vibrant, sometimes savage, and curiously anachronistic. While most modern states were discovering that they could strengthen their grip by throwing off religious convictions and the divine right of rulers, Japan alone clung determinedly, until the mid-twentieth century, to a solar mythology of the imperial dynasty whence it drew its most active principles of chauvinism. In science they could accept the most methodical doubt, the most rigorous verification, while at the same time accepting a national life based on simple, cut-and-dried ideas and fabulous legends. And (supreme irony) the throne was eventually occupied by a marine biologist who of all people was the least likely to be the dupe of his own divinity.

Looking to the future, then, they sought counsel in the ancient chronicles of divine genealogy. Tossed on the sea of time they clung to the eternity of a dynasty supposed to have remained unbroken since the birth of the sun – refusing to see that if it had so endured, it was thanks to its total impotence. The vast majority of people accepted this solar mythology, and it shaped the language of their guiding convictions. There were other beliefs based on other assumptions, liberal, democratic or socialist, but they were always marginal: intellectual speculation, sometimes deemed officially dangerous, sometimes denounced in awkward moments by chauvinist watchdogs, sometimes proscribed and hounded by the police. But how to reconcile the national belief with the scientific freedom of thought required for the modernization demanded by the period's most popular slogan, *fukoku kyohei*, 'Prosperous country, powerful army'?

Mori Arinori, Minister for Education from 1884 to 1889, made a clear distinction: in primary and secondary schools it was all discipline and orthodoxy, but in the universities there was complete freedom to learn and judge for oneself. Intellectuals were free to disbelieve in the ruling mythology so long as they did not say so, but they were not to undermine the salutary illusions which sent soldiers willingly to their deaths. Mori himself, murdered by a fanatic because he had lifted the veil of the temple of Ise with his stick, was an apt illustration of the dangers of irreverence. Thus the clearest eyes were hidden in night and silence. For the sake of national unanimity they subjected themselves to a self-censorship which would have seemed intolerable under the Tokugawa. The wordless nihilism of the intellectual, though it drive him to despair or even suicide, was as nothing compared with the clamour of imperial belief considered indispensable to the country's salvation. A few ended up by condemning themselves for not believing any of the right things, and killed themselves to expiate their resulting impotence. They were sacrifices to the national dream, leaving the people free to indulge the grandiose visions which attended their slumbers.[3]

For almost a century, the imperial creed supplied sufficient reasons for living and dying, and furnished the sacrificial altar on which generation after generation gave proof of its devotion. The warlike discipline which had once belonged to the clans now reached a wider public: Japan was about to re-enter the history of the world. Without giving any approval to the nationalist excesses which enslaved and misled a nation, we can feel a mixture of pity and admiration for the purest martyrs to that faith – as to any other. Religions, it seems, must be redeemed by the beauty and grandeur which they inspire at such a terrible price. Moreover, if we must find an excuse, we can say that the strength of feeling in the beginning was no more than the danger demanded: foreign pressure did not relax until after the victory over Russia (1905), and it was not until 1911 that Japan, freed from all the consequences of unfair treaties, was again in full control of her customs barriers. The great Western war of 1914-18 might have calmed her fears, but by then it was too late to moderate the imperial doctrine: having inspired the resistance, it now served the cause of expansionism. Korea had just been annexed (1910). The imperial doctrine (*Tenno shugi*) was perfectly adapted to the imperialist ambitions which modern states unfailingly exhibit according to their means. After unifying the Archipelago, could they not go on to Korea, then Manchuria, Mongolia, even China? This ambition was summed up in the slogan *hakko ichiu*: over all directions, one sky.

THE END OF A CASTE

The Meiji oligarchy probably felt no less inclined to expansionism than some of the Showa ministers and generals fity or sixty years later, but they were wise enough to hold back, if not to give up the idea. As far back as 1873, Saigo Takamori suggested an invasion of Korea to give the samurai something to do, resuming an unsuccessful project by Hideyoshi in 1592. But he was disowned by his more cautious colleagues and forced to quit the government. If Japan had channelled her energies into foreign conquest, she would have been spared the revolts of the samurai which devastated the south from 1873 to 1878. The caste knew it was dying and its death-throes had to be felt somehow. The peasant uprisings (*hyakusho ikki*), already frequent under the Tokugawa, had not ceased either: there were 186 in the first ten years of the new regime. Imperial taxes were no less burdensome than feudal dues; the accumulation of capital for the nascent industries had to be at somebody's expense.

The old warrior and peasant society was falling apart, but no cause could ever have united two classes which had been enemies for so long. The imperial ideology subdued resistance, and the government was actively fostering the changes in society. To relieve the imperial finances, the hereditary pensions paid to noble warrior-families had been forcibly converted into state bonds, soon to be eaten away by inflation. They were being deprived of their ways of dressing and wearing their hair; they no longer had the sole right to a patronymic; even their penal system, with *tsumebara* the jewel in its crown, was on the way out. In February 1874, 5,000 samurai, angry at the failure to invade Korea, staged an uprising in northern Kyushu, but were quickly crushed. The government flew in the face of tradition and beheaded the leader of the revolt, Eto Shimpei, disregarding his right to self-immolation.

The conscript army and imperial police were by then equal to the task of maintaining public order, but to complete the victory of the state they had to be given a monopoly of arms. A law of 1682 obliged the samurai to wear two swords in public, the 4-foot-long *katana* and the 18-inch *wakizashi*. The new state abolished this obligation in 1871 with a view to weakening the warrior class. The next step was to ban it: on 22 March 1876 a decree was issued reserving the sword to serving police and army officers. Japan's close on 3,000,000 samurai, already half-merged with the rest of society, made no protest.

But there was still life in the samurai of the south, where they had been numerous since the Mongol invasions, often desperately poor but all the prouder and more intransigent for that. In Japan as a whole less than one in ten families belonged to this class, but in Satsuma they formed more than a third of the population – two-thirds in the town of Kagoshima, where the ex-cabinet minister Saigo Takamori had just founded a school for them. There, following a philosophy based on the Confucian activism of Wang Yang-Ming, they practised the only necessary arts, fighting and farming, perpetuating a society of valorous warriors and industrious peasants in the teeth of a changing future. The southern samurai had beaten the Tokugawa, whom they accused of collaboration with foreigners; nine years later they realized they were the first victims of their own victory, for their chieftains, having fought their way into government, were speeding up the modernization of Japan, transforming its social structure by decree and abolishing its most venerable traditions. Never did the irony of history bite so cruelly. Why resist foreigners if it meant you had to become like them? Death they could accept, but not to renounce all that they were and yet remain alive. Armed invasion seemed less of a threat to them than corrupting innovation. It was not only the land, but the very spirit of the nation (*Yamato damashii*), the spirit of the warrior (*bushi no tamashii*) which was being imperilled by the government's own act.

Their class interests and political opposition were all expressed in the moral language of purity versus degradation. Everything seemed simple to this Manicheistic view, sprung of Shinto's peculiar horror of pollution and the old habit of measuring power by the Confucian rule of virtue: it was a spark to stubble. In the town of Kumamoto, in central Kyushu, angry Samurai had founded the 'League of the Divine Wind' (*Shimpuren*), *shimpu* being the Chinese pronunciation of two characters which can also be read as *kamikaze*. In 1281 the Gods of Japan had sent a tempest to disperse a Mongol armada; surely, in the present peril, they would not abandon resolute men, risking their lives to preserve the pure spirit of the nation. These zealots carried a white fan to protect themselves against overhead telegraph wires, and always carried a packet of salt to purify themselves if their eyes happened to light on one of those heinous (and, alas, ever commoner) Western innovations, trousers, jackets and hats.

The banning of the sword was the last straw. But what should they do? Should they all follow the example of the patriot from Satsuma, Yokoyama Yasutake? In the third year of Meiji he had disembowelled himself in Tokyo, before the building in which the new rulers of Japan were meeting, having first sent them a ten-point missive accusing them of confusing good and evil, forgetting their duties and wallowing in luxury. He might as well have waved his sword in the air for all the result his death-of-protest (*kanshi*) had had; admirable it was, but useless. So the League of the Divine Wind decided on a less innocent method which would shed more than their own blood. They would be heard, even if it meant killing others besides themselves. But their action, though more aggressive, was no less suicidal than that of the austere Yokoyama. They despised gunpowder as an impure Western innovation, and rejected all weapons save the sword. Killing at a distance did not fit their notions of courage. They relied on their trusty swords and on the gods – and on the advantage of surprise, which had always been part of the Japanese art of war.

One night, 200 of them climbed the ramparts of the castle at Kumamoto, slew the sentinels, rushed upon the sleeping garrison, and wrought great slaughter. But the soldiers of the imperial army were ten to one, and vastly better armed. The rebels fell to a hail of bullets. Those who were not killed that night fled at dawn, and in the next few hours most of them died by *seppuku*. This anachronistic, desperate little local incident found its Homer in Mishima Yukio. In *Runaway Horses*, second of the tetralogy of novels which was his last work, he gives a detailed description of the events, and pays fascinated and meticulous attention to their suicidal conclusion:[4]

> The comrades who had retired to Mount Kimpo did not amount to a third of what they had been when they took up arms. Others had died in the fighting, or, pursued by the regular troops as they withdrew to attend to their wounds, had heroically killed themselves.
>
> Aikyo Masamoto, one of the oldest among them, had retreated as far as the pass of Mikuni, but, closely followed by three policemen, he had suddenly sat down at the roadside, disembowelled himself, and died. He was then in his fifty-fourth year. Matsum to Saburo, aged twenty-three, and Kasuga Suehiko, twenty-two, had returned home and killed themselves there. Arao Tatenao, who was in his twenty-second year, had returned home and apologized to his mother for the grief he would cause her in leaving this life before her. He informed her of his desire to kill himself, on which, to his surprise, she warmly congratulated him. At this

he wept for joy. He went to the tomb of his father, and there nobly disembowelled himself.

Tsuruda Goichiro came down from Mount Kimpo with his seven young protégés; he conducted every one of them home, then returned to his own house, where he began the preparations for suicide. He served sake and the accompanying dishes, drank the parting cup with his wife Hideko, composed a last poem, and told her that, since she must care for Tanao, their only son, after his death, she must not be downhearted. It was already night of the second day after the uprising. Tsuruda also had two daughters, aged thirteen and nine, who had gone to bed. His wife wanted to arouse them so that they could bid farewell to their father, but he restrained her: 'No! Don't waken them!' Then he bared his body to the waist, disembowelled himself, and pierced his throat with the blade. Just as he withdrew the sword and collapsed, his elder daughter, who had chanced to awaken, came in. At the sight she burst into sobs.

The next day, at dawn, came the news that their only son Tanao had also disembowelled himself. Thus the news of his death reached Hideko the day after her husband had left her, telling her to set all her hopes upon the child!

After the conspirators were scattered at Chikozu, Tanao, with Ito Masura and Suge Buishiro, had gone to the great sanctuary of Shingai. There he had left them to go to the village of Kengun, for he had long intended to take refuge in Choshu. At Kengun he found his uncle Tateyama, of whom he sought assistance. But he learned that his father Goichiro had already passed by that afternoon, had entrusted his effects to his brother, and had left him after informing him of his decision. Doubtless his father had already killed himself. At this news, Tanao lost all desire to flee to Choshu.

With his uncle's permission, he spread a new mat under a great tree in the part of the garden nearest the house. Turning to the east, he bowed deeply three times towards the distant imperial palace; he bowed also towards the house of his parents, which was nearer. Then he seized his short sword and disembowelled himself. The news was at once carried to the house of Tsuruda.

FOR THE SOVEREIGN, AGAINST THE STATE

As we read of the death of these good fathers, good husbands and good sons, we forget that they are murderers. They themselves have forgotten it in all-expiating, all-effacing *seppuku*. Sudden brutal attack sanctioned by the duty of voluntary death had long ago been the method of the forty-seven *ronin* of the *Chushingura*. But they had died martyrs to their feudal allegiance, in the narrow cause of clan vengeance. Now the spur to action was a universal principle: the spirit of Yamato, above all reasons of state, the faith in their nation which supplied the rebels with a more demanding cause than mere obedience to the powers that be. Aggression can claim the noblest motives, but it must be paid for, and they knew it. The League of Kumamoto was a league of rebels who had transgressed the law, but voluntary death provided them with instant redemption. That was the law above all laws, the inscrutable nemesis written in all heats. Their rebellion, be it success or failure, would seem pure (if not just) because they had consented to die for it, and that showed that they had had nothing to gain. In their last moments they could look towards their sovereign, although they had just been slaughtering his garrison.[5]

Revolt was no less a sacred duty than obedience, so long as it was as prompt to self-sacrifice. The law itself required all people to face death if the state (in the name of the emperor) demanded it: the 1882 Imperial Rescript to the army and navy made this plain, and a few years later, in 1890, the Rescript on Education advised schoolchildren of their precocious responsibility: 'If need be, you must courageously offer your life to the state.' No education was of use to the country which did not include training in death. But there was another, silent law alongside the actual one, which paralleled and completed it: when the state is corrupt, you must sacrifice yourself for the sovereign. It is a duty of protest, resistance, contestation, insurrection – more bitter and more sacred than the other, certainly more arduous, more perilous and more adventurous.

In the last decades of the nineteenth century, the cause of the emperor did a great deal to stimulate devotion to authority – but the same cause had inspired the earlier fight against absolutism and the destruction of the Bakufu. European thought since Boulainvilliers and Locke had acknowledged and justified the right of reasoned resistance. The Japanese came to a not dissmiliar conclusion, for what society can live without some space for dissidence? But they used a language of self-sacrifice, with overtones of violence. For ten years, from 1858 to 1868, this duty of resistance had inspired the armed struggle of the samurai and *ronin* against the Tokugawa; from 1868 to 1878, the same principles were used to attack the Meiji state. A period of calm followed, after which the same spirit of resistance inspied a series of terrorist acts whose methods would have been familiar enough to Western nihilists, revolutionary socialists, anarchists or fascists in opposition, minus the ever more flamboyant self-sacrificial style. This dark side of the imperial ideology, imbued with religious feeling, resolutely disdainful of all reasons of state and all bureaucratic legalism, condensed into a few sharp and simple formulas.

The long Western tradition, from Boulainvilliers to Kropotkin, branched out into a diversity of revolutionary theories which divided their adherents even beyond death, irreconcilable doctrines each heretical in the others' eyes. In Japan, the struggles, the murderous attacks and the repression were all equally remorseless – but a dead enemy, especially one dead by his own hand, gave a piercingly convincing proof of his sincerity. Forgiveness could always be bought at such a price, for loyalists and rebels alike sacrificed themselves for the good of the empire. With differing means and manpower, but the same goal, they all died for the same cause which had driven them to kill, and death reunited them in the same belief.

DEATH-AGONIES

It must be said that the League of the Divine Wind was ten years too late. The Restoration was a *fait accompli*, and their uprising was merely one of the death-throes of their caste. It was less an act with a definite purpose, than a symptom, or at best a gesture. They sought to arouse the country's conscience, hoping that their sacrifice would be a clarion call; but perhaps what they really wanted was to prolong the apathy of a closed society, a self-centred caste sitting sulkily on the roadside of history. They killed others and themselves in a kind of dream, but their sleepwalking, class-conscious rage could not prevent the final transition. The Meiji state would follow, to the bitter end, along the hard path of duty on which it had set its foot. The necessity of which it had become the more or less willing agent was no less universal than the national soul invoked by the chauvinistic rebels. The time was come to acknowledge a long-rejected truth: that other things beside Japan existed. The stage of world history was set.

But the insurgents could not possibly be condemned, because they had failed. The defeated are not held guilty in Japan. The warriors themselves set no great store by victory, for they had no delusions of obtaining it; nor were they shamed by defeat. We should not have concurred with their victory. If they had even outlived the struggle, they would have failed to offer the perfect symbol of a noble end which best befitted their caste. Had they originally turned away from death and yielded to the desire to live on? No: what they would not accept was a death they had not themselves chosen and conducted. Their failure, assumed in their voluntary death, makes them part of our nostalgia for things past.

The mere fact of their existence revealed, marked down and wrote into history one of the uttermost possibilities of human nature. For history is not just the story of successful stratagems and the rightness of might. Their *seppuku*, on the pinnacle of their unique tradition, totally transcended their own chauvinism, and every man can see himself in their decision, for sacrifice is always moving and we do not need to be

Japanese to understand and admire the extreme demands it made on those willing victims. It is an image which calls to us across the cultural divide. They did not die for us, as did the saints and the prophets (or so we are told); but they did die before us, and an ethic of the will is more salutary than a promise of salvation, especially now when the desire to live is pressed upon us, endlessly, as the only good. They stand before us in the frozen perfection of that final gesture:

> Shimada Kataro was in his eighteenth year. Scarcely had he returned home than he was exhorted to disguise himself as a monk and flee. But he refused. Determined to kill himself, he drank the cup of parting; Then he summoned Uchishiba Juzo, a teacher of jodo, to teach him the technique of *seppuku*.
> When the young man had disembowelled himself, he set the point of his short sword to his throat and asked, 'Master, is this the right place?' When Uchishiba answered, 'It is', he drove in the blade with a swift and graceful gesture.

The aesthetic appreciation seems rather tasteless when descibing the mutilation of a young body, but emotion must be set in tranquillity and crowned by grace: the very horror assures us of a tragic redemption. Then, beyond any political aim, sacrifice can reach its true goal of emotional and moral perfection; and beauty can answer a call to sacrifice which does not destroy it but raises it to a blinding intensity. It is that, and not the fleeting arguments of reality, which remains as a poem graven in the memory of men.

SAIGO THE GREAT

The real test was yet to come. As long as Saigo endured, the wrath of the samurai kept its one last hope. Saigo had no illusions: he knew, none better, the power of the conscript army he had helped to create. He inveighed against his former colleagues in government, but, despite the activist principles he had borrowed from Wang Yang-Ming, he might never have entered the fight if his disciples, on fire to apply his precepts, had not taken sincerity to the point of falling for a deliberate provocation. Saigo heard of the first shots and cursed the naïvety of his supporters, reproaching them bitterly. Then he accepted his destiny: seeing defeat and death approach, he went honourably to meet them. William the Silent said that you could venture without need of hope: perhaps action without hope has a sort of unalterable purity, a mirror to reveal the lucidity of our Sisyphean condition. Courage is greatest when it knowingly serves a lost cause. Then destiny unfolds as a ritual, and sacrifice, though bloody, is innocent because it is consciously vain.

From February to September 1877, then, there was a veritable civil war in which thousands were killed. The imperial army, under the generalship of Yamagata, was 60,000 strong, eight out of ten of them young peasants, who made doughty fighters. The samurai flocked to Saigo's banner, knowing well that it was their last battle; they numbered some 25,000. But the warlike virtues allegedly conferred on them by birth were no compensation for inferior arms and manpower. In vain did Saigo justify his rebellion by the sacred duty of saving the emperor from his evil counsellors.

Ten years earlier the same argument had brought down the Bakufu, but it could scarcely have the same impact now that the restored and rejuvenated state had so evidently regained its vigour. It was no longer a struggle to save a nation, only a caste. It was a splendid last stand by a valiant, austere and virtuous nobility, but (unlike their French counterparts in the revolutionary Vendée) they had no support from their former subjects: the peasantry could admire its old masters without wishing them back. The new state triumphed, and in the last assault, Saigo, though wounded by a bullet, found the strength to honour tradition by ending himself by *seppuku* after a deep bow towards the imperial palace. His servant Beppu Shinsuke beheaded him, and the head was buried in a secret place. But the imperial troops dutifully discovered it, washed it in spring water and brought it to General Yamagata, who raised it in both hands and bowed, murmuring, 'Ah, what serenity is printed now on that noble countenance!'

Saigo's suicide began his redemption, and already the enemy was paying him homage. Enemy? Better to say 'adversary'. For these mortal struggles bore no hatred, no contempt. Both sides had the same national faith, the same values, the same tradition. The dead of both sides, the loyal and the insurgent, could sleep side by side, united by the same sacrifice. It was a civilization too noble to wish its enemies in hell, or even forgotten. In 1891 Saigo was officially rehabilitated, and the emperor conferred on him the dignity of Third Rank in the court hierarchy. A popular cult grew up in his memory and statues were raised to him. Good and evil are not, after all, decided by battle. The men of Meiji were admirers of Bismarck, but they remained uncorrupted by the nihilism of success. Secure in their tradition, they had no need to subject everything to the judgement of force.

We have seen other ways of writing history since. Stalin was no further divorced from Trotsky than Yamagata from Saigo, but with what savagery did he pursue his enemy beyond death, seeking to blot him out of human memory! Vishinsky had the same faith, the same principles as

Bukharin, but the victors were not content with the loser's life, they demanded his honour, made him falsely accuse himself of imaginary treasons and finally cast him into the rubbish-pit of history, his sacrifice eternally unknown. In comparison we can scarcely hold a tradition to be cruel which demands only the sacrifice of a life, and impartially honours every man's devotion.[6]

VIOLENCE AND POLITICS

So ended twenty turbulent years which saw the birth of a new society. The Meiji state had succeeded in imbuing its conscripts with the courage and self-sacrifice which had once been the prerogative of the ruling class. But the future was to profit still more from the wisdom of those former Samurai who, like Itagaki, Fukuzawa and Okuma, tried to transcend the sacrificial values of their early training. Was Japan condemned to veer eternally between the state absolutism incarnate in Yamagata and the rebellious sacrifice of Eto Shimpei and Saigo? Was blind violence the only answer to the blind obedience of army and police? Sacrifice which is merely an overflow of excess energy is a sure way to social stagnation. That energy had to be contained, used in the cause of progress, given a goal.

Itagaki, like Saigo and Eto Shimpei, was in favour of invading Korea, and like them he was forced out of the government in 1873. But instead of setting himself up in dualistic rivalry with his former colleagues, he chose a dialectical solution, a third way. The same year as Eto Shimpei was directing the Saga insurrection, Itagaki founded a mutual aid society, *Risshisha*, for the dispossessed samurai of the former Tosa domain. Unlike Saigo, he renounced the language of outraged virtue and turned away from class insurrection: his aim was to put a gradual brake on absolutism by arousing the Japanese people to its new right of freedom. Liberty without law is nothing, and his great aim was soon to lead to the plan for a constitution. In 1880 Itagaki founded the Freedom Party, *Jiyuto*, the first time a Japanese party had been more than a gathering of interests cemented by personal allegiance. Politics could be conducted according to a set of rules, rather than as factional warfare for the right to occupy the high offices of state. In the light of specific laws a society can learn to know itself, and so transform itself in freedom. When, in 1880, it was Okuma's turn to leave the cabinet, he followed not Saigo's example but Itagaki's: he founded a party and engaged in dialogue with his adversaries.

Such moderation took courage. Itagaki and Okuma, like many others, fell victim to the dagger and the bomb. Devotion to the emperor, even where it fell short of religious fervour, abolished all attempts to delimit a sphere of political action. Not only could it tighten the grip of absolutism or justify insurrection, it could begin by raising up a crowd of petty fanatics eager to avenge any imagined crime of *lèse-majesté*. Most were ready to sacrifice themselves at need, and all were quick to immolate the impious. Respect for the sacred sources of national life became a principle of terror. Thus political institutions were ncessary not just to limit the arbitrary power of the state and bring conflict within recognizable rules, but also to disarm, if possible, this kind of martyr.

The emperor was the first to realize that the transcendence of his sovereignty would soon menace the order it embodied if it became a licence to kill. The 1889 constitution aimed to moderate such passions. The intoxication of sacrifice had served its turn in the struggle for the Restoration; now it must bow to law. Not an easy task in a society which had accepted voluntary death as an excuse for any kind of aggression and wild enterprise, and had long seemed to forgive anything which people were ready to die for. 'Heads I win, tails I kill myself' was not exactly a responsible attitude. Rather it was an evasion which left silence as the only justification for one's acts. Neither instutution nor repression was enough, in the long run, to dissuade fanatics. Newspapers and schools had to join in the long task of overcoming and out-arguing the apathy and impatience which could lead a man to that last desperate throw; the whole people had to be invited to share not only in emotions but also in deciding the fate of the nation. This admirably lucid endeavour deserved a better fate. The Japanese public went on applauding any violent and theatrical gesture, and listened with nervous appreciation to bloodthirsty discourse – usually thirsty for the blood of other people.

It was a time of struggle, and above all of harsh apprenticeship, as the Japanese responded with admirable courage to the challenge of the West. It was the time of their first industrial revolution. The state led the way in the accumulation of capital, founding industries which it sold off to leading consortia as soon as it saw that private management would be more flexible and less onerous. The links between government, political parties and industrial groups became ever closer and more entangled.

Prosperity was an essential doctrine of the national creed, the occupation of a whole new ruling class which included leading civil servants, business managers and politicians. They did get richer; but the enriching of the rich has never been much consolation to the poor, and the poverty of the countryside was as bad as ever. This class of racketeers and (at times) corrupt *arrivistes* did not seem worthy of its newly acquired power. The army lent its strength to the acquisition of national wealth (*fukoku kyohei*), but without forming the military and industrial complex so characteristic of modern Western society: the austere officers and poor peasants of that army, so proud of its direct allegiance to the emperor, looked with disdain on the luxury of the new ruling class, unaware that of all luxuries war is the most ruinous. The army was not interested in party speeches: the Imperial Rescript of 1882 had warned them against engaging in any political activity. But already it was not quite deaf to certain national associations, for the salvation of the empire was not 'politics'.

At the same time as Itagaki and Okuma were thinking up their open-ended parties, dedicated to liberty and progress, a certain samurai of Fukuoka named Hiraoka Kotaro, who had fought alongside the rebels of Satsuma, was seeking his sole inspiration in the imperial (and imperialist) principle. In 1881 he founded the Society of the Dark Ocean (*Genyosha*) to revive Saigo's Korean dream and encourage expansionism. Twenty years later, the Association of the Black Dragon (*Kokuryukai*) was looking towards Manchuria and Siberia, giving violent and mysterious expression to the most audacious concepts of Japanese chauvinism.

WAR: THE AGONY AND THE ECSTASY

However, until the Showa era the army remained utterly loyal, not only to the imperial creed (that goes without saying), but also to the government. It was content to serve the state, with no thought yet of using or dominating it. Its grandeur was founded not in power, nor even in victory, but in sacrifice. The army guarded the state, but who would guard the guardians? Tradition, was the answer. The Imperial Rescript of 1882, which was aimed at young recruits and had Yamagata behind it, summed up the essentials of *bushido*. Its ancient maxims were solemnly inculcated into the Japanese soldier, even while industry was busily transforming the whole art of war. But the weapon was nothing without the hand, nor the hand without the heart.

This was an idealism which saw the material world purely as a stage on which human wills, stronger or weaker, purer or less pure, were to act out their destiny. And this, for the next generation, was the source of a blind adventurism which vented itself in suicidal audacity. The career of arms, they said, depended on the exercise of the will. The will to win? Indeed yes, but the will to win is doused by the first setback, and they needed to go beyond victory towards the acceptance of death, the asceticism of a heart which cared nothing for results and viewed its own death with detachment. A will to will which merges into renunciation, for the pure will wants nothing for itself. 'Remember that duty is heavier than a mountain, and death lighter than a feather.' This maxim was dinned incessantly into their ears, for the spirit of self-sacrifice seemed the source of all the military virtues: loyalty, courage, boldness, self-denial.

All these qualities mingled to create sincerity, an elusive virtue which was continually enjoined but seldom defined. 'Only let your heart be sincere, and all things are possible.' This was the ritual purity of Shinto combined with the teachings of Wang Yang-Ming: the heart instinctively seizes on its own inner truth and shows it forth at once in action.[7] Success or failure do not depend on us, and are unimportant anyway: to be sincere is to be at peace with oneself, and thus with death. Self-sacrifice and sincerity were two aspects of one virtue: the self did not count, only its inner truth, the burning conviction which consecrated every act. Yamagata admired Wang Yang-Ming via Yoshida Shoin, an elder of his domain (Choshu) who had been beheaded in 1859 in the cause of the Restoration. To put this sincerity at the heart of military theory was to subject all human relationships to the inner harmony of the individual with himself. This subjectivism, planted by the masters of *bushido* in a soil prepared by Zen, was what had helped the forty-seven *ronin* in their mission; it had helped Oshio Heihachiro to revolt against the speculators of Osaka and the heroes of the Restoration to face up to the Bakufu. Yamagata relied it to encourage devotion, refusing to see that the same principles had lain behind the rebellion of his adversary, Saigo; and he could scarcely have imagined that one day Japanese soldiers imbued with that same 'sincerity' would turn their weapons against minsters of government. And indeed, if someone believes his heart to be 'sincere', he may do absolutely anything.

A SOLDIER

Tradition was still too strong to expose such contradictions. It could still give the young empire heroes worthy of ancient Rome, soldiers whose glory would not rest on the hazards of war, but would seem the shining reflection of intrinsic purity. The best example was General Nogi, a faithful servant of the emperor Meiji, who killed himself in 1912 to accompany his master in death. He was a great soldier, but a poor leader. It was not he but Kodama who won the victory of Port Arthur. His glory reminds us that the life of the warlike heirs of *bushido* rested on an ethical tradition, rather than on the art of battle. He had no genius – nothing save will-power, the only gift which cannot be given to a man save by himself, and of which (by definition) he has as much as he will. A good and honest will, bent solely on service, too lofty to attach itself to any particular goal. What goal could count for more than a tradition in which one could merge one's individuality and become an incarnation of its ancient tenets? Nogi's greatness was no more nor less than this self-effacement, which led him to the purest, the most deliberate, the most logical of deaths.

He was born a samurai of the same domain as Yamagata, Choshu, which had played such a decisive part in the overthrow of the Bakufu. In 1868 he joined the imperial guard and soon became an officer in the conscript army. Twice he had to fight against childhood friends, other samurai or fellow clansmen who had rebelled against the decrees of the new-born state. We can only imagine the torment this caused a sensitive and affectionate man. A feeling of guilt remained with him, which he fought by becoming ever more rigorous, by a still more absolute allegiance to the emperor, of which his death was to be the final proof. On the other hand, he enjoyed the good life, wine, women and song; he was a poet and calligrapher, like the heroes of old who could handle a writing brush as ably as a sword.

At twenty-nine he fought under Yamagata against Saigo; his company lost its standard to the rebels. Nogi, wounded and evacuated to a field hospital, was inconsolable, no doubt fixing on this minor matter all his guilt for having to fight such intimate adversaries. He left his bed and disappeared. He was found, gaunt and hungry, wandering on the mountainside, having decided to starve himself to death like an ascetic of old. He consented to live, but only as a man reprieved, and the lost standard is recalled in his will made in 1912. The national flag (*hinomaru*), blood-red sun on white snow, had been invented five years earlier for the conscript army. Nogi's despair convinced everyone of the importance of national symbols, for which people could, and sometimes did, die, or wish they could. He was the first on a long roll of martyrs to the majesty of emblems: the lieutenant who killed himself after making a slip in the public reading of the Imperial Rescript; the schoolmaster who threw himself into the fire to save photographs of the imperial couple – a long litany of edifying (and sometimes rather puerile) stories of sacrificial popular devotion.

Ten years later, Nogi was sent to Germany to study the secrets of the world's best army; he returned yet more resolute, more upright, with a passion for discipline. He no longer took off his uniform even to sleep. Once his wife came from Tokyo to the garrison at Shikoku to join him for the New Year celebrations; he refused to see her, saying he was on active service, and sent a message telling her to go home. He knew well that one can command only by example. He saw army life as the inexorable exercise of personal responsibility, and for this no detail was insignificant. Later he served in the war against China (1894–5) which cemented Japanese control over Korea, and in due course retired to the country. Soon he left the plough, a second Cincinnatus, at his country's call: Japan had just launched a surprise attack on the Russian ships anchored in Port Arthur (8 February 1904). The great duel of the two empires had begun.[8]

A VOICE AGAINST THE SLAUGHTER

To the surprise of the entire world, Japan was victorious. Overnight, Western ideas of this quaintly backward nation changed completely, the delicate courtesan giving way to the fixed bayonet. The victory was complete and glorious on both land and sea. But it was dearly bought: the siege of Port Arthur, in particular, was a mighty holocaust, the most ruinous of human sacrifices to the gods of war – until Verdun twelve years later. They gave their all uncomplaining, in the name of the emperor and the nation. This war, so unpopular in Russia, seemed a just one to the Japanese, save for a handful of socialist intellectuals. But in 1904 one lonely voice was raised, quite indifferent to political speculation: the voice of a young woman named Yosano Akiko, begging her brother not to sacrifice his life to the ambitions of the state:

> My brother, for you I shed my tears:
> Do not sacrifice your life in this war!
> You are the last-born of our parents, who when they dandled you in their arms
> Did not seek to teach you how to handle a weapon.
> You whom they so cherished, it was not to kill
> That they raised you for twenty-four years, in love.
>
> Long did our house prosper in Sakai,
> A house of business, your inheritance.
> This ancient name of yours, ah, do not
> Sacrifice it, with your life, in the trenches!
> Let Port Arthur fall, stone from stone!
> You are a man of business, it is not your affair.
>
> Beloved brother, do not sacrifice your life!
> You know our Sovereign does not go to war.
> His Heart is too deep: he does not want men,
> Turned into wolves, perishing under the fire
> Which they say is glorious because it is so cruel.
> No! his Heart's wish could never be thus.[9]

Only the poets and the children can speak truths out loud which others quickly learn to pass over in silence. A quiet, amazed voice asks the old Minotaur the child's question: why? Since Confucius or even before, they had been taught that the nation was one great household, that the same virtue fulfilled both civic and family duties: a good husband, a good subject; a good son, a good soldier. Suddenly an Antigone raises her voice to tell them that the law of the state can be impious and cruel to families, and that the politics of the streets can be an unendurable threat to the affections of the heart.

The state claims to protect their homes, but at what price? What limit is there to its ambitions? to its demands? The imperial ideal was so omnipresent by that time that Yosano Akiko refers to it instinctively, as a thirteenth-century European would mention Christ as a seal on all his feelings, feelings of revolt included. The emperor, usually a sacrificial principle in himself, is invoked here to justify an opposition which savours of both the class isolationism of the past and the conscientious objections of the future. Dying, alas, was no longer a specialist art, and war was no longer warriors' business: its demands were no longer limited, for all limits had dissolved into the universal state. Yosano Akiko died in 1942: she lived long enough to hear the state, in its hubris, call ever more insistently for sacrifice, and finally (in the voice of its extremest militants) for national suicide. And long before that, in 1904, that quiet voice, sending echoes from past to future, asked in its naïve tenderness the question which now, after the bomb, haunts every human conscience.

It was General Nogi who was put in charge of the slaughter. Just before reaching the trenches around Port Arthur, he heard that his eldest son had been killed in battle. On 19 August he decided to attack the Russian fortifications, sure that they would fall in two or three days. A week later 16,000 men had fallen, and they were no further forward. Several times Nogi relaunched his frontal attack – useless, ruinous, and crazy. He had learned of the death of his second son, and had lost all desire to survive this war; he seemed to be under the death-wish (*shinigurui*) which according to the *Hagakure* was a virtue in a warrior, and he was always the first into battle. General Headquarters then put Kodama in charge of operations, but at the emperor Meiji's personal request, Nogi was allowed to retain his command. A few rare souls feel gratitude to the point of violence: Nogi proved it when he followed the emperor into death eight years later. General Kodama concentrated his efforts on the famous Hill 203, which was captured in December; from it they could bombard the harbour roads. The besieged garrison saw no point in prolonging the fight, and surrendered. The chivalrous Nogi forbade journalists to photograph the surrender, knowing that honour done to one's adversary is honour to oneself. Obedient to tradition, he was prodigal in sacrifice, but loftily indifferent to the result.

'THEY ARE GOING TO DIE, AND THEY KNOW IT'

The war over, Nogi, laden with honours, a frequent visitor to the Palace, was put in command of the School of Peers, where the ancient virtues were inculcated into the sons of the nobility. But in old age he had the feeling that all weakened bodies convey: that things were not what they had been. The death of the emperor on 30 July 1912 made his mind up for him. For the six weeks leading up to the state funeral, he went every day to meditate at the Palace. Returning home, he sorted his papers and put his affairs in order. His wife had guessed, but when did she decide to share his resolve? How did he persuade her not to oppose it? She was fifty-four, he ten years older. The day of the funeral had been set for 13 September. The deceased emperor would receive funerary honours at the sanctuary being built to his memory a few kilometres south-west of the Palace; then the body would be taken by train to Kyoto, the former imperial capital, where it was to be buried under the Hill of the Peach-Trees (*Momoyama*). Four terracotta warriors had been made to stand guard round the coffin, like the *haniwa* which had stood in for human sacrifices in the age of the Tumuli.[10]

In the morning, Nogi and his wife, in their most splendid ceremonial dress, went to the Palace, posing for one last photograph. Nogi, in his cockaded hat, chest agleam with medals; his wife, swathed in the vast court kimono, both modestly half-invisible in their magnificent clothes (for it was more modest to wear empty decorations than to refuse them), as impassible as a pair of costume dolls, with empty eyes. 'They are going to die, and they know it', wrote Roland Barthes, 'but there is no sign of it here.' Indeed they did know that they were going to kill themselves that same evening: they had willed it, with a shudder but with total resolution. Their eyes are empty as the abyss. Dignities, honours, commands, nothing would hold them back, not even memory; they knew how to let go, and nothing would make them forget that essential knowledge. Their act would make them what they already were: pure images, calm, wise and unhurried, present to our eyes and hearts, absent from themselves. Our living eyes look at them as if to learn a secret (for does not every mortal seek the impossible secret of how to die?); their eyes, once living, tell us the secret of every photograph, though it was taken only yesterday: 'I am dead, and you know it, but there is no sign of it here.'

Then they returned to their little house and dined together, alone in the world. Evening was falling, a warm September evening. They dismissed their servants and retired to the salon on the first floor. A maid saw Mrs Nogi, perfectly calm, going down to the kitchen to fetch her husband a cup of sake. At eight o'clock a cannon shot announced that the funeral cortège had left the Palace: a carriage of black laqueur, pulled by four great oxen without a blemish. Then (according to the forensic expert) Nogi helped his wife to die by guiding the dagger in her hand. Then he disembowelled himself from left to right, and from top to bottom, and with his last strength, fell upon his sword. In his clenched hand they found a photograph of his two dead sons.

The suicide caused immense astonishment, in Japan as well as abroad: the *junshi*, strictly forbidden by the Tokugawa, had gone out of use in the seventeenth century. Suddenly the remote past had returned into the light, a much more remote past than the newer imperial faith: the savage past of the feudal bands, who accompanied their master into death as a last mark of their intense devotion. Admiration mingled with a kind of uneasiness, compassion, near-horror, and sometimes even a little derision: such is the complexity of the deepest emotions. In Paris, every newspaper had a word to say, and the Catholic *L'Univers* intoned its usual credo, which was quite stupid in this case: 'Suicide is a crime. It is a profoundly cowardly act, when it is not mere madness.' *L'Humanité*, always in the van of progress, spoke of a 'manifestation of mystical fanaticism, blind and ever so slightly imbecilic' – an impertinent and summary judgement, but it was not so very different from the sarcastic comments of the novelist Akutagawa, or of the group of young artists and writers who rallied round the review *Shirakaba* ('The Silver Birch').

Even in Tokyo opinion was divided, as it had been two centuries earlier over the forty-seven *ronin*. It even divided along the same lines, some thinking that suicide, like any other act, should have some reason, rule, measure and purpose, while others thought that a pure and disinterested gesture could, by its very excessiveness, lay down its own measure and enlighten the eyes of those who could see it clearly. Acts follow one another into forgetfulness; but a few remain, empty and glorious, lonely and supreme. Nogi's death was a supreme service which was of no use to anyone or anything, bringing the whole tradition to the highest pitch of will. A fine act frozen against the sky of memory, the cold, distant glitter of a fragile and obstinate star.

12

Into the Abyss

Was Nogi right in thinking that things were not what they had been? The stubborn old warrior probably guessed that the astonishing ascent of the last forty years had put the nation – and nationalism – on the top of a slippery slope. On the surface nothing would change: the same beliefs, the same principles, the same institutions, the same speeches (rather noisier, perhaps) – but already success was corrupting absolutely, the army was dedicated to domination rather than to the spirit of service, and its aims were but a thin cloak over an adventurism which was drawing it secretly into the abyss which yawns before the will to power. Already Korea had been annexed (1910); colonists, cash and garrisons were pouring into Manchuria and Mongolia. Already, in the fateful August of 1914, the wily Yamagata had realized that the thing most to be feared was an alliance between China and America, and he begged the government to give friendly and fraternal assurances to the Chinese. But he was too late: the government no longer had the power to make all its own decisions, and the nationalism which the state had done its best to inculcate was about to turn against it.

This had already happened in 1905, when the patriotic leagues' demonstrations against the peace treaty with Russia had brought thousands of protesters on to the streets of Tokyo. So costly had the victory been that its fruits appeared derisory: in the name of the dead of Port Arthur, the diplomats were accused of throwing away so great a sacrifice for so small a result. From then on there were always people willing to hymn the sacrifices of others and brandish the argument of the dead; soon they would be telling cabinet ministers what to do, on pain of assassination.[1]

Meanwhile, the Confucian tradition of the suicide-of-reproof was by no means extinct: it had found its way via *bushido* into the army. In 1891 a lieutenant in the garrison on Hokkaido killed himself so as to alert the empire to the Russian menace so near Japan's northern isles; and when in 1895 the government had to yield to pressure from the three powers (Germany, France and Russia), who sought to deprive her of the fruits of the Chinese war, officers (about forty in all) killed themselves in protest all over Japan: having sworn to serve the state even to death, the best service they could do it at this juncture was to make it ashamed of its weakness.[2]

Death by *seppuku* could add its emotional force to the basic gesture. In 1933 the goverment refused to allow in its budget for the building of two cruisers, and a certain Lieutenant-Commander Kusuhara disembowelled himself in a sleeping-car on the way from Tokyo to Shimonoseki. The two cruisers were built. It is these militaristic martyrs who set the Japanese warrior tradition apart from all the other abuses of power in the world: their noble revolts, non-criminal if not non-violent, were perhaps worthy of a better cause, but certainly entirely disinterested. In the cause of efficiency such suicides became a normal accompaniment to assassination attempts, clothing intimidation in the shining robes of martyrdom. Later on, voluntary death would cease to be more than an outdated and optional codicil to murder. From sacrificial reproof men descended to terrorism, ethically tainted but politically much more efficacious: certainly it is no harder to kill someone else than to kill oneself, and the murder of a public figure is headline news, whereas a suicide, even the most virtuous, scarcely merits an inside page.

THE GOOD MANNERS OF TERRORISM

Many of these terrorists were still willing to sacrifice their lives. In 1898 Kurushima Tsuneki, a member of the Society of the Dark Ocean, planted an infernal device under the carriage of Marquis Okuma and then cut his own throat. Even in 1913 good conduct had still not been forgotten. A young adherent of the Society of the Black Dragon, concluding that the official attitude to China was too complaisant, shot dead the head of the Bureau of Political Affairs at the Foreign Office; he then spread out a map of China on the floor, sat on it, disembowelled himself and died. At that price a murder may still not be innocent, but it has certainly been atoned for. Such deeds had not the perfect purity of

Nogi's death, nor the high nobility of the suicide of reproof; they were convulsive, hate-filled, even crazy gestures, but while we may not admire them, we should not equate them with a mere time-bomb planted for someone else's benefit. Even now this sacrificial terrorism is not wholly extinct. In 1960 Asanuma Inejiro, leader of the Socialist Party, was making a speech in the main hall at Hibiya when a baby-faced student rushed on him, knife in hand. The murderer was overpowered, arrested and imprisoned, hanged himself, and followed hard on the heels of his victim.

The whole history of Japanese nationalism is punctuated with such attacks in which revolt (like the Malaysian tribesmen who gave us the expression *running amok*) goes to its catastrophic limits, beyond murder to death at last, and its abyss in which an atom of liberty consumes itself in a mad outbust of energy. In 1921 Asahi Heigo, a young leader in the Virtuous League of the Country of the Gods (*Shinshu gidan*), stabbed to death the banker Yasuda Zenjiro, who was guilty of being the richest man in Japan. Asahi immediately killed himself to give his act moral purity, which meant exemplary value, which meant political effectiveness. In a posthumous proclamation, he spoke of the need for a 'Taisho restoration' and fulminated against the poverty of the masses, the idleness of public figures, the inertia of the generals and the corruption of the rich. In terms we should rather expect from an anarchist, this right-wing extremist demanded the abolition of inherited wealth, the confiscation of fortunes, the nationalization of land and capital, and the suppression of all political parties together with the state bureaucracy. Above all he wanted millionaires punished for being rich. He exhorted his comrades not to speak but to keep calm and *act*, leaving the act, though dumb, to proclaim its own truth: stab, thrust, shoot! Assemblies and organizations were useless. The sacrifice of life was all. Forget your petty interests, sever all bonds, care nothing for what others say of you. To kill, to die, to sleep: no more. This ultra-nationalist anti-Hamlet was a startling synthesis of nihilist subversion *à la* Nechaev and the sacrificial maxims of the *Hagakure*.[3]

Was the emperor safe, at least? In 1910 the police claimed to have discovered a plot to kill the Emperor Meiji, led by Kotoku Shusui, a socialist with anarchist leanings. The year after, eleven people were duly investigated, tried and executed for taking part in this project. In December 1923 an anarchist made an unsuccessful attack on the young regent who was soon to become the emperor Hirohito. But left-wing violence never really caught on in Japan. In Russia, the empire next door, it was all the rage, but Japan had had her revolution in 1868, and most of her assassinations were on chauvinist principles. The amalgam of bureaucrats, politicians and capitalists who made up the new ruling class, and were gradually taking over the offices of state from the oligarchs, never enjoyed an unclouded period of power: the ultra-imperialists were after them immediately. The patriotic leagues, inheritors of the Saigo spirit, had taken it beyond expansionism and the frugality of a brotherhood of peasant-protecting warriors. These malcontents, often have-nots like the *ronin* of old (and therefore all the more rebellious and envious of the 'haves') execrated the politicians for being timid abroad and hand in glove with the big industrialists at home. They had one vice with two faces, corruption and cowardice: the state was drifting away from the warlike tradition which had given it birth. Nogi had thought the same, but his chosen way of reviving the tradition seemed a little too drastic to the patriotic leagues: most of them preferred to be agitators, contributing actively to the very disorder which they so deplored.

TERROR AND VIRTUE

Japanese terrorists never renounced their claim on moral idealism – naïve in young agitators, sometimes rather crafty in their elders. More like Robespierre than other men of their day, they all spoke the language of virtue. Leninism then, and Fascism and Stalinism later, dismissed morality as a formal illusion to which it was all too easy to succumb; but real history needed to be made, and the reality of the future would assign the descriptions 'good' and 'evil' which men seemed so resolved to bestow on everything. Japanese nationalism, however, never lost its moral stamp even in its bloodiest excesses. They killed people there as much as anywhere else, but they needed to do it with a clear conscience, feeling that the victims did not deserve to live. Western political cynicism would have shocked them.

Punishment was the usual alibi for violence, and the cruellest torturers were the most hypocritical. They believed in their own virtue: it was their licence to kill. They had little interest in socio-political programmes; the imperial utopia was the only one they needed. They were interested only in action: the exemplary act was enough for them, the act which would arouse the nation, the wind of sacrifice which would blow away the base contagious counsellors who clouded the sun of the perfect sovereign, too long surrounded by their foul and ugly mists. And so, strike! When less hardened souls felt a shadow of doubt, they always had the supreme alibi of the voluntary death: no consciousness meant no conscience. Suicide was an expiation, or rather proof (to oneself) of a pure heart and a right intention: they died justified in their own eyes, because this sacrificial morality demanded only that the individual show, or believe, himself to be disinterested. Death was proof of selflessness, and the responsibility ended there, with no inkling of a judgement from God or history. These martyrs to their own violence even seemed to excuse the crimes of others and to legitimate murders which would otherwise have been regarded with loathing.[4]

EXPLOITATION OF THE VOLUNTARY DEATH

The terrorists shamelessly exploited the age-old prestige of the voluntary death. The Leagues on the extreme right even had the impudence to lecture their intended victims on their faults, responsibilities and duty of self-immolation. They knew they would not be listened to, but they hoped to inflict some moral damage on their adversaries by accusing them of cowardice and corruption. When the Emperor Meiji died, Toyama Mitsuru, one of the founders of the Society of the Black Dragon, publicly asked the ministers why they had not advised His Majesty to take better care of his august health? And ought they not to hold themselves responsible for his death? And resign, or better still, sacrifice their lives? Toyama was no fool; he knew that Prince Saionji and his colleagues would not rush to follow his advice. He was content to expose the liberals' lack of moral fibre by bringing them up against the ancestral tradition. It was a rather underhand piece of blackmail: unless you kill yourselves you are not fit to live!

Such invitations to suicide became a ritual prelude, and anticipatory excuse, for murder: the tradition was used to confer some dignity on the trivialities of political intimidation. In 1932 Inoue Junnosuke, a former Finance Minister whose frugality had annoyed the militarists, fell victim to an assassination organized by the League of the Oath of Blood (*Ketsumeidan*); beforehand he received, through the post, a dagger carefully encased in a lacquer sheath. On 18 May 1930 Admiral Takarabe, returning from the London Naval Conference at which Japan had agreed to reduce its tonnage, disembarked at Yokohama, where a young extreme right-winger presented him with another such dagger as an invitation to *seppuku*. There was one occasion on which the voluntary death was exploited by the other side. On 21 January 1937, a member of parliament from the Seiyukai party named Hamada was brave enough to make a speech to the Diet in which he accused the army of usurping political power. General Terauchi, Minister for War, demanded a public apology on behalf of the injured military. Hamada swore to commit *seppuku* if he could not prove his accusations – provided, of course, that the Minster for War would do the same if the proof were forthcoming. Terauchi declined to accept the challenge. The still lively tradition of the *seppuku* became one more weapon in the political arsenal, much favoured by those who hoped to restore a certain *gravitas* to the jousting of parliamentarians.

THE USURPATION OF POWER

Hamada had put his finger on the problem when he talked of usurpation. For many years the army had been totally loyal, never flinching from the heaviest sacrifices. But little by little it was sinking into chauvinism. Nogis were few and far between. The military were becoming militarists. Ambitious projects, expanding budgets: the army had plenty of help, but the more it had the more it wanted, and it was now thinking of helping itself. The generals were beginning to think that politics was too important to be left to civilians. Article 11 of the 1889 constitution, inserted by Yamagata, designated the emperor supreme commander of the army. This conferred a privilege of 'direct access to the throne' which soon led to the conclusion that the army did not come under governmental authority. Yamagata had intended to make it indifferent to the choppings and changings of political power. A fatal precaution: by making the army independent (except from the emperor) he had made it irresponsible. The sovereign would not stoop to control or curb it. He was bound to remain mute and immutable and above all particular decisions.

Thus the army was growing within the state into an autonomous power, still attached to the tradition of service – but if that link were ever broken, it would be like a gun broken loose from its moorings in a storm at sea, crashing blindly about on a ship's deck, destroying everything in its path before finally falling overboard. Trying to protect the army from politics, they had subjected politics to the army. In the same year as Nogi followed his emperor into death, General Uehara, the Minister for War, resigned: he had been demanding two extra divisions for Korea, but his colleagues had refused them. So he went to the Palace and handed his resignation to the sovereign, without even informing the Prime Minister, Prince Saionji – who learned of it from the newspapers. A replacement was needed, but a decree of 1900, another brainchild of Yamagata's, stipulated that the Ministries of War and the Marine had to be held by a serving general and admiral, respectively. The generals turned a deaf ear to all Saionji's suggestions: the army was solidly behind Uehara and his two divisions. This virtual work-to-rule brought down the government; the too liberal Saionji was replaced by Katsura Taro, a creature of Yamagata's. Thus ended the Meiji era, leaving it clear that the army had the means of controlling the government.[5]

Yamagata, no mean statesman, would not have approved of this usurpation of power by the military, but it was his class-consciousness and absolutist prejudices that had made it possible. Such is the irony of history: the precautions of an authoritarian paved the way for anarchy. And yet he was tradition incarnate. He was an orphan, brought up by his grandmother; it was said that, her task ended, she had killed herself so that the child, free from all ties of filial gratitude, could devote himself entirely to his country. But oligarchs of his stamp were fast fading away, and with them all respect for authority. The numerous extreme right-wing leagues, sectarian and subdivided (and corrupted by the clandestine subsidies they received from the very financial interests they pretended to despise) were not in themselves any great danger. There were a few theorists like Kita Ikki, who dreamed of national socialism, sketched plans for national reconstruction and equality of wealth, and called for a second renaissance, *Showa ishin* (Showa Restoration). Nothing very worrying there, either, so long as the army remained firm in its traditional loyalty to the state. But little by little the whole chain of command was giving way: from lieutenants to colonels and generals, all were on their way to forgetting the maxims so nobly, but so vainly, made manifest n the death of Nogi.

THE TIME OF THE ASSASSINS

Down below, the lieutenants were listening to the ultra-patriotic ravings of the nationalist leagues, and a few of them were carried away by the excitements of conspiracy and assassination. In 1927 two hundred young officers formed a secret society to guard the safety of the empire. In 1932, others founded thee Society of the Cherry Trees (*Sakurakai*) and made a plot which was soon discovered and suppressed. A few years later, yet others plotted to drop a bomb on a cabinet meeting and so kill all the ministers at one blow. Soldiers were turning assassins. On the evening of 15 May 1932, nine officers, led by Lieutenant Koga, found their way into the residence of the Prime Minister. The elderly Inukai (he was seventy-five at the time) lit a cigarette and asked for an explanation. A second group, led by Lieutenant Yamagishi, burst in shouting, 'Don't stop to talk! Shoot!'

After this achievement they still had the audacity to invoke the old tradition of sacrifice: in a proclamation, they adjured the country to deliver the emperor from his evil counsellors, and claimed to be ready to give their lives so as to light the torch of the Showa Restoration. But suicides there were none. As good soldiers they scorned life, but in practice this evidently meant other people's lives: these uniformed killers were certainly human, all too human indeed. They tamely gave themselves up to the police. And so great, still, was the moral force of the belief which had passed from Wang Yang-Ming to Yoshida Shoin and Saigo – and so craven the connivance which terror had imposed on the army and the state – that in consideration of their evident 'sincerity' they were sentenced to a mere four years in prison. Prime Ministers' lives were cheap at that time: one could easily be spared.

It is strange. A lieutenant once killed himself, in a passion of responsibility, because he had made a mistake in the public recitation of the Imperial Rescript. If another one did murder from a conviction that the salvation of the state depends on it, did this excuse murder? They are soldiers, and have a right to our indulgence, Baron Kikuchi (himself a general) was to tell the House of Peers in 1934: those who are convinced they are acting from patriotic motives must be allowed to do what they think they have got to do. A very flexible thing after all, this rigid military ethic! The ideals of service and sincerity supplied two ways of dodging responsibility, from above and from below. One: 'I have my orders, ask my superiors, unconditional loyalty asks no questions.' Two: 'I have killed my commanding officer, but it was for that supreme purpose to which all human life is sacrificed and thereby fulfilled: this is my faith and my sufficient absolution.'

Altruism was an excuse for virtually anything and everything. No wonder the militarists were so attached to the imperial creed (*Tenno shugi*): it excused the frenzy on one level and so assisted the strategy on the other. For what was done by subalterns in their blindness was exploited by generals who could see quite well. Terror always has its uses. They deplored such juvenile excesses, but they used them as arguments to extract yet more from the state budget and control decision-making. A conspiracy was advancing, step by step: nobody was in charge of it but everybody was an accomplice, without realizing it if necessary. Year by year the army was nearer seizing power, like the Taira and Minamoto clans who gained such strength in the last days of Heian.

And (so true is it that history repeats itself) this army, like the clans, was divided. One faction, called the Imperial Way (*Kodoha*), included mostly officers from the former clans of the south, and its origins could be traced back to Saigo Takamori; it was distinctly radical, seeking profound reform, a new Restoration, the duties of expansion and renewal backed up by the imperial ideal. The rival faction, *Toseiha*, wanted to curb the southerners' enthusiasm and was ready to make a deal with the state, so long as the latter was controlled by the army. As for strategy, *Kodoha* called for war with the Soviet Union, *Toseiha* for expansion into China and southern Asia.

THE YOUNG OFFICERS

The failure of a plot backed by certain *Kodoha* generals (Araki, Mazaki, Honjo) gave victory to their more conservative, but no less chauvinistic, adversaries. On the night of 26 February 1936 the tanks came rolling through the snowy streets of Tokyo: twenty-one officers of the First Division, lieutenants and captains, had mutinied. In the name of the empire and the safety of the nation, they ordered their troops, about fifteen hundred in all, to occupy central Tokyo. At the same time, for good measure, they added murder to rebellion, sending teams of killers to shoot six leading public figures in their beds. As a subversive poem from the last years of Edo had put it, 'Life is not worth a penny': as 26 February dawned, it was by exhibiting a penny stamp that the conspirators recognized each other. Was that really the price they set on human life? As champions of a just cause, they felt their own existence was justified, and that they were qualified to sit in judgement on that of others. Nor did they find spilt blood at all disturbing, if it belonged to their victims: the murdering done, they thought the day was won, and began to drink, sing and celebrate. Young indeed they were. But as for *bushido*...?

They had rejoiced too soon. They knew that they could count on connivance in high places, but they had not anticipated that the young emperor himself would abandon his ritual reserve and firmly resist any sort of compromise. For the emperor could see through imperialism and knew how his name was being taken in vain by a certain element in the army. The more they proclaimed him a god, the more they expedited him to heaven, the less sure he felt of his own existence. It was the emperor's turn to revolt: like his ancestor, Go-Daigo, he refused to put his power at the mercy of violence and brutality. The alleged purity of the intention did not seem to him to justify the means. The rebels were camping inside a barbed-wire entanglement on the melting snow of the street. Negotiations likewise got bogged down. On 28 February the young officers had obtained none of their demands; they were surrounded; their troops were beginning to murmur. They made it known that they would surrender and kill themselves on condition that an imperial messenger (*chokushi*) delivered the order. They were refused this satisfaction: the emperor replied that they could kill themselves if they wanted to, but by their mutiny and murder they had ceased to be his soldiers, and so could expect no orders from him. Then, turning their weeping eyes toward the Palace, whose ramparts they could dimly see through the night, the rebels sang the slow and poignant national anthem, the *Kimigayo*.

A couple of miles away, in his house at Setagaya, Lieutenant Aoshima was preparing his *seppuku*. He had had no part in the mutiny, but he was friends with several officers of his own age, and could not face the thought of fighting them if they were declared rebels. His voluntary death would, as usual, resolve the conflict of loyalties. His young wife died with him, like Mrs Nogi. The flame of tradition still burned pure in such gestures: twenty-five years later Mishima Yukio, fascinated by this particular example, used it as a base for one of his most compelling stories, 'Yukoku' ('Patriotism'), which was soon afterwards filmed. Mishima himself played Lieutenant Aoshima, shedding floods of stage blood to bind him to that adamantine will. Characters shaped by tradition last longer on stage than in life, and reality meets reality through the good offices of fiction. Fiction is expiated by becoming reality, and already Mishima was conceiving the decision which, after ten years, brought him to his own sacrifice. The actor, a victim of confused identities, looked to pain and death to prove to him that he was no longer lying, and to give him an identity again.

Of the twenty-one mutineers, only two killed themselves at the moment of defeat. If Lieutenant Aoshima had thought he was going ahead of his friends to show them the way, he was sadly mistaken. After the surrender, in the morning of 29 February, they were conducted to the official residence of the Minister for War and asked if they, too, wished to kill themselves. They did. So they were left alone, possessed of their weapons, in halls carpeted with white cotton to absorb the blood. But the collective *seppuku* which had marked the fall of Kamakura in 1333 had gone out of fashion. The young officers got together and changed their minds: perhaps an overhasty death would be a betrayal of their cause? Better to go before the tribunal and denounce the abuses they had risen against – poverty in the countryside, the parsimonious military budget, the inertia of government, the corrupt politicians. Here we have samurai turned orators and defence lawyers, truly a sign of the influence of the detestable West!

In any case, the generals who had connived with them showed no suicidal inclinations; they had not even been arrested. The future beckoned, in fact. So many others before them been excused for their sincerity that they were confident of an amalgam of complicity and indulgence. They were soon to be undeceived. From May to June 1936 they were duly tried *in camera*. Most of them – thirteen out of nineteen – were condemned to death and shot. And shamed: they were told that they had disgraced *bushido* by failing to die. And since they had not, they really did not deserve to live! The argument that terrorists had so often turned on their victims was used conclusively against them; tradition was their prosecutor. No superior officer was condemned.

Toseiha, the 'control' faction, took the army in hand, and it suited everyone to present the affair as a venture by a few young hotheads. But the theoreticians were shown no mercy: Kita Ikki and Nishida Zei, who had tried to sprinkle cool socialism on the distemper of the military and give expression to the social malaise which their disturbances expressed, were accused, like Socrates, of corrupting youth. They too – they above all – were condemned to death and executed.[6]

THE CHINESE WAR

The adventure of the young officers, unsuccessful as it was, only helped the army's rise to power. The generals used the rebellion as an argument for their control of state policy, saying they alone were capable of preventing fresh disturbances. The government tacitly agreed, also, to leave the army more freedom in its external operations, for it seemed less dangerous to let it make war abroad rather than stage a *coup d'état* at home – or even an agrarian reform or a revolution, who could tell? So long as it accepted the established order, it was to have free rein. Indeed it was hard to do otherwise. Conspiring lieutenants and intriguing generals in the capital were bad enough, but colonels stirring up trouble on the imperial boundaries were no less of a worry. They had long specialized in setting up a *fait accompli* on the mainland which would sabotage official diplomacy and push the government willy-nilly along the road to further expansion.

In 1928 Colonel Komoto blew up the train in which Marshal Ch'ang Tso-lin, war-lord of Manchuria, was travelling. Nothing came of it: Tokyo thwarted this piece of provocation, for the new Prime Minister, Hamaguchi, was resolved to curb the militarists, even if it cost him his life. (In November 1930 he was shot and mortally wounded by a terrorist.) The officers had better luck with the Manchurian Incident of 18 September 1931, when the Japanese garrison at Mukden manufactured a pretext to attack Chinese troops. This time the government proved unable to restrain the army's self-promoting expansion. Japan's fate was sealed. On 7 July 1937 there was another incident near Peking which triggered the invasion of China. Nobody knew it, but the Second World War had begun. The army had no need to worry: it was going to have plenty to do.

But this army which wallowed in blood for four weeks at Nanking (14 December 1937 to 14 January 1938) was no longer the army of Nogi. Nothing lasts for ever, and man's conquest of himself, though it may found a tradition, is the least lasting of all. The varnish of *bushido* was cracking to show the old brutality of the *ashigaru* foot soldiers who in the fifteenth-century Onin War had laid waste Kyoto with fire and sword. In 1941 and 1942 the same cruelty laid waste Hong Kong, the Philippines, Indonesia, Malaysia, Burma. It was the very ecstasy of force. Only with the approach of defeat would the military, before being engulfed in the abyss they themselves had opened up, regain their dignity and attempt, by openly suicidal exploits, to grasp not at victory – an impossibility – but at the memory of their own honour, perhaps to expiate their newest outrages by the very excess of sacrifice.

ON THE THEORETICAL FRONT

The Chinese War gave the army a chance to superimpose its decision-making organs on the civil government, as Minamoto no Yoritomo had done by founding the Kamakura *Bakufu*. The government was losing control of operations, which from 20 November 1937 had been directed by a General Headquarters directly responsible to the emperor. In August 1938, mainland diplomacy was withdrawn from the Foreign Office and invested in an Asian Development Bureau set up and directed by the generals. The whole country was laid under requisition by a Law of National Mobilization passed on 16 March 1938. State orthodoxy was to be reaffirmed and with it the principles of national structure (*kokutai no hongi*).

A few months after the 26 February mutiny, two million copies of a leaflet appeared celebrating the unanimity of the nation: those who renounced themselves and rose above their private interests would immediately be bathed in the universal grace proceeding from the *Tenno*. The new Minister for Education, General Araki, had a favourite slogan, *ichioku isshin*: a hundred million minds with but a single thought. On the theoretical front he ruthlessly opposed Western concepts like the class struggle and bourgeois individualism. All the trouble came from egoism, in families, clans and social classes as much as in individuals. All that was good came from self-forgetfulness. Thus truly to live was to die to this illusory self: a distant echo of Buddhist teachings, inflected, distorted and bent towards sacrificial demands quite alien to the Buddhist spirit.

So long as nobody noticed the egoism of an army well on the way to subjugating the nation, or the egoism of a nation well on the way to subjugating its neighbours, this unanimist utopia could deny the existence of conflicts which were rending both Japanese society and the whole of Asia. Political parties were to set an example of self-forgetfulness: in 1940 they were officially dissolved and amalgamated (or lumped together) into a National Association for the Service of the Empire

(*Taisei yokusankai*), in which rooted factional divisions were disguised in the most anodyne phraseology. As for the subjects of the empire, they were exhorted to merge themselves in the collective soul.

Such was the mania for resolving everything in imaginary theories: solution, dissolution, the ego identified with its ideal and forced to merge its real being in a totality free from all contradiction. It is always reappearing and is always the same under its different guises – Komsomols, Hitler Youth, Red Guards. One day the excitement always drops before the stark face of reality and the maniacal agitation collapses into depression, bringing back the ego more detestable than ever. In such cases it is safer, if you do not want to kill yourself in despair, to forget yourself entirely by dying on the crest of the wave. The War in the Pacific would be prodigal of opportunities for that.[7]

THE LEAP INTO THE VOID

Unlike the Chinese War, this was not a venture by one or two colonels. The rulers of the army and the state hesitated and debated for two long years. But no authority could get the army to pull back out of the Chinese morass, while discussions with the United States led up a blind alley. Prince Konoe, the brilliant young Prime Minister, surrounded by national socialists, was overflowing with good intentions, but every peace initiative foundered and was bogged down in the generals' determined blindness. Sometimes individual life has to go through these desert periods in which contradictions are so extreme that they paralyse instead of stimulating, all dialectical horizons are obscured and everything is ominous and grey. Thus for two years Japan watched war come sleepwalking towards it and was powerless to awake. In such situations suicide can look like the only gesture which might shake off the lethargy. Often it is an appeal, someone taking a grip on himself and defying death, or rather gambling with his life, killing himself just to make something happens, leaping into the void.

Such was Pearl Harbor. A few days prior to the attack the new Prime Minister, General Tojo, a man of war, said with perfect naïvety to Prince Konoe that 'once in his life, a man must dare to throw himself off the terrace of Kiyomizu Temple'. Did he think he could justify his venture by boasting of it? Risk-taking is after all a military virture. Tojo saw himself as heir to Yamagata, the great founder of the Japanese army, but lacked Yamagata's statesmanship: adventurism can serve, but not make decisions, it is all boldness in tactics and prudence in strategy. Here again the tradition was forgotten, or worse, misunderstood. They saw Pearl Harbor as a repetition of the attack on Port Arthur. Repetition may always be reassuring, but it baulks any intention which goes along with it.

The day of Pearl Harbor, 7 December 1941, was the army's bold stroke which risked everything, all the gains of two generations. A power which could not contain itself, and so could neither know nor master itself, could grow only by spending itself, its all. It is noble to risk everything, *quantum potes tantum aude*. But should one go further even than that? In militarist Japan they no longer knew what 'further' would mean: too long had their ideology proclaimed that the will was the only measure of power. Admiral Yamamoto, as he made his plans for Pearl Harbor in the summer of 1941, knew that the navy could sustain only a single year of war. But it had become sacrilegious to obey the truth, it was an insult to the will. He concluded that it was all the more urgent to attack and strike terror into the enemy.

The voluntarist illusion, Japan's version of idealism, led to a sort of collective solipsism. The will, and the will to will, and the denial of all limits to the will, ended in a void which dismissed the world and had no final wish save death. If will be the measure of power, then death is the measure of will. If the war was to continue it had to be extended; to conquer China they had to conquer south-east Asia and its oilfields. In this perpetual self-transcendence there still was a limit to expansion – the abyss into which it was unsuspectingly rushing. Any adventure has this ambivalence at its core: at the height of vitality, the summit of the upward rush, the risk of fall must be accepted – in advance. That is the price of true resolution. Does a will which so ventures know what it really wants? Or is it fascinated by the coming conflagration, already conniving at the waiting catastrophe and the abomination of desolation which will follow?

Until 1931 the expansion of the empire had been slow, careful, regular; then, for another ten years, bold and hazardous. Suddenly, in a few months, it exploded as far as the confines of India and Australia. But in June 1942 the navy met defeat at Midway. In the first days of 1943 the long ebb-tide began at Guadalcanal, withdrawing from island to island up to the battle of Okinawa in April, May and June 1945. The numbers of dead grew inexorably, but not the numbers of prisoners. 'Victory or death' was a slogan taken literally by the Japanese soldier. If a position became untenable they rushed on machine-guns and flame-throwers with a shout of *banzai*! Wounded men would unpin a hand grenade or ask their best friend to kill them. Often officers would make a point of disembowelling themselves or falling on their swords, for they always trailed this powerful emblem after them through the jungle, immutable in its perfection through ten centuries, completely useless in modern battle but handy for that last honourable office. Unlike Saigo, and so many others before him, they could not hope to capture the enemy's admiration thereby, for they knew that the gesture would be imputed to fanaticism and cause even greater horror, even revulsion. But they no longer hoped for victory or recognition; the consciousness of rejoining the long tradition of suicide in defeat, escaping the shame of captivity, sufficed as a last consolation.

THE LONG ROLL OF SACRIFICE

Civilians, too, rushed to death in hordes, either fatalistic or panicking at the approach of the victors. In July 1944 the little island of Saipan finally fell to superior American firepower. Admiral Nagumo, the skilled architect of Pearl Harbor, killed himself, and the elderly General Saito performed *seppuku* before his officers, having ordered the survivors to make one final assault. The Japanese settlers took refuge in caves over the sea, and many of them, especially women with babies in arms, hurled themselves from the cliffs. The Tokyo press, with the approval of the censors, did nothing to reduce the toll of human lives, but did its best to increase it, praising the martyrs to the skies as if to urge others in their wake. And in battle after battle, on island after island, the same bloody outcome was seen, until Okinawa was reached a few months later. When on 22 June 1945 the joint *seppuku* of Generals Ushijima and Cho marked the end of that battle, 130,000 Japanese had died, as against 12,000 Americans.

As the war neared the Japanese homeland the resistance became bloodier and more bitter. General Tojo had been demoted after the fall of Saipan, and the government knew well that there was no hope of securing victory or avoiding defeat. But how to end the long roll of sacrifice? As the number of dead grew, the living, not wishing to seem grudging of their lives, hastened to follow them. In 1869, the Emperor Meiji had founded in Tokyo, his new capital, a temple for the repose of the souls of soliders killed in battle: *Yasukuni jinja*, the Sanctuary of the Nation at Peace. For (to be fair) your militarist so loves peace that he will always make war to gain it. 'We shall meet at Yasukuni', soldiers would smile to one another before the assault.

The Pacific War was now simply the path leading innumerable victims to that final peace. The perpetrator of Pearl Harbor was no longer in power, but no negotiator would have dared to insult all those sacrificed lives by a premature surrender like that of the Italians under Badoglio. The argument of the dead was used to the bitter end to stifle any thoughts of stopping the war. There were shortages of everything, famine threatened, the bombs rained down, but nobody spoke of anything save ever greater sacrifice: the inertia of despair could see no other way out.

Once the euphoria of the early victories had disperesed, the army had seen defeat staring it in the face, but refused to acknowledge it. They knew that the army would not survive it. At the time of the Russo-Japanese war, Nogi's army and Togo's navy could have undergone any reversal of fortune and survived, because there were politicians available to shoulder the responsibility. But now the army had murdered or intimidated the politicians, sabotaged diplomacy, subjugated authority, unleashed hostilities: how could they endure the shame of capitulation before the silent emperor, the wounded nation, the wordless dead? The Japanese army had staked its very existence in the Pacific, and defeat meant death – death not only for the army but for Japan, for the army made no distinction between them.

It was at that same time that the foundering Hitler regime was struggling to throw off its guilt on to its victims, or deny it altogether by proclaiming that the victors are always right, and that only the defeated are ever found guilty by the tribunal of history. The Japanese militarists had too lively a conscience to feel this anxiety to justify themselves, however cynically. But shame is no less strong, and can lead to the same revages as guilt. Never were human beings more rigid and stubborn in their pride. Their martial tradition suggested the solution: dying to become invincible. Every soldier can do this freely enough; the Pacific added a novelty, careful planning – most suitable, after all, in a century where every freedom is organized.

THE SECRET WEAPON

In 1994 America was working on the Manhattan Project, while Hitler hurled his V1s and V2s. The Japanese army was also pluming itself on its ultimate weapon, one to strike terror into any enemy: the voluntary death, the invisible weapon, the spiritual secret of the Yamato race, a recipe for invincibility due not to scientific cunning but to the remote past, the allegedly immutable identity of the nation, the pure self-sacrifice of youth. The secret of victory was really to want it, even to death, and to make the most of the ensuing willingness for sacrifice. When the Americans landed on Saipan, a few pilots, aware of the strategic importance of this (bombers could now reach the homeland), aware also of the inferiority of the Japanese forces, resolved to crash-land on the enemy ships. The squadron took off from its base at Iwojima on 20 June 1944. Most of them were shot down and none reached their target; five pilots (out of seventeen) got lost and returned to base, determined on a second attempt.

The idea caught on in the naval air force. It was not the first time that a suicide mission had been suggested: there was even a word, *jibaku*, for such belligerent self-destruction, and every Japanese schoolchild knew the names of the three heroes of Shanghai, who on 20 February 1932 had armed themselves with bamboos stuffed with dynamite and hurled themselves on the Chinese barbed wire in order to breach it. But now, for the first time, such exploits were deliberately planned: not on-the-spot impulses but massive, regular, systematic attacks.[8]

On 19 October 1944 Vice-Admiral Onishi, commanding the naval air force in the Philippines, went to the base of Mabalacat and briefed the assembled pilots. The Americans had just made a successful landing; a decisive naval battle was in prospect; orthodox methods were no longer sufficient, but there was still hope if a number of Zero fighters, each carrying a single 250-kg bomb, would crash-land on the American aircraft carriers. Could volunteers be found for such a mission? he asked. Never in the long history of human warfare had soldiers been asked to do such a thing. Every battle has its perilous volunteer missions with small chance of coming back alive: the volunteer knows that, but the little voice which whispers 'You might make it', illusory as it may be, is a large part of physical courage. And it does happen that a man will suddenly court certain death in the heat of battle, like Fleming, an American pilot who during the battle of Midway, on 5 June 1942, crashed his plane on the turret of the Japanese cruiser *Mikuma*.

Despair, too, can give the vanquished the strength to kill themselves, like the Jewish fighters besieged by the Romans at Masada; and suicides of that type, sometimes on a huge scale, had taken place all through Japanese history, culminating in the massacres of Saipan three months earlier, which the very pilots addressed by Onishi had perforce witnessed. But now, for the first time, it meant deliberately choosing absolutely certain death, a few days or even weeks in advance. It was an appeal to pure, free good will, devoid of any illusion, any emotion. The ethic of war had attained a Kantian severity. And as Kant is always accompanied by Sade, the result of such a choice would be the sacrificial annihilation of an innocent life, the brutal dissolution of a young body shattered to fragments amidst the silence of the indifferent ocean.

THE SYLLOGISM OF VOLUNTARY DEATH

The pilots of Mabalacat heard Onishi out, thought for a moment, considered their decision and agreed. On 20 October 1944, three days after the first American landing in the Philippines, three days before the terrible naval battle at Leyte, they created the first four 'Special body-shock attack units' (*Taiatari tokubetsu kogekitai, Tokkotai* for short). On the morning of 25 October a first venture seemed to justify the new tactic: of the five planes in the *Shikishima* flight, four reached their targets, and the aircraft-carrier *Saint-Lo* was sunk. When he was informed of this, the emperor expressed a reserved and ambiguous approval: 'Was it really necessary to go so far? Well, it was a noble deed.' Onishi himself had his doubts – but it was the only hope, as the name given to these units showed: *shimpu, kamikaze,* the Wind of the Gods, the Divine Typhoon, the unhoped-for hope which might scatter the invaders as it had scattered the Mongol ships in 1281.

There was no shortage of volunteers, in fact there was a waiting list. The unheard-of notion, which no commander before Onishi had dared even pronounce, seemed quite obvious to them. It was the fiery and perfectly logical conclusion to the whole tradition of sacrifice. Fanaticism? Rather a totally lucid syllogism: premise, the will to win; second premise, enemy superiority; conclusion: voluntary death. The ardour of sacrifice merged with the most rigorous logic, in an amalgam of fire and ice. Why deceive oneself? The pilots knew that they would be killed sooner or later in such an unequal combat, and preferred to choose their own premature, but more useful death. They looked for no reward, no paradise, soon not even for victory, nothing to blunt the steely edge of death. Japan's military tradition had always despised illusions: in this it comes close to a scientific ethic of truth. If something is inevitable, one must learn to see it and then to will it, forging one's heart in the heat of necessity.

This was the basis for their recruitment and training. The Battle of the Philippines was lost, but the management of the voluntary death had been institutionalized. The air force organized its own special units in imitation of the naval force. In the beginning they chose only the best and put off those who were not superlative pilots. A few months later they were calling for volunteers. In principle it was always voluntary, but there was a certain amount of moral blackmail. A squadron leader would gather thirty or so apprentice officers, talk of the anguish of their country and the necessity of sacrifice, and invite them to give their reply that evening, one by one. Seldom did any of them decline the honour thus offered; perhaps it took no less courage to stand aside from the common destiny than to accept it. Solidarity and rivalry, strong feelings for a boy of twenty, bound them into one exalted will. So they would call in the commander's office, receive his congratulations, sign on, and start their training – petrol supplies permitting, that is, for the shortages were getting worse and worse.

There was a shortage of everything, except human lives. Soon there were twice as many volunteers as available planes. Experienced pilots, now few and getting fewer, were kept on escort duty, using their skill in air combat while the youngest made the fatal dive. The latter were told to keep a cool head and be sure to make the best use of their precious aeroplane. They had to select their prey, dodge the enemy fire and come in almost at sea level, or dive on it vertically: with mind alert, quiet heart, eyes wide open, they could not miss. No haste, no anxiety, no impulsiveness, no discouragement: they had to commit suicide without any suicidal feelings, and die in a perfection of self-mastery.

DYING AT TWENTY

These twenty-year-olds had opted for death some weeks or even months before. They had chosen, and had to live (or die) up to their choice. Most were university students, of law or literature for the most part, because scientists were considered too important to the country's future to be spent in this fashion. How long would the respite be, with so many of their comrades already gone? One evening they would learn that the next day was to be the last of their short lives. They wrote their last letters, one or two poems, and slept – if they could. At sunrise a table was set up on the breezy aerodrome, the selected flight was assembled, and while the planes were being cleared of camouflage, the squadron leader would share a last cup of sake with the chosen few.

We have a few photographs from just before the take-off, the pilots smiling and waving from their cabins, their foreheads hound with a cotton strip bearing a red sun. Lambs to the slaughter? No: it would insult them to deny their perfect concord with their own destiny. No need to force or cajole or even indoctrinate them. They were entirely free, their decision springing from their country's agony. However well-organized this death, they had chosen it and willed it unceasingly, from day to day, proud of it, and finding in it all their reasons for *living*. If they wavered it was furtively and in secret: a feeling of apprehension, the memory of a loved one, a sharp awareness of the beauty of the world. They did not seem any more thoughtful than other young men of their age, certainly cheerful enough, but occasionally their thoughts mights swerve: when I see the enemy ship growing larger by the second, the sailors runing on to the deck, shall I have the strength to keep my eyes open?

A sacrifice must be useful: however cruel, it is justified by its efficacity. And at first the attacks of the *tokkotai* were indeed fearsomely effective. The enemy ship had no idea how to react: zigzag, or hold steady for the anti-aircraft gunners? Then they learned how to defend themselves, the surprise wore off and the losses diminished. Fewer than one in eight suicide planes hit their targets: it was not the ultimate weapon, but it was still considerably more productive than orthodox methods, and that was justification enough. The Battle of Okinawa saw their fiercest attacks: they hit three hundred ships and sank thirty-four. It was not enough to save the empire.

Afterwards the experienced pilots were gone, training was abbreviated by shortage of fuel, and they were using elderly aircraft which could never have survived air combat. Their petrol tanks were half-empty, since they were not expected to return. They even invented a crude flying torpedo which was launched by another plane, like a glider: the pilot, sitting on a ton of explosive, lit three rockets which propelled him rapidly towards his target. The first mission of this type took place on 21 March 1945, but American air superiority was too overwhelming, and the bombers carrying these 'torpedoes' were intercepted and shot down. Anothe attack, on 21 April, accounted for a single destroyer – not much of a return for these elite units solemnly baptized *Jinrai oka*, the Cherry Blossoms of the Thunder of the Gods. Inventors dreamed up various other suicidal devices: small boats laden with dynamite, frogmen, pocket submarines. All of them proved ineffective in practice, but were ritually employed to the death. They accounted for five thousand kamikaze – five thousand twenty-year-olds sacrificed in a matter of months.

They no longer believed they could win the war by cowing the enemy, nor destroy an invasion fleet, nor even put off the landings on Japanese soil. But sacrifice had to remain part of the general agony, like a flame for all eyes to see, for the glory of Greater Japan on point of death. Did the imperial sun, like the sun god of the Aztecs, need to be reborn in human blood? Whether effective or not, General Onishi would say, these attacks are giving the world and ourselves a spectacle of heroism and pride; whatever happens they are the safeguard of our spiritual heritage. The day came when the sacrifice knew itself to be void and vain, but it reigned on without a purpose, pluming itself on its heroic prestige, continuing on its course by pure inertia.

THE IMPARTIAL MARTYR

In letters of consolation written to their parents, the young volunteers often took up well-worn themes: do not weep for me, I shall die, proud and happy, for the emperor and for victory. They really had to appear convinced of the efficacity of their devotion. In their private notebooks some doubts made themselves felt, and they dared to contemplate defeat, and with it the chill absurdity of their death. (Absurd? A death that is willed, and not simply endured, is not absurd: it has the meaning its sufferer gives it, however vain that meaning may be.) Anti-militaristic accents are often heard: see what the pride of these strutting generals has brought upon us! Thus Sasaki Hachiro, who died off Okinawa on 14 April 1945, intent on keeping an equitable frame of mind to the end. An unusual martyr – lucid, sceptical, impartial:

> To tell the truth, what the generals say sounds hollow in my ears, aimed only at exciting the masses. I have always tried to be on the side of the just, and I hate the unjust and the proud, whether on our side or on the enemy's. Good and Evil, love and hate, in my eyes are simply aspects of humanity, and I cannot love or hate along national boundaries. Of course, the problem changes when a difference of nationality or racial origin causes mutual incomprehension or antagonism. But a mere difference in nationality does not make me deny my respect to what is truly humanly noble and beautiful, or shut my eyes to what is base and ugly.

In the officers' mess, those who encouraged themselves by repeating propaganda from the radio were jokingly called *kichigai*: madmen, loonies. The great surge of national feeling was past, leaving it to the present generation of sacrifices to expiate the excesses of others. They went to their deaths at the height of their health and strength, and most of them openly avowed their love of life, which they had to renounce as if waking from a dream. A beautiful dream: they did not stoop to despise what they could no longer have, and their sacrifice was all the more poignant for being devoid of pessimism and bitterness. When they looked back on the brief time which had been allowed them, they were grateful for it, remembering only the happy hours. In a supreme refinement of feeling they blessed the world they were leaving. Without complaint, they renounced everything but refused nothing – the opposite of our modern rebels who contest everything but will not give up an atom of it.

Pilot Officer Nagatsuka had the gentle, but now for ever unrealizable, ambition of reading the whole of George Sand's *The Master Bellringers*. He thought of his mother and sisters, who must be protected from invasion. A good son, a good student, a good soldier, the young pilot of the Special Units was martyr less to his faith than to his good will. He was no daredevil and no boaster: he was serious, industrious, a good child who always did what was expected of him. Not only the enemy but the whole world, longing for the peace which their sacrifice was postponing, cursed their frenzied fanaticism.

But what reaches us is their sense, their calm, their lucidity. From the outside they looked like raving madmen, or robots, those eager hearts too aware of the ills of their time to cling to their own lives. No one could understand what they were doing, but for them it was simple and spontaneous. People believed they were forced, inveigled, brainwashed, fed on promises, illusions and drugs; people's eyes went through the crystal clarity of their self-denial, so clear it was impossible to perceive. It is this purity which is so unbearably moving. These young men, learning to die well at an age when life might have been so fair, were misunderstood. It is for us to give them the tribute of admiration and compassion which they deserve. They died for Japan, but we do not need to be Japanese to understand them – only mortal. Their prodigies of resolution are summed up by Sasaki Hachiro in a few lines. In their struggle with and into death, it was good will alone which gave them a profound peace at heart:

> I should like to dedicate all my strength to living as a man in conformity with the decrees of destiny. That is my state of mind. Must we not all assume the destiny which was conferred on us at birth, work with all our strength, fight with all our strength, each in the way that is set before him? To quibble, to turn aside from that way, is the act of a coward. Let us resolve the clash of arms as Heaven decrees, by choosing to follow the way which has been set before us. I am convinced that only by each of us accomplishing the task we have been given can the history of the world move forward. I want to live as a man among men, human to the end, and without cowardice.

Destiny must not only be endured, it must be loved and conquered, for that is the price of serenity – *amor fati*. Then one can die, like Kusunoki Masashige, wishing to be reborn again, even seven times, to such a life. The will has peace when it understands that it can only will, and go on willing, what it has once willed. There is no need for other worlds besides this one.

ON THE BRINK

Every week of reprieve brought the volunteers nearer the outer limits of the human condition, to the roots. They were no supermen, nor desired to be; they were radically, unreservedly human. They drew their courage not from improbable promises of victory, but from the friendship born of the common will which united them, and from that friendship with the past which is called tradition. Like the scholars of Heian, endlessly reformulating the eternal *mono no aware* of beings cast adrift in time, Admiral Onishi had sounded the old note of impermanence in a poem dedicated to the first kamikaze flights:

> Blossoming now,
> Tomorrow scattered on the winds,
> Such is the flower of life.
> So delicate a perfume
> Cannot last long.

The volunteers could echo tradition and say that it is good to serve even to death, even if it is useless – and to die young, like the cherry blossom which does not wait to wither on the tree. Of course they would have liked to live, and perhaps forget death; but it was there, and had to be faced. They strove, therefore, to live as those already dead, transcending opposites as the aims of Zen required, and as the *Hagakure* commanded. Usually they went through a critical phase a few hours after signing on: it was the beginning of mourning. They they reached a plateau of serenity, detachment, almost humour. They could laugh again, and those who remember the officers' messes say that they rang with gaiety at times. Their calm was not disturbed by any impatience to die, if a proposed mission happened to be put off. If it was not, they remained even-tempered, both resolute and resigned. Still alive and lively, they were distanced from life, or at least from that obdurate desire to live which holds us all in thrall. Thus they could be alive to all the details of life: rain, wind, leaves on a tree, everything was more beautiful for them, as if seen in a mirror. And the commonest theme of their last letters is gratitude for having lived. They stood on the brink of the abyss, their faces turned to what cannot be seen, cannot even be thought. Chained to a single moment in history, nailed to an overweening and temporary crisis – and yet running before the wind of freedom. Beleagered by chauvinism, most of them were aware of its abuses, and certainly well aware of bearing witness, in this extremity of experience, to the deepest essence of our common nature.

> *22 February 1945*   Now at long last I am a member of the Special Units. Will the next thirty days be my real life? Here is my chance! I am to train for death: an intensive training for a noble death.
> I leave for war with the tragedy of my country before my eyes. My youth concentrated into thirty days, my life rushing to its end.
> *A few days before leaving for battle*   I am a man among men. Neither good nor evil. Neither a superior being nor an imbecile. Decidedly a man. I, a wanderer who will live his life, to the very end, as a quest, I should like to die resigned to that, a man among men, a human story.

Those were the words of Okabe Hirakazu, soon to die at the age of twenty-four, awakening to the unequivocal destiny of a being who knows himself totally mortal, and so radically equal to all other beings.

The decision to die ushered in a period of respite which pared away the inessentials. Death so eludes thought that words cannot convey – can scarcely even indicate – the experience. But as his last moment approaches, if he knows it is so and desires it to be so, a man is made new.

NATIONAL SUICIDE: THE PAYMENT FALLS DUE

Thus the volunteers rose to the universal, while the high priests of chauvinism at headquarters and in the newspapers wrapped their deeds in glossy declamation. The best of them, in the thick of the action, kept a sense of proportion. Extremism was, as one would expect, the heroism of those who led from the rear, and the most strident speeches came from behind office desks. The sight of sacrifice inflamed them, they found the example some consolation in the midst of disaster: every subject of the empire would have to follow it, and become a human bomb. There were even those who still dreamed of victory. Saipan had been called the turning-point; so had Leyte, Iwojima, Okinawa – and no one had dared to draw a final political conclusion from those successive defeats. Now they were proclaiming that the decisive battle would take place on the soil of Japan. Twenty million voluntary deaths, said Onishi, would be enough to save the empire. Long before the war, General Araki had been fond of saying that a people armed with sticks is invincible if it knows really how to desire it; the moment had now come to apply this impressive 'Doctrine of the Bamboo Lance' (*takeyari shugi*). A steel and concrete shelter had been built in the mountains of Nagano for the imperial family.[9]

The ego, if too harshly tested, may split, recognizing reality, but at the same time denying it with all its strength. The leaders of Japan were split into two factions, for peace and for war, but the boundary was uncertain, with people passing from one to another, so deep was the divide in each man's heart. The elderly Admiral Suzuki, venerable and valiant Prime Minister, veteran of many a tempest, was following his Taoist principles of non-action and letting himself drift. On 6 June 1945 he was telling his parliament about the range of possible suicidal reactions to a landing on Japanese soil – but the day before he had authorized his diplomats to put out peace feelers to the Soviet attaché. Very discreetly, of course, because a minister openly in favour of an armistice would not have survived for long; the militarists might have been unable to defend the country, but they could still terrorize it.

The nation seemed doomed to inevitable strangulation in the twin nooses of the enemy army and its own. Everything was sinking, the social body was gripped with a paralysing lethargy, the abyss yawned and it seemed easiest to slide into it and let oneself die. The only audible voices were those advocating national suicide.[10] Never had voluntary death been more vastly insistent. And yet it was voluntary death which offered the solution and brought peace to Japan. At the emperor's call the army finally decided to capitulate – to die alone, to fade away like the samurai of old. The will-power which was its proudest boast went to the limit, where the will is consummated by willing its own annihilation.

The last week of imperial Japan began with three terrible blows: Hiroshima on 6 August, the declaration of war by the USSR on the 8th, and Nagasaki on the 9th. Must they renounce the final battle and accept the Potsdam Declaration, which meant capitulation, occupation and a war crimes tribunal? The navy bowed to the inevitable, but the army still hoped for the impossible. For a few days everything hung on the Minister for War, General Anami. Had he resigned he could have brought down the Suzuki cabinet, and formed his own, committed to war to the death, amidst a welter of denunciations of defeatists, traitors and Badoglios. The young officers in his ministry, who worshipped him, begged him to let them stage a *coup d'état* which would give him supreme power. He was indeed an admirable figure, a suitable subject for Plutarch in some respects; but he showed his true greatness by accepting death rather than dictatorship, even his own. He would not have won the war; the die had been cast since Leyte, or even Saipan. But he could have delayed the final reckoning for a few months, postponing his own death at the cost of many others – like Hitler. Anami decided not to kill the peace; he killed himself for its sake. Twice he gave his signature to Imperial Conferences (on 9 and 14 August), knowing that peace would be the outcome. Twice he heard the emperor speak against any war on Japanese soil, and against the suicide of his country. He killed himself at dawn on 15 August.

THE EMPEROR'S WISH

Usually the emperor was presented with a unanimous decision of government and asked merely to ratify it. This had happened with Pearl Harbor. But this time he had to decide, as the divided ministers begged him to. Twice, Suzuki, Yonai and Togo pleaded for an immediate peace, while the hawks, Anami and Umezu, spoke of the dead and of defending the national structure (*kokutai*) to postpone the capitulation. Twice the emperor made his wishes clear in simple, moving terms: he wanted an end to the sacrifice, and he was ready to sacrifice himself for the peace, to yield himself to the victor: 'Whatever may happen to me, I am resolved to endure the unendurable. I am putting an end to this war on my own authority.'

The army could never of itself have accepted defeat: the supreme will, publicly declared for the first and last time, was at least giving it a chance to obey another principle than its own will, to rediscover the meaning of service and to endure the surrender as a proof of loyalty. Peace would be reached through self-transcendence, the army would capitulate and cease to be part of the national life. The country, restored by the emperor, would not die but be changed. Endure the unendurable: they would have to waken from their bad dream and stand up to the impossible – to reality – and then the gulf would turn aside. The nation, so long hypnotized by the imperial ideal, would be roused by the imperial decision. Perhaps a future could be born out of the agonies of the present. Not death but change, much harder and no less glorious: that was the sovereign's express wish. A will accustomed to prove itself by death was invited to put itself to the long test of reality which lay ahead.

LEARN TO DIE

Those days of tears and agony make one of the saddest tales in human history – whereas the bunker in Berlin owes its fascination solely to its horror. Both have been called a *Götterdammerung* for the smoky twilight which envelops them, but in Hitler's case this is hardly fair to Wagner: if Wotan wills to die, it is because he yields to the future, to the freedom to which mankind will accede after him. Even by suicide, Hitler's soul was incapable of the silent nobility of one who has accepted his destiny. The void was his emergency exit; it taught him nothing, he renounced nothing, remained obstinate, dictated his will in such a was as to shuffle off all blame and even all defeat, admitting to only one weakness – he had been too kind! It was all the fault of the German nation, which had proved unable to conquer. Was his racial obsession then no more than a pretext for the old hatreds he repeated so tirelessly?

A man in a cellar, judging all without mercy to avoid having to judge himself, as incapable of self-forgetfulness as of self-knowledge, powerless to transcend himself even in death, powerless to cease his evil talk even on the brink of the abyss of silence. Still he dreamed of vengeance and denied responsibility, error, fault, expiation and pardon, then whole of human destiny, the tribunal of history which no force can suppress and no victory interrupt. Except for Eva Braun, who showed some nobility by willingly returning to the beleaguered city, there was nothing in the bunker which was not horrible or derisory.

What a difference between the Nazi suicides and those which accompanied the defeat of Japan! Not all such acts must be judged on their outcome alone: death is always the same, but no two suicides are alike. Some are lucid and productive, others sordid and confused. Each must be understood and evaluated separately. Nero's death was not Cato's. The militarists of Greater Japan were no less cruel and brutal than any others, but they had learned to die, and kept the best of themselves for that final moment.

Shortly before midnight on 14 August, General Anami returned to his official residence at Miyakezaka. He knew that a few hours later, at midday on 15 August, the emperor would broadcast to the whole people announcing the end of the war. He had spoken to his collaborators and the young officers in his ministry. Some of them, like Colonel Ida, were suggesting a mass suicide of army officers. Anami pointed out that their duty was rather to live for their country's future. He took his usual dose of vitamins and his usual hot bath, then retired to his room. There he composed two farewell poems. At about one o'clock in the morning his brother-in-law, Colonel Takishita, entered the room. Anami made no secret of the fact that he intended to kill himself: his decision had been taken long ago and the moment had now arrived. Then he called for sake, and the two men drank together.

At two in the morning, shots were heard from the Palace: a few young officers from the Ministry of War were attempting a final coup. They had just shot General Mori, commanding the Imperial Guard, and were using his seal on orders which would admit them to the palace itself. Falsities and forgeries were the unedifying methods of these last superpatriots. While murder squads went off, as they had on 26 February, to mow down some leaders of the peace party, the young officers searched the palace rooms for the record carrying the emperor's speech, wrenching off cupboard doors like burglars – but in vain. The attempt was quickly crushed and concluded with the suicide of the perpetrators, but it showed clearly enough what could be expected in the last throes of ultra-nationalist anarchy.

When Anami learned of it he remained calm: 'That, too, will be expiated by my death.' Then he put on a white robe which the emperor had given him some years before, and seated himself on the veranda of his room. He seized his dagger and disembowelled himself from left to right. Takeshita offered to give him the *coup de grâce*, but he refused. With his left hand he felt for his carotid artery and stabbed himself below the ear. He then sank down unconscious, but he was still breathing. Takeshita, to end his agony, guided his hand and struck again at the artery, but still death did not come. As the bleak dawn of accepted defeat rose on Japan, Anami writhed under the steel. He was slowly dying. A doctor was called and certified the death when it finally took place at eight o'clock. A poem found near the body explained that laborious agony:

> Our country, protected by its gods,
> Will not perish. Let my death be offered
> To the emperor to expiate our great crime.

With this one man died the army of Greater Japan, its eyes opened by death to its abuses and overweening pride. Where is the nobility, on Hitler's side or Anami's? Nobility goes with responsibility, and willingly bears the burden it assumes. Oedipus too punished himself, and accepted guilt so as to find peace and give it to his people. Beyond impermanent victory, the warrior's dream is peace: he fights for peace, and finds it in death, happy to give it away at this price. Anami's great soul stands, like Janus, between the past and the future, peace and war, error and forgiveness. Hitler looked to hatred to give him a bogus survival; hence the idea of sending his body up in petrol smoke, to live on as a phantom (or bogeyman) and haunt history for evermore. He tried to elude the dialectic by which the future rests on a death accepted, noted and acknowledged, the death which is deliverance. The Japanese army long refused to admit defeat, but when the time came it was great enough not to try to avoid it, realizing that it would be the expiation for what the army had been. Dying, it knew itself. It realized there was no place for it in the future, and disappeared of its own accord. Many men died by their own hand. Others, in silence and labour, did endure the unendurable, to become what they were not.

THE STORM IS OVER

The emperor's speech to the nation, the first he ever made, so just, so dignified, tapped the source of tears in people's hearts, and all drank of the at bitter and purifying stream. In the next few hours, many indeed were the men and women who came to the palace gate to bow or kneel on the gravel of the vast precinct, and weep their fill of mourning and distress. Quite a few killed themselves there, under the ramparts: some thirty in all. That evening, General Onishi summoned a few friends, officers on his general staff, and bade them farewell. At three in the morning he took a sword and disembowelled himself with two cuts in the shape of a cross (*jumonji*), as Nogi had once done – from left to right, then upwards. Shortly before dawn, a servant in the building where he lodged saw the light in his room and found him sprawling in his own blood, but still alive. They laid him on his bed. A few friends hurried up; he refused any help but spoke to them, told them not to kill themselves, begged them to live for their country. On the table was his farewell poem:

> In a clear and cloudless sky
> Now shines the moon.
> The storm is over.

Onishi, creator of the Typhoon of the Gods, had devoted his last thought to serenity. By joining in the sacrifice he had inspired, his soul had found peace. He even had the strength to smile! Even his poem... not a bad attempt for an old man (he was fifty-eight). But he was in agony and could not die. *Seppuku*, without the *coup de grâce*, is not for those in a hurry. His agony, attended by so many of the youthful dead who seemed to await him, was restoring him to innocence. A fanatic? Never was anyone more so, but resolved from the beginning to give his life in payment. He finally expired at six o'clock in the evening.

Many chose death, that day or shortly afterward. Each one sought it in his own fashion. Vice-Admiral Ugaki, for example, who commanded the Fifth Airborne Division at Kyushu and a large *tokkotai* force, concluded (like Onishi) that it was his duty to follow into death all the young pilots whom he had sent to their organized sacrifice. Some twenty of his men requested permission to escort him: he would not die alone. An airborne *junshi*, sacrifices not to the hope of victory or the shame of defeat, but to friendship, eager to rejoin their lost comrades. Eleven planes took off in the evening in the direction of Okinawa. Nobody knows what became of them: they were lost in the ocean and the night.

The ultra-nationalists were resigned, forgetting their most recent declarations and obeying the sovereign will. But in the night of 15–16 August, a little group made an unsuccessful attack on the residence of Marquis Kido, Keeper of the Privy Seal, who was said to have proposed the peace to the emperor. These youngsters, students for the most part, some ten boys and three girls, made out that traitors had compelled the emperor to make his speech of capitulation. Denial of reality could scarcely have gone further without sinking into psychosis. The transcendence of the sovereign, which was the core of the imperial system, was producing its final confusions: that much-vaunted 'national structure' did indeed give full licence to suppose that the emperor was detached from the acts of his own government. After wandering through Tokyo for a few days and realizing the full extent of their isolation, they met on the night of 22 August on the little hill of Atago, joined hands in a ring – and all unpinned hand grenades, dying thus to avoid living a truth which they could not accept.

The demobilization of the armed forces continued without incident. Some officers committed suicide rather than surrender their arms – an unequivocal gesture which had the merit of showing the rest a clear path from war to peace. It was like the sudden change from cold to heat which characterizes the Japanese climate: to every season its own weather in the eternal cycle of time. War and peace, storm and calm, are part of nature, seasons of the heart.

The only hitch took place at the air force base of Atsugi, not far from Tokyo, where the commander (he really *was* psychotic) maintained that the emperor's speech was a forgery perpetrated by the Badoglios in the government. He distrusted everything and everybody and would not even answer the telephone; he spoke only of annihilating the American navy. He had to be taken to hospital. He had 2,000 kamikaze in reserve for the final battle; their mothers and fathers came to persuade the young recruits that their duty was to make better use of their good will, and live on.

THE SECOND WAVE

The process of disarmament occupied the army chiefs for several weeks, during which suicide was forgotten, or at least postponed by the urgency of the task. When it was over, all these men of once-Greater Japan were reduced to inaction and despondency. Several were about to be tried as war criminals. A second wave of suicides took place. Valiant old General Tanaka, commanding the Army of the East which was responsible for the defence of Tokyo, had had to stand idly by and watch the flames attack the sanctuary of the Emperor Meiji and the imperial palace itself, partially destroyed in the bombings. The memory was unbearable. He also had another care: for this worthy follower of Nogi, the standard could not be lost and the captain remain alive. Therefore Tanaka took upon himself to have the flags of all the units under his command transferred to army headquarters, to be burned before the victors arrived.

His voluntary death was to expiate this holocaust of the standards and make it possible for his subordinates to live without having to deny their principles, useless as the latter would be from then on. On the evening of 24 August General Tanaka, in his full-dress uniform, seated himself in a chair in front of his desk and in a loud voice thanked his aide de camp, who was working in the next room, for services rendered. Then he shot himself through the heart. Before him he had laid a few farewell letters, a sword once given him by the emperor, his cap, a pair of white gloves, some Buddhist sutras, and his false teeth.

In those last days of August, fear of the occupying army was at its height: they were expected to land at any moment. Those who remembered the atrocities committed by certain Japanese invading armies since the sack of Nanking had reason to fear the worst. The director of an aviation factory in Utsunomiya, for example, thought it expedient to issue his (female) workers with cyanide capsules, on the grounds that death was preferable to rape. The Japanese maidens were more fortunate than that St Pelagia who once jumped off a roof to escape the soldier of Diocletian: they were not called upon to die in defence of their virtue. The American troops arrived in good order, and there was no violence.

Tojo, who was chiefly answerable for the Pacific War, was widely expected to kill himself. But he seemed to be in no hurry about it. On 11 September American military police arrived at his house; he asked them, from a first-floor windown, on whose orders they were acting. Then a gun went off: he had shot himself in the chest. But he did not die. A few journalists, who had arrived to cover the arrest of the villain of Pearl Harbor, soaked handkerchiefs in his blood for their collection of wartime souvenirs, while a doctor bandaged the wound. He was taken to hospital, and with the help of numerous transfusions, dragged back to life – to be imprisoned, tried, and hanged.

General Sugiyama, army chief of staff at the time of Pearl Harbor, had been so busy with the demobilization that he forgot about dying. His wife reminded him of his duty. He had certainly decided to die, but in such cases there is a gulf between the decision on principle and the actual moment of truth: this evening, tomorrow or in a month or two? 'Well', she told him, 'I shall die before you if need be.' Throughout Japanese history, women have risen to the circumstances, however terrible. Sugiyama promised that he *would* kill himself, so long as she did not. Tojo's failed suicide made up his mind for him. The next day, 12 September, in his office at the Ministry of War, he shot himself four times with a pistol and died instantly. His wife was told; she hung up the receiver, went to her room and knelt before the Buddhist altar to the family dead. Then she prepared a cup of cyanide, drank it and stabbed herself in the breast with a little dagger.

A few weeks later Prince Konoe, hearing that he was to be indicted for war crimes among other Japanese civil and military leaders, also decided honourably to escape the tribunal. The generals' friend, he had been their dupe and accomplice between 1937 and 1941, disguising their preparations under idle talk of peace. He belonged to the ancestral aristocracy of Heian which had always detested the gory methods of the warrior aristocracy: he opted for poison.

TRIAL BY HISTORY

The war was over. It was time to judge, to explore, to try to understand. The Tokyo trials had begun, and of those leaders who had not pre-empted them by death, about thirty were accused, arrested, and subjected to precisely such a detailed examination of events, and of their own decisions. Perhaps it took no less courage to endure the lengthy trial than to elude it, as Sugiyama and Konoe had done. Week by week Tojo sat impassively, earphones over his bald head, following the sometimes confusing exchange of arguments. At the last, he bowed in salute to the tribunal when, three years after his attempted suicide, it handed down a death sentence based on abundant evidence.

'Judge not' is a good maxim if God, or karma, will do the judging for you at no extra expense. But no man of our times can refuse to collaborate, as best he can, with the stumbling search after truth which is our history. A people has the right, not to avenge itself, but to know what it has lived through and suffered – the vanquished as much as the victors. They are equal before death, but before that, equal before the truth. Voluntary death has its grandeur, but too often it drowns everything in instant night and silence, leading others up the same blind alley. It honoured the end of the war with men like Anami and Ugaki – and even war itself must be saved from total nihilism. And yet the most demanding war ethic must yield to the only struggle really worthy of humanity, in which the arms, the rules and the goal are all dictated by the truth.

The militarists were defeated, but what of militarism? Its defeat was enshrined in the new constitution – and people who talk of the Japanese as warmongers, as if to crush a whole people under a part of their past, should first make sure that their own country is bound by a law as strict as Japan's Article 9. The workers also played their part: ten years after the defeat, the highest level of prosperity achieved before the war had already been equalled and surpassed. The ruinous (and eventually catastrophic) nature of expansionist militarism, the cruelly disappointing emptiness of its solutions, was a truth learned from bitter experience. For a few more years, like the tidal waves that follow at long intervals after an earthequake, a fresh wave of suicides overtook the young men who could have – should have – died in the war. In hard times many of them were tempted to identify themselves with their many brothers and friends, eternally unwithered in memory, so soon delivered by death from the ugliness and sluggishness of living; to identify so closely that they went to join them.

Long afterwards, in 1970, Mishima Yukio was the last Japanese survivor to feel the nostalgic spell of the all-devouring Minotaur. Even effects such as these faded away with time. The young of today, who have nothing to forget because they have had nothing to endure, have little chance to judge the frenzies of nationalism. Poster-hung vans belonging to the Patriotic Party (*Aikokuto*) or some other little extreme right-wing group are more of an inoculation, a dissuasion, than an attraction as they parade through the indifferent Tokyo streets to the piercing rhythm of the melancholy, stubborn songs of Greater Japan.

If the tradition of sacrifice lingers on it is transformed, sublimated, appeased, in the work ethic binding modern Japan. It is, ironically, in the underworld that it keeps its old fire, amongst the famous criminal gangs, the *yakuza*.[11] They make no jokes about allegiance and devotion. The most disgusting criminal activities are decently clad in the most touchy ethic of honour. Like a rudimentary bone subsisting in the skeleton of a species which has evolved beyond the need of it, the pride of the ancient warriors lives on in the quarrels staged in the more disreputable bars. When one of these gentlemen feels the need to bare his soul then he acts – but it is not by searching his bowels for proofs and excuses. A cut finger or a shaven head is quite sufficient. What better way to serve tradition? And indubitably at a bargain price.

13

Some Nihilist Vignettes

The tradition of sacrifice was to have a last defender, illustrator and restorer in the writer Mishima Yukio, who gave his life for it. His suicide recalls Nogi's, but a Nogi well versed in Nietzsche, trying to bar the road to nihilism which is traced in *The Will to Power*.[1] In the modern civilization which had triumphed through Japan's defeat, Mishima saw a dismal decadence which favoured the reign of the egalitarian tarantulas denounced by Zarathustra: quietism, permissive egoism, hidden resentment. All the values which men were once justly prepared to die for have faded away, immanence is unlimited, death is a nothingness which concerns us not at all, everything has gone flat. Nothing exists for us but our own life, and when it turns out to be nothing worth having, what safeguard have we against the scandalous, anguished absurdity of despair?

Modernism, according to Mishima, has withered transcendence by banishing sacrifice, leaving no sovereign principle to give meaning to life. We may have no further illusions, but also no transcendent goal to unite and exalt us. Under our busy everyday life lurks apathy; even revolt, now sunk to mere protest, is no longer self-justifying. Life, by cutting loose from death, has lost its *élan*, its vitality. With no risk and no sacrifice we are left with both boredom and anger, spurts of lawless violence pointlessly and uselessly disturbing the torpor of official pacifism. Insanity is only answered by insanity. Such was Mishima's diagnosis under its veil of romantic nostalgia. Even in this desert there had to be some way of restoring transcendence and the sacrifice on which it feeds. Discourse is vain: one must act and rely on the silent eloquence of gesture. Like Dostoevsky's Kirilov,[2] Mishima killed himself to show that there was a way out, his voluntary death a stake laid down to win the prize of a healthy future. On 25 November 1970 he struck his last blow against the nothingness of modernism.

THE CONSEQUENCES OF THOUGHT

Kirilov and Zarathustra, familiar figures for Mishima, should not be allowed to mask what is specifically Japanese in his case. Perhaps the whole modern world *is* destined for nihilism; perhaps it is the ransom already paid for the increase of power conferred by technology – but every nation beats its own path to the same goal. Dostoevsky and Nietszche saw it as the natural aftermath of Christianity: God is dead, and how can that loss be avoided, expiated, compensated or consummated? It was thus that Barbey d'Aurevilly gave Huysmans the choice between the pistol barrel and the foot of the cross.[3] Is it a real dilemma?

If, as Kirilov averred, men over the centuries merely imagined God as an escape from despair, was he not obliged to kill himself if he really wanted to follow his new conviction to its logical conclusion? The ancient Greeks and Romans had followed their eudaemonic bent and justified suicide as a 'reasonable way out', the surest way to escape unnecessary evils. Stoicism had given it an ethical function by entrusting it with the dignity of the sage. The warlike tradition of Japan, by ritualizing its proceedings, had codified its relationship to honour and self-sacrifice.

Romanticism brings in a new complication. Whether it puts the final seal on nihilism or aims to transcend it, voluntary death becomes part of a spiritual struggle. It is no longer a mere product of circumstances, convention, mood or custom, or of an art or duty of dying well: it becomes the proof of an essential disillusionment, part of the thinker's journey towards his conclusion. A pure philosophical act, as Novalis called it. A preliminary question, as Camus called it. The only really important question, which must be answered before any other question, now that God is dead and we can no longer avoid it by denying the sovereignty of the human will. Might one be logically obliged to kill oneself after reaching a certain level of lucidity? In a world where there is no life except the present one, no other will than the indiviudal will, man has become the sole judge of the totality of being balanced on the knife-point of his decision. The sun of divine omnipotence has imploded into the black hole of nihilist suicide, ready to swallow up the absolute of freedom.

Japan never knew the Western God; why should it be troubled by his disappearance? Akutagawa confirms that the Japanese never knew a supreme and all-powerful being worth killing off! To them, the metaphysical revolt which, over two centuries, extinguished the heaven of the West might have remained a distant event. The rulers of Meiji's time thought it was. Their slogan was *wakon yosai*: keep the spirit of Japan and borrow from the West only its military and industrial expertise – the better to oppose it. Did they have some inkling of the profoundly subversive and destructive impact of Western ideology? They still saw Christianity as a force for conquest, and remembering Shimabara, feared lest it introduce fresh dissensions.

They were surprised to find that this foreign religion had lost much of its bite. There was no harm in letting the missionaries preach, but other dangers gradually did appear: more to be feared than catechisms were novels, the thousand and one scattered episodes in the odyssey of freedom seeking freedom. Soon it became clear that they could not dissociate scientific techniques from the science of institutions and the institution of ideas and customs. Step by step the whole of Western civilization, with its trail of contradictions, enigmas and seductions, was creeping in. Curiosity and courage, sound Japanese virtues, found work here, with the keenest intellects folowing untrodden paths between East and West and striving to travel, in a few decades, the road which the men of the West had taken two centuries to complete. Many failed and despaired, but all emerged with the idea that thought can be both bold and tragic. The literature of the last years of Edo reflects an exhausted world: theatre sinks into melodrama, poetry into mere prettiness, novels are divided between lumbering moralism and empty frivolity. The plays of Shakespeare and Goethe, the poetry of Baudelaire, the novels of Tolstoy, gave the readers of the new Japan some idea of the dangerous power which books can have over the destiny of mankind.

REASON IN A PADDED CELL

It was Fukuzawa Yukichi, the most brilliant advocate of openness to the West, who incarnated the spirit of the Enlightenment, from Voltaire to Bentham. He preached liberty, so long as it served the common good. Among the twenty-nine articles of the moral code he published on 11 February 1900 as a résumé of his convictions was a total condemnation of voluntary death: 'Man's duty is to live his allotted span to the end; to dispose of one's own life, in whatever circumstances, and for whatever alleged reasons, is always an irrational and cowardly act, altogether abominable and unworthy of the principles of Independence and Self-Respect.'[4]

Before Fukuzawa, most eighteenth-century European philosophers had also endeavoured to exclude the right to die from the panoply of the rights of man – that simple 'right to leave' claimed by Baudelaire. Kant said that man could not logically think it good to destroy his own power to choose between good and evil, and had not the right to eliminate that consciousness which is the foundation of all rights: no licence for a freedom so opposed to all freedom. That was the decree of reason, and the barriers it raised seemed high enough, even without the sanction of divine punishment, to those who felt no pressing need to have done with life. But it can happen that such arguments are refuted in action, as the Eleatics' arguments are refuted by the action of walking. A philosopher may even be found to forgive each individual suicide while condemning all suicide, supposing he is willing to understand it and not be blinded by his own theorems.[5]

Fukuzawa, a samurai by birth, was an admirer of Saigo, but he had vowed to destroy the ethic of the warrior aristocracy, which he blamed for Japan's backwardness. He knew perfectly well that by decrying the voluntary death he was dealing that tradition a body-blow, and in this struggle he was convinced that he had reason and progress on his side, with all the weight of the West. And yet in 1900, other forms of voluntary death, alien to *bushido* and the sacrificial tradition, were already beginning to appear, inspired by that same West of which Fukuzawa had made himself the mouthpiece. He himself, as he defended his principles, was paving the way for unforeseen consequences. He advocated independence and emancipation – and to a growing number of students, intellectuals and authors who followed the lead of romanticism and anarchy towards radical forms of individual liberty. He advocated utilitarianism; it was a first step towards materialism. Exalt the freedom of the individual and decry the constraints of his environment: nineteenth-century Europe had devoted itself to first the one and then the other.

The liveliest strain in the Japanese culture of 1900 was inspired by both at once. Translations introduced people to Wordsworth and Flaubert, Rousseau and Maupassant, all at the same time. In the productive genre of the autobiographical novel (*shishosetsu*) naturalism rubs shoulders with romanticism, which in European literary histories is described as its natural enemy. A single writer – Shimazaki Toson for example – could imitate both Shelley and Zola. Such writers ignored Western boundaries – though not more so than did geniuses in European literature who, like Baudelaire, were capable of combining the most piercing idealism with the most implacable realism. These tendencies, born of Enlightenment rationalism, all converge on nihilism and its assertion that nothing in reality confirms the vital illusions of the heart. At which point suicide, representing the clash of life's demands with our dreams, begins to look like the recoil of a mind beseeching death to deliver it from nothingness.[6]

DESTINY OF A ROMANTIC

Fukuzawa's apparently robust optimism did have its precarious moments. In 1894, everything conspired to justify him: Japan was on the way up, it was shaking off the extra-territoriality clauses which shackled it; it made an alliance with Britain and entered into a war with China which was to show how well it had assimilated its Western borrowings. But a chance event of that same year, the suicide of a young poet aged twenty-seven named Kitamura Tokoku, expressed a malaise which could never be dissipated by any great events in the country's history.

On the surface, the will to power engaged in ever bolder ventures; but the intellectuals, stubbornly indifferent to such projects, were sinking into ever deeper gloom. The intellectual, if he is more than just a technician or bureaucrat, always tends to feel isolated from immediate social intercourse: he observes himself and others, criticizes himself and others, is of divided mind and has no spontaneous adherence to anything. In Meiji Japan this alienation was much more marked: intellectuals employed in the work of modernization saw turning to the West as an ideal still imperfectly understood and overestimated. Many of them, like Don Quixote or Madame Bovary, felt sadly that they had been born in the wrong time or place. They became strangers to their own society, drifting between two worlds. Kitamura was tormented by a feeling of inadequacy. 'In everything we are inferior', he would say; 'never will we produce a work like *Les Misérables* or the *Divine Comedy*, not to speak of *Paradise Lost*!'

Thus the openness to the West which had stimulated Fukuzawa could also provoke a depressing feeling of rootlessness. Hölderlin, in his fascination with Greece, had realized the danger, and advocated a 'return to the homeland' (*vaterländische Umkehr*) which would retore the European, child of the modern Hesperides, to the cultivation of qualities more natural to him, without envy or nostalgia. What is foreign to us should teach us to become what we are. Japanese intellectuals sometimes performed this volte-face (*tenko*) simply in order to fit back into their milieu. Some denied themselves, and became, like Barrès, mere voices of chauvinism. But from one generation to the next most of them, grown wiser with the years, inevitably became bourgeois and respectable and lost their early fervour.

Kitamura disdained such equivocations; his tormented conscience remained pure and alert, and if he finally chose death, it was also because he, like so many of the young, wanted to remain faithful to the fragile intensity of feelings and convictions which time would inevitably obscure. At a very early stage he campaigned for civic freedoms, but intrigue and violence killed his taste for political action. His hero, Lord Byron, had been lucky to find a cause like Greek independence to soothe his spleen. In a society which seemed too narrow for him, Kitamura could see no undertaking worth risking his life for. For some months he was a Christian, or thought he was, like so many other intellectuals of his time; but it only gave him a still greater scorn for this world, and a feeling of failure: the God he would have liked to love had not come alive within him.

Ardent and thoughtful, a devotee of the inner life, he was the incarnation of a noble soul disappointed and embittered, aware of its growing solitude. At least most noble souls are satisfied with their own perfection, and their vanity preserves them from despair; Kitamura was too lucid to fall for such deceits. He might have endured disappointment and deceit from vile men and an ungrateful world, but to deceive *himself* was intolerable to this son of a samurai, fed on Byron and Emerson. He had dreamed wonderful dreams, planned books and exploits which he could never perform: it was a failure which had to be expiated.

In an essay published a year before his death, he noted that suicide could have an element of vengeance: it could be self-punishment for self-inflicted injuries. What injury was worse than failing to become what one ought to be? Idealism paved the way for nihilism and nourished resentment, measuring the gulf between what existed and what ought to exist. Came the time when the dreamer avenged his dream by sacrificing himself to it. Most idealists manage to avoid this conclusion by blaming someone else: their condemnation of the world always turns into self-satisfaction. Evil has its uses, since combating it gives one something to do. Kitamura scorned such evasions. One value might have saved him, if he had ever seen it incarnate: love. He thought it justified life and might even explain its enigmas. He had had the courage – very rare in the society of his time – to marry for love at the age of twenty, but he had seen love wear away in marriage. When, a few years later, he suggested to his wife that they commit suicide together, it was too late: she could no longer understand him. If she had accepted, would it have restored his taste for living? Through disappointment to disillusionment, he was retreating from this world in which 'action is not the sister of dreams.' On 28 December 1893, he tried to cut his throat with a dagger, but he was found and taken to hospital, and the wound healed. His melancholy was not so easily cured, and on 16 May 1894 this poet, impatient with the prosaic world, hanged himself very simply from a tree in his garden.

THE IMPULSIVENESS OF YOUTH

Kitamura's short life breathed the spirit of the new era, with its promises and perils, the longing to live at last and break every fetter – a project as doomed as the flight of Icarus. A soul that burns too brightly consumes itself and dies, like Werther, Emma Bovary or Anna Karenina. Idealism and passion fall broken-winged into voluntary death. It was in the early years of the twentieth century, not long before Meiji's death, that romanticism and philosophical pessimism together worked most powerfully on young Japanese, seduced by Western books into trying the adventure of liberty.[7] Perhaps ideas would have been an insufficient attraction in themselves, but they were decisive when added to the depressing material conditions which many students and intellectuals had to endure: poverty, rootlessness, solitude, the tuberculosis which was so common at the time, any of them could become unbearable under the goading of a book. The most consistent among them wondered whether to attack the very root, the will to live which (according to Schopenhauer) produces the contradictory world to which we are doomed. And their conclusion was suicide, although Schopenhauer, faithful to his Buddhist antecedents, rejected suicide as a violent gesture unconducive to deliverance. For him, chastity, detachment, asceticism, resignation, at the worst death by starvation, were the best ways to deny the will to live.

It was too much to expect a young creature to keep to those cold methods: he must show his vitality even in the way he died! Fashion also took a part, for suicide, even in the depths of solitude, is still open to imitation. A forest, volcano or river shore might become a favourite place for a few months or years, a place where death seemed easier, where you felt surrounded by friendly presences who had trodden the dark road before you. In 1903, in the forest of Nikko, an eighteen-year-old schoolboy carved his last message on a tree: 'I am killing myself because I don't understand what things mean.' Then he leapt into the waterfall of Kegon. Others followed. In this confrontation of the thinking mind with the silent world, a sombre exaltation can be felt under the revolt, the exaltation of Hölderlin's Empedocles in his farewell to the world:

> And the glad bow of Iris the bright-blossoming
> Flexed, rises up where those quick billows fall;
> So from my heart it [joy] billows and bows down.[8]

Could death ever be a celebration, as Zarathustra wished? A savage and solitary one if so: the green grass, the sun, the crashing waters, and the palpitations of a youthful heart, pierced with anguish but dizzy and drunk with liberty and that curiosity about death which fades with age, the desire to pluck out the heart of its mystery and find what is hidden there. No doubt it was that curiosity which pushed a very young poet called Oka Masafumi – he was twelve – off a high building on the evening of 17 July 1975. 'I may kill myself one day', said one of his poems. 'But I cannot die.' Perhaps that is what he wanted to ascertain, once and for all.[9] The purest beings, always athirst for understanding and always amazed at their own existence, are virtually convinced that they have nothing to lose by dying. At the other end of life you have to be feeling very worn, very ill, to regain that same liberty and turn back to the 'reasonable way out', knowing that you have nothing to lose but your pains.

A SOCIAL SCOURGE

In that same year, 1903, Japanese suicide rates reached their highest level, with over twenty suicides per 100,000 of the population per year. Statistics had been compiled and published since 1882, and the numbers were steadily rising: 14.4 in 1884, 17.2 in 1895, 20.6 in 1903. They were not to know that this figure represented a ceiling, and that the rate would soon fall to around the 15 mark. In 1939 the rate was the same as in 1884 – nothing too alarming. But at the turn of the century, all the Cassandras out to foretell the awful consequences of modernism had some support for their anxieties: the wave of suicides detected over about twenty years seemed unstoppable. Could there be a surer criterion for judging a civilization?

A few years earlier, in 1897, Durkheim had conferred scientific value on that indicator, and with his new concept of *anomie* he had described the modern fever which was undermining the health of society. Sacrifice, called altruistic suicide by Durkheim, was in decline, but unbridled individualism and anarchic desire were much more ominous: the individual was breaking away from his family and whatever secular and religious groups were restraining – and also protecting – him; his freedom, i.e. his solitude, then laid him open to an anguish which he would often terminate by suicide. Perfect nihilism is attained when every self denies the existence of every other self, a solipsism whose result is revealed by the statistics.

In the first decade of the twentieth century an awareness of nihilist death, fed by suicide stories in the daily press and given intellectual respectability by the new scientific study of suicide, became perceptible, especially among students, teachers and writers, who felt themselves most intimately concerned in this curious menace whose victims were all volunteers – this ill which was the cure for all other ills. The intellectual, teetering between the past and the future, the near and the far, the familiar and the strange, inevitably ran risks. Though it might be calm on the surface, his life was beset with grave dangers, and the statistics show that suicide struck ten times harder at this section of the population.

The greatest novelist of the period, Natsume Soseki, expressed the general anxiety. In *I Am a Cat* (1905) he lovingly transcribes an interminable discussion as it might fall upon the ironical ears of a favourite cat. Once, says one speaker, people were taught self-forgetfulness, but nowadays individualism is triumphant, and there is no peace of soul any more. One must die – but how? Our times are asking each one of us that question, and it is becoming more and more insistent:

'Most people are not particularly intelligent, and they let things follow their natural course; then eventually the world and its difficulties puts an end to them. But men of character are not satisfied with death over the slow fire of the world's wickednesses. They meditate on the means of their death, and after long deliberation they come up with an original idea. So I can assure you that, in future, the general tendency will be for more suicides, and that those who commit suicide will leave this world in a fashion all their own.'

'Life will be frightening, then.'

'No doubt it will. [Henry] Arthur Jones often brings on a philosopher advocating suicide in his plays...'

'And he commits suicide?'

'Unfortunately not. But in a thousand years' time, everyone will. In ten thousand years' time, people will think of suicide as the only way to die.'

'What a terrible thought!'

'Indeed it is. Then people will really begin to make a serious study of suicide, which will become a science in its own right, and in schools like the School of the Descending Cloud you will have suicide studies instead of moral science.'[10]

A sarcastic sort of philosophy, cooked up over a cup of sake, but with a real cross-current of apprehension at such nihilism. What is the remedy? The same year that saw Soseki's novel published also saw Japan fighting the empire of the Tsars and forgetting its dissensions in sacrifice: a society was being reforged in war, as Hegel had said could happen – and Durkheim had just been showing that at such times the suicide rate usually falls. If that was the remedy, was it not worse than the disease? Soseki put his hopes in another solution, the morality of self-sacrifice, luckily still well alive in Japan. Perhaps it was not too late to look to traditional disciplines for a protection against the dangers of unbridled individualism?

> I am saying that Western society may seem attractive, but in reality it is doomed to failure. Conversely, the East has always gone in for the discipline of the mind, and the East is right. You see: everyone is turning neurotic because of this cult of the personality.

Would a free spirit like Soseki have approved of the distrustful officialdom which, since the beginning of the Meiji era, had been warning teachers and intellectuals against Western influence? Hardly: censorship cannot really be asked to combat nihilism, it is more likely to justify it. If tradition were to be a refuge it would have to be reconquered by every individual, defended and illustrated by a personal commitment. General Nogi was to be an example. After presiding over the slaughter of Port Arthur he was entrusted with the education of the sons of the nobility, where he was to find some already very sceptical minds. Perhaps we should add one more to the reasons for dying he gives in his will: it gave real weight to speeches which had sounded empty and stereotyped in youthful ears. The irrefutable act would silence all the quibbles of decadence. Words were vain; they played into the adversary's hands. Only a free and wordless sacrifice could win the fight against nihilism, with its libertarian siren call luring the young into the abyss of despair.

THE NOBILITY OF THE ACT

Japanese traditional thinking kept up the same opposition as Christianity between sacrifice and suicide, Jesus and Judas. Voluntary death could not be divorced from its intentions: it was good if it had a goal, an ideal, and drew people together by affirming certain values; it was bad if it was only the conclusion of despair, solitude and negation. But the study of suicide which had developed in the nineteenth century on the fringes of the humane sciences had had the effect of cancelling that opposition. Even seen as aspects of behaviour, suicide and sacrifice became confused, and their more or less illusory (and sometimes crazed) motivations had to be deciphered as pathological symptoms. A student of ethics might have replied that to consider the intention as a symptom was to display that very nihilism which they were supposed to be resisting. While the scientists set up their clinical statistical tables, it was important to keep open the possibility of an ethics of voluntary death, whereby it would still have meaning and might have a use. It was the nobility (if any) of the act which would be decisive, alerting those minds which could understand and rally round.

Indeed the writer Mori Ogai, who had translated Goethe, Strindberg and Ibsen, heard the death of Nogi as a clarion call. He turned to the composition of austere tales of olden times. A writer's first goal should perhaps be lucidity; but if he dedicates himself (as Ibsen did, for example) to revealing the Pharisee and hypocrite under the virtuous exterior he must also be able, when the time comes, to recognize and hail acts of true nobility. Otherwise Ibsen and all who seek to imitate him are doomed to moral nihilism. Human actions can be beautiful – pointlessly so perhaps, but they can at least set a limit to utilitarianism and show the existence of higher values than individual happiness. If morality consists of talking and talking to show one's obedience to duty, then the sceptics are right. But the obligation to act out your duty even to death, as the customs of old Japan required, eliminates false pseudo-Kantian virtue without destroying morality.

An ethic of voluntary death, such as Mori Ogai develops in his tales, *is* an answer to scepticism. Why live on in a world where everyone cheats, where everyone pursues his own petty interests under cover of morality, like a businessman trading on his reputation for honesty? Such cheating cannot stand up to the duty of death. Its distinctions are irrefutable and irreducible to mere utility. Mori Ogai was determined to grasp the implicit morality of bygone custom and give it contemporary relevance.

It was at that time that Gandhi, heir to a completely different tradition, was preparing to fight imperialism with the non-violent weapon of a fast to the death. But in Japan the state was too strong and its aim too sure: it had monopolized tradition for its own ends. Before 1945 there was no way to unloose the bond which had enslaved self-sacrifice to the power of the state and its spirit of conquest. In 1912 the government censors got busy over the Nogi affair, trimming the event to fit into a mythology of blind obedience, effacing its useless nobility, its calm and empty beauty, and turning it into an echoing recitation of the militarist catechism they had instilled into the masses.

DESPAIR OF A WEALTHY BOURGEOIS

It is not surprising, therefore, if Japanese free-thinkers took a generally detached attitude to the suicide of Nogi: its annexation by officialdom had compromised it. Among the young intellectuals associated with the review *Shirakaba* between 1910 and 1923 were several who came from the very School of Peers over which Nogi had presided, but their attitude remained unsympathetic: they were far more touched by the suicide of (for example) Van Gogh. To these readers of Tolstoy, Whitman, Maeterlinck and Romain Rolland, Nogi's principles seemed cramped, sour, anachronistic. They were sensitive souls, fed on humanism and aestheticism; they were not worried by nihilism, and if they looked on decadence they saw only its splendid exuberance. They were impassioned dilettantes who felt there would never be time enough to explore all the cultural treasures which the world had to offer. The fertility of the human spirit seemed to them safeguard enough against the attraction of the void.

However, when in 1923 one of the most famous of their number, Arishima Takeo, committed suicide, the fragility of humanist principles was exposed. Perhaps they could remain unassailable only so long as they remained abstract and theoretical: as soon as anyone really tried to practise them in society, the contradictions appeared, and discouragement loomed. But knowing without doing, as Wang Yang-Ming had remarked, was not knowledge. Arishima, following Faust, asked, 'In the beginning was there the Word? or the Act?' The answer was, of course, the Act. Something must be done – but what?

For Arishima, son of a senior civil servant, the intellectual life had begun with his conversion to Christianity. It presented him with a contradiction: the notion of love raised to a supreme ideal, and the awareness that the flesh was enslaved to sin. Later, while studying in the USA, he became interested in revolutionary doctrines, read Marx and met Kropotkin. Thereafter he was torn between the desire to free the creative impulses of the individual, and the idea of a social revolution. (A few years later André Breton and his circle were also to try, with no better success, to reconcile life here and now with the austere meditations of political commitment.) What distinguished Arishima was his uneasy conscience; he could invent a course of action but not feel part of it, saw the need for a combat which he could not conclude or even undertake. As a wealthy landowner and bourgeois intellectual, what could he do to deliver himself from what he was – from what he had? In 1922 he divested himself of his lands, sharing them among his tenant farmers, but he knew that this experiment in rural communism in a capitalist society was doomed to failure. One individual could achieve nothing, perhaps not even appease his own conscience.

Arishima was never to escape from his original sin of being born bourgeois; he would never be numbered amongst the elect. In his discouragement he turned again to Marxism; his paradox was to have a faith and find nothing in it but despair. It remained only to put his pessimism into action. In July 1922 a yong woman attached herself to him; already a widower at forty-four, he saw this liaison as his last chance of love. In his writings he had often talked of the shattering, if also creative, force of passion; he knew what he was risking by giving way to it. When he wanted to end the relationship he could not: she threatened to kill herself. The wronged husband burst on the scene demanding financial compensation, emphasizing the intolerable triviality of bourgeois adultery. On 8 June 1923 the two lovers took the train to the mountain station of Karuizawa, a few hours' journey from Tokyo, where Arishima owned a villa. There, a month later, their putrefying bodies were found hanging side by side from the ceiling.

In this much publicized event the newspapers sought evidence of the looseness of modern morals so characteristic of the new Taisho era. But what is really striking is the intellectual's loss of heart as he stands frozen on the threshold of action, aware of his solitude face to face with a distrustful party, a repressive state, and an indifferent public. One month later there was the terrible Kanto earthquake. People were gripped with a savage madness and sought scapegoats: Koreans and left-wingers. Ten anarcho-syndicalists were massacred in the courtyard of a Tokyo police station, and a police officer took it on himself to strangle Osugi, an anarchist, his mistress and his young nephew in the cell where they had been detained. Such details show the extent of the social pressure weighing on intellectuals – and their enemies gained fresh ammunition from a law on 'dangerous thinking' passed on 6 May 1925. Three years later 1,500 people were arrested at the same time for casting doubt on the sacred principles of national structure (*kokutai*) and private property.

THE ART OF TAKING NOTHING SERIOUSLY

Many intellectuals, despairing of a world whose violence was equalled only by its inertia, sought consolation in aestheticism. They accepted their solitude and decided to view it as a sign of election. They fell back on the enjoyment of the privileges of which Arishima had been so ashamed. Thus, long ago, had the aristocracy of Heian shut itself in its refined little world. Some of the greatest writers of modern Japan, like Nagai Kafu, Tanizaki or Kawabata, opted for this contemplative retreat and took refuge from the present in the past. It was not an unwise preference. While most people dutifully shouted for war in the Pacific, Tanizaki was following the light-hearted detours of the *Tale of Genji*: the Japan of the old romances was probably preferable to the Japan of the newspapers of the day. If they sought an escape from nihilism, then the religion of art could grant the soothing, appeasing, healing, gift of beauty.

A wordsmith can earn the esteem due to any honest craftsman. Diligent work will always be the safest refuge, from which one can view the human comedy and feel the weight of reality less heavy, since it is no more than an illusion to be described. That was Flaubert's recipe for enduring his conviction that nothing was worth anything. The Absurd is blunted to the merely ridiculous. Others might, like Zola, take their stand on scientific objectivity: life is not so worrying if it comes neatly done up in psycho-sociological parcels. Goethe had avoided a similar fate by describing the sufferings of the young Werther. Gide claimed that he did not drown himself in the morass because he wrote *Paludes* instead; perhaps we should believe him. There may indeed be no better way to escape the menace of suicide: to be freed from all illusion, but to keep one's distance and learn to be detached from everything, even despair. Suicides commit the folly of forgetting that the world is a game without a prize, an innocent game indifferent to good and evil. The strongest argument against them is that they lack sang-froid and a sense of humour. Life is not serious enough to be worth cursing. The smile of the Buddha reminds us of that lesson, and Zen drives it home.

Of all Japanese writers, none was more inclined than Akutagawa to seek refuge in art. He recalls how as a bookish young man he would perch on a library ladder, looking down on passers-by: 'The whole of life is not worth a single line of Baudelaire!' His novellas, whose subject matter is often borrowed from ancient chronicless (as in *Rashomon*), are distinguished by the elegant irony of their construction, somewhere between Wilde and Swift. He was indifferent to the traditional ethic and had nothing but scorn for the brutality and sentimentalism of Nogi. He was wholly modern in spirit, but he was unsatisfied with the optimism of *Shirakaba*, which seemed to him naïve. He had understood very early on that beauty is the accomplice of evil, and that nothing truly delightful is done without help from a demon. Art works hand in glove with cruelty.

One of his stories gives a striking example of this. Yoshihide, a screen painter, anxious to give an accurate depiction of the torments of hell, wants a human being burned alive before his eyes, and his feudal employer grants his request. In the victim, bound and gagged in a burning cart, Yoshihide recognizes his own daughter. Transfixed with horror, he remains capable of appreciating the beauty of the flames and the piteousness of human suffering. He finishes his masterpiece, then hangs himself the following night. Can life be a mere spectacle? All is illusion; suffering alone cannot be denied. Art does not bring salvation, or even physical well-being; it is a crime which has to be expiated. What writer does not feel called upon to share the agonies he is describing? If the path to truth leads through misfortune, then, like Oscar Wilde in prison, he will follow it.

Akutagawa's aestheticism, confident at first, became hesitant and uneasy: life was baying at this heels. After 1922 his stories became more emotional and intimate. The work of art was no longer a crystal but a flame, which needed living fuel. And the artist felt honour-bound to offer himself as its victim. On the surface he was protected by irony, but deeper down his sensibility delivered him up entirely. If only, like Geothe, he could have found some sort of equilibrium through his work . . . but more often, his modernist demand for authenticity made of art an insatiable search, inconceivably dangerous. Zola, basing *L'Oeuvre* on his friend Cézanne, shows a painter so obsessed with the absolute that he hangs himself; Mallarmé, in 'Igitur', describes the annihilation of self-consciousness at the moment of its supreme achievement.

THE ANTECHAMBER OF THE VOID

Akutagawa, frail and feverish, seemed to be consuming himself year by year in the flame of his art. His sojourn in hell was a long one. He envied those who, like Verlaine or Claudel or Strindberg or Max Jacob, had escaped into religious conversion. He himself felt too alienated from Christianity, but too Westernized to look elsewhere. The last pages he ever wrote are devoted to Jesus, but to Jesus the man, a doomed intellectual, son of the Spirit (that is, of Inspiration), dedicated to the struggle against the Pharisees, determined to live intensely, which meant to venture as far as death and defeat – *Eli, Eli, lama sabachthani?*

In his last months, Akatagawa's anguish grew. He used sleeping pills and complained that his mind was never clear for more than an hour a day. He thought his inspiration had run out, although these last months were among his most fertile; and worse, he feared he was going mad, as his mother had done. Death was preferable: for two years, he said, he had thought of little else but suicide. What other refuge was there when even sleep, dream-haunted, gave no rest? He was never impulsive or crazy. His was a cool-headed distress, with eyes open on the approaching abyss.

The act had been anticipated for a long time, meditated and premeditated. Long ago, out of childish curiosity, he had experimented with timed strangulation and discovered that it was painful for one minute and twenty seconds, after which one began to lose consciousness. Now he had to choose a method. Most of them he thought were ghastly, and he opted for pills, which would not disfigure the body. With a flicker of humour he wished that he was rich enough to possess a villa at Karuizawa; he would have to hide his decision and preparations from his nearest and dearest, and pretend there was nothing wrong. A woman had once offered to accompany him, but he thought it would be simpler to go alone. He said nothing to anybody, but wrote more and more, a writer to the end, as if writing was stimulated by the approach of death. Those black, silent, unmoving marks which would outlive the hand that wrote them would be his testament, life's attestation and farewell. We are reminded of the condemned man in the story by Victor Hugo, still scribbling his last few lines on the very steps of the guillotine. Every writer must feel close to that condemned man, even if his own last day lasts fifty years: all writers are in a hurry, all at the foot of the scaffold.

Perhaps Akutagawa remembered that his beloved Voltaire had exhorted would-be suicides to leave a note of their motives, 'with a word concerning their philosophy', as a contribution to the history of the human spirit. He undertook to write notes for an old friend, still faithful to his trust which was to understand and explain. And Akutagawa obediently tried to explain himself. Undoubtedly he had a feeling of necessity: he knew he could do no other than kill himself. But his reasons faded and eluded him when he tried to formulate them. 'In my case', he said, 'it is no more than a vague anxiety. Yes, a vague anxiety about the future. Perhaps you won't be able to believe me.' This was the end of all his lucidity. Death seemed to escape the snares of words, it was elusive, conjured one to write and then frustrated the writing. One gets the same impression from Drieu la Rochelle's *Récit secret*. Foolish is he who tries to tie it to a meaning, bend it to reason, harness it to any other goal than the void. This is the culmination of nihilism: the will which is bound for the void wants nothing beyond.

> The world in which I presently live is as transparent as ice, a world of sickly neurosis. Yesterday evening, I spoke to a prostitute about her wages [!], and I felt to the marrow of my bones how pitiable we are, we poor humans who 'live to live'. If we could be content to enter into eternal sleep, surely we would find peace at least, if not happiness. I am not too sure when I shall have the courage to kill myself. Putting it simply, in my present state nature seems to be more beautiful than ever before. You will laugh at my contradictions, since I want to kill myself and yet love nature; but if nature seems fair to me it is because I am seeing her with eyes that are about to close forever. More than anyone, I have seen, loved, understood. That at least, in the midst of the sufferings heaped upon me, is a cause for satisfaction.[11]

At long last, on the hot and humid night of 24 July 1927, a fatal dose of veronal snatched this man of thirty-five from his wife, his three sons, his great fame, his many friends, his books and manuscripts, his plans, dreams and anxieties. With Akutagawa, as once with Nogi, people felt that it was the end of an era, a schism in the history of modern Japan. The event had widespread repercussions precisely because of its ambiguity.

There was no lack of hasty interpretations, as if to fill up the gulf of silence with clichés. Indeed Akutagawa had granted himself the sour pleasure of mocking them in advance in *Kappa*, published some months earlier, which describes the suicide of Mr Toc, a poet by trade: 'He was selfish', 'He was suffering from a disease of the stomach', 'He had become subject to fits of melancholy', 'His poetic inspiration had dried up', 'He was suffering from loneliness', 'Mr Toc was not a believer.'

ILLS OF A BOURGEOIS

The only coherent interpretation came from a young intellectual well versed in Marxist-Lenininst dogma, Miyamoto Kenji; he drew his strength from the already well-established ascendancy of this new orthodoxy in Japanese intellectual circles. He saw in Akutagawa's death the twilight of the bourgeois consciousness. A class condemned by history, vanquished or about to be so, must perforce have a nihilistic and suicidal ideology. The aesthete who professed indifference to good and evil thought he had broken away from the interests of his class, but in fact he was their victim: he had condemned himself to immobility, solitude, all the twists of an uneasy conscience. Aestheticism and immorality were, like nihilism, symptoms of bourgeois decadence. The only way out was political action: the categories of 'good' and 'evil' are rooted in the history of societies, and by action one can infuse a new content into them, and so give a new meaning to life, create, as it were, the future.

Miyamoto seemed to be taking up Barbey d'Aurevilly's ultimatum: 'The pistol barrel or the revolutionary party!' A righteous brutality which aroused some idle spirits. Every doctrine is selective, choosing its elect, giving some the hope it denies to others who are too weak or too sceptical. Let them die if that is all they are capable of, if even truth cannot convince them! If something is tottering on the brink it still had to be pushed, an edifying principle adopted by many of our ideologists. Nietzsche, for example, was quite convinced that the progressive diffusion of ideas such as the Death of God, the Will to Power, and the Eternal Return would unleash tremendous bouts of contagious nihilism: the weak, the out of place, bereft of their comforting illusions, would plunge into the void in self-disgust – and relieved of this ballast, our bourgeois world of masterless slaves would be transformed into a new world of slaveless masters. After which, with weakness eliminated and despair consumed, the only form of voluntary death remaining would be the free and festal farewell to life.[12]

Suicide has always furnished arguments to both left and right; revolution, no less than tradition, thought it had the answer to the scourge.

'Courage, my young friends, study, spread the idea, work honestly, and the taste for life will be born like a beautiful hollyhock [sic] in your hearts', proclaimed an article in *Le Libertaire* which was quoted, not without ironic intent, in a 1924 number of *La Révolution Surréaliste*. Starting from Akutagawa's case, Miyamoto took up the dream, or utopia, of a society of 'hollyhocks', purged of nihilism, still open to sacrificial enthusiasm, but free from the shameful disease of suicide. An attractive ideal, soon to be belied by the death of Mayakovsky, a son of the Leninist revolution and one of its most famous – and formerly most fervent – poets, who killed himself on 14 April 1930 at the age of thirty-seven.[13]

Was there no end to this supposedly bourgeois defect, to loneliness and despair, burdens inherited from the past? André Breton remarked at the time that existence is not just unanimous and collective, and that the mind can be defeated by the contradictions of so-called 'private' life: a timid protest against the totalitarian design which was even then working to combine the individual and the social in a single organized state which would banish suicide along with every other deviation. Large numbers of Japanese intellectuals still looked for a revolution – though they felt powerless to hasten it – which would put an end to all their ills. The frail Akutagawa, so cruelly treated by the Marxists (for whom he had actually had some sympathy) was to have some sort of revenge: he thought that in a world where nobody speaks the truth, a writer should be like a microphone, picking up and amplifying murmurs, whispers and rumours. And it happened: away from the epics which won all the prizes, far from the long novels teeming with positive, healthy, robust heroes oozing brotherly love, there came a day when an unknown Solzhenitsyn began his scribbling in the house of the dead. Literature really is incorrigible.

AN ARDENT SOUL

In the strife-ridden Japan of the 1930s, intellectuals seeking protection against the vague anguish of the soul which had killed Akutagawa looked first and foremost to political commitment. Marxist doctrine satisfied that need to act which might offer salvation to the spirit. Revolt and revolution, refusal and hope, might give meaning to life and afford an escape from the ego and the void. Perhaps Marxism is the opium of the intellectual; certainly it is the cup which cheers, justifies, organizes, and harnesses them to history, arousing them to the realities of poverty and the Struggle. A cup of life. It soothes their solitude and comforts their alienation: the masses may not be following us, but one day they will know that we were right. Indeed the Japanese masses were not following them: the state was threatened and suborned by terrorism and adventurism from the militarists, not by tracts from the militants.

Marxism remained for the most part the prerogative of teachers and students with a taste for the clandestine, obsessed with doctrinal squabbles and reciprocal excommunications. Some, like Kawakami Hajime, were wholly sincere in their devotion. In his youth, under the influence of Tolstoy, the Gospels and the Pure Land, he had practised an uncompromising altruism. His motto was 'Do nothing which will do no good to others.' He denied himself and dedicated himself utterly to suffering humanity. He left his wife, his children and his goods to live among the poor. He even decided that he must waste no more time in sleeping. He knew that it would mean death in the fairly short term, but he was on fire to give his life. Not to kill himself; to dispose freely of himself he would have had to acknowledge that he had the right to do so, and his life was no longer his own: he had received it from universal Love and he was going to pay it back, not hang on to it. Then he turned to Zen, which moderated his ideas a little. He lived. Becoming a professor of political economy, he turned Marxist and joined the Communist Party. In 1928 he was expelled from the University of Kyoto, where he was teaching. He aspired to martyrdom, and would have sacrificed his life a hundred times over to prevent the war which he foresaw. Martyrdom was granted him, but he had plenty of time to realize its uselessness. In 1933 he was thrown in prison, and he died in 1946 of the ill-treatment he had received, after having witnessed the ravages of war and the hopelessness of defeat – miserable, powerless and broken.[14]

While Marxism could foster the noblest of sacrificial ardours, it could also foster the most outrageous cynicism, as we know only too well. Even Marx had a smack of Bismarck about him; it came out strongly in his successors. Ultimately truth is part of the power struggle, and the final blow to the vanquished is calumny. This is one form of nihilism: reality, if it be imposed, will be officially declared rational, and will always be right. Realism, no less than idealism, can lead to crushing despair. For the idealist nothing real is worthy of the ideal; for the realist all ideals are the phantasms of a deluded consciousness. The conquest of power justifies everything, from calculated pessimism to fruitful compromise – at the time. Later, when power is achieved, the void gapes under the morality of success: did the will to power desire nothing beyond?

This let-down played some part in the suicides of Essenin and Mayakovsky. In such circumstances it is less trouble to slide down the gentle slope of opportunism, and many Japanese Marxists ended by doing just that. If something is on the brink, but refuses to fall in when you push it, too bad. Be strong against the weak and weak against the strong, such is the realism of the power struggle. Thus some of them rallied to nationalism as it became more pervasive and more extreme, even if they decorated it with some preliminary socialism. Under pressure from the state, its laws and its police, such volte-faces (*tenko*) became numerous. When war finally broke out, the dissidents ceased their struggle in the face of the *fait accompli*, and the great majority of them could think of nothing to do save rally to the cause of the empire, which just then happened to be preening itself on the anti-imperialism of its diatribes against the colonialism of the white man.[15] At the same time the suicide rate, in obedience to Durkheim's law, was declining: 13.51 in 1940, 13.11 in 1941, 12.50 in 1942, 11.49 in 1943. Akutagawa's torments were out of fashion, for the death-wish had plenty of scope elsewhere. Amidst such oceans of sacrifice suicide faded into anodyne pettiness. Battles and bombings made violent death so commonplace that in 1944 and 1945 they did not even bother to compile the statistics on suicide. Catastrophe had dried up the well of despair.

14

Mishima: The Last Act

When the war ended the despair broke out anew. Japan was in ruins. So were the hearts of its mourning people. So severe a defeat could not but cause a dismay initially coloured by self-disgust. Japan resolved to become the perpetual Switzerland of the Far East; but to rise so high, it seemed it would have to jettison its identity. It was at this juncture that Shiga Naoya, one of Japan's most famous writers, sometime member of the *Shirakaba* group, laid the blame on the very structure of the Japanese spirit, its language. Japan must die to itself and be transformed. They must choose a sensible language – French, for example – and teach it to adults and children, then make it the one, compulsory, everyday language, while after a few months or years Japanese would become a dead language of hateful memories.[1]

Much earlier, when Meiji ascended the throne, some people had asked themselves if it would not be a good idea to ban Buddhism and Shinto and make Christianity the state religion. Desire for change and shame for the past made Shiga Naoya suggest an excessive plan for cultural revolution – more than that, cultural autogenocide, a pendant to the national suicide (*ichioku gyokusai*, a hundred million willing Japanese sacrifices) advocated a few months earlier by nationalist fanatics.

THE GREYNESS OF DAWN

This was the darkest hour of the nihilist night. The survivors of heroism were dabbling in the black market, widows were looking for a suitable replacement. At every ruined street corner the war wounded, wearing their white hospital kimonos, were playing their harmonicas to earn a few pence. Nevertheless the dawn wind was blowing, and the future was coming to birth. It was in that grey and urgent hour that the Japanese had to accomplish the 'transvaluation of values' of which Nietzsche once spoke. Everything which, only yesterday, had been great, noble and sacred was suddenly despised, decried and discredited. New values – pacifism, equality, democracy, liberty, tolerance – were now to enlighten people's minds and shape the customs of a reconstructed society. They seemed to have been dictated by the victors, but they would not have survived if they had not dwelt for so long in the old Japan: what society had ever been more peaceful than Heian, what reforms more egalitarian than those of Taika, what democrary more assured than the village communities, what tolerance more generous than Buddhism?

So it was that Japan broke with a whole segment – the loudest one – of its history and limited its miltary freedom. Article 9 of the 1947 constitution renounces any use of armed force in international relations, though it is the essential attribute of a sovereign state of which no other state has ever deprived itself voluntarily.[2] A nation can survive, and even fight, without weapons if it can remain united, surmounting internal divisions. Would fear, which had once pricked on the courage of warriors, join militarism in the gutter? Or, rather, would the new Japan end up by transposing Gandhi's principles (for example), and introduce a new policy into international relations, a policy of truth and non-violence worthy of the great Buddhist tradition? Certainly truth was progressing. On 1 January 1946, the emperor spoke on the radio, denied his alleged divinity and declared the absolute sovereignty imputed to him as emperor (an ancient and anodyne myth, skilfully manipulated by the militarist factions to subjugate the state) to be invalid.

In the consciousness of the West, the death of god had been announced by Nietzsche, by Dostoevsky, by Feuerbach, and before them by Diderot and Spinoza: it had left an aching void, but it had had two or three centuries to take its progressive, indirect and sometimes imperceptible effect. The Japanese consciousness had a few weeks to go through a similar crisis. Of course, the *Tenno* had never been a metaphysical being; he had never laid claim to omnipotence, omniscience or another world, nor to personal immortality. But he was undeniably transcendent, and every emperor from Meiji onwards had been the symbolic focus of all undertakings. He was the supreme signifier in the mind of every Japanese: every act, from the most banal to the costliest sacrifice, could be mentally dedicated to him, as if his silent presence had made the whole Empire into one immense altar for the perpetual service of good intentions. Now, in the place of that harmonious unity, there was a man like other men, and each individual will was left to its solitary disintegration.

AWAKENING TO LIFE

In the years following the defeat, with sacrifice discredited by its very excesses, suicide regained its former ascendancy – slowly at first, 15.6 in 1947, 15.9 in 1948. For, as Durkheim said, poverty is a protection against it: difficulties can be stimulating, great misfortunes provoke silent but determined resistance. It is when life becomes easier, and so loses its savour, that people think of killing themselves. The commonest feeling in Japan at that time was amazement at the inexplicable miracle of having survived at all. It was the writer Sakaguchi Ango who expressed the truth of this, in hopeful tones: 'Living, that's the only miracle.' Men needed an ideal, but they could maintain it only at the price of death: if they lived, their illusions would prove false, just as beauty fades with time.

The ideal could haunt the imagination only by doing violence to truth, to nature and to life. The forty-seven faithful retainers, for example, owed the perfection commonly attributed to them to the *seppuku* which redeemed them from all-devouring time: they were asked to kill themselves, and this saved them from self-forgetfulness. Only the dead could rise to the dream for which they were content to die; only in death could they be sure not to play it false. They gave fresh impetus to the fascination which killed them, and it was this impetus which turned the wheel of sacrifice. *Bushido*, the Empire, Greater Asia, World History were all mirages feeding on the lives of their devotees. But when the wheel stopped turning, should we really be sorry to lose such ruinous dreams? Man, freed from the alienating power of history, aroused from his falsifying ideal, would perhaps be born at last, and know himself under an empty sky:

> It is a grandiose image of man which the ending of the war has vouchsafed us: sixty- and seventy-year-old generals dragged before the tribunals instead of committing *seppuku*! Japan is defeated, *bushido* is no more; but our decadence is the true womb whence man has at long last been born. Living is a progressive imperfection: is there any quicker and more

convenient way to save mankind than that natural process? Harakiri does not appeal to me.[3]

You give yourself to life, which gives itself to you, and accept it for what it is: a gradual wearing away, a deterioration, dispersion, forgetting; and also a birth, a flowering, a becoming. Sakaguchi's view of the future, formulated when his people were in the deepest pit of distress, takes us back to the intuitions of the Buddhist Greater Vehicle: the understanding that the further bank is the same as the hither bank, that salvation must be in this world, that you can save yourself here and now if you can see yourself and accept yourself as you really are: a fallen being, perhaps, but ready for redemption – which is metamorphosis, the law of all life.

DISTRESS AND DISARRAY

One can probably find good in all things, including (or especially) defeat, if one looks hard enough: for the first time since Heian, Japan could say it had shaken off the warrior caste. But even allowing for this more positive tinge, the feeling of decline and chaos was overwhelming: the people fumbled their way from day to day. In literature, an openly nihilist tradition gave some shape to the feeling of helplessness: 'Philosophy? All lies. Principles? All lies. Ideals? All lies. Order? A lie. Sincerity, truth, purity? All lies.'

The greatest writer of the time, Dazai Osamu, was making a clean sweep. It was at that time that he went through a respite of two of three years, in which he brought out his finest works, *Villon's Wife*, *The Setting Sun* and *No Longer Human*, before taking the final plunge on 13 June 1948. By agreeing to be symptomatic of his times, swimming with the current, putting his despair in tune with what everyone else was feeling, he managed to give his work an unequalled depth and resonance. His inner firmament gave back an unsurpassable reflection of the thick darkness of a hopeless heart and the light of proffered love – like the night once conjured up by Chikamatsu, the quivering, anguished night just before dawn, when lovers die.

The tone which Dazai adds to the ancient melody is one of decadence and decay, a progressively more abject weakness. In this fleeting world everything seems to be dissolving, life drifts gently downstream. But a man aware of his weakness, even his degradation, can be forgiven. Dazai's characters are not selfishly shut up in themselves, injured by evil, alone in the depths of malaise and misery: they communicate, open up in floods of tears, deliver themselves and depart. Perhaps this is a sort of hell, and indeed few writers are more harsh or bitter – but perhaps it is only in hell that we can find the holy goodness which advances, offering itself, loving and saving. This is the voice of hope and compassion, the voice of the Pure Land whence Amida comes to the dying, Kannon to the drowning, Jizo to the damned: it promises salvation to all beings, even the vilest and most degraded, if only they will acknowledge themselves.

When he died, still young, at thirty-nine, Dazai was already an experienced would-be suicide. He made his first attempt at twenty. The recent death of Akutagawa, whom he admired, may have had something to do with it. It was the day before an examination: he took an overdose and spent the next dey in a coma. The next year, 1930, he met a barmaid who was tired of life: they went to the seaside, near Enoshima, and together took an overdose of sleeping pills. He got it wrong and survived; the girl died. The failure hypnotized him, and he wasted his gifts, incapable of making anything of his life. Perhaps this incapacity to get on in the world is part of the writer's vocation – witness Baudelaire, Verlaine, Proust, Kafka and many others. If Dazai was any different it was because of the truly monumental hash he made of his life; debts, women, drink, and soon tuberculosis, which he carefully nurtured by drinking still more, and a whole pharmacopoeia of drugs, like a litany of barbarous gods: 'Morphine, atromol, narcopon, phillipon, pantopon, panopine, atropine . . .'[4] It was a kind of wrong-headed dandyism, made up of weakness and degradation, its only sacrament suicide.

If he had been asked to reply to the disturbing enquiry in the first issue of *La Révolution Surréaliste* (December 1924), namely 'Is suicide a solution?' there is no doubt of what his reply would have been. Did he already know of Jacques Vache and Jacques Rigaut, or of René Crevel, whose description of the final gesture has a chilling humour which Dazai would have savoured? 'A saucepan on the cooker; the window tightly shut; I turn on the gas; I forget to light a match.'[5] One of Dazai's first novels (1936) opens on the same tone of detachment: 'I was thinking about killing myself. But somebody gave me a New Year present of a piece of material for a kimono. It's linen, with fine grey stripes. For a summer kimono. I told myself that I might just as well go on living until summertime.'[6]

A MONUMENTAL HASH

Much to the displeasure of his family, and purely in order to annoy them, Dazai joined the Communist Party for a few months, with abundance of tracts, posters and empty words. Then he backtracked and confessed himself to the local police commissioner. It left him with nothing but an increased distaste for himself, his irresolutions and his reversals. His attempts at a proletarian literature remained unfinished, but he did retain from Marxism a sense of belonging to a doomed social class. (Cesare Pavese, who sometimes seems to be Dazai's masochistic *alter ego*, and who committed suicide two years after him, gleaned the same guilt feeling from communism and the anti-fascist resistance.) Dazai made his third attempt when he was twenty-six. He had just been turned down for a job by a big newspaper; he went up into the hills of Kamakura and hanged himself from a tree. The rope broke. Two years later, in 1937, he planned another attempt, again with the help of a woman, this time an ex-geisha whom he had secretly married in the teeth of his family's disapproval. He had soon left her: he loved her enough to die with her, but not to live with her.

After that the vast spectacle of war kept him busy for a few years – kept him alive, in fact. By then, in spite of all the failures, success had finally arrived: he was famous. He could have gone on living, or rather, gone on dying, with the help of tuberculosis and drink; there was no particular hurry. But he felt compelled to force the pace of destiny once again, as if to make a real gesture to authenticate the tales of misery and love born of his imagination. He is the culmination of the *shishosetsu*, the tradition of frank, direct, intimate and sometimes indecent confession. His life and work were inseparable, and he would have though it unworthy of a writer to keep at a polite distance from the creatures of his imagination. More than drink or tuberculosis, it was writing which was killing him: his obscure call to face up to life, explore its furthest bounds, ravish and reveal its secrets and enigmas. A writer is a writer not only in his books, but also in his letters and diaries: step by step, his whole life story becomes part of literature, and therefore open to curious eyes. The life contains the works, that is true, but it is also part of them, it completes them. Rimbaud's sojourn in Harar is no less disturbing, no less a piece of 'writing', than his *Saison en enfer*.

Dazai, for his part, could well have written up his own ending and made his last day into his last story. In 1948 a war widow, a hairdresser by trade, fell in love with him. Did she suggest the idea? The feeling of solidarity, when all hope is gone, runs through his stories, and may have brought him closer to her; or perhaps he was looking once again for compliant female help in dying. Be that as it may, both of them – probably slightly drunk – went wandering around a distant suburb, one warm and muddy night, till they came to the banks of a narrow water conduit swollen because of the rainy season. There their drowned bodies were found a few days later. His sardonic spirit would doubtless have rejoiced to know that people saw this concluding episode as a failed attempt, more inept even than all the others.

Writers write so as to be loved. This man, who never loved himself, can now be loved by others, so close and immediate is the voice which speaks through his work. He loved to outrage the timid conformism of the modern Japanese bourgeoisie. His shyness and sensitivity made him a cynic. He wanted to be punished so as to be forgiven, and wallow in the indulgent love and dependence (*amae*) which lurks in the heart of the Japanese Oedipus. Death would be a mother to him, giving him peace and forgetfulness. His attitude was less one of revolt than one of provocation, the provocation which Sartre quite wrongly attributed to Baudelaire.[7] Such immaturity is not incompatible with literature, which (as Kafka remarked) is both a joke and a desperation; it may spring from the silence of the will while remaing indifferent to grand designs, knowing that caprices have their fascination, and that it is failure which really gives depth to life.[8] Any adolescent aware of the inertia and indifference of his fellows without being able to shake free of them will always find a kindred spirit in Dazai, and a protection against the morality of success. His life and work are romantic ruins, with the additional attraction of suicide.

Like Werther, he had his imitators. A student was found dead with his head resting on a book by his favourite author. A somewhat eccentric young writer called Tanaka Hidemitsu, whom Dazai had noticed and encouraged, was so upset by the news of his death that he decided to follow him without delay: he went and threw himself into the same conduit, but he was fished out again. For a few months he did his best to live and get over it; then, on 3 November 1949, he felt impelled to go to Zenrinji, a temple in a Tokyo suburb called Mitaka, where Dazai was buried. He was very drunk. His pockets were crammed with razor blades and sleeping pills. It was night. He teetered among the tombs, found Dazai's and opened his veins on top of it. A passing child saw him lying there, at his last gasp. 'Kill me and forgive me' were his last words to the doctors who tried in vain to reconnect him to life.

I THINK, THEREFORE I SHALL NOT BE

'Forgive me for having been born', Dazai had said. Many young Japanese about that time sought the same forgiveness – from death. Two or three years earlier the war would have accounted for them all. The peace was no peace to them, for they could see no reason why they should have survived. One of the clearest cases is that of a student at the University of Tokyo called Haraguchi Tozo, who drowned himself in the sea at Zushi on 26 October 1946, aged twenty. He left a few notebooks which bear shining witness to his lucidity and intransigence, although he was suspicious of the act of writing and felt the need to explain and excuse it, as if it were a weakness. He spoke, paradoxically, to say that it would have been better to remain silent. He had already decided that the silence of nothingness was the best reply to the silence of being. To ask questions was to ask a favour – it was degrading. To express oneself was to be in trade. Haraguchi avowed that he would have liked to be the ghost of one of those old warriors who despised both transactions and explanations.

He never mentioned the war and the defeat in his writings, nor disputed the *fait accompli*, as Mishima was to do. But it almost seems as if in him the ideal of *bushido* survived the catastrophe and became, albeit sublimated to the uttermost, the guide of his thoughts. The only combat he was involved in was a spiritual one, but it was 'as savage as a battle among men', and it demanded just as much courage, blodness and self-sacrifice, for the adversary was life itself and the fear of nothingness. He had no illusions and expected no salvation; he had renounced the ideologists and all their works. What was there that needed to be understood? He had measured the absurdity of all things, and had decided on a fitting reply, which was voluntary death. He followed the schoolboy who, in 1903, threw himself into the Kegon waterfall.

Proud and unbending, like any other twenty-year-old Saint-Just, he followed his thoughts to their logical ending. He cut through the Gordian knot of modern nihilist problematics with the coolness of an expert in the martial arts. Unlike Sisyphus, he refused to play along with the cruel game of being, for he had realized what a silly game it was. Beside him Kirilov would look verbose, nervy and febrile. He felt that his impatience, laconicism and revolt brought him closer to Arthur Rimbaud. But although Rimbaud cursed life, he ended by consenting to a life of the most sordid description, getting rich on drug trafficking. Haraguchi could never have lived with such inconsistency. Had he been less lucid he might have been content to live and love: he called himself 'life's unhappy lover'. But life always betrays her lovers, for so she must, and it is better to know it and evade her perfidy. Loving is not enough, even being happy is not enough: one must act as one should and will what one wants.[9]

Haraguchi came to the conclusion as Dazai, death by drowning. But two more contrasting attitudes could scarcely be imagined. Dazai collaborated with his own ruin to the gain of his work. Haraguchi turned his back on both. Solitude, purity, silence: he allowed himself only the few words necessary to indicate the transparency of his decision. He laughed at the seductions of writing and the subtleties of fiction. We can feel him tense, screwing his will-power to the sticking place till it saw itself endlessly reflected in the will to *will*. Dazai was different: confused, pathetic, he abdicated all intention, let go, kept hope and ceased upon the midnight.

In the Heian period the mandala was imported from India by followers of esoteric Buddhist sects, as a focus for their meditations and prayers. A mandala is a metaphysical diagram which represents the universal order under its two governing aspects, the womb world and the diamond world. This dualism gained a fresh lease of life later in the Zen and Pure Land sects. Both travelled through the centuries along the pathways of the Japanese mind, and the moderns spontaneously turned their steps back on to those same paths. The nihilist consciousness was their point of departure, and at the other end they reached the voluntary death, but the ways in between were wholly different, worlds apart.

A VERY GIFTED YOUNG MAN

The young men who had not been decimated by the war were threatened by the attraction of suicide, which reached a peak in the fifties. Of this generation Mishima was the most famous, but not the quickest in answering the call of the dead: this old young man, who died at forty-five of his adolescent dreams, was wise enough to give himself a lengthy reprieve. He was a year older than Haraguchi, who had been his fellow student at the University of Tokyo. When he killed himself, a quarter of a century later, did he spare a thought for the quiet comrade who had travelled the same way so long before? In any case he, like Haraguchi, had lost faith in anything save the most intransigent of acts.

His scorn of life – shameless, chattering life – grew year by year, and in the end he followed up the consequences of his thoughts. But in 1946 the youthful Mishima was still a long way away from Haraguchi's conclusions. He had survived, so he would go on living, with an ardour inflamed by his narrow escape from death. His talent as a writer, already recognized, seemed to make life even better. Mishima, bubbling over with intelligence and energy, was to know victories in that defeated Japan which any young man might envy. His will to success, based on a severe working discipline, readily lent itself to any available means of publicity. He was not at all displeased to annoy pallid Sartrean intellectuals by his cynical conformism and ostentatious success: at thirty-four he built himself a vast 'anti-Zen' residence of positively kitschy opulence, complete with wrought-iron staircase and chandeliers, statue of Apollo on the lawn, and a pretty young maid in black dress and white apron to answer the door.[10]

It is possible that this attitude, in its very ostentation, was a kind of psychic safety barrier. The appetite for success can become a kind of

Pavlov reaction: 'I am *not* going to be beaten!' Mishima seemed to be clinging determinedly to this resolve, wrong-footing the acknowledged defeat of 1945, and especially the defeatism so widespread among intellectuals from Akutagawa to Dazai. But he would not have reacted so violently had he not already felt the stirrings of nihilism and the taste for destruction astir within himself.

Perhaps becoming a writer means dedicating oneself to one's own inner night, and even being lost in it for ever. The young Mishima flattered himself he had found a better use for it: he would be his own clinician and take a scalpel to dissect his own darkness. At twenty-four, the boldly minute descriptions in *Confessions of a Mask* made him into one of the most famous writers of his age. All the confessions in the personal novels, the *shishosetsu* of the last fifty years, seem banal alongside the luxuriant sado-masochistic fantasies of this outwardly well-disciplined young man, who had attained to his first sexual satisfaction in front of a picture of the violated and swooning body of St Sebastian. It is a paradox of literature that by confessing what most people would rather hide, it wins the recognition of all, and by its alchemy transforms solitude and shame into the glory of universal sympathetic attention. Did Mishima confound his own darkness by bringing it so boldly into the light? He knew the Aristotelian catharsis, the purging of passion by the exhibition of passion. Perhaps by describing the abyss he quieted the vertigo of looking into it. In any case, having told all he felt an incrased appetite for life.

THE SUN AND THE NIGHT

'I hate people who commit suicide.' So he said in 1954, in an article on Akutagawa. Warriors were another matter: they were only doing their duty. But for a writer to commit suicide seemed to him an intolerable failure, a public admission of incompetence. Mishima proclaimed Goethe's ideal of health through art: a writer may be both patient and physician, but the physician must have the upper hand. Mishima was quite definite on this point. He claimed he felt nothing but repulsion for Dazai – he would not even mention his name – but he did feel some esteem for Akutagawa, appreciating the perfection of his writing and his hyper-elaborate narrative technique. All the more deplorable was Akutagawa's self-inflicted end: his suicide must have been an accident, a pathological impulse from outside which art ought to have vanquished and sublimated.

Clearly Mishima was putting himself on guard against a similar fate. He was now going beyond Goethe and seeking his precepts for living in ancient Greece; in 1952 he had visited the country and came back full of enthusiasm. He went to Greece a puny youth of elegiac disposition, and there he met Apollo, god of art, god of health, god of the sun. Nietzsche had said that we are all Greek-loving phantoms, but one day we may become 'physically' Greek. Mishima set out to realize Nietzsche's dream literally, in his own body. From 1955 onwards, when he was thirty, he was regularly to be seen in the gymnasium and on the running-track. And as he always succeeded in what he set out to do, his disciplined body slowly clothed itself in the sort of muscles immortalized on the statues of the Parthenon and Olympia. The thin, pale, fearful, shameful, rancorous, cruel and sickly child had been the chrysalis from which a new Mishima had emerged. He justified his will to success, strength, health and happiness with a philosophy of vitality inspired by the Nietzschean *Lebensbejahung*. Never did any one have a more self-confident, ardent and unshakeable will to live.[11]

But even in the first flush of enthusiasm, it would be unfair to see Mishima as a prototype of Jane Fonda. His organized cult of life was like a mask deliberately placed over darker impulses. When, in *The Sound of Waves* (1954), he does his best to celebrate the innocence of the flesh, a certain insipidity shows that he is not writing from a profound inner conviction. Certainly he loved the body he had made for himself, and found it a reason for living, having always found it difficult to love anything outside himself. But his narcissism could not have the fatuous simplicity of the bronzed beach divinities calmly on the look-out for the first wrinkles under a Californian sun. His conquered body embodied not only his will, but also (and first and foremost) his dreams, and he still took a morose delight in the idea of striking it, cutting into it. He had managed to identify with the object of his fantasy (killing a young man), bending it back on itself. Thus there was a tragic element in his narcissism: he had made himself beautiful, but he had an obstinate urge to persecute beauty.

Mishima was above all a writer, not because there was anything very singular about his fantasies (nothing is more profoundly human than sado-masochism in all its different guises), but because of his determined devotion to them and enjoyment of them. All his works were a variation on this theme; all his thoughts echoed it. Japanese classical poetry reminded him that beauty is a fragile flower; Sade told him that it would pass beneath the juggernaut of sacrifice. European romanticism suggested that it was noble to give in gracefully. The examples of Keats, Rimbaud and, above all, Radiguet, showed him that genius spends itself and dies young. But it was from Nietzsche, commenting on the civilization of Greece, that Mishima sought an ideal of tragedy which could claim his entire allegiance. Under Apollo lurks Dionysus, sombre, howling, torn to pieces. High points draw the lightning, which crowns their grandeur; the glory of the void is the crown of the noblest life.

Japanese culture was unsympathetic to individual transgression; it acknowledged destiny and commiserated with it, celebrated the nobility of failure, but also accepted it, on Buddhist terms, as a fitting reward which gave the lesson of inevitable renunciation. Thus it tended to mute tragedy into elegy. Japan could have produced an *Oedipus at Colonus*, but never an *Oedipus Rex*. The fascination of tragedy, stirred up in Mishima by his early fantasies and by the catastrophe of 1945, could feed only on western literature. On these imported concepts he built a fabric of native materials, and offered his life as the keystone which might bind Western tragic individualism to the moral abnegation of Japanese tradition.

THE WILL TO TRAGEDY

In *The Temple of the Golden Pavilion* (1956) he is still exploring the pyschology of nihilist crime in the style of Dostoevsky. The elements of Japanese tradition, such as the Buddhist hierarchy, the enigmas of Zen and the tea ceremony, are purely decorative, and the essence comes from the dark corners of the soul as explored in the Russian novels: the stammering incendiary who burns down the radiant pavilion, like the schoolboy in *Confessions of a Mask*, is tormented by the resentment he feels at the untouchable purity of the Beautiful.

Meanwhile Mishima was amusing himself by playing a petty criminal in a very bad film; like Jean Genet and Pasolini, he occasionally felt the attraction of the gutter. And Sade fascinated him. None the less he was to find his destiny not in crime but in sacrifice, which is the other side of the same coin. In 1960 he turned from evil to good. He began a story, 'Patriotism', and his whole being, from its brightest to its darkest, crystallized in love for the young lieutenant who killed himself, followed by his wife, the day after the failed coup of 26 Febraury 1936 so as to reconcile his duty to his friends with his duty to the army. It brings in the theme of *seppuku*, obstinate, obsessive, described in the minutest and most horrible detail, later to be acted on screen, and repeated insatiably until it was finally translated into action.[12]

Can ethics and tragedy be reconciled? Mishima drew on the sacrificial tradition as transposed in the Kabuki: the sight of the harsh demands of duty provoked feelings of horror, pity and admiration. His attempted synthesis does not lack grandeur, but it feels artificial. He was going beyond health, success and vigour, and climbing towards the higher peak of tragedy. But was there not a contradiction here? To be authentic, tragedy must be unforeseen, gratuitous, and as capricious as lightning. Oedipus may accept his accomplished destiny, but not will it in advance. The unthinkable happens, the impossible strikes, appalling and inevitable: in fact, the Absurd.

If the will is not suited to tragic catastrophe, it is suited to moral heroism, and Mishima was perfectly entitled to look for a duty and serve it. But did he have the right to invent a duty and make it serve him? In *Sun and Steel* he described, with his usual frankness, the moment of illumination which came to him when his fantasy of destruction decided to don the uniform of duty and sally forth into the light. The costume was not far to seek, in the burned-out slogans lying in the ashes of the last war, the songs he had sung twenty years before, all the devalued values, the outdated, outworn, suspect virtues, all the good which had wrought such evil.

At forty, a cosmopolitan soaked in Westernism, he 'came home', endlessly proclaiming his ethnic and cultural difference, apparently taking pride in a 'Japaneseness' inaccessible to foreigners – as if the eyes of a stranger could never see clearly at a distance, as if the untranscendable human condition had not always permitted and commanded cultures to give one another that profound and receptive attention of which Japan had given such a shining example. He was not a chauvinist, but he did his best to acquire a chauvinistic attitude. He gave himself the mission of restoring the imperial doctrine which the emperor himself had denied on 1 January 1946, and defending the much criticized code of *bushido*, whose darker and more violent aspects he compared to the Dionysiac cult of ancient Greece as interpreted by Nietzsche.

The *Hagakure* became his vade-mecum. He needed a cause to sacrifice himself to, and here it was. He devoted himself to it. But what were the means, and what the end? The extremist faction before the war had often enough confused devotion to the imperial cause with the will to sectarian power. Mishima's most vehement political writings have a specious after-taste: they were the mask covering his steadily advancing death-wish. If it is deeds alone which give the measure of truth, then his *seppuku* gave incontestable proof of the purity of his intention and the sincerity of his conviction. Even then, the *seppuku* can look like an end which he had admired, desired, fantasized about and premeditated, so that its execution casts some suspicion on its previous justification.

Who would not want to escape from old age and death? But old age was coming. Mishima knew that he would soon run out of steam; already a voice was following along the running-track and whispering, 'How long?' Growing old is hard, and moreover undignified. Zarathustra had told people to 'die in time'. Mishima took this to mean before decline set in. Moreover, in this dull world he felt the call to battle. He was tired of muscles which bulged only before the mirror or the camera. Without risk of death the flesh becomes dull and insipid; only the unity of strength with fragility can be really moving. He dropped his dumb-bells and took up the martial arts, and later military training, as if he wanted to carry out the military service which twenty years earlier he had avoided by alleging lung trouble.

In 1945 he had not been well enough to die. Sacrifice would have none of him then; now that his vigour had made him worth having, it returned to claim him. He thought about his own generation, decimated, immolated to the empire, betrayed by the emperor when he renounced his sovereignty, and now swallowed up in the modern prosperity. Like a fantasizing sybil he gave his voice to the noble dead in *Eirei no koe* (1966): 'Why has the sovereign lowered himself to the rank of a human being?' Complaisant acceptance of defeat had destroyed transcendence, and nihilism reigned; there was no longer anything worth sacrificing oneself for. The world no longer recognized any value higher than individual survival: with no higher goal, bereft of inequality, life could only lose its meaning. But although it had no meaning, would love be enough to give it intensity? Mishima maintained that two people could not love each other, or agree, unless they were united by some principle. Not long ago the beloved Other had been the emperor, the guarantor of good and duty and the pledged word, the recipient of the sacrifice on which harmony was founded. Now he was as dead as the Christian god.[13]

BIRTH OF A FACTION

Mishima's plan was crystallizing at last, the exact opposite of the lucid sobriety advocated in 1946 by Sakaguchi Ango. It was to combat the world of the present in the name of the dreams of the past and appeal against it to the future; to goad the young (or perhaps only the elite among them) into an assault on a society which had turned its back on anything which transcended humanity. He drew on the Maoist upheaval, but only as an opposite, setting up the cultural Defence in opposition to the Cultural Revolution, hoping to reunite the chrysanthemum and the sword under the aegis of the empire. He was Nietzschean in his reverence for hierarchy as against destructive egalitarianism, and a Romantic in his nostalgia for a glorious past.

But a cause is no good in isolation: it needs a group of dedicated supporters. Mishima was looking for a way out of solitude and singularity. As a good Japanese, he looked to a living community to constitute a principle of duty and an euphoric solidarity. In 1967 he recruited dozens of young twenty-year-olds, most of them students, and forged them into the Society of the Shield (*Tate no kai*), which was intended to protect the emperor, having first re-established his transcendence by their example of sacrifice and faith. The principles seemed clear enough, but the details remained vague, for the plan left a great deal of room for its founder's imaginings. A blood-brotherhood, worthy of the ancient *bushi* or the *yakuza* gangs, bound together the first of the elect: they would each cut a finger, and collectively fill a goblet with blood, of which each drank a few drops. But after these sensational beginnings, Mishima turned enthusiastically to designing his young acolytes a pretty mustard-coloured uniform decorated with gold braid, stripes, epaulettes and a plethora of brass buttons, the sort of thing Pierre Cardin might have dreamed up if he had been asked to treat Tokyo to a Viennese operetta.[14]

The writer was bored with his pen and had gone for a naïve splash in the fountain of youth. But what was he going to make of his Society of the Shield? An extreme right-wing group, an agency for violence and fanaticism? Hardly likely: Mishima did not approve of terrorism, and he despised right-wing parties as much as left-wing ones, because he was above them all: the imperial principle transcending politics and making himself into a shield against every type of totalitarian party hegemony. Mishima's young patriots ended up looking so inoffensive that the Self-Defence Force let them use its training grounds. Thereafter they were to be seen at the foot of Mount Fuji, marching in step, saluting the flag, sleeping rough and wading through the snow with the touching enthusiasm of a Boy Scout troup. Mishima told them to Be Prepared. But for what? To defend the emperor? But there was no threat to the emperor. To save Nippon culture? But where was Nippon culture? To vanquish nihilism? But nihilism was everywhere. Where *could* they find an identifiable enemy who would provide them with a meaningful struggle?

Student agitation, which reached its height in 1969, came along just in time. They would fight against 'communism' (a convenient abstraction!), practice counter-guerrilla warfare, oppose the leftist *Zengakuren* movement. But in May 1969 Mishima had a talk with the rebellious students of Tokyo University, and suddenly realized that if he had been a little younger, he would have been with them. Their anger could be his anger, if their rebelliousness showed itself able to choose a supreme cause and fight to the death for it. But it did not: the students shared the values of the society they were rebelling against; they valued nothing more than life, and they could only bargain, with no intention of killing or being killed for any goal.

Mishima's quarrel was with society *en bloc*: in the name of the imperial principle, universal and absolute, he cursed all the little individual egos – satisfied or not – which intertwined into what Hegel had called the way of the world. Against petty individual interests, all scratching each other's backs under the umbrella of competition, he set up the lofty image of self-sacrificing Virtue. The *Phenomenology* seemed to have anticipated the impasse into which Mishiam had come: Virtue, emerging from her quixotic struggle, is obliged to acknowledge her own vanity and bow to the rich concrete virtualities which the way of the world has brought out into the full daylight of reality. The individual who talks of sacrificing himself to the Good would do better to exercise his innate capacities for the *common* good. That was Hegel's verdict, and, as usual with Hegel, it was a very sensible one.[15]

THE PENITENT IN SPIRIT

But Mishima was past making amends. Under the eye of his young followers he had to go forward, bear his own burdens and give some content (however arbitrary) to his incessant speeches about self-sacrifice. Meanwhile he continued with his writer's vocation, every night until dawn. Since 1965 he had been engaged on a long work, *The Sea of Fertility*, a series of four novels intended to contain the quintessence of his genius. For the last time he poured out the potentialities of his own being into this fictional characters. But as he proceeded with this ambitious project, he felt a mounting distaste for words and fables. One person can become any number of other people in his imagination, but only his deeds will show him what he really is.[16] Only by doing can he face up to reality; reality is irremediable; therefore, reality is death; therefore, only by doing can he reveal the truth of reality and death. By writing he remains in the labyrinth of images, where he forgets himself and floats away on the current of phrases, neither true nor false, neither dead nor alive. An unintentional lie, perhaps, but it had to be paid for: it is among the poets that we find those 'penitents in spirit' of whom Zarathustra spoke, who look to action to fill the vacuum left by words.[17]

Mishima felt the need to produce a decisive act more acutely than the need to produce a great work. Moreover, he was too lucid not to realize that what little attention was being given to the Society of the Shield was slightly sardonic: a rich author playing with his favourite toy, a cohort of youthful admirers. Every day they spent playing at soldiers increased his impression of a great gale of surreptitious laughter. Meanwhile the left-wing rebellion was running out of steam: in the violent demonstrations of 21 October 1969, the state showed itself more than capable of dealing with subversion unaided. There was no further hope of street warfare, a counter-guerrilla action in which one might be able to give one's life. Mishima performed a volte-face and decided to attack the state, since the state was triumphant. It was to be attacked at its root, the 1947 constitution. The regime born of defeat was to be swept away, which was a sufficiently grandiose project, even if it was perfectly impossible – and Mishima had no illusions about that. But if it failed, death would be no less glorious than the undertaking itself. He who, like Icarus, aims high can consent to the abyss which awaits him.

PLANS AND PREPARATIONS

Through 1970 they secretly made their plans. Mishima had gathered together four young men who belonged to him body and soul: first Morita, then Chibi-Koga, Ogawa and Furu-Koga. Innumerable meetings in hotels, saunas and restaurants all over Tokyo enabled the consirators to plan out their coup, with a typically Japanese penchant for extreme audacity in combination with the most meticulous preparation, a miniature Pearl Harbor. They were still a bit vague, however. From the autumn of 1969 onwards Morita had been proposing a large-scale insurrection in the style of 26 February 1936: the Society of the Shield, supported by elements of the Self-Defence Force, would storm the Diet. But they could not count on the complicity of the officers, still less that of the men, and it would not be easy for a few dozen students to put Tokyo under siege. Very soon the plan had been whittled down to a commando raid: they would have a try at stirring up the soldiers against this constitution which forbade them to be real warriors.

It is certain that Mishima never cherished any fond hopes of succeeding: what miracle could have saved him? He went in search of suicide from the start, and the whole political adventure, however intense and sincere, which he used to cloak his desire for death seems to have been conceived with that end in mind, as a novelist designs his plots – back to front. The screenplay had been written and was to be followed to the letter: Mishima had always been a meticulous writer, and his imagination was now working directly on reality, composing not sentences but facts. This real-life novel had its novelistic, even romantic, aspect: three weeks before the appointed day, Mishima made Ogawa and the two Kogas swear to live on after it, for only Morita was to follow him into death. Morita, a robust and placid student from Waseda University, had become his friend, and probably his lover, like one of the seventeenth-century samurai whose passions are described by Saikaku.

The public and political demonstration was cover for a *shinju*. There was nothing that the author of *Confessions of a Mask* would not confess, if he had to, but he had learned from the *Hagakure* that love is deeper if it remains a secret. It was another way of going against modern tendencies, this time towards the open admission, and therefore devaluation, of feeling. Moreover, he was instinctively aware of Freudian group psychology and knew that the unity of the Society of the Shield, which, like the *bushi* clans or the brotherhood of knights in *Parsifal*, was bound together by sublimated homosexuality, would never have stood up to any show of favouritism. The only, noble and refined preference he showed his beloved was to die with him.

FROM WORDS TO ACTION

After the lengthy preparations, the deed was prompt and quick, and in a couple of hours it was all over. On 25 November 1970, at eleven o'clock in the morning, Mishima, along with his four companions, presented himself at the military base at Ichigaya in the centre of Tokyo. He had arranged a meeting with General Mashita, commanding the armies of the east, in his office at the general headquarters of the Self-Defence Force. Ten minutes later, the incredulous General Mashita had been bound, gagged, taken hostage, and lay, with a knife at his throat, at Mishima's mercy. A few subordinates who tried to come to his rescue were chased away by a sword – a very precious, sixteenth-century sword which, apart from a few daggers, constituted the commandos' entire arsenal. Like the League of the Divine Wind attacking the castle of Kumamoto in 1876, Mishima made it a point of honour to use only cold steel. Then he laid down his conditions: the hostage's life would be spared if the soldiers on the base, about a thousand strong, were assembled to listen in silence to a speech from the balcony of Mashita's first-floor office.[18]

This was the Balcony Scene, the second scene in the last act of Mishima. He appeared in the full glare of the midday sun, dominating the amazed and quivering crowd from a height of about 30 feet. Suddenly they saw his small figure in its invented uniform spring on to the parapet and draw itself upright. Hands on hips, he launched into his speech.

The absolute silence he had demanded does not exist nowadays: police and press helicopters, cars coming and going, and ambulance sirens drowned him out more than once. But even if they had heard it perfectly they would have understood it no better, and acepted it no more readily. His remarks on Article 9, the national spirit, the military ideal and the decadence of the modern world seemed confused and abstract. His appeal to them as soldiers was received with indifference and hostility. Sarcasms and gibes were hurled at him: 'Come down from up there!' 'That's enough!' 'He's crazy!' The idea of a military rebellion to force the abolition of the constitution was instantly seen for what it was, a political fiction.

Mishima was losing his sang-froid: 'Silence! Listen! A man is appealing to you. Are you men?' Men of war? Will no single one of you arise with me?' The question 'Are you men?' hurled with the full force of his lungs, was really addressed to himself: it came out of his subconsciousness and had been troubling him all his life, hence his fascination with virility. His imminent sacrifice was the only way of getting an answer and silencing the question for ever. The man he was seeking could be found only within him, in his own entrails, whence alone he could appear before the eyes of others. Eventually he spoke in resignation and disdain: 'I see that you are not men. You'll do nothing. I have no further illusions about you.' He ended with a thrice-repeated cry of *Tenno Heika banzai*, 'Long live the emperor!' with arms spread wide and white-gloved hands held up to heaven.

He went back into Mashita's office and immediately unbuttoned his uniform to expose the naked torso which age would not wither. He took off his shoes and knelt on the floor, 6 feet away from the hostage still tied to his chair. He undid his belt and drew his trousers down to his thighs. He had dreamed for so long of those gestures, and rehearsed them so often: now it was for the last time. He sat back on his heels, seized a dagger and put the tip to his left side. Behind him Morita, his face bathed in sweat, was brandishing the sword, ready to give the *coup de grâce*. Mishima gave the ritual cry *Tenno Heika banzai*. Then he took a deep breath, expelled it with a violent cry, and thrust in the dagger. With both hands he pushed the blade across his stomach, under the navel, towards his right side. An interminable journey of a few inches, through the shrieking pain, through blood and organs and intestines and their contents. Finally, Morita struck him with the sword, but his hand was trembling and Mishima's body was sagging sideways: the blade sank into his shoulder. A second ill-aimed blow sank into the still living flesh. The third attempt severed the neck and the jerkings of the ravaged body ceased. Morita in his turn took off his tunic, sat on his heels and seized the bloody dagger. He made only a small cut before Furu-Koga beheaded him with a single blow. The surviving commandos gathered up the heads, set them upright next to the two bodies and dedicated a few moments of tears and prayer to their dead. Then they untied General Mashita and gave themselves up to the police.

EVERY MAN IS A LABYRINTH

The event – or should we say the performance? – was instantly seized on by journalists, and the first quake was followed by numerous aftershocks – as Mishima had anticipated. At first nobody could make head or tail of it. 'I believe', said Prime Minister Sato, 'that he was seized with a sudden attack of madness.' Later, people made only too much of it, or at least tried too hard to explain it: there was a plethora of interpretations, each of them partially true.

The deed of Mishima appeared little by little in all its fugitive complexity, like a composition which had been long meditated and scrupulously performed: a polyphony of diverse motifs, a résumé of the contradictions of a living man. The treble line, the highest and most penetrating, was political and ideological, but more insistent was the *basso continuo* of sado-masochism which had initiated the performance and given it such a peculiar frenzy. It was a deliberate transgression of a perverse kind, but constructed according to a neurotic logic which impelled the individual to expiate his fantasies by the very act of indulging them. The *shinju* which united him to Morita was also a *junshi*: the tradition was dead, the emperor's sovereignty abolished, the heroes all forgotten, and Mishima went into death in search of them.

It was the suicide of an adolescent refusing to survive his shattered dreams, refusing to fit in with a society which he had resolved to reject; it was the suicide of an ageing man whose pleasures and successes and joys were already behind him, and who was resigned to fleeing the decline which was all the future offered. He still had every reason to be happy? – All the more reason to leave this life, not, perhaps, without regret, but without bitterness. Plutarch would have agreed: when a man is in possession of all his goods, that is the time for him to leave.[19] To jump from a height is a noble resolve. For a soul aspiring to grandeur, like Mishima's, happiness could never be enough; the supreme challenge was to live, as Nietzsche recommended, in such a way as to have the will to die at the fitting hour, and the honour of closing with one's own hand the perfect circle of a chosen destiny.

So was this the supreme leap towards the summit of the will? Or was it a romantic fascination with the abyss? Heroic daring may be one of the tangled threads in Mishima's motivation, but another equally obvious one is self-punishment. For a start, there was the reluctant soldier's need to punish himself for the half-lie which had saved him from the call-up in 1945 by alleging tuberculosis. Then there was all the literature he had loved too well, so that he lost his own being under the masks of his imagination. And lastly, he would have liked to believe that he had found a creed; but warlike heroism was, after all, only the most beguiling of his many roles.

All writers since the Romantics had been obliged to construct their attitudes no less carefully than their sentences, and Mishima took the task seriously. He would have liked to be a statue – a monument. But at the same time his frank and transparent writings obstinately refused to hide anything in the wings of his mental theatre. He would have been the first to laugh at the attitudes he was striking if death had not been there to remind everyone that it was no joke. Or was it rather death which stopped anything in this world from being really serious? He wrote his own death-scene into his own last act: it was the price he was willing to pay for an incontestable identity. If only he had believed in truth... but he believed, with Nietzsche, that there is nothing in this world save appearances and interpretations. So he would die as a soldier of the empire. Or as a writer playing at soldiers?

If he was prepared to pay so dearly for the last of his masks, it was to expiate the empty space left in him by his dream; to satisfy the need to punish himself for the vanity of his imagination, which was both his torment and his joy. Moreover he would have the satisfaction of playing yet another part, that of a censorious Confucian lambasting modern morals. His death would be a reproach to everything and everybody: the emperor first and foremost for betraying his own sovereignty, then the nation which had fallen away from its tradition, the soldiers unworthy of their arms, the degradation and shamefulness of the modern world, and all those who think they are alive and have not learned to die.

THE SPIRIT OF THE AGE

But the world had left its mark on him, whatever he believed, and even his last act admitted to that: it was a public piece of self-advertisement, the story of the century, a convenience food for the television society, duly spiced with the violence which is more and more sought after on our screens. Compare this noisy death with that of a soldier of the old, genuine tradition like Nogi, and Mishima's begins to look both turbid and tawdry, a bit of 1920s kitsch, tradition reduced to parodying itself. The suicide of another author, Kawabata, two years later in 1972 (so discreet that some people took it for an accident) was a reminder that silence has its own grandeur: in our increasingly noisy society, we need it.[20] Mishima needed a bit of self-censorship: he stooped to blackmail, and by taking a hostage he exploited for his own ends the respect for life which elsewhere he had repudiated. This was the logic of the terrorist whose weapon is the abuse of rights and values which he refuses to recognize.

Did his example help to justify the suicidal rage of the Red Army Faction extremists (*sekigunha*) who machine-gunned the crowds in the airport at Tel Aviv?[21] Probably not: Mishima was not in favour of terrorism and gave no support to those nihilists who believed that fear is the only emotion which can rule over human beings. He could be indignant and vituperative, but not vengeful. He was a fanatic, yet he was innocent: his cause called for sacrifice, but would accept none which was not voluntary. He was more demanding even than the pre-war terrorists who paid with their lives for the life they had taken, for he saw to it that he and Morita were the only victims of his coup. In that, his violence showed itself pure and deserves our respect if not our sympathy. Excessive and flamboyant as it was, the act still obeyed certain principles and conformed to its self-imposed rules. It was in this sublimation of violence into a moral law, far more than in the literal imitation of the evisceration, that Mishima showed himself a worthy heir of *bushido* and an adversary of nihilism.

The whole world received the news with stupefaction, more or less mingled with horror. There was more uneasiness than admiration, for it was all too clear that the act was in some way phoney. And yet Mishima had often cherished the illusion of tapping some collective devotion that would sweep away the loneliness and singularity which, in his vocation as a writer, he was rather inclined to luxuriate in. Like T. E. Lawrence in the RAF, he savoured the peace of being unrecognizable under a uniform, the bliss of having no more self, like a prelude to the ecstasy of annihilation: he dreamed of dying anonymously among a like-minded group. But his narcissistic excitability and his taste for the flamboyant proved too strong. The script for his dazzling and solitary death was more amazing than the most complex of his novels. In other countries which cherished the mistaken idea that harakiri was a kind of Japanese folk-art, the surprise was less marked. Thus Mishima's last act was, like many of his novels, more easily accepted (if not better understood) outside his own country, as can happen with goods designed for export. His penchant for living in the public eye was so strong that he determined to die as a tourist would imagine a real Japanese *ought* to do it.

CATHARSIS AND SOVEREIGNTY

It was in the real Japan that the emotion and uneasiness were greatest. The Japanese felt that they were the real target of Mishima's scoldings. He had stirred up too many ashes and put a finger on too many sore places. They had witnessed a drastically abridged revival of the extremist coups of the pre-war years, and a rapid evocation, allusive as a seventeen-syllable poem, of the imperial and militarist themes of a whole century which had ended in catastrophe. Marx once said that the great events of history were doomed to be repeated on a parodic scale, and this is what had happened to what had originally been a collective tragedy. Some people were worried by this revival of the old obsessions, the return of a past which had been suppressed, troubling the decency of official pacifism. But such risings against suppression, however agonized they may be, bring some promise of liberation. It was thus that the hysterical subjects who came to Breuer and Freud in Vienna helped to cure themselves by abreacting the pathogenic traumas from their past. Mishima's gesture, in its sumptuous theatricality (despite its lack of future promise) and its monumental aestheticism, had a sort of cathartic power. The Japanese people were profoundly shocked, but also enlightened and purified, as the Athenian people may once have been when *Oedipus Rex* re-enacted for them the downfall of the proud tyrants of the past.

In Japan, and everywhere else, suicide was to go on, more or less, with its own dark business; but in Mishima there was a sort of exaltation, a fitting subject for Japanese eyes with their unique way of looking on death: in him it burned too brightly not to conquer him altogether. He was determined to die, and to die voluntarily: his self-awareness aimed to be a reflection of the awareness of all the ages, and he tried to dissolve his own singularity in a vaster sea of time by becoming one with the pure decision 'not to be'. It was the end of a life, and the end of a story of which that life had been the fruit. Mishima's brief splendour was the quintessence of the Japanese tradition of the voluntary death, and the last bloody gleam of its setting sun.

Perhaps it was, after all, the strange deed of a frenzied man who had merged reality with imagination; we cannot stop the Pharisees from dismissing it as senseless and insignificant. But the frenzy needs to be understood for what it really was. The history of mankind, which involves the spending, as well as the getting, of life and the means of life, is periodically shaken by that same frenzy, and sooner or later every individual meets his share of it. From it springs that savage and mysterious element in man which is more than human. The singularity of Mishima, like the solitude of every man, is universal, and it reaches, seizes and convinces us at a stroke, whether we are Japanese or not. There are times when death's challenge to the will can seem to sleep and be forgotten; but at any moment something may happen which will arouse it. That is the time for extraordinary and exaggerated acts. Against the keen anguish of the void, the impenetrable enigma of existence, a man affirms his immeasurable sovereignty. It is the sovereignty of one who dares give himself the gift of death.

Notes

CHAPTER 1 CATO'S HARAKIRI

1 The description of Cato's death is quoted from *North's Plutarch*, ed. G. Wyndham, vol. V (London, 1896), pp. 177–8. Four years later Cato's nephew Brutus chose to die in the same way. So, later, did Antony, in a still more heart-rending and muddled fashion.

2 In the Bible (2 Maccabees 14), one of the Elders of Jerusalem, Razi by name, is suspected by the Greek occupying forces of stirring up resistance in the name of the Jewish faith, and is threatened with arrest by the soldiers of the Greek general, Nicanor. He prefers to fall on his sword. As he dies he tears out his entrails with both hands and throws them towards his enemies. Fourteen centuries later the *bushi* reinvented this defiant gesture. In an earlier book (1 Chronicles 10:4) Saul, vanquished by the Philistines, also falls on his sword.

3 There is an enormously long list of people who have pronounced for or against Cato, from Seneca and Lucan via St Augustine and Montaigne to Victor Hugo (who disapproved) and Lamartine (who claimed he preferred 'the patient death of the lowliest beggar on his paillasse of straw', *Cours familier de littérature*, p. 73). Thiers's opinion was delightfully opportunistic: Cato ought to have manoeuvered and temporized so that later he could have resumed the struggle with Brutus and Cassius. Those who judge Cato judge themselves.

4 The classic study by Albert Bayet, *Le suicide et la morale* (Paris, 1922) resumes the differing judgements and rationalizations, hostile and favourable, which suicide has provoked through centuries of Western civilization. There is a chapter on suicide among the Romans in Gabriel Matzneff's *Le Défi* (Paris, 1965): it adopts and extends the arguments of Montherlant. There are many studies of suicide in antiquity. The latest light on the subject is thrown by the work of Paul Veyne, in an article in *L'Histoire* 27 (October 1980) and a brilliant study in *Latomus* (April/June 1981) called 'Suicide, fisc, esclavage, capital et droit romain'.

5 Aristotle, *Nicomachean Ethics*, book V, 1138a; Plato, *Phaedo*, 62b (tr. D. Gallop, Oxford, 1975, p. 6); *Laws*, 873c (tr. R. G. Bury, Loeb edn, Cambridge, Mass., 1926, p. 267).

6 The indifference to metaphysics in Japanese culture is examined in Nakamura Hajime, *Ways of Thinking of Eastern Peoples* (Hawaii, 1964). In Part IV, chapter 5, he quotes from Dogen, 'Hossho' in *Shobogenzo*, and the little poem of Otomo no Tabito, from *Man'yoshu* (p. 541). The will of a businessman called Shimai Soshitsu, in 1610, accuses Christians of being too preoccupied with their salvation and the next life: it is a kind of egoism, and such a faith leads to neglect of the duties of this world. (J. Mark Ramseyer, 'Thrift and diligence: house codes of the Tokugawa merchant families', *Monumenta Nipponica*, 1979.)

CHAPTER 2 THE ARITHMETIC OF SUICIDE

1 Japanese demographic and economic statistics are compiled by a statistical unit attached to the Prime Minister's office and are published every year, in Japanese and English, in a volume entitled *Japan Statistical Yearbook*.

2 An article by René Duchac in *Revue Française de Sociologie* (1965, no. 5), 'Suicide au Japon, suicide à la japonaise', gives a very full picture of the situation at this time. For an older sociological viewpoint see *Archives d'Anthropologie Criminelle* (1907), p. 809: 'Le suicide et la criminalité au Japon' by E. Tarnowski, who emphasizes the marked rise in suicide rates up to the end of the twentieth century: 'The feeble and the excitable are wiping themselves out.'

3 Again in *Archives d'Anthropologie Criminelle* (1897, p. 365), a French doctor named Jean-Jacques Matignon, observing the slow collapse of the old Chinese empire, published an article on suicide in China, where its frequency reflected the general confusion. He elaborated on the theme in two further works, *Superstition, crime et misère en Chine* (Paris, 1909) and *La Chine hermétique* (Paris, 1936). In the decadence of the empire suicide was very common, and Matignon's ingenuous racism saw the reason ready to hand: 'The Chinese is a fundamentally selfish being', and all the varieties of suicide

could be reduced to one of the 'numerous examples of unbridled egoism which is one of the characteristics of the race'. It was no use expecting too much of a Chinese: 'Do not seek in him the sentiments of humanity and philanthropy so well developed in Western nations.' For example, it was no good expecting the poor to spare the rich the banal, but still annoying, spectacle of their despair: 'Sometimes an ill-disciplined beggar will be revenged on you by cutting his thoat on your doorstep' (*La Chine hermétique*, p. 103).

CHAPTER 3 TOWARDS A THEORY OF SUICIDE

1 A critical bibliography of suicide through the centuries would fill a volume. We refer the reader to the stimulating and wide-ranging work of a sociologist determined to shake off routine views of suicide: Jean Baechler, *Les Suicides* (Paris, 1975). His eleven categories could be represented more simply by a six-pointed star.

2 The reference to Gall, the phrenologist, is in G. Deshaies, *Psychologie du suicide* (Paris, 1947).

3 In *The Phenomenology of the Mind,* Hegel shows that observant reason, in the example of allegedly scientific objectivization supplied by phrenology, arrives at the conclusion that 'the being of the mind is a bone'. Gall has gone out of fashion, but rationalizing objectivization is taking on new and more sophisticated forms.

4 Durkheim's *Suicide: A Study in Sociology* (1897), tr. J. A. Spaulding and J. Simpson, London, 1968) is required reading, but in Masaryk's excellent *Der Selbstmord als soziale Massenerscheinung* ('Suicide as a Social Mass Phenomenon', 1881), one of the first studies of the urban collective mentality, there is a clearer echo of the debate introduced by Dostoevsky in his diary for October 1876 (*The Unpublished Dostoevsky: Diaries and Notebooks, 1860–1881,* ed. T. S. Berczynski, Ann Arbor, 1973–6).

5 As Antonin Artaud, following Durkheim, said of Van Gogh, can one commit suicide for any other reason than 'society'? I kill myself? No: they kill me. The accusation of society becomes positively judicial in *Les Dossiers noirs du suicide* (Paris, 1976), in which Denis Langlois encourages each one of us to be indignant at everyone else's selfishness.

CHAPTER 4 SUICIDE AS SYMPTOM

1 Some of the malaise in Japan's economic society is explained in Christian Sutter, *Japon, le prix de la puissance* (Paris, 1973).

2 George De Vos (*Socialization for Achievement: Essays on the Cultural Psychology of the Japanese,* Berkeley and Los Angeles, 1973) stresses the

Japanese individual's identification with his social role; on this see also Nakane Chie, *La Société japonaise* (Paris, 1974).

3 An article by Philippe Pons (*Le Monde*, 24 December 1978) pointed out the responsibility of these usurers, called *sarakin*. He claimed there was some talk of curbing their activities.

4 A film by Imamura Shohei which won at the Cannes Festival in 1983, based on a story by Fukazawa called *Narayama bushiko* (1956, tr. D. Keene as 'The Old Woman' in *Three Modern Japanese Short Novels*, London, 1961), dramatizes the semi-voluntary deaths of old people in situations of extreme poverty which might once have occurred at times of famine.

5 Every year the Japanese press publishes a mass of stories, statistics and commentaries illustrating essential aspects of suicide in modern Japanese society. Suicides of whole families (*oyako shinju*) are an ever-recurring theme. In 1977, 1978 and 1979 the press laid special stress on juvenile suicides. In 1983 and 1984 it took more interest in violence by schoolchildren. The psychiatrist Ohara Kenshiro has studied the family aspect of suicide. Iga Minoru has published a detailed article, 'Japanese Adolescent Suicide and Social Structure' in a collective work called *Essays in Self-Destruction* (New York, 1967). There is also a general study on suicide in Japan, culturalist in inspiration, in Takie Sugiyama Lebra's *Japanese Patterns of Behaviour* (Honolulu, 1976).

6 Dr Kosawa Heisaku, the first of the Japanese psychoanalysts, had already noted the arousal of guilt feelings in the son by the mother's masochism. In 1932 he presented Freud with a study on the 'Ajax complex' which had been inspired by a Buddhist legend. A generation later, the psychiatrist and psychoanalyst Doi Takeo revealed the role of dependence in his 1971 book *Amae no kozo* ('Structure of Dependence'), translated into French by E. Dale Saunders as *Le Jeu de l'indulgence* (1982). On the early progress of psychoanalysis in Japan see James Clark Moloney, *Understanding the Japanese Mind* (Rutland, Vt., 1954).

7 The remark about St Peter and Judas, quoted in Duchac, 'Suicide au Japon', was made by a Japanese university professor who had been a Christian for thirty years.

8 There is a penetrating study by William Caudill and David W. Platt on family life: 'Who Sleeps by Whom? Parent–Child Involvement in Urban Japanese Families', in *Japanese Culture and Behaviour* (Honolulu, 1974). In the same collection is an article by Kato Masaaki, 'Self-Destruction in Japan: A Cross-Cultural Epidemiological Analysis of Suicide'.

9 The conflict between daughter-in-law (*yome*) and mother-in-law (*shutome*) was no less insidious in China than in Japan: 'If the law took an interest in

these private suicides, one might tell it to "Look for the mother-in-law". In Europe she is a comic figure; in China she is better suited to melodrama' (Matignon, *Chine hermétique*, p. 114).

10 In the foreword to *Genealogy of Morals* (tr. F. Golffing, Garden City, 1956), Nietzsche speaks of this deciphering of the past of human morality which the historians of mental attitudes now seem to be engaged in: 'the object is to explore the huge, distant and thoroughly hidden country of morality, morality as it has actually existed and actually been lived, with new questions in mind and with fresh eyes' (pp. 155-6).

11 An article by William Wetherall, 'Anti-Suicide Traditions in Japan: Past and Present', which appeared in *The Japan Times* for 14 February 1981, is an interesting reaction against a clichéd image of Japanese society, which has incorrectly been seen (on the basis of imperfect Western understanding of the *bushis' seppuku*) as being massively tolerant of any kind of suicide and indifferent to death. A thesis presented at the University of Illinois by Robert George Sewell in 1976, 'The Theme of Suicide: A Study of Human Values in Japanese and Western Literature', attempts to open up some comparative horizons. In 1978 an international symposium on the prevention of suicide gave rise to a Japanese Association for the Prevention of Suicide with Mr Koto Masaaki, director of the National Institute for Mental Health, as its president. Its aim is, in particular, to alert the public to distress signals and to promote communication with individuals considered to be at risk so as to improve their idea of themselves.

CHAPTER 5 THE DAWN OF HISTORY

1 An article by Charles Haguenauer, 'Du caractère de la représentation de la mort dans le Japon antique', *Études Chinoises*, 2 (Leiden, 1977), helps us understand the sentiments in the myths of the *Kojiki* and the *Nihongi*. The horror of corpses is redoubled in the case of suicide; even today there are nervous superstitions attached to the place where a suicide has taken place, which give rise to propitiatory rites.

2 In *La Part maudite*, Georges Bataille transcribes and comments on the Aztec myth according to which the sun shines in answer to a voluntary sacrifice.

3 The story of the Lady Ototachibana is taken from *Nihongi*, VII. The *Kojiki* gives a briefer version.

4 The combat of modesty between the two princes and the suicide of the brother of the future Emperor Nintoku are in *Nihongi*, XI.

5 The suicide of the maid of Unahi, which in the fifteenth century inspired the No play *Motomezuka*, features in a famous poem (no. 1809) in the

NOTES 291

Man'yoshu, and anthology put together in the eighth century, but which contains poems already several centuries old at the time. There is a study by Jacqueline Pigeot, 'Les suicides de femmes par noyade dans la littérature narrative du Japon ancien', in *Mélanges offerts à M. Charles Hagaenauer* (Paris, 1980).

6 The invention of terracotta images as substitutes for human sacrifice is in *Nihongi*, VI.

7 *Junshi* (called *oibara* if it involves disembowelling) is a Japanese institution, but the feelings behind it are universal. In 1 Chronicles 10:5 Saul's armour-bearer falls on his sword after his master dies. Plutarch tells us that Eros, Antony's slave, made death easier for him by killing himself before his eyes. Arria did the same to encourage her husband (*Paete, non dolet*), a story recalled by Montaigne in *Essays*, book II, chapter xxxv, 'Concerning three good women'. When Otho died several of his soldiers also killed themselves in 'profound affection', according to Tacitus. Thus, accompanying someone in death is a universal human practice which Japan has only codified, intensified and ritualized. In China it was thought a splendid thing for a widow to commit suicide, and it was commemorated by inscriptions, sometimes even a triumphal arch. In 1729 these honours were forbidden by imperial decree. In India, voluntary self-immolation by the wife, called suttee or 'faithful wife', was still practised after the British had forbidden it, and has continued down to our own time. The conjugal bond is considerably looser in Japanese society, less close than the link between lord and vassal, and never made such demands. As early as 834, a commentary on the existing law, *Ryo no gige*, strictly prohibited the semi-voluntary sacrifice of widows, some examples of which had been seen in Shinano province.

8 Under the influence of Buddhism, *junshi* became somewhat less drastic. In 1219, at the death of the shogun and poet Minamoto no Sanetamo, about a hundred of his vassals retired to monasteries.

CHAPTER 6 VIOLENCE AT A DISTANCE

1 The edict limiting funeral expenses is in *Nihongi*, XXV.

2 On the character, fall and posthumous vengeance of Sugawara no Michizane see Jacqueline Pigeot, *Michiyuki-bun: poétique de l'itinéraire dans la littérature du Japon ancien* (Paris, 1982): in four very informative pages (289–92) she throws a good deal of light on these legendary archetypes. There is a chapter on the disgrace of Michizane in Ivan Morris's study of vanquished heroes in Japanese history, *The Nobility of Failure* (New York, 1975).

3 The story of the Lady Ukifune ('Storm-tossed ship') and her miraculously unsuccessful suicide is told in chapter 51 of *Genji monogatari*. There are

several English translations of the *Tale of Genji*. (A *genji* is a prince of the blood, the founder of a line descended from the imperial family but thereafter distinct from it.)

4 It will be noted that the suspicious and reserved attitude of Ukifune and the young daughter of Unani makes them more desirable. This is a recurrent aspect of Japanese sensibility which is analysed in the magnificent essay by Tanizaki, *In Praise of Shadows* (London, 1991).

CHAPTER 7 THE MARTIAL ART OF DYING WELL

1 The very earliest text to describe a voluntary death by incision of the stomach concerns a female character. The story is found in one of the monographs or *fudoki* compiled in the eighth century to give an account of the landscapes, resources, customs, legends and other particulars of every province in the empire. According to the *Harima fudoki* there is in that region a lake called Harasaki. Once upon a time a female divinity, Omi no kami, went in search of her husband, who was also a god; furious and in despair at not being able to find him, she came to the banks of the lake, seized a sword, disembowelled herself and threw herself into the water. Since then the lake has been called *hara-saki* (cloven belly), and the fish in it have no entrails. Cf. a passage from *Kojiki*, I, in which the god Susanoo, the *enfant terrible* of the pantheon, throws a newly-flayed horse into the room in which some ladies are weaving. They are so scared that they smite themselves in the stomach with their shuttles and so perish! In *Nihongi*, V, there is another legend, peculiar as a dream, concerning a princess called Yamato-toto-hime, who is married to a god who visits her only at night. Once she asks him to stay a little so that she can look on his beauty. 'So be it!' says the god. 'Tomorrow I shall be in your toilet bag, but take care you are not frightened!' At dawn, when the princess opens the bag, there is a pretty little snake inside. She cannot restrain a cry of fright. The god regains his human form, reproaches her bitterly, and takes flight. The princess, left alone with her shame, sticks so many wands into her abdomen that she dies. This tale, which seems expressly written for psychoanalysts, suggests that the suicide attack on the belly, before being monopolized by vanquished warriors, was performed by women succumbing to solitude, shame and anger, cursing their sex. It may be that her sterility has put her at risk of repudiation (the Japanese family has never focused on the married couple, but on the need to continue the family line), or that she has proved too fertile too early and thus dishonoured herself, as it might be a *miko*, who were, like vestals, vowed to virginity. Most often women commit suicide by drowning, but these legends show that death can sometimes be connected with a laceration fantasy directed at the womb as a cause of misery.

2 The *seppuku* of Yorimasa is described in book IV of the *Heike monogatari*, a chronicle of the twelfth-century civil war between the Taira and the Minamoto. English translation by B. T. Tsuchido (Tokyo, 1975).

NOTES 293

3 The first three stories are in *Heike monogatari*: Imai's suicide, book IX; the drowning of lady Kozaisho, ibid.; the death of the child-emperor Antoku in his grandmother's arms, book XI. The *seppuku* of Yoshitsune is translated from the romantic story of his life in *Gikeiki*, book VIII.

4 For prince Morinaga and Yoshiteru see *Taiheiki*, book VII. *Taiheiki* is a story of savage civil wars whose euphemistic title means 'Chronicle of the Great Peace'. The mass *seppuku* of 1333 around Nakatoki and Takatoki are in books IX and X; the criticism of *seppuku* by Sadanao in book X, and the attempted *seppuku* by the son of Kusunoki Masashige in book XVI.

5 On *seppuku* in general there is a study in Japanese by Chiba Tokuji, *Seppuku no hanashi* ('Some Remarks on *Seppuku*', Tokyo, 1972) which was evidently prompted by the deed of Mishima in 1970 that revived historians' interests in the practice. Jack Seward (*Hara-kiri, Japanese Ritual Suicide*, Rutland, Vt., 1968) gives a rapid survey, concentrating on the penal *tsumebara*.

CHAPTER 8 GIVING UP THE BODY

1 The dialogue between the Kunusoki brothers, Masasue and Masashige, is in *Taiheiki*, XVI.

2 The world of the fighting *Ashura* is described at the end of the No play *Kiyotsune*, by Zeami (1363–1443), whose theme is the fall of the Taira. Kiyotsune is a clan warrior who drowns himself when an oracle tells him that defeat is inevitable. He reappears as a dream or ghost at the bedside of his wife, who reproaches him for his suicide, but then forgives him. After reliving in the hell of the *Ashura* the battles which he experienced on earth, he is finally delivered by the grace of the Buddha Amida.

3 The early Buddhism of the Theravada is clearly explained in Walpola Rahula, *What the Buddha Taught* (Bedford, 1967). For the condemnation of self-destruction (*vibhava tanha*) see p. 37.

4 See Henri de Montherlant, *Essais* (Paris, 1963), p. 247.

5 Augustine's condemnation of suicide did not deter the Abbé de Saint-Cyran, despite his friendship with the author of the *Augustinus*, from pronouncing in 1608 in favour of voluntary death, if it was inspired by reason, which was a ray of the Eternal Light. Here Saint-Cyran was taking Augustine's concept of a direct message by God to the conscience so far that he met up again with the stoic idea that hopeless defeat, incurable illness and implacable enmity were all signs sent by god to the reasonable man telling him that it was time to take his leave of life. Saint-Cyran and the Jansenists, worried at the progress of absolutism under Richelieu and Louis XIV, rejected contemporary Christian pro-authoritarianism and reawoke the

spirit of resistance and liberty which had inspired Cato's suicide in opposition to Casear, and Seneca's and Lucan's against Nero.

6 The very useful anthology of Buddhist texts by Edward Conze, *Buddhist Scriptures* (Harmondsworth, 1959), includes the encounter with Mara, god of death (p. 59) and the Buddha's *Parinirvana* (p. 62).

7 The legendary tale of the death of Kukai (774–835), posthumously named Kobo-Daishi, is from *Konjaku monogatari*, XI, 25. There is a French translation by Bernard Frank (*Histoires qui sont maintenant du passé*, Paris, 1968, p. 263), from which the present English version is translated; so far as I am aware, there is no published English translation of this particular tale. In fact, Kukai was cremated, but other Buddhist deaths from starvation or burial alive did undoubtedly produce mummies which were venerated: as recently as 1829 an ascetic called Tetsumonkai took this path to perpetual immobility (*nyujo*). On the mummification see Paul Demieville, 'Momies d'Extrême-Orient', *Journal des Savants* (1965), and Ando Kosei, 'Des momies au Japon et de leur culte', *L'Homme*, 8/2 (1968).

8 The story of the bodhisattva who cut his own throat so that the tigress could devour him is in Conze, *Buddhist Scriptures*, p. 26, after the Mahayana sutra *Suvarnaprabhasa*.

9 In Brahmanism, the creation of the universe is attributed to the sacrifice of Prajapati: see Sylvain Lévi, *La Doctrine du sacrifice dans les Brahmanas* (Paris, 1898). There was no sacrifice in early Buddhism, and it maintained a determined agnosticism regarding the origins of the cosmos. But the return of the spirit of sacrifice and of metaphysical speculation is evident five centuries after the Buddha's death, in the sutra of the Lotus of the True Law (*Saddmarmapundarika-sutra*), which relates the voluntary cremation of the bodhisattva Bhaisajyaraja with the shining of the sun (L. de La Vallée-Poussin, *Bouddhisme*, Paris, 1925, p. 326). Thus returned the theme which the Aztecs, a world away, practised with their cruellest rites: since the sun was born of sacrifice, the life which it nourishes must also accept sacrifice.

10 The aphorisms of the monks are in *Ichigon hodan*, in the series 'Nihon Shiso', published by Chikuma-shobo, vol. V.

11 There are two excellent French studies of Buddhist self-cremation. Jacques Gernet's 'Les suicides par le feu chez les bouddhistes chinois du ve au xe siècle', *Mélanges publiés par l'Institut des Hautes Études Chinoises*, vol. II (1960), points to eleven solemn ceremonial suicides by fire between 451 and 501, when Buddhist fervour in China was at its height. Jean Filliozat's 'La mort volontaire par le feu et la tradition bouddhique indienne', *Journal Asiatique*, 251 (1964), points out that before yielding to the intoxication of devotion, the disciple of the Buddha is a yogi, impassible and supremely indifferent to his own body. Both views are equally valid and there is no

need to prefer one to the other: Gernet's applies to the Chinese version of the Mahayana, Fillozat's to the Theravada. What is worth noting is the flexibility of Buddhism, which nevertheless remained one faith all the way from the Benares to Heian. An article by Monseigneur Etienne Lamotte, 'Le suicide religieux dans le bouddhisme ancien', *Bulletin de l'Académie Royale de Belgique, Séance du 7 mai 1965*, gives a succinct summary of the question. In China, even after the first great solemn self-cremations, a rite of 'burning the skull' persisted as part of Buddhist ordination: sticks on incense were stuck on the shaven scalp of the future monk with vegetable gum. It was a rite of passage and a test of endurance, a diminished echo of past exploits (La Vallée-Poussin, *Bouddhisme*, p. 327). But in Japan, from the eleventh century onwards, the *Ryo no gige* strictly forbade monks to give their bodies to the flames: it was illegal. In China, however, Jean-Jacques Matignon drew attention to a double Buddhist self-cremation in Tche-Kiang Province as late as 1888 (see *La Chine hermétique*). The sutra of the Lotus of the True Law (in Japanese Hokkekyo) was, however, venerated in the archipelago, by the Tendai sect in the eleventh century and even more by Nichiren in the thirteenth. But Japanese readers did not pay much attention to ch. 22, which describes the immolation by fire of Bhaisajyaraja, a bodhisattva who, under his Japanese name of Yakuo, excited no particular devotion. The Japanese preferred to address their prayers to the bodhisattva Avalokiteshvara who figures in chapter 25 of the Lotus, and who enjoyed immense prestige in Japan under the name of Kannon.

12 Angela of Foligno's *Book of Visions*, admired by Georges Bataille, sketched the essentials of Christian mysticism three centuries in advance of St Theresa: 'Oh, let me languish no longer! Oh, death, death! For life is a death to me.' In her ecstasies of love she claims to love 'imps, toads, serpents and even demons'.

13 The drowning of Taira no Koremori is recounted in *Heike monogatari*, X.

14 The passage by Pierre Charlevoix is from his *Histoire et description générale du Japon* (Paris, 1736), vol. I, p. 224.

15 The ascetic's failed attempt to drown himself in the river Katsura is from *Uji-shui monogatari*, IX/9; the story of the devotee who burned himself with red-hot iron before embarking for Fudaraku is from *Hosshin-shu*, III/12.

16 The quotation from Dogen, in which he equates life in this world with the life of the Buddha, is in the 'Shoji' chapter of *Shobogenzo* ('The Treasure of the True Law'). There is a French translation by Nakamura Ryoji and René de Ceccaty (Éditions de la Différence, 1980) under the abstruse title of *Réserve visuelle des événements dans leur justesse*. In Georges Renondeau's *Le Bouddhisme japonais* (Paris, 1965) there are some notes on the *Shobogenzo* by a disciple of Dogen's called Ejo.

17 Shinohara Shiro's description of the voluntary death of the *yamabushi* Jitsukaga was translated into French by a ethnologist, Anne-Marie Bouchy; the English translation is from hers. She also wrote an excellent article, 'Jitsukaga, *yamabushi* des premières annees de Meiji et le *shugendo*', *Revue de l'Histoire des Religions*, 2 (1978). By the same author is a work in Japanese on Jitsukaga, *Shashin gyoja Jitsukaga no shugendo* (Tokyo, 1977). On this grandiose and ascetic aspect of Japanese Buddhism see also G. Renondeau, *Le Shugendo* (Paris, 1965). Kukai (ninth century) maintained in a celebrated little work called *Sokushin-jobutsu-gi* that it was possible to become a Buddha in this body and in this life. Despite the diversity of methods, Zen, the schools of Heian, Tendai and Shingon, and *shugendo* all draw inspiration from the same monism.

CHAPTER 9 THE THEATRE OF CRUELTY

1 The laws of the *bushi* emphasize the virtue of loyalty so heavily that it makes one suspect that treason was commonplace during the civil wars. A battle was often decided by a defection. One of the most celebrated was that of Akechi Mitsuhide, who on 21 June 1582 used this method of avenging himself on his lord, Oda Nobunaga.

2 There is a chapter on the Shimabara revolt, and the brief career of Amakusa Shiro, in Morris' *The Nobility of Failure*.

3 In *Seppuku no Hanashi* Chiba Tokuji mentions certain *seppuku* performed in the Edo period by people who were not members of the warrior class, but these were very much the exception.

4 *Junshi* reappeared in the civil wars of the fifteenth and sixteenth centuries, when the clans became more cohesive and the princes more powerful and more demanding.

5 In *Sources of Japanese Tradition* (New York, 1958), a very useful anthology of historical documents, there are some edicts relating to Hideyoshi's great Sword-Hunt (I, p. 320) and to the closure of Edo society (I, p. 326). The secret of Tokugawa Ieyasu's success is given on page 331.

6 The story of the cane which was asked for by the young prince Nabeshima Tsunashige is in *Hagakure*, VIII.

7 The suicide of protest had a long and glorious history in China. Matignon recalls (*Chine hermétique*, pp. 123, 180) that the Imperial Censor Ou-Kou-Tou hanged himself in 1879, aged sixty-six, to protest against the choice of an incompetent Son of Heaven by the dowager empress Tseu-Hi (Cixi). Tseu-Hi was quite unaffected, and twenty years later, on 23 July 1900, she forestalled any further protests by having the Censors who had begged her to dismiss her xenophobic and opportunistic ministers executed *en masse*.

8 In his *Dictionnaire philosophique*, Voltaire notes that in Japan a man of honour who has suffered an injustice does not challenge his enemy to a duel, but kills himself. 'The aggressor is forever dishonoured if he does not forthwith plunge a great knife into his belly.' What astonished Western observers was the principle of a second suicide in answer to the first, obeying a code of honour even more costly than that of the familiar duel.

9 On the penal system in the Edo period see J. C. Hall, 'Japanese Feudal Laws', in *Transactions of the Asiatic Society of Japan*, 41 (Tokyo, 1913).

10 The *Hagakure*, which was recommended reading during the War in the Pacific and restored to honour by Mishima, gives us an idea of the purest and most untamed aspects of the *bushi* spirit. From the *Hagakure* are: using condemned men for sword-practice (VII/14); Makiguchi Yohei as *kaishaku* (VIII/81), the samurai in the latrines during the quarrel of the *hatamoto* (X/126), Lord Matsudaira's retainer (X/65), the identification of *Bushido* with death or the intoxication of death (I/2, I/114) and the marriage of Lord Ryuzoji Takanobu's daughter (VIII/47). There is no complete English translation of the *Hagakure*, although excerpts are found in Mishima's own *On Hagakure* (Harmondsworth, 1979).

11 Montesquieu, an avid reader of books like Père Charlevoix's which drew on stories from persecuted missionaries, saw the Tokugawa regime as the blackest kind of despotism: see *L'Esprit des Lois*, VI/13 and XIV/15. The Chinese regime was also more or less despotic, but it was much more tolerant, enlightened and open to reason. The authoritative opinion of George Sansom (*History of Japan, 1334–1615*, Rutland, Vt., 1961, p. 371) is that Nobunaga and Hideyoshi were dictators, and could be violent, but fell far short of the atrocities of Tiberius, Caligula or Nero.

12 The 'three precious gifts' of the emperor of China are described by Matignon in *La Chine hermétique* (p. 154). The great advantage of such a death, to the Chinese, was that it left the body intact, whereas it would have been mutilated by decapitation.

13 On the Chinese School of Laws, see Marcel Granet, *La Pensée chinoise* (Paris, 1934, IV/1), where he discusses the cauldrons on which the penal laws were written.

14 To Confucian scholars, *junshi* was no more than an irrational waste of life, but in fact it had its reasons, like any other aspect of reality. When a lord died, his ministers and closest advisers disappeared along with him, into death or into a monastery, and no more was heard of them. It was in fact a way of changing governments, a process which in Western society is subject to the caprices of the electorate. It was also a curb on the gerontocratic and conservative tendencies of absolutism.

15 After the *junshi* of Nogi in 1912 (see chapter 11), Mori Ogai wrote a novella called *Abe ichizoku* ('The Abe Clan') which contains a casuistic justification of honorouble suicide, similar to the justifications of duelling which were familiar in the West. If vassals made it a point of honour to kill themselves, and were mortally hurt if not allowed to do so, it was because they were afraid of looking afraid – a common source of courage.

16 Quarrels between lords (daimyo) were decided by the Bakufu, but every lord had an absolute power over his vassals. Quarrels between lords and vassals were not admitted and could not be submitted to arbitration. In the seventeenth century the absolutism of the daimyo was so well established that a *bushi* could no more appeal against the lord who employed and paid him than a child could appeal against his father. Quarrelsomeness and rebelliousness were despised, but when people ran out of patience they were none the less obliged to resort to some catastrophic solution, without arbitration, as happens in the closing pages of *Abe ichizoku*.

17 On feudal vengeance see D. E. Mills, '*Kataki-uchi*: The Practice of Blood Revenge in Pre-Modern Japan', *Modern Asian Studies*, X/4 (1976). On the famous vendetta of the forty-seven loyal vassals see the translation and commentary by René Sieffert and Michel Wasserman, *Le Mythe des quarante-sept ronin* (Paris, 1981). There is a superb re-telling of the legend in A. B. Mitford, *Tales of Old Japan* (London, 1871; 2nd edn 1903). The author of the *Hagakure* condemned the *ronin's* slow and calculating approach (I/55). The contrary opinion was formulated by Ogyu Sorai (1666–1728) in a pamphlet on the Ako affair called *Shijushichi shi no koto o ronzu*. In the same spirit, but based on Western rather than Confucian rationalism, was the opinion of Fukuzawa Yukichi (1834–1901) half a century later: in *Gakumon no susume*, chapter 6, he declares against clan vengeance in the name of state justice.

18 Sakuma Sogoro, so pitilessly crucified, was the incarnation of the submissive peasantry of the period. On their sporadic revolts see Hugh Burton, 'Peasant Uprisings in Japan of the Tokugawa Period', *Transactions of the Asiatic Society of Japan*, 16 (May 1938).

19 Morris, *Nobility of Failure*, has a chapter on the abortive attempt at urban rebellion by Oshio Heihachiro in 1837.

20 The English diplomat A. B. Mitford (later Lord Redesdale) was one of the Westerners who observed the death-agony of feudal Japan. He witnessed Zenzaburo's *tsumebara* and gives a description of it, quoted below, in *Tales of Old Japan*, pp. 357–8. The Sakai affair, when thirteen French sailors were massacred near Osaka, took place the same year, 1868, on 15 February. The French consul, Léon Roches, demanded an exemplary punishment, which was granted by the brand-new imperial government: twenty soldiers of the Sakai garrison were to be condemned to *tsumebara*. The ceremony

took place in the presence of the consul and a delegation of French sailors. The eviscerations commenced. At the eleventh Roches, perhaps feeling unwell, got up and left. The ceremony was called off, and later the nine survivors were pardoned. Mori Ogai, who described these events in *Sakai Jiken* (1914), is discreetly but perceptibly proud of the prowess of the Japanese in contrast to the flinching – attributable to weak nerves – of the foreign consul. The soldiers concerned were not samurai by birth; they were ennobled posthumously. Such were the last prodigies of feudal *seppuku*: it had begun to devour commoners. Five years later, in the new penal code of 1873, capital punishment by *tsumebara* was abolished, leaving *seppuku* as a freely chosen gesture independent of any written law. On the transformation of Japanese law under French, German and American influence see Noda Yoshiyuki's excellent *Introduction au droit japonais* (Paris, 1965).

CHAPTER 10 LOVE AND DEATH

1 The story of Ocho and Ryushichi is from *Shinju okagami*, I/4.

2 The double suicide proposed by Minagawa to Seijuro is in book I, chapter 1 of *Koshoku gonin onna* (*Five Women who Loved Love*, tr. W. T. de Bary, London, 1969). Quotations are from this translation.

3 On the organization of the Yoshiwara district and on prostitution in the Edo period see J. E. de Becker, *The Sexual Life of Japan: Being an Exhaustive Study of the Nightless City* (1899). The Kabuki theatre, whose modern repertoire seems quite blameless, was originally (in the early seventeenth century) a series of lascivious dances very much concerned with sexual adventures, and male and female prostitution. All through the seventeenth and eighteenth centuries the Bakufu strove to contain, moralize and control such performances. At just that time Molière was fighting it out with the French authorities. On this mini-war of prohibitions and infringements see Donald H. Shively, '*Bakufu* versus *Kabuki*', *Harvard Journal of Asiatic Studies* (December 1955).

4 In his commentary on the *Hagakure*, Mishima Yukio quoted this passage on secret love with approval. Did he put it into practice with his young friend Morita, who died with him three years later, on 25 November 1970? Love needs silence as much as truth: love that is known is no longer special.

5 Fujimoto Kizan's remarks on love-tokens are quoted along with other extracts from works of the Edo period in Donald Keene, *World Within Walls: Japanese Literature of the Pre-Modern Era 1600–1867* (New York, 1976), p. 163.

6 See *La Dame aux camélias*, tr. B. Bray (London, 1975), p. 31, where Marguerite's lover Armand Duval pronounces on the ways of redemption

offered to the fallen woman. The *dame aux camélias* (*Tsubakihime*) is one of the most popular of the Western fictional characters imported into Japan: she appealed readily to minds already sensitized to the sacrificial resignation of womankind.

7 The trials of the fair Mikasa are recounted in Part II of Saikaku's *Koshoku ichidai otoko* ('The Life of an Amorous Man', 1682), tr. K. Hamada (Tokyo, 1964); see pp. 230–2.

8 This idea of avenging oneself by suicide also occurs in ancient Greece, where the victim's ghost persecutes its persecutor. Ajax falls on his sword in order to attract the attention of the Furies, goddesses of vengeance (and therefore of justice) to his wrongs. *Ajax furens*: is his suicidal violence the height of unrighteous presumption or righteous indignation? See Marie Delcourt, 'Le suicide par vengeance dans la Grèce ancienne', *Revue de l'Histoire des Religions* (1939), 154–71. The victim can become quite a menace, as Sugawara no Michizane did; he may even affect and bend the will of the gods. In Euripides' *Iphigenia in Tauris* (line 973) Orestes tells how he has influenced Apollo by threatening to starve himself to death in front of his temple.

9 The threat of suicide can be stratagem or blackmail. When the Christian reprehension of suicide was at its height Molière extracted some amusement from it in *Georges Dandin* (1668), III/6. (It drew him a few thunderbolts from the Church, especially Père Bourdaloue, outraged by a performance of 'naked impudence'.) Angélique alarms her imbecilic husband by threatening suicide: 'I shall have courage to carry out the extremest resolutions, and with this knife I shall kill myself on the spot.' She pretends to stab herself. 'Oh dear!' say Georges Dandin to himself. 'Could she really be nasty enough to kill herself just to get me hanged?' And he falls neatly for his wife's trick. Saikaku shows the same mocking spirit when his Osan, and her lover Moemon, fake a *shinju* (see below).

10 On *shinju* see Serge Elisséeff's article in *Japon et Extrême-Orient* (September 1924).

11 Likewise, in China, there was nothing wrong with taking one's pleasure in a brothel, but falling in love was the mark of a dissolute character: R. Van Gulik, *Sexual Life in Ancient China* (Leiden, 1961), p. 308.

12 On the new-style *joruri* invented by Miyakoji Bungonojo in 1730, see the article by Pierre Faure in *Mélanges offerts à M. Charles Haguenauer*. The scholar who denounced this 'epidemic of lust' was Dazai Shundai (1680–1747).

13 Eventually the Kabuki became bogged down in melodrama, though the suicide theme persisted and indeed became more prominent: this can be

gauged in the French translation by Pierre Faure of a play by Mokuami (1816-93) in *Le Kabuki et ses écrivains, suivi de 'Izayoi et Seishin' ou l'histoire amoureuse et tragique d'une courtisane et d'un bonze* (Paris, 1977).

14 Bonaparte's order for the day condemning the suicide of Grenadier Gobain is quoted in *Roland Barthes par lui-même* (Paris, 1975), p. 94.

15 There are stories of homosexual love in several of Saikaku's works, especially *Nanshoku okagami* ('The Great Mirror of Masculine Love', 1687) and also *Budo Denraiki* and *Buki Giri monogatari*, which concern the manners and customs of the warrior class. There is a French translation of some of these stories in Ken Sato, *Contes d'amour des samourais* (1927).

16 The adulterous love of Osan, the almanach maker's wife, and Moemon the salesman is the third of the true stories in *Five Women who Loved Love*.

CHAPTER 11 THE TRADITION OF SACRIFICE

1 There is a convenient collection of documents on the nationalist and imperialist ideologies in vol. II of *Sources of Japanese Tradition*. Another anthology, *Imperial Japan 1800-1945*, ed. Livingstone, Moore and Oldfather (New York, 1973), gathers together some of the best studies in English on this period.

2 In *Le Japon* (Paris, 1966), Jean Lequiller presents a clear and wide-ranging panorama of the political history of Japan from the fall of the Bakufu to the end of the Pacific War. Studies on modern Japan have appeared in such numbers, and are of such excellence, that it would not be possible to list even the best ones here, though we might mention Paul Akamatsu, *Meiji 1868: Révolution et contre-révolution au Japon* (Paris, 1968); Jacques Mutel, *La Fin du Shogunat et le Japon de Meiji 1853-1912* (Paris, 1970) and the short but concentrated precis by Michel Vié, *Le Japon contemporain* in the 'Que sais-je?' collection (Paris, 1971).

3 In *The Intellectual Foundations of Modern Japanese Politics* (Chicago, 1974), Tetsuo Najita gives a vivid depiction of Japanese politics from the Edo period to the dawn of the twentieth century. He shows their diversity, but in the process he rather tends to minimize the religious, and certainly sacrificial, intensity of the imperial creed, which was more deeply rooted than any kind of theoretical rationalization.

4 The second volume in Mishima's tetralogy, *Runaway Horses*, was written in the first half of 1967, and contains a story-within-a-story devoted to the Society of the Divine Wind and the assault on the castle of Kumamoto. This story is a pastiche of the austere Meiji style, and shows the influence of the stories of feudal life written by Mori Ogai after Nogi's death. There is a translation by M. Gallager (London, 1971).

5 During these years of crisis and transition, political terrorism was rife. In his autobiography, Fukuzawa Yukichi has a great deal to say about the danger of assassination which hung over supporters of modernization from 1860 to 1875.

6 There is a chapter on Saigo Takamori in Morris, *Nobility of Failure*.

7 Japanese Confucianism was a conservative philosophy based on the rationalism of Chu Hsi (1131–1200) and was made official by the Tokugawa. But Confucianism as interpreted by Wang Yang-Ming (1472–1528), known as O Yomei in Japan, stressed intuition and active intransigence. The thoughts of Wang Yang-Ming (*Yomeigaku*) inspired Oshio Heihachiro in 1837, Yoshida Shoin in 1859, Saigo Takamori in 1877, and Mishima Yukio in 1970.

8 The comparison of Nogi to Cincinnatus springs naturally to mind, as all Western historians of Japan – at least in the seventeenth and eighteenth centuries – imitated the style of Livy or Tacitus, finding something Roman about the acts and deeds of the Japanese.

9 Yosano's poem has a quaint charm of its own which is hard to render into English.

10 There is an abundant literature on Nogi. A recent work by Lifton, Kato and Reich, *Six Lives and Six Deaths* (New Haven, 1979), does its best to demystify the official version. The photographs of Nogi and his wife, taken on the day of their deaths, are reproduced in Roland Barthes, *The Empire of Signs* (London, 1983), on the edge of a road of thought which eventually led to *Camera Lucida* (London, 1982).

CHAPTER 12 INTO THE ABYSS

1 On the contradictory currents of the Taisho era see the collection of historical studies *Japan in Crisis, Essays in Taisho Democracy*, ed. Silbermann and Harootunian (Princeton, 1974).

2 In his witty catalogue *Things Japanese* (London and Tokyo, 1890), Basil Hall Chamberlain includes an article on 'Harakiri' in which he notes several recent cases of *seppuku* by soldiers which were probably symptomatic of the tension during the approach to the Russo-Japanese war. In the next generation this military propensity for sacrifice allied itself to the terrorism of the nationalist groups.

3 The posthumous manifesto of Asahi Heigo, who killed himself on 3 September 1921 after murdering the banker Yasuda, figures in *Sources of Japanese Tradition*, II, p. 260. Another suicide-murder of the same berserk

type, with an ideological coloration, took place in France much more recently, on 14 May 1976. A young man of twenty-two called Jean Bilski murdered a banker named Chaine, chairman of the Crédit Lyonnais, on the Boulevard des Italiens and then killed himself. The 19 May issue of *Libération* reproduced a lengthy interview given by Bilski a year earlier, in which he had announced his desire to die after killing a banker.

4 In *Les Justes* and *L'Homme révolté*, Albert Camus described the link between suicide and terrorism, using as illustration the terrorist attacks in Russia which culminated between 1903 and 1905. In Malraux's *La Condition humaine*, Chen, carrying a bomb, throws himself under a car in which he believes Chiang Kai-Shek to be travelling.

5 The best historian of the nationalist, militarist and imperialistic tendencies of the early Showa era is Maruyama Masao, *Thought and Behaviour in Modern Japanese Politics* (Oxford, 1963). The inevitable comparison with Fascism and Nazism should not be allowed to obscure the unique aspects of the Japanese situation.

6 The events of 26 February 1936 have been described by Ben-Ami Shillony in *Revolt in Japan* (Princeton, 1973). On the theories of Kita Ikki which the young officers claimed to be following, see George Wilson, *Radical Nationalists in Japan: Kita Ikki (1883–1937)* (Cambridge, Mass., 1969). But the most dramatic evidence of this moment in Japanese history is to be found in the journals of General Honjo, then the emperor's aide-de-camp. They were published in Tokyo in 1967 as *Honjo Nikki* and translated by Mikiso Hane: *Emperor Hirohito and his Chief Aide de Camp: The Honjo Diary 1933–1936* (Tokyo, 1982). David Bergamini's *Japan's Imperial Conspiracy* (London, 1971) is observant and interesting, but his theory of the emperor's involvement should be treated with caution.

7 There are very many accounts, commentaries and analyses of the Pacific War. For an eye-witness account of the run-up to the war see Joseph C. Grew (the US ambassador), *Ten Years in Japan* (London, 1944). Another eye-witness of the war as experienced by the people of Tokyo is Robert Guillain, *Le Peuple japonais et la guerre: Choses vues, 1936–1946*, published very soon after the events, in 1947.

8 Since the end of the war over 200 works on the Special Units (*tokkotai*, kamikaze) have appeared in Japanese, an indication of abiding public interest. A first anthology of letters and journals, *Kike Wadatsumi no Koe*, was published a few years after the war and translated into French by Jean Lartéguy as *Les Voix qui nous viennent de la mer* (Paris, 1954). There is also a moving account of his anguish written in French by a survivor, Nagatsuka Ryuji: *J'étais un kamikaze* (Paris, 1972). A wider view is given by Bernard Millot, *L'Épopée kamikaze* (Paris, 1969).

9 The story of the last days of the Pacific War has often been retold. A detailed impression can be built up from Robert J. C. Butow, *Japan's Decision to Surrender* (Stanford, 1954), Willian Craig, *The Fall of Japan* (London, 1954) and Lester Brooks, *Behind Japan's Surrender* (New York, 1968).

10 The idea of national suicide was succinctly expressed in the slogan *ichioku gyokusai*, 'A hundred million men as diamond-dust'. The word *gyokusai* (broken jewel, crushed diamond) meant death in the heat of battle, a death one rushes into and which is pure, sudden and sublime. All hundred million inhabitants (*ichioku*) of Greater Japan were invited to join in.

11 On the *yakuza* and their affectation of traditionalism see Philippe Pons's article in *L'Histoire* 51 (December 1982), and chapter 10 of Takie Sugiyama Lebra, *Japanese Patterns of Behaviour*.

CHAPTER 13 SOME NIHILIST VIGNETTES

1 The word 'nihilism' was popularized by Turgenev in 1862. The attitude is incarnated in several of Dostoevsky's most famous characters; according to Nietzsche it was the crucial problem of modern civilization, the 'danger of dangers', the 'second Buddhism', the evil which had to be hammered out of society. See 'European Nihilism', Book I of *The Will to Power* in Walter Kaufmann's translation (New York, 1968; the original text is dated 10 June 1887). Nietzche's final thoughts on the human condition, in so far as they can be gleaned from his notebooks, seem to be based on this diagnosis of nihilism. At this time (1887), Nietzsche was rereading *The Possessed* with the greatest concentration: he copied out the arguments of Kirilov (see *Fragments posthumes, automne 1887–mars 1888*, Paris, 1976, p. 323). Paul Claudel, in his early stages, was the poet of nihilism, which he expresses with unsurpassable vigour in the 1890 version of *La Ville*.

2 The long-meditated suicide of Kirilov should not make us forget that of the youthful Ippolit in *The Idiot*, which was as well conceived as it was badly executed.

3 André Breton quotes the 'bizarre ultimatum' of Barbey to Huysmans in *Les Vases communicants* (1932), p. 133. He was then at the height of his devotion to dialectical materialism, and saw suicide as a 'bad remedy' and 'the result of a system of subjective idealism pushed to the limit'. But subjectivity proved resistant to the excellent arguments of dialectic: passionate love, dreams and suicide went on existing, even in Soviet Russia. Therefore (Breton went on) it was not enough to transform the world; it was necessary to change life itself, and to start by 'rehabilitating the study of the self'.

4 The moral code of Fukuzawa Yukichi (1835–1901), which appeared on 11 February 1900 in the newspaper *Jiji Shimpo*, is quoted in John W. Morrison, *Modern Japanese Fiction* (Utah Press, 1955), p. 29.

NOTES 305

5 The return of the problem of voluntary death in European romanticism is illustrated particularly clearly in Letter XLI of Senancour's *Oberman*, in which the author, through his hero, debates at some length whether human beings have an a priori right to kill themselves.

6 There is abundant material on suicide by modern Japanese writers in a special number of the review *Kokubungaku Kaishaku to Kansho* ('Interpretation and Appreciation of National Literature', Tokyo, December 1971). Obviously this collection of studies was inspired by the suicide of Mishima a year earlier. A. Alvarez, *The Savage God* (Harmondsworth, 1971) gives a succinct but very illuminating overview of suicide in Western writers from Dante to Sylvia Plath.

7 In *Things Japanese*, Basil Hall Chamberlain rather flippantly lists suicide among the 'fashionable crazes' to which the Japanese are so susceptible, along with stamp-collecting and garden parties. In 1903, he writes (p. 259), 'youths nourished on Schopenhauer and Niezsche took to practising "the denial of the will to live" by jumping into the great waterfall of Kegon at Nikko.' This is a disrespectful allusion to the pure death of the schoolboy Fujimura Masao, which had caused a good deal of comment. Such suicides among students, enlarged by the imagination, were a leading theme at the time, which was taken up and developed by Western observers. A contemporary author, E. Vincent (quoted by Matignon, *Chine hermétique*, p. 97), thought he was not exaggerating when he said that suicide was epidemic among students at the University of Tokyo, who would throw themselves into the cataracts of Kegon or into the crater of the volcano Asama. It was, he said, a silent and unpremeditated death. In a single month, 2,000 people had jumped into the volcano of Asama. Japanese people might kill themselves at any age, for any reason and by any means to hand. The statistics given by Tarnowski in his 1907 article in *Archives d'Archéologie* go some way towards correcting Vincent's exaggerations: Japan's suicide rate of 20.6 per 100,000 was about the same as France's or Germany's. But voluntary death, like all insidious evils, has to be someone else's problem. For eighteenth-century France it was the English disease; when *japonisme* came in, it was the Japanese disease.

8 See Hölderlin, *Empedokles*, in *Poems and Fragments*, with translation by M. Hamburger (London, 1966), p. 34. The three versions of this unfinished drama are perhaps the noblest expression ever given to the theme of the voluntary death.

9 The poems of Oka Masafumi (1962–75) were published by the Japanese firm Chikuma Shobo as *Boku Wa Junisai* ('I am Twelve'). We may be reminded of the suicide of the boy Boris in Gide's *The Counterfeiters* (*Les Faux-Monnayeurs*, 1925). Gide based his story on a real event: in June 1909, a boy of fifteen blew his brains out in a classroom of the Lycée Blaise-Pascal in Clermont-Ferrand. According to an appendix to Gide's notes on

the composition of his novel, the *Journal des Débats* blamed 'the assiduous and uncontrolled reading of the more pessimistic German philosophers'.

10 Natsume Soseki's *I Am a Cat* (*Wagahai Wa Neko De Aru*) was translated into English by Katsui Shibata and Motonari Kai (Tokyo, 1961); see pp. 409-11.

11 Akutagawa's *Rashomon and Other Stories* can be read in the translation by Takashi Kojima (New York, 1952). The passage translated here is from *Aru Kyuyu e Okuru Shuki* ('Notes to an Old Friend'), which has never been published in English.

12 The contagious nihilism on which Nietzsche remarked was probably an effect of drugs. 'Problem: with what means could one attain to a severe form of really contagious nihilism, such as teaches and practices voluntary death with scientific conscientiousness?' (*The Will to Power*, tr. Kaufmann, p. 143). The idea which weak minds find most unendurable, and which Nietzsche himself could scarcely bear to think about, was the 'eternal return' of the same life.

13 In July 1930, André Breton wrote a short account of Mayakovsky (which was published in *Point du Jour*), defending him against an article in *L'Humanité* which stigmatized him as a retarded bourgeois, whose bogusness as a revolutionary was exposed by his suicide.

14 There is a chapter on Kawakami Hajime in Lifton, Kato and Reich, *Six Lives and Six Deaths*.

15 The reactions of Japanese writers to the War in the Pacific is described in Donald Keene, 'Japanese Writers and the East Asia War', *Journal of Asian Studies* (February 1964).

CHAPTER 14 MISHIMA: THE LAST ACT

1 Shiga Naoya's suggestion was put forward in an article entitled 'Kokugo Mondai' ('The Problem of our National Language') in the April 1946 number of *Kaizo* ('Reconstruction').

2 Article 9 of the 1947 constitution reads: 'Aspiring sincerely to an international peace based on justice and order, the Japanese people forever renounce war as a sovereign right of the nation and the threat or use of force as a means of settling international disputes.

In order to accomplish the aim of the preceding paragraph, land, sea, and air forces, as well as other war potential, will never be maintained. The right of belligerency of the State will not be recognized' (D. F. Henderson (ed.), *The Constitution of Japan: Its First Twenty Years, 1947-1967*, Washington, 1968).

By a law of 1954 a Self-Defence Force (*jieitai*) was set up. By 1980 the land, sea and air Forces had risen to a total of 265,000 men. The budgetary allowance of the Self-Defence Force was at first voluntarily kept below a ceiling of 1 per cent of GNP.

3   From Sakaguchi Ango (1906–55), *Darakuron* ('Essay on decadence', 1946).

4   The above quotations are from *Shayo (The Setting Sun*, tr. D. Keene, Norforlk, Conn., 1958). They are from the diary of Naoji, a character clearly reflecting the author, who kills himself at the end of the novel.

5   'Une tisane sur le fourneau à gaze', by René Crevel (1900–35), from *Détours* (1924).

6   This description of the grey-striped kimono is from the beginning of one of Dazai's earliest works, *Bannen* ('Old Age'), written at the age of twenty-six after his third attempt at suicide.

7   For a critical account of Sartre's celebrated study of Baudelaire see Georges Bataille, *La Littérature et le mal* (Paris, 1957).

8   In his diary for 6 December 1921, Kafka describes literature as 'a mockery and a despair' (Maurice Blanchot, *Kafka*, Paris, 1981).

9   Haraguchi Tozo's notebooks were published in Tokyo under the title *Nijusai No Echudo* ('Studies from his Twentieth Year').

10 Most of Mishima Yukio's novels are available in English translations, several published by Penguin. John Nathan, *Mishima: A Biography* (London, 1975) is excellent; there is also an essay by Marguerite Yourcenar, *Mishima, a Vision of the Void* (Henley, 1986).

11 The wish for us all to become 'physically Greeks' is in *The Will to Power*.

12 Mishima's story 'Patriotism' is included in *Death in Midsummer and Other Stories* (Harmondsworth, 1977). The film Mishima himself based on the story, in which he paid the leading role, was very well received at the Tours Film Festival in January 1966. The rather flashy title *Rites of Love and Death* was chosen by Mishima himself for foreign consumption.

13 Two works published by Mishima in 1968, within a few months of each other, are essential for understanding his development in his last years. *Bunka Boei Ron* ('On the Defence of Culture') challenges the values of modern civilization. The philosophical position assumed in that work would have remained purely theoretical without the description in *Taiyo to Tetsu (Sun and Steel*, New York, 1970) of the emotions which made it a vital part of his own existence.

14 There is a very beguiling biography of Mishima by Henry Scott Stokes, *The Life and Death of Yukio Mishima* (Rutland, Vt., 1975), which gives a detailed description of the paramilitary exercises performed by the Society of the Shield at the foot of Mount Fuji.

15 The dialectic of virtue and the 'way of the world' is detailed in *The Phenomenology of Mind* (tr. J. B. Baillie, London and New York, 1931): 'its [individuality's] action is at the same time one that is universal and with an inherent being of its own' (p. 411). Thus it is no longer necessary for the individual to sacrifice himself so as to produce good. It is not by dying, but by living and realizing his own potential that the individual can contribute to the general good; therefore the tradition of sacrifice is out of date according to Hegel's notions of the evolution of reason in history.

16 Behind Mishima's activism we can detect the thoughts of Wang Yang-Ming. In a letter written to his friend and translator Ivan Morris shortly before his death, Mishima emphasized how important *Yomeigaku* was to him (see Stokes, *Life and Death*, p. 249). In *Runaway Horses* the pure, young and beautiful Isao, who is obviously an avatar of Mishima, is passionately interested in an essay on Yang-Ming by the nationalist philosopher Inoue Tetsujiro (1855–1944).

17 'Already I have seen poets transformed and turning their eyes on themselves. I have seen the coming of spiritual penitents, who were born of them' (*Thus Spake Zarathustra*, Part II, 'On Poets').

18 Stokes gives a very detailed account of events on 25 November 1970, which were also described at length in the newspapers.

19 Valerius Maximus (*Facta et dicta memorabilia* II.6) opines that it is better to die while one is still happy, and so avoid reversals of fortune. He may have a point. A little later, Plutarch took up the idea in *De communibus*: 'When a man is in possession of all his goods, when he lacks nothing needful for happiness and content, it is fitting for him to take his leave of life.' Paul Valéry echoed Plutarch's paradox in *Tel Quel*: 'Permission to kill himself given only to perfectly happy man' (*Oeuvres*, Paris, 1957, p. 1179). The possibility of committing suicide on a peak of joy, at the best moment of one's life, in sheer 'enthusiasm' (as Dmitri Karamazov puts it) is illustrated by Olivier's suicide attempt in Gide's *The Counterfeiters* (tr. D. Bussy, London, 1931, p. 273).

20 Kawabata Yasunari (1899–1972), novelist, awarded the Nobel Prize for Literature in 1968, was Mishima's literary mentor and always remained one of his closest friends. On 16 April 1972 he was found dead, asphyxiated by gas, in a little apartment he owned near his house in Kamakura. He left no will, no farewell poem – not even a line to his nearest and dearest. At least it let them talk about the event as an accident – a comforting illusion which

his silence had perhaps been deliberately intended to foster. Kawabata, too, had put on the saucepan and then 'forgotten' to light the gas.

21 More even than Mishima's exploit, it was the raid on Tel Aviv airport on 30 May 1972 which called into question the relationship between ethics and politics, and the possibility of making self-sacrifice into an apologia for terrorism. Verkhovensky, in *The Possessed*, was already exploiting Kirilov's death for his own subversive ends. Some real people have given the impression of incarnating both of Dostoevsky's characters in themselves. An example is the sensational incident in Stammheim prison on 18 October 1977, when Andreas Baader, Gudrun Esslin and Jan-Carl Raspe were found dead. Probably it was a threefold suicide, the victims attempting to throw the blame on the forces of repression as a farewell political gesture. One wonders if sacrificing one's life for a cause really confers the right to sacrifice the truth along with it. According to Gandhi, *satyagraha*, the truth (*not* what one believes to be true, but what can be proved to be so) must struggle to establish itself, but always within the bounds of non-violence and non-harmfulness (*ahimsa*) – which bars terrorism. The political struggle had to be kept within stern moral limits. In summer 1981, Bobby Sands and nine of his comrades, young Irishmen aged between twenty-three and thirty, in the Maze prison for terrorist outrages, died voluntarily one after another in a seven-month hunger strike. Their martyrdom did not induce Margaret Thatcher's government to bow to their demands. Sacrificial starvation failed where Gandhi, by submitting politics to ethics (i.e. by refusing to be obsessed by success) did, in fact, succeed. In an article published in 1939, 'Le suicide de vengeance dans la Grèce ancienne', Marie Delcourt brings together two traditions of fasting to the death, in India and in Ireland, i.e. at opposite ends of the expansion of Indo-European peoples. In medieval Ireland a Christian might even fast against God, having blamed him for the injustices of this world.

Glossary of Japanese Terms

ABE NO YORITOKI (?–1057). Around the year AD 1000, the Abe clan was so securely established in the province of Mutsu, in northern Japan, that Yoritoki dared to defy the court of Heian; in 1051 the latter sent Minamoto no Yoriyoshi to punish him. The war lasted for several years and Yoritoki was killed in battle.

AIKOKUTO, more accurately DAI NIHON AIKOKUTO, the Party of the Patriots of Greater Japan, an extreme right-wing movement.

AKUTAGAWA RYUNOSUKE (1892–1927), writer of essays and short stories.

AMAE, dependence. The adjective *amai* means 'sweet' as sugar is sweet. The noun *amae* means 'sweetness', 'tenderness', and the verb *amaeru* 'to be childish, to wheedle, to submit to caresses'. It means relying on someone's indulgence, using an instinctive strategy of subordination and abdication of responsibility. The psychiatrist Doi Takeo relates this feeling to a regressive desire for symbiosis with the mother which Japanese educational practices tend to foster in children. Western individualism is based on the precocious repression of the very dependence which Japanese society encourages and perpetuates by its vertical conception of social relationships according to the *oyabun–kobun* (parent–child) model. This implies inequality of status, with the desire to dominate answering the infantile desire to be protected, relieved of responsibility and merged with a group.

GLOSSARY OF JAPANESE TERMS

AMAKUSA SHIRO (1622–38). Dubbed 'child of heaven' by his supporters, the youthful Shiro became the messianic leader of the uprising of Christian peasants which broke out on 11 December 1637 in the Shimabara and Amakusa regions, west of Kyushu. He was killed on 12 April 1638, aged sixteen, when the castle of Hara fell. Thirty-seven thousand rebels were slaughtered along with him.

AMA (or AME) NO UZUME, a female divinity who, according to the myths in the *Kojiki* and the *Nihongi*, danced before the assembled gods and so brought Amaterasu out of the Celestial Cave.

AMATERASU OMIKAMI, the 'August Goddess of Heavenly Light', the chief divinity of Japanese mythology, identified with the sun. She was born when the god Izanagi washed his left eye after returning from the world of the dead. Her task was to reign over the Plain of Heaven. Outraged by the bad behaviour of her younger brother, Susanoo no Mikoto, she withdrew into a cave. Intrigued by the music and laughter which accompanied the dance of Ama no Uzume, she eventually came out, and restored light to the world. She sent her grandson, Ninigi no Mikoto, to pacify the isles of Japan. Her great-grandson was Jimmu, first emperor of Japan, ancestor of the sole ruling dynasty.

AMIDA BUTSU, the Buddha Amida, in Sanskrit Amitabha ('infinite light'), who according to the scriptures of the Greater Vehicle dwells in the paradise of the Pure Land in the west. When he was a bodhisattva, Amida-to-be made forty-eight solemn vows, promising to succour all suffering beings. In China, and in Japan from the eighth century onwards, Amida became the most venerated member of the Mahayana pantheon. In the Heian period (794–1185) he was often shown fetching a dying person away to the paradise in the west. In the Kamakura era (1185–1333) the sects of the Pure Land emphasized his importance as a universal saviour.

ANAMI KORECHIKA (1887–1945). General Anami was appointed Minister for War in the Suzuki cabinet formed in April 1945. At the imperial conference on 14 August he advised rejecting the Potsdam Declaration and continuing the war to the bitter end. He killed himself a few hours later, at dawn on 15 August.

ANNEN (841–89), a monk of the Tendai sect with a self-appointed mission to bring in the teachings and rites of esoteric Buddhism.

ANTOKU TENNO (1178–85), emperor of Japan who reigned from the age of two to the age of seven. His mother was the daughter of Taira no Kiyomori. When in 1183 the Taira were forced to pull out of the capital, they took the child-emperor with them to the western provinces. After the naval battle of Dan no Ura in 1185, his grandmother, Kiyomori's widow, leapt into the sea with the emperor in her arms.

ARAGOTO, 'unpolished manner', a dramatic style created by the actor Ichikawa Janjuro (1660–1704) to act superhuman heroes of a type much admired in Edo, whereas in and about Kyoto and Osaka the tender and natural style (*wagoto, jitsugoto*) was preferred.

ARAKI SADAO (1877–1966), an ultra-nationalist officer, one of the leaders of the faction of the Imperial Way (*kodoha*) in the 1930s. After the failure of the mutiny on 26 February 1936 he was suspended. In 1938 Prince Konoe chose him as Minister for Education, and he developed militaristic propaganda for schools. He was condemned to life imprisonment by the Tokyo tribunal, but was freed for health reasons in 1954.

ARISHIMA TAKEO (1878–1923), a writer interested in the social and progressive ideas of his time.

ASAHI HEIGO (1890–1931), leader of a small ultra-nationalist group which demanded a 'Taisho restoration' and the transformation of the economy. He killed himself on 3 September 1921 after murdering Yasuda Zenjiro.

ASANO NAGANORI (1667–1701), daimyo of the small fief of Ako in the Harima region. He lost patience with the insolence of Kira Yoshinaka, master of ceremonies at the shogun's court, and tried to kill him. He was immediately arrested and condemned to execution by *tsumebara*. Two years later, forty-seven retainers from his clan burst into Kira's residence and beheaded him to avenge their master.

ASANUMA INEJIRO (1898–1960), chairman of the Socialist Party, stabbed to death on 12 October 1960 by a young ultra-nationalist of the patriotic party (*Aikokuto*).

ASHIGARU, literally 'light feet', lightly armed infantry, peasants bearing lances, sometimes mere brigands recruited by local lords in the civil wars. With the introduction of Portuguese muskets in 1543, their tactical importance supplanted that of the knights armed with bows and swords.

ASHIKAGA TAKAUJI (1305–58), head of the Ashikaga family, descendants of the Minamoto, whose power base was in the eastern provinces. In 1333 the Kamakura Bakufu put him in command of the army intended to crush the supporters of the Emperor Go-Daigo, but he went over to the imperial cause. Two years later he changed sides again, forcing Go-Daigo to flee into the mountains of Yoshino. Thanks to these turncoat tactics, supplemented by the odd murder, he succeeded in founding a new military government (*Bakufu*) which kept the Ashikaga in power through the Muromachi era (1338–1573) until the rise of Oda Nobunaga.

ASHURA, Mazdeist god of light. In Indian mythology Ahura Mazda (Sanskrit *asura*) becomes plural and malefic, the *asura* demons fighting against the gods (*deva*). In Buddhism the *ashura* represent the spirit of quarrelsomeness and violence and have their own world, one of the six worlds (*rokudo*) into which one may be reborn.

AWAZU. In 1183, Minamoto no Yoshinaka (1154–84), lord of Kiso, expelled the Taira from the capital, but his abuse of power made him hated. His cousin, Minamoto no Yoritomo, sent an army against him; he was defeated and killed at the Battle of Awazu, and his four inseparable companions, of whom Imai was one, died with him.

BAKUFU, literally 'government of the tent', general headquarters: the military government of the shogun as distinct from the government of the imperial court, which had been reduced to virtual impotence. The word is used for the three shogun regimes of Kamakura (1192–1333), Muromachi (1338–1573) and Edo (1600–1868).

BANKA, literally 'poem sung while pulling [a coffin]': funeral hymn, death-poem.

BONSAI, literally 'plant on a tray': dwarf tree, miniature plant. The art of miniature trees was introduced from China in the thirteenth century, along with (e.g.) tea, wash-drawing and Zen Buddhism.

BUNGOBUSHI. *Fushi* (*-bushi*) is the name for any declamatory style used for *joruri* (dialogue poems), which sometimes accompany puppet actions in the Bunraku theatre. Some of these styles are named after great declaimers of the past, e.g. Myakoji Bungonojo, who from 1730 practised the style called *bungobushi*, and Myakoji Sonohachi, who in the next generation created *sonohachibushi*.

BUNRAKU, puppet theatre, in which the narrator recited a dialogue in verse while the puppets performed the appropriate actions. It reached its perfection in the early eighteenth century when the narrator Takemoto Gidayu (1651–1714) performed the plays of Chikamatsu in Osaka.

BUSHI (or SAMURAI). Both words mean 'warrior', i.e. the martial elite which in the twelfth century became the ruling class, relegating the old imperial aristocracy to a purely ceremonial role. The word *bushi* carries a connotation of nobility, like our 'knight'. *Samurai* is 'he who serves', any man with a function or office. *Bushi* is the word commonly used in Japan itself; *samurai* has caught on abroad, along with *harakiri* and *kamikaze*.

BUSHIDO, the Way of the Warrior. *Do* means road or journey, method, discipline. What way must be followed by those wishing to become true warriors? Can the use of arms be a way towards a certain ethic, a kind of wisdom? Such questions as these arose when the warrior class became pre-eminent in twelfth-century Japan. Already the *bushi* were codifying their activities along three axes: technically, they had to practise to improve their skill in the martial arts; morally, they had to serve their master devotedly and remain loyal through any ordeal; spiritually, they had to face death with impassibility and self-sacrifice. But it was only under the peace of the Tokugawa that the word *bushido* became current to mean the exaltation of warlike virtues, which were all the more necessary now that the warriors were no longer called upon to fight. *Bushido*, in this sense, was founded in the seventeenth century by Yamaga Soko under the influence of Confucian rationalism. In the *Hagakure* (1716) *bushido* becomes more radical and intransigent. It did not disappear with the Bakufu: the privileges of the aristocarcy were abolished, but not their values. Inoue Tetsujiro, the philosopher of *kokutai*, put them at the service of nationalism. In 1900 Nitobe Inazo, himself a convert to Quaker belief and a great cosmopolitan, wrote (in English) *Bushido: The Soul of Japan* to explain the persistence of the tradition and its role in the modernization of Japan. During the Pacific War, the reading of the *Hagakure* was encouraged. Mishima, the novelist, vowed to consecrate, and finally sacrifice, his life to the renaissance of *bushido*, which had been tainted by the defeat of Japan.

CHIKAMATSU MONZAEMON (1653–1724), reckoned to be Japan's greatest dramatist. He wrote about a hundred plays in all, for the Kabuki, and in particular the Bunraku, initially for the narrator Takemoto Gidayu of the Takemotoza puppet theatre in Osaka. Some were historical (*jidaimono*), some domestic (*sewamono*).

CHINKONSAI, Shinto ceremony for the appeasement of souls, an originally shamanic ritual designed to pacify the spirits of the dead, and sometimes to revive nature-spirits (e.g. at the winter solstice), through music and dancing.

CHOKUSHI, an imperial order direct from the sovereign, transmitted by a special messenger.

CHONIN, townsman, bourgeois. It is the opposite of *bushi*, samurai, and in the Edo period meant the common people, artisans or merchants, living in urban areas. The growth of towns in the seventeenth and eighteenth century brought about a great increase in their numbers. But although the great merchants became rich, and a new urban culture developed, the *chonin*, unlike their Western couterparts, never attempted to throw off the control of the aristocracy.

CHU, loyalty, the cardinal virtue of fidelity, the devotion of a vassal to his suzerain or a samurai to his master, greatly exalted in *bushido*.

CHUSHINGURA ('The Treasury of Faithful Vassals'), a play by Takeda Izumo (1691–1756) in collaboration with Miyoshi Shosaku and Namili Senryo, first acted in the puppet theatre in 1748, forty-five years after the events on which it is based, and later in the Kabuki. It is the most famous of many stage works inspired by the vendetta of the forty-seven *ronin*, and is still very popular today.

DAIGO TENNO, emperor of Japan from 897 to 930. At the instigation of his minister, Sugawara no Michizane, he attempted to rule in person and curb the power of the Fijuwara regents. Michizane's exile in 901 marked the triumph of the Fujiwara. In 902 Daigo promulgated the reforms of the Engi era, which vainly sought to strengthen the central power of the court by limiting the importance of private estates.

DAIMYO, literally 'great name': a prince of the warrior aristocracy. At the end of the sixteenth century, the word was used for feudal lords who controlled a territory large and fetile enough to produce at least 10,000 measures of rice in annual taxes. During the civil wars these estates became independent principalities, and even after the three dictators, Oda Nobunaga, Toyotomi Hideyoshi and Tokugawa Ieyasu, had established their hegemony, the daimyo kept a large measure of self-government. In the Edo period there were 266 daimyo, all vassals of the shogun. Their intrigues and coalitions brought about the fall of the Tokugawa and the restoration of the imperial regime, but at their own expense: in 1869 they all yielded to the emperor full authority over their principalities, which became provinces from 1871. This ended the historical importance of the daimyo.

DAN NO URA, a naval battle which took place in the straits of Shimonoseki on 25 April 1185, in which the Minamoto fleet destroyed that of the Taira.

DAZAI OSAMU (1901–48), writer of novels and short stories.

DOGEN (1200–53), monk of the Kamakura era, considered one of the greatest masters of Zen Buddhism. Born in Kyoto of a noble court family, he chose the monastic life at the age of thirteen. He first studied Tendai Buddhism, then came under the influence of the Zen Rinzai sect which had just been brought to Japan by the monk Eisai (1141–1215). In 1223 Dogen went to China and became the disciple of a Zen master of the Soto sect whose essential practice was seated meditation (*zazen*). Two months later he experienced the awakening (*satori*). He returned to Kyoto in 1227 and established this new sect in Japan. It was then that he wrote his first treatises, saying that the experience of *satori* is accessible to anyone, monk or layman, man or woman, irrespective of age, social status and intelligence, through the practice of *zazen*. In 1243 he went to the province of Echizen, where he founded the temple of Eiheiji. After lecturing on Zen to the heads of the Bakufu at Kamakura, he returned to Kyoto, where he died in 1253.

DOKYO (?–772), a monk of the Hosso sect who wielded great political power at the Nara court because of his influence over the Empress Koken.

ECHIGO, a former province, now the prefecture of Niigata.

EZOSHI, 'illustrated broadsheets', printed by the woodblock process imported from Korea in the late sixteenth century, sold on the streets of big towns in the Edo period.

FUDARAKU (Sanskrit *Potalaka*), in Buddhist Mahayana mythology, the name of a mountain or island supposed to be inhabited by the bodhisattva of compassion, Avalokiteshvara (Japanese *Kannon bosatsu*).

FUDOKI, descriptions of provinces: compilations made on the emperor's orders in the eighth century to describe about sixty different regions of the archipelago, their climate, landscape, resources, population, legends, customs, etc. Most of them are preserved only in fragments, the only complete ones relating to Bungo, Harima, Hitachi, Hizen and Izumo.

FUJIWARA, an aristocratic court family which dominated the imperial government in the tenth and eleventh centuries. From generation to generation its menfolk held the highest court offices, in particular the regency, created in 866; the women married successive emperors as their principal wives. Sugawara no Michizane tried in vain to shake this monopoly. The power of the Fujiwara was limited only by the simulacrum of government by emperors living in retirement from 1087 onwards. Fujiwara no Michinaga (966–1027) raised the clan to the height of its power: father of four empresses, he dominated the court for some thirty years.

FUKOKU KYOHEI, 'Prosperous nation, powerful army', a slogan of Chinese origin adopted by the Meiji government to define the twofold purpose of its modernization project.

FUKUZAWA YUKICHI (1835–1901), eminent educationalist, prolific writer and journalist, a free and lofty spirit, pioneer of Japanese modernization. Born into a poor samurai family, the young Fukuzawa learned first Dutch (in Nagasaki), then English. In 1860 he went with the first Japanese mission to America, and two years later, with the first to Europe. At the Meiji Restoration he realized his purpose in life: Japan could not attain its intended power and prosperity unless every Japanese shook off feudal routine and adopted the values of liberty and knowledge preached by the eighteenth-century West. A huge educational project had to be undertaken; Fukuzawa pursued it in his many writings and his teaching at the University of Keio, which he founded. He gave an example of independence by declining all official functions and retaining an alert and critical attitude toward governments.

FUNSHI, voluntary death with aggressive intent, motivated by anger, resentment, frustration or indignation.

GEISHA, literally 'artists'. Orignally, in the seventeenth century, male flute-players and drummers who enlivened parties in the houses of pleasure; later, women skilled in music and dancing (*onna geisha*). In principle, courtesans (*yujo, joro*) and *geisha* performed different functions, which did not overlap, but in fact the courtesans used every art as an embellishment to their beauty, and despite many reproofs the *geisha* were not always deaf to male blandishments.

During the decadence under Yoshiwara, in the late eighteenth century, the best clients preferred the restaurants in the Fukugawa district, beside the River Sumida. But it was the nineteenth century which saw the *geisha* in all their glory. In the Taisho era (1912–26), there were still some 80,000 of them. Nowadays there are fewer than 17,000. They suffer from competition by professional hostesses, and tend to confine themselves to the traditional arts of music and dancing, emphasizing (sometimes to a pedantic extent) the difference between these and hastier, easier pleasures.

GEKOKUJO, literally 'The inferior supplants the superior.' A slogan often used in the Muromachi era (1338–1573) to refer to the social mobility caused by the civil wars: the old families were becoming weaker, new forces were emerging, vassals were becoming independent, the peasants were in revolt and the parvenus had it all their own way. It was this mobility which Hideyoshi (himself a parvenu) and Ieyasu wished to check by fixing social barriers, at the turn of the seventeenth century.

GENJI MONOGATARI, *The Tale of Genji*, a long story (over 1,000 pages) written in the early years of the eleventh century by Murasaki Shikibu, a woman of genius at the court of Heian. The most famous of all Japanese novels and one of the best ever written – nine centuries before Proust. Two-thirds of the work tell about the life of a brilliant prince of the imperial blood, his joys, sorrows and loves. The last twelve of the fifty-four chapters are devoted to characters from the next generation. *Genji Monogatari* is a wonderful and faithful mirror of the most perfect courtly civilization ever created by mankind.

GENROKU, the era from 1688 to 1704, under the government of the fifth shogun, Tokugawa Tsunayoshi: the most prosperous years of the Edo period (1600–1868). Peace brought a rapid growth in the economy and in population, and the townsmen (*chonin*) created a lively culture of their own in the great cities; all the arts, from ceramics to drama and from poetry to textiles, reached their heights. Despite the sumptuary laws passed by the Bakufu, expenditure became ostentatious, especially around the great courtesans and the famous Kabuki actors. This sensual and light-headed Genroku world was aware of its own precariousness, calling itself *ukiyo*, the floating world – frivolous, unstable, ominous in its very brilliance.

GENYOSHA, Society of the Dark Ocean, an ultra-nationalist league founded in 1881 by samurai in the Fukuoka region who admired Saigo Takamori. Its goal was to encourage Japanese expansion into Korea. Under the cover of devotion to the emperor and pan-Asiaticism, the society, often clandestine in its operations, inclined to terror and corruption, filling the mainland with adventurers and secret agents.

GIRI, obligation, duty, a moral debt binding an individual to anyone who has done him a good turn. *Giri* is not based on any universal law, like justice in the Western sense; nor is it a precarious contract between two individuals which lapses once its aim is attained. It links precise individuals who may be of differing status (parent and child, master and pupil, suzerain and vassal, employer and worker) or of equal status (neighbours, allies, friends, colleagues, comrades). The link is long-lasting and unbreakable, involving the individual's idea of himself and the esteem in which he is held: it rests on his discretion and sensitivity. One good turn deserves another, or rather must not be forgotten, and it can be repaid – without cancelling the relationship, rather the reverse – in any one of a thousand freely chosen and often symbolic ways. Sometimes, particularly in the Kabuki, *giri* is so strict that it can go as far as suicide. But it can also be tempered by the human feelings of compassion and sympathy (*ninjo*). An individual bound by *giri* knows that he can rely on the goodwill of his benefactor, and if he is willing to utter some formal words of allegiance, he can even fall back into infantile dependence (*amae*).

GO-DAIGO TENNO (1288–1339), emperor of Japan from 1318 to 1339, famous for having briefly restored the imperial function to full political importance: the Kemmu restoration (1333–6). The Hojo exiled him to the Oki islands after he conspired against the Bakufu of Kamakura, much like the emperor Go-Toba a century earlier. He escaped, and Ashikaga Takauji went over to him. Kamakura fell, but Go-Daigo's government proved ineffective and Takauji withdrew his support. Go-Daigo was forced to flee south of the capital into the mountains of Yoshino. Another emperor was set up in his place, so that from 1336 to 1392 Japan had two emperors and two rival courts, Kyoto in the north and Yoshino in the south.

GORYO-E, a ceremony in honour of souls, a Buddhist ritual to appease angry ghosts. Animism, which Buddhism made no attempt to eliminate, taught that the dead were able to avenge themselves and cause various catastrophes. In the Nara and Heian periods (710–94, 794–1185) monks and well-known ascetics were often asked to conduct rituals aimed at soothing the resentment of dead souls.

GO-TOBA TENNO (1180–1239). In 1183 the Minamoto took over the capital and set this three-year-old child on the throne as a rival to his brother, the emperor Antoku (then aged five), whom the Taira had taken with them when they fled westwards. Go-Toba reigned for fifteen years, then abdicated so as to take a more active part in politics: he wanted to get rid of the Bakufu of Kamakura and restore the lost authority of the imperial court. In 1221, in the Shokyu era, he went into action, but his troops were overwhelmed by those of the Hojo, and he was exiled to the Oki islands, where he died.

HAGAKURE (literally 'In the Leafy Shade'), a collection of 1,300 reflections and anecdotes taken down by the young Tashiro Tsuramoto (1687–1748) between 1710 and 1716 from the mouth of a *samurai*, Yamamoto Tsunetomo (1659–1719), who had become a monk after the death of his master Nabeshima Mitsushige (1632–1700), daimyo of the province of Hizen in north-west Kyushu. This very rich and varied work gives a radical interpretation of *bushido* and boils it down to the resolute acceptance of death.

HAKKO ICHIU, 'In all eight directions, one single heaven': a saying, attributed in the *Nihongi* to the Emperor Jimmu when he founded his capital, and taken up by Prime Minister Konoe Fumimaro when outlining his policy of a New Order in Greater Eastern Asia; it was kept as a slogan until the end of the war. It can be taken as the affirmation of universal order, peace in the whole world; or as the decision to put the whole world in order by a limitless expansion.

HANIWA, literally 'clay circles'. From the fourth to the seventh century there grew up a custom of surrounding burial mounds (*kofun*) with hollow terracotta cylinders at least three feet high, with their bases sunk in the soil and with the top part sometimes modelled as a human being, an animal or some everyday object.

HARA, the stomach. In Sino-Japanese the same character is pronounced *fuku*, as in *seppuku* (= *setsu-fuku*). Expressions still widely current in Japanese to denote feelings and virtues such as anger, vigour, courage, honesty and generosity show that in traditional psychology the stomach was considered as the seat of personality and the source of virtues necessary for action. Cf. English, 'he that hath no *stomach* for the fight . . .'

HARAGUCHI TOZO (1927–47), pupil in the preparatory class at Tokyo University who drowned himself at the age of twenty.

HATAMOTO, standard-bearer, officer. Direct vassals of the Tokugawa house who received a hereditary pension of at least 100 measures (*koku*) of rice per year. There were about 5,000 of them, and some, with a revenue of several thousand measures, were almost as rich as a daimyo. They were high officials of the Bakufu, descended from warriors who had helped Ieyasu in his long struggle for the supreme power.

HEIAN KYO, literally 'Capital of Serene Peace', the name given to the town where the Emperor Kyoto decided to transfer his capital in 794. From the eleventh century onwards the town was commonly called Kyoto, a word simply meaning 'the capital'. The imperial court resided there until 1868, when the Emperor Meiji settled in Edo, henceforward to be known as *Tokyo*, 'the capital of the east'.

HEIJO KYO, literally 'Capital of the Citadel of Peace', name given to the town of Nara in Yamato when it was chosen as capital of the empire and residence of the court from 710 to 784.

HEIJO TENNO, emperor of Japan from 806 to 809. He succeeded his father, the Emperor Kammu, and after reigning for four years abdicated in favour of his brother, the Emperor Saga. But he plotted to regain the throne and restore the capital to Nara. His intrigues were discovered, and he was forced to become a monk, in which guise he lived for another fourteen years.

HIEI, a mountain north-east of Kyoto. When in the late eighth century the Emperor Kammu was looking for a new site for a capital, the presence of this mountain, blocking the supposedly evil influences from the north-east, was pronounced lucky by experts in geomancy. There was a Tendai monastery there, Enryakuji, which prospered so greatly that later it even proved a threat to the peace of the capital.

HIJIRI, holy man. While the bonzes lived in communities under a rule, there were also Buddhist ascetics, hermits and travelling monks who lived on alms; they might preach the *nembutsu*, sell amulets, certificates for paradise, charms and horoscopes, or practise exorcism or medicine. They were hard to classify: religious *ronin* among whom one might find the best – and the worst.

HIKIME, literally 'eye of toad', the name for an esoteric Buddhist ritual of exorcism practised by *yamabushi*.

HININ, literally 'non-human': a beggar, a pariah. Edo society had two categories of pariahs, the *eta* and the *hinin*, racially identical with the rest of the population, but generally excluded from it. The *eta* were confined to work considered impure, for instance in slaughterhouses or tanneries. Still lower down were the *hinin* – executioners, pallbearers, gravediggers, or simply beggars. People could be condemned to *hinin* status as a punishment. This legalized discrimination was abolished in 1871.

HINOMARU, the disk of the rising sun, the national emblem. At the end of the thirteenth century, at the time of the Mongol invasions, Nichiren presented such a banner to the shogun. During the civil wars, several daimyo used it. In the nineteenth century the Bakufu ordered Japanese ships to fly it as identification. Finally, on 27 January 1870 the new Meiji government passed a decree making the red disk on white the national flag of Japan.

HITOBASHIRA, human pillar. There are legends about human beings who were buried alive under bridges, dikes or fortresses to appease the divinities of earth or water.

HOBEN, expedient (Sanskrit *upaya*), a Buddhist term for images, legends, devotions and any useful procedure, pious subterfuge or recipe for salvation which could take a living being on to purer and purer levels of the knowledge of truth.

HOJO, an aristocratic warrior clan from the Izu region. At the end of the twelfth century it helped Minamoto no Yoritomo to establish his military government at Kamakura. After Yoritomo's death the Hojo dominated the

Bakufu as regents to the shogun. Thus they were masters of Japan for over a century. In 1333 the emperor Go-Daigo put an end to their power.

HONEN (1133–1212). Son of a samurai, he entered a monastery at the age of eight. First he studied the Tendai doctrine on Mount Hiei; later he became convinced that calling on the name of Amida (the *nembutsu*) was sufficient to ensure salvation, i.e. rebirth in the Pure Land. Though he was driven out of the capital from 1207 to 1211, the sect of the Pure Land, which he founded in 1175, was a big success. Faith, hope and the *nembutsu*, which Honen used to repeat 60,000 times a day, replaced meditation, ascesis and lengthy ceremonies. A solid conviction, with no other merit, was enough to secure Paradise.

HORYUJI, a Buddhist temple near the town of Nara. Founded in 607 by Prince Shotoku, it housed works of art from the Asuka era (552–710), relics of the coming of Buddhism to Japan.

HYAKUSHO IKKI, a peasants' revolt against crushing taxes and obligations. Between 1600 and 1868 there were 2,500 of them. They became more frequent and more violent in the 1780s, 1830s and 1860s, decades of economic and political difficulty. It is hard to tell whether (as Marxist Japanese historians believe) they were genuine anti-feudal class struggles or just local and scattered reactions to some intolerable situation.

HYOGO, nowadays the name of a prefecture, once the region of Kobe. It was the scene of the battle of Minatogawa (July 1336) at which Kusunoki Masashige was killed.

ICHIGON HODAN ('Sentences and Propositions'), a collection of Buddhist aphorisms compiled at the end of the Kamakura era.

ICHI NO TANI, a place near Hyogo, in the former province of Settsu, where Minamoto no Yoshitsune defeated the Taira in 1184.

ICHIOKU ISSHIN, 'A hundred million men with but a single thought', an ultra-nationalist slogan disseminated by General Araki, Minister for Education. In 1938 posters were distributed bearing these words illustrated by an enlarged picture of a worker ant.

IHARA SAIKAKU (1642–93), a writer of the Edo period, born and died in Osaka. Member of a family of wealthy shopkeepers, he initially became famous as a virtuoso of *haikai*. In 1684 he beat his own record by improvising 23,500 poems during an uninterrupted session of 24 hours. In 1682 he published the first of his *ukiyozoshi*, 'tales of the floating world': *Koshoku ichidai otoko* (*The Life of an Amorous Man*). Others were *Koshoku gonin onna* (*Five Women who Loved Love*, 1686) and *Koshokou ichidai onna* (*The Life of an Amorous Woman*). Saikaku also published several collections of novellas on various subjects, such as love between men, traditions of the warrior aristocracy and the tribulations of townsfolk.

IKI, SUI, elegance, chic: two terms very similar in meaning, written in the same way, and used by cultured townsmen of the Edo period to refer to refinement and good taste; *sui* was used chiefly in Osaka from the Genroku era onwards, and *iki* in Edo at the beginning of the nineteenth century.

IMIBE, IMBE. IMI means 'taboo' and BE a hereditary corporation. At the ancient court of Yamato, from the fourth to the seventh century, a family in charge of religious duties bore the name 'Imibe' or 'Imbe', which recalled all the importance which Shinto laid on ritual purity and taboo.

INGA, cause and effect, an essential concept of Buddhism, and of Indian thought even before that: every act, good or evil, has good or evil consequences sooner or later, in this life or another one, and so is fairly repaid. This is the immanent law of existence: every piece of good or bad fortune is the effect of a cause, the result of a previous act.

INOUE FUNNOSUKE (1869–1932), banker and politician, the representative of financial orthodoxy in government circles under Taisho and Showa. He drew the enmity of the army by his policy of austerity and his refusal to increase military spending. In February 1932 he was assassinated by a young ultranationalist aged twenty-one, a member of the League of the Oath of Blood (*Ketsumeidan*).

INUKAI TSUYOKI (1855–1932). A student of Keio University and pupil of Fukuzawa Yukichi, Inukai defended the principles of liberal and constitutional government. Under Meiji he fought against the absolutist cliques of the former clans of Choshu and Satsuma. In 1932 he was asked to form a government. He tried to settle the Manchuria affair by controlling the army, and drew the hatred of the expansionists. On 15 May 1932 he was assassinated by a group of young officers.

IPPEN (1239–89). After studying the Tendai school, the monk Ippen turned to the doctrine of the Pure Land and became a wandering preacher. On his journeyings, like Kuya (903–72) three centuries earlier, he spread the chanting and dancing of the *nembutsu* among the common people. He preached quietism, a trusting self-abandonment to the mercy of Amica. He died in a trance. His last words were, 'No funerary rites: give my body to the wild beasts.'

ISE, the most important Shinto sanctuary, the residence of the ancestral divinities of the Imperial House. The cult consists essentially of ritual food-offerings. The main building, dating from the third century, shelters the solar goddess Amaterasu Omikami, who is represented by a mirror. This building of bare wood, the purest prototype of Japanese architecture, is dismantled and rebuilt avery twenty-one years. From the fifteenth century onward Ise was a very popular place of pilgrimage.

ISHIHARA SHINTARO, novelist, born in 1932; became a politician. He became famous in 1955 with *Taiyo no kisetsu* ('The Sun Season'), a novel which earned him the Akutagawa prize. It is a description of the disillusioned, free, libertarian lives of young people after the defeat. Ishihara has since become an important member of the Liberal Democratic Party.

ISHIKAWA GOEMON (1558–95) belonged to a samurai family. At the age of sixteen he burgled his master's house and killed three men who tried to detain him. He fled and became a famous brigand. In 1595, Toyotomi Hideyoshi's henchmen laid hands on him and he was boiled in oil, along with his brother Ichiro, on the banks of the River Kamo in Kyoto. Before dying he composed a poem of farewell to this world.

ITAGAKI TAISUKE (1837–1919). In the last years of the Bakufu the young Itagaki headed the progressive faction in the principality of Tosa in Shikoku. He attached himself to Saigo Takimori and took part in the armed struggle against the Tokugawa. From 1869 to 1873 he was in the imperial government, but resigned when the plan for an expedition to Korea, which he (like Saigo) had supported, was rejected. In 1874, in Tosa, he founded a mutual aid society for samurai, *Risshisha*, which combined the values of *bushido* with Western notions of liberty and equality. He defended the rights of the people (*minken*) against the ruling oligarchy and fought for the establishment of a constitutional regime. In 1881 he founded the freedom party *Jiyuto*. In the last years of the nineteenth century he and Okuma were the most untiring advocates of a liberal government untainted by the absolutism of the ruling cliques.

JIBAKU, literally 'self-detonation', the deed of a combatant who destroys himself along with his enemy. The word *taiatari* is also used to mean the direct contact of a body with its objective. This sacrificial death-of-attack can also be called *gyokusai*, giving the image of a jewel – a diamond – exploding into a thousand splinters.

JIDAIMONO, history play. In the Kabuki and Bunraku repertoires, from the Genroku era onwards, *jidaimono*, whose characters were court nobles or *bushi* of olden times, were contrasted to *sewamono*, realistic domestic dramas.

JINRAI OKA, the Cherry Blossom of the Thunder of the Gods: name for elite units formed in the spring of 1945, young volunteers whose mission was to steer a flying, rocket-propelled torpedo on to its target after it had been dropped from a bomber.

JIMMU TENNO, the Emperor Jimmu, a more or less legendary personage whose exploits are recounted in the *Kojiki* (712) and the *Nihongi* (720). His father was the great-grandson of the goddess Amaterasu, his mother the daughter of a sea god. After living for a time on Kyushu, he resolved to conquer the plain of Yamato. The expedition lasted several years. After subjugating the hostile tribes, Jimmu was finally proclaimed emperor of Japan, the first to assume this title.

JISATSU, suicide: a recent, general and neutral word, sometimes accompanied by a determinant indicating the motive, e.g. *sekinin jisatsu* (responsibility suicide), *shikarare jisatsu* (suicide provoked by a reprimand). Usually the ancient practices of voluntary death have their own names, e.g. *junshi, seppuku, shinju* etc.

JITSUKAGA (1843–84), an ascetic of the Meiji era who tried to maintain and restore the traditions of the *yamabushi* in spite of a government proscription of *shugendo* enacted in 1873. At the age of twenty-five he left his family to live as a hermit in the mountains of the Kii peninsula and practise Buddhist austerities, such as sitting under a waterfall in winter. From 1861 to 1880 he performed a long pilgrimage into north-eastern Japan before returning to the region about Mount Omine. In 1884 he drowned himself by jumping down the waterfall of Nachi.

JIYUTO, Freedom Party, Liberal Party. There have been three political groupings with this name. The earliest Japanese political party was the *Jiyuto* founded on 29 October 1881 by Itagaki Taisuke and other leaders of the movement for the rights of the people (*minken*). This party campaigned for the creation of a constitutional parliamentary system. It was dissolved in 1884 because of internal dissension. In 1890, Itagaki briefly re-created another *Jiyuto*. Finally, in 1945, Hatoyama Ichiro founded a *Jiyuto* party which in 1955, under the leadership of Yoshida Shigeru, merged with the *Minshuto* to become the Liberal Democratic Party, *Jiyu Minshuto*, which has dominated Japanese political life ever since.

JIZO BOSATSU, the bodhisattva Jizo (Sanskrit 'Ksitigarbha', 'Womb of the Earth'). Like Kannon, he vowed to aid all suffering beings. He is very popular in Japan, where he is represented as a young, shaven-headed monk with a jewel in one hand and a pilgrim's staff in the other. He is the protector of children, and succours both lost travellers and dead men in hell.

JODO, the Pure Land. In certain Buddhist scriptures of the Greater Vehicle, the Pure Land is described as another world, without any imperfection, inhabited by the Buddhas and bodhisattvas, where human beings may be reborn after death. The Pure Land was created by the accumulated merits of the Buddha Amida, and he promised to receive there all those who died calling on his name. This consoling belief, already very strong in the Heian period (794–1185), became a veritable doctrine of salvation by faith in the Kamakura era (1185–1333), when the monks Honen and Shinran founded the sects of the Pure Land (*Jodoshu* and *Jodoshinshu*).

JOKAMACHI, a town at the foot of a castle, capital of a principality. During the civil wars of the sixteenth century, the war-lords built castles in the centre of their territories. When peace returned under the Tokugawa, towns developed at the foot of such castles. In the castle lived the daimyo with his administration and garrison, and all round, in hierarchical order, spread the residences of his principal vassals, then the dwellings of samurai of lower rank, and finally those of the common people (*chonin*), the artisans and merchants. Edo, with its immense fortress and its rapidly increasing population, was the chief of these 250 capitals of varying sizes. In the eighteenth century, one fifth of the population of Japan was crowded into these *jokamachi*.

JORURI. Princess Joruri is a legendary personage associated with Yoshitsune. In the fifteenth century she became the heroine of lyrical tales performed by a singer accompanied by a lute-player, or later by a player upon the *shamisen*. These tales contained dialogue passages which became progressively more important: the *joruri* evolved from epic into drama, and from the seventeenth century onwards puppets were used to represent the characters alluded to by the narrator. Thus arose the Bunraku, also known as *ningyo joruri*.

JOSHI, dying for love: equivalent to *shinju*.

JUKAI, the Sea of Trees: a forest covering the slopes of Mount Fuji.

JUNSHI, sacrificial death; dying to accompany someone else. This sacrifice of a servant at his master's death was originally obligatory, if we are to believe the *Nihongi*'s probably legendary account of the origin of the *haniwa*; it was most commonly practised voluntarily, in the warrior clans and in battle. Under the peace of the Tokugawa, in the early years of the seventeenth century, *junshi* was allowed only if a daimyo died from natural causes. The Bakufu put an end to the custom in the 1660s. The case of General Nogi, who followed the Emperor Meiji into death in 1912, remains entirely exceptional.

JUSHA, a Confucian scholar. Confucianism was introduced into Japan in 404 by a Korean scholar; it inspired the reformers of the Taika era in the seventh century and the authors of the *Nihongi* in the eighth. Sugawara no Michizane (845–903) was another great scholar in the Confucian mould. After the tenth century Confucianism gave ground before Buddhism. A second flowering took place in the Edo period: Confucian scholars became the official theoreticians of the Bakufu. Except for the activist tendency inspired by Wang Yang-Ming (*Yomeigaku*), the scholars were generally conservatives, and under Meiji they were respected defenders of tradition; their tradition was behind texts such as the Imperial Rescript on education.

JUSUI OJO, death by drowning followed by rebirth in Paradise. *Ojo*, which means letting go of life, is an Amidist term implying hope of a rebirth in the Pure Land, as in the title of a celebrated treaty on the grace of Amida published in 985 by the monk Genshin, *Ojo yoshu* ('Essential Principles for Letting go of Life').

KAIDAN, a fantastic tale or extraordinary story, especially a ghost story.

KAIKEN, literally 'pocket dagger': a small dagger worn under one's clothes.

KAISHAKUNIN, an assistant who beheads the protagonist of a *seppuku*.

KAIZOEBARA, assisted *seppuku*, terminated by the intervention of the *kaishakunin*; from the Muromachi era (1338–1573) onward this was the norm.

KAMI. In Shinto, the work *kami* (also pronounced *shin* in Chinese fashion) is used for the innumerable gods, spirits, powers and energies which govern various aspects of the natural world and the social order. Sanctuaries and cults are dedicated to them.

KAMIKAZE TOKUBETSU KOGEKITAI, 'special attack forces of the wind of the gods', *Tokkotai* for short: special units usually called kamikaze by foreigners. Name for various navy and army corps which were formed for suicide attacks in the last ten months of the Pacific War. The first attack took place on 25 October 1944. In all, 2,198 pilots sacrificed themselves, thirty-four American ships were sunk and 288 damaged.

KANNON, literally 'he who hears our cries', the Buddhist deity of supernatural help, the bodhisattva designated by the sutra of the lotus under the Sanskrit name of Avalokiteshvara. He vowed to give aid and assistance to all those who called to him. He is the incarnation of help and compassion and can intervene in the real world under any form and through any medium. He is the assistant of the Buddha Amida, whose cult merges with his.

KANSHI, death of protest, a voluntary death to show blame.

KARATE, literally 'empty hand': the art of unarmed self-defence. According to the legend, in the sixth century the Indian master Bodhidharma established both Zen and the tecnhique of unarmed combat in the Chinese temple of Shaolin; it later developed in Okinawa, and went from there to Japan, where it was preserved, and has enjoyed a brilliant renaissance in the twentieth century.

KATAKIUCHI, literally 'enemy attack': blood-vengeance, vendetta. *Bushi* morality recognized a duty of vengeance inspired by filial or vassalic loyalty. In the Edo period it was regulated: the daimyo or shogun had to be asked for permission to attack and kill the murderer of one's parent or suzerain, and the vendetta had to stop after this one murder: reprisals were forbidden. Between 1600 and 1868 about a hundred cases were duly registered. Vengeance always played an important part in the repertoire of the Kabuki theatre. In 1873 a government decree made vengeance illegal in all cases: it now belonged to the state.

KATANA, sword. Ever since the eighth century, Japanese smiths, practising ascetic rites and regarded with awe, have produced very high-quality steel. The apogee of this art was reached in the long blades (*tachi*) belonging to knights of the Kamakura era. In the Muromachi era the sword became shorter and easier to handle: the blade of a *katana* was less than 3 feet long. The *bushi* of the Edo area could not appear in public ungirded with *katana* and *wakizashi*.

KATSURAGAWA, a river running west of Kyoto.

KATSURA TARO (1847–1913), a military leader and politician of the Meiji era, born in the principality of Choshu, like Yamagata Aritomo whose protégé and ally he was. In the 1880s he modernized the Japanese army on the German model. In 1898 he became Minister for War, and in 1901 he assumed the functions of Prime Minister, which he retained throughout the Russo-Japanese war. In 1908 he formed a second cabinet which decided on the annexation of Korea in 1910. His third cabinet, formed in 1912, succumbed to the opposition of political parties hostile to the power of cliques full of ex-members of the Choshu and Satsuma clans.

KAWABATA YASUNARI (1899–1972), novelist, winner of the Nobel Prize for literature in 1968.

KAWAKAMI HAJIME (1879–1946), writer and economist. In 1906 he joined a Buddhist society called *Mugaen*, the Garden of Self-Sacrifice. He was professor of political economy at the University of Kyoto from 1908 to 1928, and was one of the Japanese interpreters of Marxism. He was forced to resign his post, and imprisoned from 1933 to 1937. He attempted to reconcile Marxism with his youthful belief in self-sacrifice.

KEGON NO TAKI, the waterfall of Kegon, 300 feet high, near Lake Chuzenji in the Nikko region.

KEGONSHU, the Kegon sect, based on the Avatamsaka sutra (in Japanese, *Kegonkyo*). Introduced from China and Korea in the eighth century, it prospered in the Nara era (710–94), but not thereafter, despite the efforts of the monk Myoe to revive it in the thirteenth century.

KETSUMEIDAN, League of the Blood-Oath, a small ultra-nationalist and terrorist group of about fifteen young peasants recruited by Inoue Nissho under the slogan *ichinin issatsu*, 'One murder each'. On 9 February 1932 they killed Inoue Yunosuke, the former Finance Minister; on 5 March, Dan Takuma, the managing director of the Mitsui group.

KII HANTO, the Kii peninsula, a mountainous region to the south of the plain of Yamoto.

KIMIGAYO, 'The Reign of the Sovereign', Japan's national anthem, composed in 1880 to words from an anonymous poem in the *Kokinsu*, a tenth-century anthology.

KIRA YOSHINAKA, master of ceremonies in the shogun's palace at Edo; in 1700 he was entrusted with the organization of a solemn reception for the emperor's envoy. He publicly reprimanded the daimyo of Ako, Asano Naganori, who, in his anger, wounded him with his sword. This incident sparked off the vendetta of the forty-seven *ronin*.

KIRISUTE GOMEN, licence to stab (with a sword): in the Edo period, samurai were entitled to cut down any peasant or lower-class townsman whom they considered to have insulted them. If the blow was mortal the samurai had to report it to the authorities.

KITA IKKI (1883–1937), theorist of Japanese national socialism. When revolution broke out in China in 1911, he tried to take part, and came back with the idea that the army would have a vital part to play in future Asian revolutions. Back in Japan, from 1919 he developed his theories of revolutionary nationalism, and in 1923 published his 'Plan for the Reorganization of Japan' (*Nihon kaizo hoan taiko*). The imperial national structure (*kokutai*) must take a socialist form (nationalization, agrarian reform), after which a revitalized Japan would be able to head the Asian nations in their struggle against Western colonialism. The young officers who mutinied on 26 February 1936 got from Kita Ikki the idea of demanding a restoration of Showa (*Showa ishin*).

KITAMURA TOKOKU (1868–1894), essayist and poet influenced by romanticism.

KITANO JINJA, the Shinto sanctuary of Kitano, in Kyoto, built for the forty-fourth anniversary of the death of Sugawara no Michizane (845–903) in an attempt to appease his angry ghost.

KODAMA GENTARO (1852–1906), soldier who fought against the Tokugawa in 1868, then against the rebellious samurai of Saga and Kumamoto, and finally against the Satsuma rebellion of 1877. In his capacity as commander-in-chief he was important in the Chinese War, and especially in the Russo-Japanese war, at Port Arthur and at Mukden.

KODOHA, faction of the Imperial Way, one of the two factions (the other being *Toseiha*) which fought for influence in the Japanese army in the 1930s. The *Kodoha* faction, led by General Araki and General Mazaki, attracted mostly officers from the former Saga and Tosa clans. Its aims were a thorough reform of the nation and expansion northwards at the expense of Russia. After the repression of the mutiny on 26 February 1936 it lost ground to the *Toseiha*.

KOFUN, tumuli built between the third and the seventh centuries to house the coffins of important personages along with funerary offerings. When Buddhism took a hold the custom yielded to the building of temples. In Japanese chronology the *kofun* age corresponds to the protohistoric stage (300–710) which saw the emergence of social classes, the supremacy of the imperial court of Yamato, the first towns, and finally the introduction of writing and Buddhism.

KOJIKI ('Chronicle of Deeds of Yore'), completed in 712: a collection of Japanese oral traditions recorded in Chinese script, including myths about the creation of the world and the founding of the ruling dynasty, genealogies, legends and annals.

KOKURYKAI, Society of the Black Dragon, i.e. of the River Amur: an ultranationalist league founded in 1901 as an offshoot of the *Genyosha*, with the aim of thrusting the Russians back north of the Amur and encouraging Japanese expansion in Manchuria and Siberia.

KOKUTAI NO HONGI ('Fundamental Principles of National Structure'), a pamphlet published on 30 March 1937 by the Ministry of Education and circulated on a huge scale (more than 2,000,000 copies) in educational establishments with the aim of countering various Western ideologies, encouraging patriotism, combating individualism and exalting the spirit of sacrifice. The inspiration of *kokutai*, which as a political structure is believed to be the only one of its kind, comes from notions of imperial sovereignty and the celestial origins of an unbroken dynasty.

KONISHI YUKINAGA (1556–1600). One of the chief lieutenants of Toyotomi Hideyoshi, he was baptized by Christian missionaries, and appears in their chronicles under the name of Dom Agostinho. From 1592 to 1598 he played a vital part in military and diplomatic operations in Korea. After the death of Hideyoshi he fought against Tokugawa Ieyasu; after the battle of Sakigara (1600) he refused to kill himself and was beheaded in Kyoto.

KONOE FUMIMARO (1891–1945), a descendant of a family related to the Fujiwara, he long kept the reputation of a reformer open to new ideas. In 1937 he formed a government, and after the incident at the Bridge of Marco Polo, he was dragged into a war against China which was not stopped by his promise of a 'new order in East Asia' (*Toa Shinchitsujo*). Prime Minister again in 1940, he signed the tripartite pact with the Axis powers and proclaimed a 'Sphere of Co-prosperity in Greater East Asia' (*Dai Toa Kyoeiken*). He formed a third government in 1941, attempted to halt the march towards war, but was forced to resign in favour of General Tojo.

KOROMOGAWA, a fortress in the Mutsu region, in northern Japan, where Minamoto no Yoshitsune took refuge when persecuted by his brother Yoritomo. He was attacked there a few months later, in 1189, and killed himself.

KOTOKU SHUSUI (1871–1911), militant socialist and anarchist. In 1901 he was one of the founders of the Social Democratic Party (*Shakai minshuto*), which was immediately proscribed by the government. He opposed the Russo-Japanese war and in 1904 published the first translation of Marx and Engels's *Communist Manifesto*. While staying in the USA in 1906 he was converted to anarchism and returned to Japan dedicated to the general strike and to direct action. He became involved in the plots of a group of young extremists to assassinate the Emperor Meiji, was condemned to death, and was hanged on 24 January 1911.

KOYASAN, Mount Koya, in the centre of the Kii peninsula, where in 816 Kukai founded the Kongobuji, the principal temple of the Shingon sect; many monasteries grew up around it, and there are still 110 today. Set in a lonely and mountainous region, it became a place of pilgrimage, refuge in defeat, and banishment, especially for the victims of Sekigahara. Many tombs and cenotaphs gathered around the grave of Kukai.

KUGAI, 'this world of suffering', a Buddhist expression applied by courtesans to their unhappy fate.

KUKAI (774–835), literally 'Ocean of the Void', name for the monk also known posthumously as Kobo Daishi. After studying for the civil service, Kukai became convinced of the superiority of Buddhism over Confucianism and became a wandering hermit, practising asceticism and meditation. In 804 he sailed for China, and returned in 806 equipped with a knowledge of the esoteric Buddhism recently arrived from India. He founded the Shingon sect and became an important personage in the religious and cultural life of Heian. In 816 he began the building of a monastic centre in the remote region of Mount Koya, where he died.

KUMANO, a mountainous region on the Pacific seaboard, in the south-east of the Kii peninsula, where there are three famous Shinto sanctuaries. With the advance of religious syncretism in the Heian period (794–1185), the *kami* worshipped there were seen as incarnations of Buddhas and bodhisattvas, and Kumano became an active centre of the cult of Amida and Kannon, and a famous place of pilgrimage; it was also closely connected with the ascetic practices of *yamabushi* and *shugendo*.

KURUSHIMA TSUNEKI, a militant member of the Society of the Dark Ocean (*Genyosha*). In 1889 he threw a bomb at Okuma Shigenobu, Minister for Foreign Affairs, who was accused of being too conciliatory when renegotiating unfair treaties with foreign powers.

KUSUNOKI MASASHIGE (1294-1336), a faithful warrior for the Emperor Go-Daigo in his struggle to restore the imperial power. During Go-Daigo's exile he helped Prince Morinaga carry on a guerrilla war against the Hojo. After the fall of the latter he was, with Nitta Yoshisada, leader of the loyalist forces opposed to Ashikaga Takauji. In July 1336 he was defeated at the battle of Minatogawa. His son Masatsura continued the struggle in the service of the court of the South at Yoshino. Under the Meiji Restoration, Kusunoki Masashige became a byword for loyalty, and in the first decades of Showa he was a highly praised figure in school textbooks.

KYUBA NO MICHI, 'the way of the bow and the horse', i.e. the art of shooting at full gallop. The warrior clans attached great importance to training their horsemen in the use of the bow, which remained the most important weapon (along with the sword) until the introduction of the musket in the sixteenth century. In so far as this training was connected with self-mastery, it was one of the sources of the codified *bushido* of the seventeenth century.

MAKOTO, sincerity, loyalty, genuineness. In native Japanese tradition the word *makoto* (*ma* 'truth', *koto* 'conduct') meant the purity of the heart as demonstrated in action. In Confucian thinking, sincerity is also seen as a cardinal virtue which guarantees the other four. From the seventeenth century moral philosophers, particularly writers on *bushido*, referred continually to *makoto* as an essential principle.

MAN'YOSHU ('Collection of Ten Thousand Pages'), the first of the great poetic anthologies, containing 4,516 poems dating from the fourth to the eighth centuries, mostly short *tanha* of thirty-one syllables.

MASAKADO (?-940), a warrior of the Taira family, based in the western provinces, who in the tenth century rebelled against the court of Heian and even went as far as to call himself the 'new emperor'. He aimed to make Kanto an independent state. He was killed in battle on 25 March 940. His adventure was the first real warning of the growing power of the warrior aristocracy.

MEKAKE, concubine. The husband's duty to be faithful in marriage (unlike the wife's) was not legally established until the civil code of 1947.

MICHIYUKI, journey, itinerary, travel. Many Japanese literary works have lyrical episodes describing a journey.

MIKAWA, a former province south-east of the modern town of Nagoya.

MIKO, originally female shamans who could, while in a trance, communicate with the *kami*, spirits of the dead or forces of nature, and who performed rituals such as the *kagura* dances. Their importance diminished with the introduction of Buddhist ceremonies confined to the masculine clergy. Today, *miko* are girls in the service of a Shinto sanctuary.

MIMANA, a territory to the south of the Korean peninsula, controlled by the Yamato state from the fourth to the sixth century.

MINAMOTO or GENJI, a surname for branches pruned from the imperial family tree, the origin of new princely lines. The polygamous emperors produced vast numbers of princes, who had to be pruned away to save money on pensions and limit quarrelling over the succession. In 814, for example, the emperor Saga gave thirty-four of his fifty offspring the family name of Minamoto. Another name, Taira, was given to several descendants of the emperor Kammu. Some branches of the Minamoto and Taira families settled in the eastern provinces and ruled as lords over the local warriors.

MINAMOTO NO YORIMASA (1104–80), courtier, warrior and poet. At first he supported Taira no Kiyomori, but later plotted against him. Under attack by a Taira army in Uji, he killed himself by *seppuku*.

MINAMOTO NO YORITOMO (1147–99), principal architect of the victory of the Minamoto over the Taira in 1185, he continued to build up his power by setting up a military government (Bakufu) in Kamakura. In 1192 he was given the title *shogun*, making him supreme over the warrior aristocracy and *de facto* master of Japan. The power structure set up by Yoritomo lasted for seven centuries until the Meiji Restoration in 1868.

MINAMOTO NO YOSHINAKA (1154–84), a warrior born and bred in the mountains of Kiso, who rebelled against Taira no Kiyomori in 1180. In 1183 he expelled the Taira from the capital, but his excesses made him hated: the next year, he was attacked on the orders of his cousin, Minamoto no Yoritomo, and killed in battle.

MINAMOTO NO YOSHITOMO (1123–60). His power spread over the eastern provinces. With Taira no Kiyomori, he supported the emperor Go-Shirakawa in the quarrel over the succession in 1156, but took offence at receiving fewer favours than Kiyomori and in 1160 began a struggle against Taira supremacy. He was killed as he fled towards his estates in the east, but his sons, Yoritomo and Yoshitsune, avenged him twenty-five years later with a crushing victory over the Taira.

MINAMOTO NO YOSHITSUNE (1159–89), son of Yoshimoto and brother of Yoritomo. In 1180 he answered Yoritomo's call to arms against the Taira and became the most brilliant general of his house. He routed the Taira at the naval battle of Dan no Ura (1185). Afterwards Yoritomo regarded him with fear and suspicion, and he went into hiding in the mountains of Yohino and later fled to the northern provinces. He was attacked in the fortress of Koromogawa and killed his wife and daughter, then himself.

MINATOGAWA, a hamlet near the present-day town of Kobe (formerly Hyogo), where in July 1336 Ashikaga Takauji triumphed over the supporters of the Emperor Go-Daigo, led by Kusunoki Masashige and Nitta Yoshishada.

MISHIMA YUKIO (1925-70), writer.

MIYAKOJI BUNGONOJO (1660-1740), narrator of *joruri*. He invented a new style of interpretation which was officially forbidden in 1739.

MIYAMOTO KENJI, essayist and politician, born in 1908; while still a student he became famous for a Marxist criticism of Akutagawa Ryunosoke. In 1931 he joined the clandestine Communist Party; he was arrested in 1933 and remained in prison until the end of the war. Later he became one of the most influential figures in the Japanese Communist Party.

MONO NO AWARE, sorrow felt at the fragility of existing things. The word *aware* is used more than 1,000 times in the *Genji monogatari* to mean both the aesthetic tone of the Heian court and the Buddhist notion of ineluctable transience. It implies a sensitive mind capable of appreciating beauty not only in its perfection of form, but also in its intrinsic evanescence.

MORI ARINORI (1847-89), statesman of the Meiji era. He encouraged modernization, progress, enlightenment and a social order based on choosing the best possible men for the service of the state. From 1885 to 1889 he played an important part as Minister for Education. He was assassinated by a Shinto fanatic.

MORI OGAI (1862-1922), writer.

MORINAGA SHINNO (1308-35), Prince Morinaga, eldest son of the Emperor Go-Daigo. He fought a guerrilla war against the Hojo in the Kii peninsula on behalf of the exiled emperor. After the 1333 restoration he was regarded with distrust by Ashinaga, who imprisoned him at Kamakura and eventually had him murdered.

MUGA, 'not-I', negation of the self, Sanskrit *anatman*. A fundamental aspect of the materialist atomist doctrine in primitive Buddhism: there is no such thing as a substantial, and therefore unalterable and permanent, 'self'. The existing self is a temporary effect of the union of the five types of aggregate, and its unity is a delusion. This doctrine can be supplemented or supplanted by a moral interpretation: it is better that the self should not exist and that the individual should be freed from his spontaneous egoism. In this derivative sense *muga* means the supreme virtue of self-sacrifice.

MUNENBURA, protest *seppuku* in order to wipe out an affront or avenge an insult or injustice.

MURASAKI SHIKIBU, author of the *Genji monogatari*, a lady of the court belonging to a cadet branch of the Fujiwara. She was the daughter of a provincial governor, and it was doubtless because of her fame as a poet and writer that she was summoned to the imperial court as lady-in-waiting to the Empress Akiko.

MUTSU, former province in the north, now the prefecture of Aomori.

MYOE (1173-1232), religious reformer of the Kegon sect. He accused the Amidists of reducing all practices to the single one of reciting the *nembutsu*. He attempted to restore ascesis and meditation.

NABESHIMA NAOSHIGE (1537-1619), initially a vassal of the house of Ryuzoji. With Hideyoshi's consent he took over his lords' principality and became daimyo of Hizen in north-west Kyushu (now the districts of Saga and Nagasaki).

NACHI NO TAKI, the waterfall of Nachi, in the south-east of the Kii peninsula in the Kumano region, much frequented by ascetics and pilgrims.

NAGAI KAFU (1879-1959), novelist and essayist, a lover of old Edo.

NANIWA, a region now part of Osaka, where the Emperor Nintoku resided, and later the Emperor Temmu established his capital.

NANORI, a profession of faith during a chivalric combat; proclamation by a warrior introducing himself, making his intentions known or issuing a challenge.

NATSUME SOSEKI (1867-1916), professor of English literature, novelist, one of the leading writers of the last years of Meiji.

NEMBUTSU, the invocation to the Buddha Amida, brought from China in the ninth century by the founders of the Tendai sect. In the twelfth century, Nonen maintained that the mere recitation of the homage to Amida, even without any meditation or ceremony, was enough to ensure a rebirth in the Pure Land.

NICHIREN (1222-82), originally a Tendai monk. His veneration of the sutra of the Lotus (*Myohorenge-kyo*, Sanskrit *Saddharmapundarika-sutra*) became exclusive, and his disdain for other sects, such as Zen and, especially, the Pure Land, became pugnacious. In 1253 he began to preach the urgency of a reform based on the orthodoxy of the Lotus. He was exiled for his intolerance in 1261 and 1271, and threatened with execution. The sect he founded is known for its invocation of and homage to the sutra of the Lotus, *Namu Myohorenge-kyo*. Nichiren's example inspired many other aspects of militant Buddhism, such as the *Soka gakkai* society.

NIHONGI or NIHONSHOKI (Annals of Japan), a compilation, begun on the emperor's orders and completed in 720, narrating the mythical and historical events from the creation of the world down to the seventh century. After the *Kojiki*, this is the oldest source for the history of Japan.

NINJO, human feelings, humanity, sensibility. A principle of conduct founded on sympathy with the sufferings of the heart and with human failings in general, a potential for mitigating the severity of the *giri*.

NINTOKU TENNO, emperor of Japan, the sixteenth according to the traditional chronology, whose reign probably belongs to the first half of the fifth century. The *Nihongi*, under Chinese influence, endows him with all the virtues of moderation and benevolence required by the Confucian ideal. His mausoleum (*kofun*) covers 32 hectares near Osaka: it is the largest grave-mound in Japan.

NO, literally 'talent', 'skill'. A kind of theatre accompanied by music and dancing, which, after its first appearance in the fourteenth century, was favoured by the shogun Ashikaga Yoshimitsu (1358-1408). It was then that the best plays in the repertoire were written by Zeami (1363-1443). During the Edo era the No, under Tokugawa patronage, showed a tendency to standardization and sluggishness, at a time when urban audiences were turning to the Kabuki. After six uninterrupted centuries, the No has come down to us in all its ceremonious fascination.

NOGI MARESUKE (1849-1912), a warrior famous more for his moral exellence than his strategical skill, a worthy incarnation of *bushido*.

NOKOGIRIBIKI, 'torment of the saw': cutting through the neck of a condemned man with a bamboo saw.

ODA NOBUNAGA (1534-82), a war-lord, who, at the end of the Age of the Warring Kingdoms (*Sengokujidai*), gained the supreme power by means of cunning, violence, intelligence and courage. He was the first of the three dictators who ruled a united Japan, the others being Toyotomi Hideyoshi and Tokugawa Ieyasu.

OGYU SORAI (1666-1728), thinker, scholar, philologist and teacher of the Edo era, who tried to return to the very sources of Confucian doctrine.

OIBARA, voluntary self-disembowelling in order to follow a beloved individual into death.

OKA MASAFUMI (1962-75), a youthful poet: committed suicide.

OKUMA SHIGENOBU (1838-1922), progressive politician, founder of Waseda University. He was in the earliest governments of the Meiji era, but was disowned by his colleagues and forced to resign in 1881 for supporting the immediate introduction of a constitution on the British model. A year later he founded the constitutional reform party *Rikken Kaishinto*. In 1889 he escaped an assassination attempt by Kurushima Tsuneki, who thought he had been unduly conciliatory when renegotiating unfair treaties. Prime Minister in 1898 and again in 1914, he declared war on Germany and presented China with the 'Twenty-One Demands' which formulated Japanese pressure on the mainland.

OKUSAMA, literally 'inside person': housewife, spouse.

ONIN NO RAN, the civil war of the Onin era (1467–9), which took place in Kyoto from 1467 to 1477 and, together with the weakening in the power of the shogun Ashikaga, ushered in the turbulent epoch called *sengokujidai*, 'the Age of Warring Kingdoms'.

ONISHI TAKIJIRO (1891–1945), vice-admiral of the navy and air force, who organized the first squadrons of suicide pilots in October 1944.

ONRYO, angry ghost, a vengeful spirit, much feared.

OSHIO HEIHACHIRO (1793–1837), son of a police officer from Osaka. He succeeded his father, but gave up his job to study and teach the thought of Wang Yang-Ming. Wang gave him the idea that the ruling classes are responsible for the evils afflicting the lower classes. In 1836 there was famine in the Kansai region; Oshio sold his books to help the hungry. In protest against the inaction of the authorities he started an insurrection on 19 February 1837. There were two days of rioting, during which Osaka was set on fire. The insurrection was crushed. Oshio and his son were hunted by the police; they killed themselves on 27 March 1837.

OSUGI SAKAE (1885–1923), anarchist militant. He was influenced by Kotoku Shusui, but was not implicated in the 1910 conspiracy. Two weeks after the Kanto earthquake, he was arrested and put to death by a police officer.

OTOMO NO TABITO (665–731), a warrior and courtier, high official, scholar and poet of the Nara era (710–94), the leading light in the spread of Chinese cultural influence. After subduing the rebel tribes south of Kyushu, he was appointed governor of Dazaifu in 727, settled in that distant province and surrounded himself with Chinese scholars. Several of his works appear in the *Man'yoshu*, notably a group of thirteen poems in praise of wine and intoxication.

OYAKO SHINJU, suicide of parent and child together, also called *ikka shinju*, family suicide. The same word, *shinju*, is used for the suicide of two lovers together.

RASHOMON, a long short story by Akutagawa Ryunosuke (1892–1927) which gave its title to the celebrated film by Kurosawa Akira that won the prize at the Venice Festival in 1951.

RISSHISHA, a mutual aid society founded in 1874 by Itagaki Taisuke in the former principality of Tosa, for samurai impoverished by the changes in

Japanese society. The society eventually acquired political aims such as the calling of a national assembly, the reduction of land taxes and the revision of unfair treaties; it paved the way for political parties. It showed a positive response by the former ruling class to the challenge of inevitable transition.

RONIN, literally 'floating man'. Initially it meant peasants who temporarily deserted their land to become soldiers; during and after the Muromachi period (1336–1568) it was the name for professional samurai who, either because they had belonged to a defeated and disbanded army or because they had been dismissed by a daimyo anxious to reduce his wage bill, were left masterless, jobless and penniless. At the beginning of the Edo era, after the battle of Sekigahara, there were about 400,000 of them. Some turned to farming, many found work in the rapidly expanding towns, but others remained on the outer fringes of organized society and resorted to violence, adventure and criminality.

RYUZOJI TAKANOBU (1529–84), daimyo of the principality of Hizen, he managed to extend his power north of Kyushu. He was defeated and killed in a skirmish with the Shimazu of Satsuma. His lands was granted to one of his vassals, Nabeshima Naoshige.

SAIGO TAKAMORI (1827–77). Born into a poor samurai family in the principality of Satsuma, south of Kyushu, Saigo played a prominent part in the struggle against the Tokugawa. In 1867 he overcame the shogun's troops at Toba and Fushimi and marched on Edo. He was military chargé d'affaires in the imperial government. In 1873 he advocated an expedition into Korea, but was disowned by most of his colleagues and forced to resign. Returning to Kagoshima, he started to organize the local samurai and perfect their training. After an incident in which his supporters clashed with the regular authorities, he headed the rebellion of Satsuma, which ended in his defeat and suicide on 24 September 1877.

SAIONJI KINMOCHI (1849–1940), statesman, born into a court family descended from the Fujiwara. Prime Minister from 1906 to 1908 and from 1911 to 1912, he was influential in politics to the end of his life. After the death of Yamagata Aritomo in 1922, Prince Saionji was the last of the *genro* ('former rulers') whose task it was to advise the emperor in his choice of Prime Minister. He had studied in France from 1871 to 1880 and he had liberal and moderate sympathies: he opposed the ultra-nationalists, but altogether too moderately and with small success.

SAKAGUCHI ANGO (1906–55), author of essays and short stories; along with Dazai Osamu he was the voice of the years following the defeat.

SAKURAKAI, Society of the Cherry Blossom, a secret society of some fifty young officers bent on a military *coup d'état*. Founded in 1930, the society planned the ultra-nationalist conspiracies of March and October 1931 before it was dissolved and its organization shattered.

SAKURA SOGORO, a legendary personage, a village headsman from the Sakura dominions, in the modern Chiba district near Tokyo. In 1655 he agreed to head the protest of 200 villages which had revolted against the abuses of the local daimyo, the youthful Hotta Masanobu (1629–77). Sogoro presented his petition directly to the shogun Tokugawa Ietsuna. For this he was crucified along with his wife after seeing his children beheaded. Hotta Masanobu was deprived of his dominions and banished to Tokushima.

SATO EISAKU (1901–75), president of the Liberal Democrat Party, Prime Minister from 1964 to 1972.

SATORI, awakening, enlightenment: an essential concept in Zen Buddhism. A sudden realization of the Buddha inherent in every being. A transcendent experience, ineffable and yet concrete and irrefutable, of uncontradicted unity. A shining entry into the truth of being.

SEIYUKAI, a moderate constitutional party which played an important part in parliamentary life from 1900 to 1940.

SEKIGAHARA, a village in the Gifu region, site of the decisive battle which assured the hegemony of Tokugawa Ieyasu (11 October 1600).

SEKIGUNHA, Red Army Faction, an extremist group founded in 1969 by radical students aiming at world revolution via the armed struggle. Among the actions of organized terror perpetrated by the Japanese Red Army is the machine-gunning of the Lod airport terminal in Tel Aviv (30 May 1972) by a commando unit of three young Japanese. Twenty-four people were killed.

SENDATSU, literally 'guide': in the *yamabushi* hierarchy, a title conferred on confirmed ascetics who lived in the mountains and directed *shugendo* exercises in endurance and mortification.

SENGAKUJI, a Buddhist temple south of Edo, where in 1703 the servants who avenged their master Asano Naganori were buried alongside him.

SENGOKUJIDAI, 'Age of the Warring Kingdoms', a term borrowed from Chinese history to designate the century of civil war, from 1467 to 1568, from the War of Onin to the supremacy of Oda Nobunaga. During this period the daimyo ruling various provinces in the empire fought each other incessantly and made an unending series of hostile coalitions.

SEPPUKU, 'incision of the abdomen'; HARAKIRI 'belly cut open': two names for the same act; two different pronunciations of the same pictograms, the Chinese being *seppuku* and the Japanese *harakiri*. The difference is like that between our 'incision' and 'cut', 'abdomen' and 'belly'. Foreigners have adopted *harakiri*, but the Japanese stick to *seppuku*, which is more dignified.

SEWAMONO, kitchen-sink drama, a category within the repertoire of the Kabuki and the Bunraku containing plays with contemporary subjects, often inspired by minor news items, whose characters are citizens of modest means (*chonin*); cf. the category of historical drama, *jidaimono*.

SHASHIN, giving up the body, rejecting the body: a Buddhist term for taking holy orders.

SHIGA NAOYA (1883-1971), a writer associated with the *Shirakaba* group, a leading author of autobiographical novels (*shishosetsu*).

SHIKARABA, 'The Silver Birch', a magazine of art and literature which ran from 1910 to 1923.

SHIKIDO OKAGAMI ('The Great Mirror of the Way of Amorous Pleasures'), an erudite work by Fujimoto Kizan, published in 1678, describing life in the pleasure districts and detailing the rules of good behaviour which were to be observed there.

SHIMABARA, a peninsula near Nagasaki. On 11 December 1637 an insurrection broke out there among the peasants and the *ronin*, many of them Christians, who gave the revolt a touch of millenarianism by choosing, as their leader and messiah, the youthful Amakusa Shiro. The insurrection, which had spread instantaneously to the Amakusa Islands, was crushed four months later.

SHIMAZAKI TOSON (1872-1943), a Romantic poet and naturalist novelist, one of the first to become prominent in the autobiographical genre of *shishosetsu*.

SHIMPUREN, League of the Divine Wind, an association formed in 1872 by samurai from the Kumamoto region opposed to modernization. On 24 October 1876 they attacked the garrison there.

SHINGON SHU, a Buddhist sect founded in the early ninth century by the monk Kukai (774-835) on his return from China. *Shin-gon* means 'true word', 'spell that works', in Sanskrit *mantra*. *Shingon* is an esoteric form of Buddhism, with complex ceremonies, magical rites, and practices of devotion, ascesis and meditation in which it makes use of mantras, mudras and mandalas which came from India via China.

SHINJU, literally 'depths of the heart': any behaviour likely to make one's true feelings known. In particular, a type of suicide motivated by passionate love or love of family. Lover's *shinju*, which reached its apogee in the theatre of the early eighteenth century, is also called *joshi*, dying for love. *Shinju* for the family is called *oyako shinju* or *ikka shinju*.

SHINJU OKAGAMI ('The Great Mirror of the Suicide of Lovers'), a collection of seventeen stories by Shokoken, published in 1704.

SHINJU TEN NO AMIJIMA ('Lover's Suicide in Amijima'), a play by Chikamatsu performed on 3 January 1721 at the Osaka puppet theatre.

SHINRAN (1173–1263), founder of the True Sect of the Pure Land (*Jodo shinshu*). A disciple of Honen (1133–1212) from 1201, he was exiled along with his master in 1207. He was the first of the Japanese bonzes to take a wife. He lived in Kanto, then returned to Kyoto in 1235. His doctrine of salvation by faith explains the rebirth in the Pure Land as a rebirth, here and now, of the heart enlightened by the compassion of Amida made manifest in his Original Vow.

SHINSHU GIDAN, League of the Virtue of the Country of the Gods, a small ultra-nationalist group led by Ashi Heigo (1890–1921).

SHINTO, the Way of the Gods, a native Japanese religion based on various local nature cults, over which is superimposed a divine genealogy of the imperial dynasty which made it possible to create a religion of national unity and the state, as was done from Meiji onwards.

SHISHOSETSU or WATAKUSHISHOSETSU, personal novel, novel of the self, autobiography.

SHOEN OKAGAMI ('The Great Mirror of Pleasure'), a book by Ihara Saikaku, published in 1684 as a sequel to 'The Life of an Amorous Man (*Koshoku ichidai otoko*, 1682).

SHOGUN, generalissimo: a title conferred by the emperor on warriors entrusted with the task of making and keeping the peace in the empire. In 1192 it was given to Minamoto no Yoritomo, who had overcome his enemies and set up a military government at Kamakura, where nine successive shoguns ruled up to 1333. After the fall of Kamakura, Ashikaga Takauji assumed the title of shogun and passed it on to his descendants, who chose to reside in the Muromachi quarter of Kyoto. There were fifteen Ashikaga shoguns between 1338 and 1573. Finally, in 1603, Tokugawa Ieyasu received the office of shogun, which stayed in his family for generations: there were fifteen Tokugawa shoguns up to the restoration of imperial power in 1868.

SHOKYU or JOKYU, name of an era which lasted from 1219 to 1221, marked by an unsuccessful attempt by the emperor Go-Toba to restore the imperial power. His army was defeated by the Hojo, whose influence lasted for more than a century thereafter.

SHOWA ISHIN, 'Restoration of the Showa era', a slogan used between 1926 and 1936 by radical army officers and ultra-nationalist militants who planned a *coup d'état* to transform all economic and political structures and bring about a rebirth of the pure Japanese spirit. After the failure of the mutiny of the Young Officers in 1936 the slogan passed out of use.

SOGA, an aristocratic family which dominated the court of Yamato for four generations in the sixth and seventh centuries. The Soga actively promoted the introduction of Buddhism. In 645 a *coup d'état* put an end to their supremacy.

SOKOSUSHI, 'death for negligence', a voluntary death intended to expiate a careless error.

SOKUSHIN JOBUTSU, 'Becoming a Buddha while still in this Body', a doctrine explained in a short treatise written in 817 by Kukai (774–835). He says that all beings have it in them to become Buddhas because this capacity is not transcendent, but immanent in existence.

SONEZAKI SHINJU ('Lover's Suicide in Sonekazi'), a play by Chikamatsu performed at the Osaka puppet theatre on 20 June 1703. It was the first of his *sewamono*. At the time Sonezaki, like Shinmachi, was one of the pleasure districts of Osaka.

SONNO JOI, 'Honour the emperor and expel the barbarians', a slogan which summed up the intentions of the advocates of imperial restoration towards the end of the Edo era.

SOTO SHU, the Zen *soto* sect, founded by Dogen on his return from China in 1227; it is one of the two great schools of Japanese Zen, the other being Rinzai. It stresses meditation without thought (*mokusho-zen*), and attributes less importance than Rinzai to the *koan*.

SUGAWARA NO MICHIZANE (845–903), a learned admirer of Chinese culture, a high official, poet and courtier of the Heian period who as minister to the Emperor Daigo attempted to curb the power of the Fujiwara and thus fell out of favour. He died in exile and was later rehabilitated, canonized and deified; today he is venerated as the patron of learning, and invoked in examinations and competitions.

SUGIYAMA HAJIME (1880–1945), general in the imperial army, chief of staff from 1940 to 1944. In July 1945 he was put in charge of the defence of Japan in the eventuality of an allied landing. He killed himself on 12 September 1945 after helping to complete the demobilization of the army.

SUININ TENNO, eleventh emperor of Japan, who, according to the (probably legendary) account in the *Nihongi*, decided to replace funerary sacrifices by earthenware images (*haniwa*).

SUSANOO NO MIKOTO, a Shinto god, son of Izanagi, younger brother of Amaterasu. He was banished from the Celestial Plain for bad behaviour, came down to earth, and settled in the province of Izumo, in western Japan.

SUZUKI KANTARO (1867–1948), admiral, veteran of the Sino-Japanese and Russo-Japanese wars, navy chief of staff in 1925, asked to form a government in 1945. On 14 August, after a series of conferences with the emperor, the Suzuki cabinet accepted the Potsdam Declaration and ended hostilities.

TACHIYAKU, leading masculine role in the Kabuki, who must show energy whether for good or ill, whereas the second role (*nimaime*) must be tender and pathetic.

TAIHEIKI ('Chronicle of the Great Peace'), anonymous story finished in 1370, telling of the fall of the Hojo in 1333, the restoration of the Kemmu era, the rise to power of Ashikaga Takauji and the rivalry of the two courts of the North and the South. The text, heavily stylistically influenced by Chinese, was acted out in public by monks, instrumentalists and story-tellers.

TAIHO RITSURYO, code of the Taiho era (701–4), promulgated in 702, comprising six volumes of penal law (*ritsu*) and eleven volumes of administrative law (*ryo*), all heavily influenced by Tang China.

TAIKA NO KAISHIN, reform in the Taika era: from 646 onwards imperial decrees and codes were promulgated with the aim of strengthening bureaucratic centralization on the Chinese Tang model and clinching the Yamato state's control over the land and people.

TAIRA (or HEIKE or HEISHI), an aristocratic family of imperial origin and bellicose inclinations which in the twelfth century reached its apogee under Kiyomori; his fall and destruction followed soon after. The Taira, like the Minamoto, grew from buds pruned from the imperial family tree.

TAIRA NO KIYOMORI (1118–81), head of the Taira family, who successfully dominated the imperial court after emerging victorious from the troubles of the Hogen (1156) and Heiji (1160) eras. For twenty years his influence was supreme, and he abused it. A few months before his death, he managed to place his grandson on the throne as the emperor Antoku.

TAIRA NO KOREMORI, son of the eldest son of Taira no Kiyomori, who after the defeat of his clan took refuge on Mount Koya, and later drowned himself in the sea off Kumano.

TAISEI YOKUSANKAI, Association of Assistance to the Imperial Reign, a political mass movement created on 12 October 1940 on the initiative of the Prime Minister Konoe Fumimaro to replace the former political parties and mobilize the energies of the population in the service of the state, in imitation of the totalitarian parties in Europe. The Association relayed official propaganda but never had any decisive weight in political decisions.

TAKARABE TAKESHI (1867–1949), Minister of Marine from 1923 to 1927 and from 1929 to 1930, represented Japan at the London conference on limitation of naval weaponry. He accepted a compromise which was disputed by the ultra-nationalists.

TAKASHIMADAIRA, a new town north-west of Tokyo.

TAKEYARI SHUGI, 'doctrine of the bamboo lance', a do-or-die theory according to which a resolute people is invincible, however poorly armed.

TAKI ZENZABURO, the officer who in February 1868 gave the order to open fire on the foreign enclaves of Kobe and for this was condemned to death by *seppuku*.

TAMAMUSHI ZUSHI ('Beetle Reliquary'), a work of the mid-seventh century, the Asuka period (552–710), a miniature model of a temple whose walls are decorated with Buddhist scenes painted in oils. Its name comes from the iridescent beetles' wings (*tamamushi*) which originally decorated its uprights.

TAMESHIMONO, literally 'object for experiment': a corpse or living body (prisoner or condemned man) on whom (or which) the sharpness of a blade could be tested.

TANAKA HIDEMITSU (1913–49), novelist, disciple and friend of Sazai Osamu.

TANDEN, the 'field of cinnabar': in Buddhist textbooks of meditation, a metaphor for the space under the navel, comparing it to an alchemist's furnace.

TANIZAKI JUN'ICHIRO (1886–1965), novelist.

TATARI, vengeance by the spirit of a dead person. Rites of appeasement, or exorcism, were necessary to put an end to it.

TATE NO KAI, the Society of the Shield, a paramilitary organization founded in 1967 by the writer Mishima Yukio, and dissolved after his death.

TAYU, leading actor in the No theatre. Metaphorically, a top-ranking courtesan in the brothel hierarchy of the Edo age.

TENDAI, a Buddhist sect founded by the monk Saicho (767–822) on his return from China, equivalent to the Chinese *tiantai* sect which, following the sutra of the Lotus (*myohorengekyo*), declared that the world of absolutes and the world of phenomena were inseparable. The Enryakuji temple, on top of Mount Hiei to the north-east of Kyoto, was the centre of *tendai* teaching from the beginning, when they were noted for an esoteric Buddhism which a rival sect, the *shingon*, claimed as its monopoly. From the twelfth century onwards, the monks of Enryakuji and their mercenaries meddled more and more in politics. In 1572 Oda Nobunaga destroyed the powerful monasteries on Mount Hiei and massacred 3,000 monks.

TENKO, reversal, inversion, change of direction, i.e. turning from Marxism back to patriotism. During the first few decades of the Showa era, many Japanese communists, alarmed by the repression of 'dangerous notions' organized under the Law for the Preservation of Civil Peace of 1925, publicly proclaimed that they had rejected their former ideas as being contrary to the national interest.

TENNO, the 'Celestial Sovereign', the emperor. From the beginning, his ritual authority took precedence over his political power, which varied from century to century and was usually delegated. The institution of empire, rooted in a legendary past, has shown itself to be flexible, enduring and adaptable. Alongside its power and resources, it allows some space for the encouragement of disinterested devotion, which is indispensable to the social fabric.

TERAUCHI HISAICHI (1879–1946), a general and the son of a general, member of the Choshu clan. Minister for War in the Hirota cabinet formed immediately after the mutiny of 26 February 1936, he engaged in a polemic against the parliamentarian Hamada Kunimatsu (1869–1939), member of the Seiyukai Party. This struggle aggravated the ill-feeling between the army and the political parties.

TOGO HEIHACHIRO (1848–1934). In his youth, in 1863, he witnessed the bombardment of Kagoshima by a British squadron; later he fought against the Tokugawa. From 1871 to 1878 he studied naval science in England. During the Russo-Japanese war he was commander-in-chief of the Japanese navy, and at the battle of Tsushima (27 May 1905) his strategy brought about the defeat and destruction of the Russian Baltic fleet.

TOJO HIDEKI (1884–1948), soldier and statesman, held chiefly responsible for the opening of hostilities at Pearl Harbor. At the GHQ of the army of Kwantung, in Manchuria, he always advocated total war. In the ministerial posts which he occupied, he advocated opposition to Chiang Kai-Shek and supported the Tripartite Alliance. He opposed Prince Konoe's inconsequential efforts to reconcile Japan and the United States. In October 1941 he was entrusted with the formation of a cabinet which unleashed the 'War of Greater Oriental Asia' (*Dai Toa Senso*) at Pearl Harbor. After the fall of Saipan, in July 1944, he was compelled to resign. On his arrest he attempted suicide, and was one of the chief defendants at the Tokyo trial. He was condemned to death and hanged on 23 December 1948.

TOKAIDO, 'road of the eastern sea', which since the dawn of Japanese history has linked Yamato, seat of the imperial government, to the eastern regions of Kanto, originally scantily cleared and pacified. When the Bakufu was installed at Kamakura at the end of the twelfth century, the Tokaido's importance increased. It played its most important part in the life of the country in the Edo period, when it was well maintained and policed.

TOKUGAWA, an aristocratic warrior family which, after the victories of Tokugawa Ieyasu in the early seventeenth century, ruled Japan until 1868.

TOKUGAWA HIDETADA (1597–1632), third son of Tokugawa Ieyasu, second shogun of his line; he pursued his father's policies of control and isolation.

TOKUGAWA IEMITSU (1604–51), third of the Tokugawa shoguns, invested in 1623. He intensified the persecution of the Christians and succeeded in sealing off the country. Under his rule, the Bakufu reached the height of its power.

TOKUGAWA IEYASU (1453–1616), a war-lord who, by making an alliance with Oda Nobunaga and later with Toyotomi Hideyoshi, managed to extend his power over the east. After Hideyoshi's death, the victory of Sekigahara (1600) assured his supremacy over the whole of Japan. In 1603 the emperor granted him the title *shogun* which conferred authority over the warrior class and legitimized the military government he had set up at Edo. In 1604 he destroyed the castle of Osaka, where Hideyoshi's son was threatening to rally the opposition. When he died he was canonized, and by imperial decree his ashes were interred in the sanctuary of Nikko. He gave the country peace through his many wars.

TOKUGAWA TSUNAYOSHI (1646–1709), fifth of the Tokugawa shoguns, who presided over the brilliant age of the Genroku.

TOSEIHA, controlling faction, a coalition of officers hostile to the rule of General Araki, Minister for War from 1931 to 1934; they accused him of weakening the army by dragging it into ideological conflict, thus hampering its modernization.

TOYAMA MITSURU (1855–1944), a militant supporter of expansionism and extreme nationalism. In 1879 he founded an action group for the 'rights of the people' (*minken*). In 1881 it became the Society of the Dark Ocean (*Genyosha*), which was to encourage expansion into Korea; twenty years later it was succeeded by the Society of the Black Dragon (*Kokuryukai*), which set its sights on Manchuria. Toyama Mitsuru took it upon himself to maintain the link between the ultra-nationalists and government circles. In his last years he was highly respected by the ruling classes as a veteran of the nationalist cause.

TOYOTOMI HIDEYOSHI (1537–98), a war-lord of humble origins, Oda Nobunaga's lieutenant, who in 1590 rose to be the second dictator capable of dominating the entire country.

TSU, competence, skill, expertise of a man of pleasure.

TSUJIGIRI, street attack – sometimes perpetrated by young samurai in adventurous mood.

TSUMEBARA, compulsory disembowelling, forced *seppuku*: in the Edo age, samurai condemned to death had to employ this method of self-execution.

UDAIJIN, 'minister of the right'. The imperial government as organized by the laws of the Taibho era in 702 was led, under the presidency of a great minister of state (*dajo daijin*), by a minister of the left (*sadaijin*) and a minister of the right (*udaijin*); the other ministries came under them.

UEDA AKINARI (1734–1809), scholar, poet and author of short stories, doctor, master of the tea ceremony, altogether an open-minded and enlightened man.

UEHARA YUSAKU (1856–1933), general, Minister for War, whose resignation in 1912 caused the fall of the Saionji cabinet.

UGETSU MONOGATARI ('Tales of Rain and Moonshine'), a collection of fantastical tales published in 1776 by Ueda Akinari.

UJI, a town a few miles south of Kyoto, beside the River Ujigawa.

UKIFUNE, 'Storm-tossed ship', title of the fifty-first chapter of *Genji monogatari*, which tells of a girl tossed by indecision between two princes.

UKIYO, 'floating world', originally a medieval Buddhist expression, adopted in the Edo period to mean the tempting and deceptive world of pleasure, which inspired *ukiyo-ye* painting and *ukiyo-zoshi* narrative.

UMEZU YOSHIJIRO (1882–1949), a general in the imperial army who in 1944 succeeded General Sugiyama as army chief of staff. As such he was one of the signatories of the surrender on board the aircraft carrier *Missouri*, 2 September 1945. He was found guilty by the Tokyo tribunal and died of disease in prison.

WAKIZASHI, 'side-dagger', an auxiliary weapon about a foot long, made (like the *katana*) of the highest-quality steel; the *bushi* of the Edo age had to bear both blades, the long and the short (*dai-sho*), in public, thrust through their belts.

WAKON YOSAI, 'Japanese spirit, Western knowledge', a slogan frequently used in the Meiji period by supporters of modernization combined with a careful preservation of Japanese identity.

YAKUO BOSATSU, the bodhisattva King-of-Healing-Medicines (Sanskrit *Bhasajya-raja*). In one of his previous existences, following the sutra of the Lotus, he abandoned his body by casting it into the flames.

YAKUZA, gangster, a member of one of the 2,500 organized gangs making up the Japanese underworld. There are thought to be over 100,000 *yakuza*.

YAMABUSHI, mountain-dwelling hermit, a name given to holy men who combine Shinto shamanism and Buddhist asceticism, striving to acquire superhuman powers by the practice of austerity. In the Heian age (794–1185), these ascetic mountain-dwellers gathered in a religious order called *shugendo*, which transmitted esoteric Buddhist teaching and secret ritual. Shugendo *yamabushi* were called upon to perform exorcisms and supply medicines.

YAMAGA SOKO (1622–85), savant, man of letters and historian, moralist in the Confucian tradition; in 1656 he published a study reflecting on the duties of the warrior class. He became friends with the first theoretician of *bushido*.

YAMAGATA ARITOMO (1838–1922). In his youth he took part on the struggle against the Tokugawa and became an important statesman under Meiji; after crushing the rebellion of Saigo Takamori he reorganized the army on the German model and strove to distance it from all political parties. He always acted in the interests of authoritarian conservatism, as formulated in the Imperial Rescripts of 1882 and 1890. As *genro* he controlled the appointment of Prime Ministers until his death.

YAMAMOTO ISOROKU (1884–1943), commander-in-chief of the navy during the Pacific War. He took a pessimistic view of the comparative strengths of the two armies and conceived the attack on Pearl Harbor so that at least he would enjoy the advantage of surprise. His plan of attack foundered at Midway Island in June 1942. The aeroplane carrying him on a tour of inspection was shot down on 18 April 1943.

YAMATO DAMASHII, the spirit of Yamato, the true spirit of Japan. This expression, which covers the virtues of courage, self-sacrifice, and sincerity conferred by nature on all those belonging to the Japanese race, was often used in the earliest years of Showa by ultra-nationalist demagogues playing on the native chauvinism of the mob.

YAMATO TAKERU NO MIKOTO, the Prince Brave-of-Yamato, a legendary character in the *Kojiki* and *Nihongi*, son of the emperor Keiko. He pacified Kyushu, and later the plain of Kano which was still peopled by barbarian tribes. On his way back to Yamato, he fell sick and died.

YANAGIDA KUNIO (1875–1962), the father of Japanese folklore studies, a talented writer. If there is such as a thing as the Japanese spirit, Yanagida thinks its origins should be sought in the ordinary people of past ages, and in popular tradition.

YASUDA ZENJIRO (1838–1921), financier, founder of the Yasuda banking and industrial group. He came from nowhere to build a fortune on speculation in the monetary fluctuations of the early Meiji years. He was at the head of the most powerful of the *zaibatsu* when he was killed by an ultra-nationalist.

YASUKUNI JINJA, sanctuary founded in Tokyo in 1869 by the Emperor Meiji for the repose of the souls of Japanese soldiers killed in battle. There are over 2,400,000 names inscribed on the tablets in the temple.

YAYOI BUNKA, Yayoi culture, name given to the period following the Jomon culture, three centuries before the birth of Christ, characterized by rice-growing in irrigated paddy-fields and by bronze and iron working, techniques brought over from the mainland.

YODOYA, a family of merchants from Osaka which made its fortune in the seventeenth century. In 1705, the head of the family was indicted for his ostentation; his fortune was confiscated and the whole family was banished from Osaka.

YONAI MITSUMASA (1880-1948), commander-in-chief of the imperial navy in 1936 and Minister of Marine in the Hayashi, Konoe and Hiranuma cabinets; he unsuccessfully opposed the Tripartite Alliance with the Axis powers. In January 1940, as Prime Minister, he was compelled to resign under army pressure. Minister of Marine in the Suzuki cabinet in 1945, he was one of the principal advocates of peace, in opposition to General Anami.

YOSANO AKIKO (1878-1942). In the early years of the twentieth century she vowed to renew Japanese poetry by giving sincere expression to feelings of love and personal convictions. Together with her husband, Yosano Tekkan, she always kept open house for new literary talent.

YOSHIDA SHOIN (1830-59), youthful patriot, teacher, tactician, sentimentalist and man of action, he alerted the elite of the Choshu principality to the need for a national awakening, in the spirit of the slogan *sonno joi*. He became involved in a plot against an officer of the shogun and was arrested, condemned to death and executed at Edo. His example inspired the struggle against the Tokugawa.

YOSHINO, a mountainous region on the Kii peninsula, in the south of Nara, where in 1336 the Emperor Go-Daigo established the court of the South, which strove to rival the court of the North (in Kyoto) until 1392. Yoshino has always been an important rallying-point for the *yamabushi*.

YOSHIWARA, the pleasure district of Edo, founded in 1617: it contained some 200 establishments and two or three thousand courtesans. It reached its apogee in the Genroku period (1688-1704) and declined towards the end of the eighteenth century.

YUI SHOSETSU (1605-51), professor of martial arts and military science, well known in Edo. He surrounded himself with unemployed *ronin*, and together with Marubashi Chuya, he plotted to overturn the Tokugawa government after the death of the shogun Iemitsu. When the conspiracy was discovered he killed himself.

YUJO, woman of pleasure, courtesan. In the Heian period, *asobine* prostitutes were travelling dancers, or conversely might be attached to travellers' hostelries. With the civil wars of the twelfth century appeared the first camp-followers. From the same period comes the earliest evidence of organized male prostitution. Under the Tokugawa organized pleasure districts grew up, controlled by the authorities. The law of 1872, liberating prostitutes, had little effect, and on this point the Meiji government followed the policies of Edo. In 1956 the law *Baishun boshi ho* outlawed prostitution and put an end to official tolerance.

YUKAKU, pleasure district containing numerous brothels. *Yuri* and *kuruwa* are used in the same sense. In 1585, Toyotomi Hideyoshi allowed the establishment of a pleasure district in Kyoto. The Tokugawa extended this: twenty-five strictly delimited pleasure districts were officially set up. The most famous were Yoshiwara in Edo, Shimabara in Kyoto, and Shinmachi in Osaka.

YUKOKU, 'Patriotism', a short story by Mishima Yukio written in summer 1960, narrating the *seppuku* of Lieutenant Aoshima at the end of the mutiny of the Young Officers in February 1936. In 1965, Mishima wrote and acted in a short film on the same theme; under the title *Rites of Love and Death* it won an award at the Tours Festival in January 1966.

ZEGEN, pander, seller of women. The sale of human beings had been officially illegal since the seventh century, so the *zegen*, who roved the countryside as agents for the brothels, would offer the family a lump sum in exchange for a contract of hire for the services of a girl over ten years.

ZEN, meditation, from the Sanskrit *dhyana*, a Buddhist school whose followers were bound to reach the awakening of *satori* by the exercise of mental concentration. The two leading Zen sects were introduced to Japan from China: *Rinzai* by Eisai in the twelfth century and *Soto* by Dogen in the thirteenth.

ZENGAKUREN, General Federation of Students, founded on 18 September 1948 to unite extreme left-wing student groups and co-ordinate their activities.

Index

Abelard 47
abortion 34
Abraham 110
action *see* phenomenalism
adultery 179–83
Aeschylus 4
Age of Warring Kingdoms (*sengoku jidai*) (1467–1568) 122–3
Ako affair *see* Forty-Seven *ronin*
Akutagawa Ryunosoke (author) 209, 245, 260, 267, 272
  suicide of 257–9
Alexander the Great 100
alienation 28–9, 33, 173
  see also nihilism
Amakusa Shiro 124
Ama no Uzume (goddess) 43, 52
Amaterasu Omikami (goddess) 43, 52
Amida Butsu (Buddha) 81, 110–11, 113–14, 116, 156, 176, 267
  Amidism 12, 108, 110–13, 115, 118, 126, 156, 167, 186: *see also* Pure Land sects
Amijinta 177

Amitabha *see* Amida Butsu (Buddha)
Anami Korechika, General 234, 236–7
anarchism *see* nihilism
Ancient Tombs, Age of 61, 208
Angela of Foligno 111, 167
animism 71, 119–21, 171
Annen (Buddhist monk) *quoted* 12
'anomie' (Durkheim) def 29, 250
  see also nihilism
Antigone (Sophocles) 5, 143, 176, 207
Antoku, Emperor 82–4
Aoshima, Lt 219
Apollinides 3
Araki Sadao, General 218, 221, 233
Arishima Takeo (author) 254
Aristotle 9, 119
Arles, Council of (452) 4–5, 8–9, 80, 100, 102, 172
Artaud, A. *quoted* 28
Asahi Heigo 212
Asakusa 133
Asano Naganori 141, 144–5
Asanuma Inejiro 212

Asashige Takauji 94
asceticism 106, 108–9, 112–13, 115–17, 119–20, 249
Ashikaga shogunate 94
Ashikaga Takauji 90
Ashura (demons) 98, 122
assassinations 78, 192, 201, 212–13, 216–17
Assembly in Honour of Souls 71
assisted suicides 2, 80–1, 88, 124, 131–2, 151–2, 200, 281
Association of the Black Dragon (*Kokurukai*) 203
Athens 5, 172
Atraud, A. 123
Atsugi 239
Augustine, St 87, 100–1, 110
  prohibition of suicide 3, 95, 102, 115, 119
Augustus, Emperor 4
Australia 223
Austria 14, 17
authority, Japanese concept of 43–4, 63
Auxerre, Council of 100
Awazu, battle of 81
Aztecs 52, 229

Barbey d'Aurevilly, J. A. 244, 259
Barrès, M. 247
Barthes, R. 208
Bateson, G. 137
Baudelaire, C. 245–6, 256, 267, 269
Beppo Shinsuke 200
Bismarck, Prince Otto von 191, 200, 261
Bizen, lord of 151
Boissonade, Gustave 135
Braga, Council of 100
Brahmins 106
Braun, Eva 235
Breton, André 254
Breuer, J. 285
Britain 191, 247
Buddhism 11–13, 48, 66, 68–71, 74, 97–101, 103–21, 148, 154, 156, 186–7, 221, 240, 264, 274

arrival in Japan 11–12, 67: and decline of violence 67–8, 138; proposal to ban 263
'becoming' (*samsara*) 12, 98–9, 103, 118
and death 51–2, 98–9, 99–100, 104, 107–8, 109–11, 188: antagonism to suicide 67–8, 71–5, 99, 249, 256, 266; ambiguity of antagonism to suicide 83, 103–4, 109–11; and other world 11–12, 52, 94, 115, 171–2
and love 156, 176
and suicide 249
see also Amida; Amidism; Jains; Siddhartha Gautama Buddha; *ukiyo*; Zen Buddhism; Pure Land sects
see also Ashura
Bukharin, N. 201
Bunraku puppet theatre 175
burial 181
  voluntary 104–6
Burma 221
bushi see samurai
bushido 2, 126–7, 127–30, 129–30, 137–40, 144–5, 265
  in Meiji era 189
  and Japanese army 203–4, 211, 218–20: *see also* Nogi Maresuke, General
  and Mishima 270, 275
see also samurai
Byron, Lord 248

Caligula, Emperor 7–8
Camus, A. 144, 244
capitalism
  Japanese and Western compared 31
Cathars 101, 156
Cato, Marcus Porcius (Uticensis) 1–4, 7, 11, 80, 101, 236
Cervantes, S. M. de 247
Cézanne, P. 257
Ch'ang Tso-Lin, Marshal 220

Charlevoix, Father 114
Chibi-Koga 279
Chikamatsu Monzaemon (playwright) 143, 146, 153–7, 160, 172–9, 182–5, 266
children 35–43
 as obligation on wife 46–7
 suicides of 35–9: with parent (*oyako shinju*) 48–9, 83–4; statistics 36
 see also education
China 11, 61, 109, 128, 134, 148
 cultural influence on Japan 66–7, 69–70, 104–5, 134–6, 140, 154–5, 180
 invasion of (1937) 193, 210, 217, 220–1, 223
 suicide statistics 17, 19
 see also Confucius; Manchuria; Sino-Japanese War
Cho, General 224
Choshu clan 150, 189, 204
Christianity 11, 13, 24, 39, 86, 100–4, 110–11, 117–18, 122, 126–7, 190, 207, 244–5
 Christ as sacrifice 54, 62, 110, 129, 257
 condemnation of suicide 3–5, 8–9, 22–3, 34–5, 44, 80, 100–1, 100–3, 107, 115, 124, 172–3, 181; distinction between self-sacrifice and suicide 29, 156, 252
 guilt and responsibility 46–7
 and homosexuality 162
 in Japan 114–15, 124–5, 133, 245, 248, 254, 257, 261, 263: persecution of 102, 133
 and love 156, 159, 167, 176
 see also crucifixion; Jesuits; Jesus Christ
Chushingura (Takeda Izumo) 196
clan loyalty 63–5, 76, 79–80, 95, 139–40, 142–6, 148–9
class struggle 31
Claudel, P. 99, 257
Cold War 16

collective suicides 79, 90–1, 248
Commodus, Emperor 133
companionship suicides (*junshi*) 62–4, 83–4, 127–9, 139, 204, 208–9, 281–2
 decline of 127–9, 140–1
 prohibition of 65–6
Confessions of a Mask (Mishima) 272, 274
Confucianism 61, 63–4, 94, 126, 128, 142, 148, 182, 186, 194, 283
 official ideology in Japan 140
 on government 67, 71, 134, 137–8, 145, 153, 191, 207
 on responsibility 38, 155
 and suicide: of accompaniment in death 139; lovers' 156, 176, 179; of reproof 211
 see also Wang Yang-Ming
Constant, B. 165
Corneille, P. 102, 155–6
courtesans *see* prostitution
cremation 66
Crevel, R. 267
crime 242, 276
 followed by suicide 40
 suicide as 172
crucifixion 133, 135, 143, 147, 185
Cynics 3, 100, 117

daggers 88
Daigo, Emperor 69
Dame aux Camélias, La 168
Dan no ura, battle of (1185) 83
Dazai Osamu 16, 266–72
dead, vengeance of 69–71, 171
death, Japanese attitudes to 13, 27, 51–3, 111–12, 190
 see also suicide
defeat
 as motive 3, 67, 78, 80, 233–4, 236–42
Demetrius 3
Democritus 106
Denmark, suicide rate in 14
 for women 46

despair
  as motive 5–6
Dezai (author) 16
Diderot 175, 264
Diocletian, Emperor 4–5, 133
disembowelling (*seppuku*) 33, 64, 86, 88, 95, 131, 182–3, 183, 211, 214–15, 222–4, 265
  ceremony of 96, 124, 130–3, 146–7
  collective 90–3, 219
  criticism and decline 93–6, 140–1, 144–7
  individual acts of 80–2, 89–90, 195–6, 198–9, 200, 209, 236–8, 281
  institution of 87–8
  as punishment 130, 133–6, 142–4, 151–2
  as samurai privilege 96, 124–5, 127–30
disguised suicides 26–7
Dogen (Buddhist monk) 12–13, 118–19
Dokyo (Buddhist monk) 67
Dolto, Françoise (author) 41
Doman (monk) 68
Donatist heresy 101
Dostoevsky, F. 24, 111, 243, 264, 274
dragons 119–21
drowning (*Jusui ojo*) 83–4, 112–15, 117, 119–21, 186–7, 268
  failure at 115–17
drunkenness 41
Duchac, R. (author) 15
duelling 73, 128, 141
Durkheim, E. 16, 21, 26, 28–30, 250–1, 262, 265
  see also '*anomie*'

economy, Japanese 181–2, 193, 202
  postwar economic revival 31–3, 242, 265: and suicide 265;
  suicide statistics 16–17, 19–20
'Edict of a Hundred Articles' (1742) 134, 136

Edo
  city 54, 133, 135–6, 142, 144, 162, 174, 179, 186: Yoshiwara district 162–4; see also Tokyo
  era see Tokugawa era
education 36–8, 49, 188, 192, 221, 252
  in China 148
  1890 Rescript 197
  suicide during 37
educational competition
  as motive 37–8
Eijumaru 91
Eirai no koe (Mishima) 276
Emerson, R. 248
Emperor of Japan see under Japan
endura 101
Enki (monk) 92
Enoshima 267
Epaminondas 183
Epictetus 6
Epicurus 8
error (*sokotsushi*)
  as motive 129
Esquirol, J. *quoted* 23
Essenin, S. 261
Etchu province 160
Eto Shipei 193, 201
evisceration see disembowelling
executions 78, 193, 204
  use of saw 136
exile 67, 69, 78
exorcism 68, 74, 172

Fa Hsien 104
failure
  as motive 38
families
  family suicides (*oyako shinju*) 48–9
  pressure on children 36–44
  pressure on lovers 156–9
  in West and Japan contrasted 33–4
Fascism 213
Feuerbach, L. A. 264
fire 100, 109, 117, 124

in Vietnam 109
Five Women who Loved Love (Saikaku) 184
flag, Japanese 205
Flaubert, G. 246–7, 255
Fleming (US pilot) 226
'Forty-Seven *ronin*' 141–6, 150, 174, 196, 204, 209, 265
 criticism of 144–6
France 32, 63, 126, 128, 141, 150, 181, 183, 191, 200, 209, 211
 suicide rates *tables* 14, 15, 17, 19, 22, 29
Francis Xavier, St 114–15, 122
Freedom Party (*Jiyuto*) 201
Freud, S. 23, 26–8, 40, 42, 47, 159, 164, 280, 285
 see also Oedipus
Fudaraku, Mt 114, 117, 187
Fudoki 51
Fuji, Mt 32
Fujimoto Kizan 165–6
Fujiwara clan 69, 76, 78
 Fujiwara no Akimitsu 68
 Fujiwara no Korechika 68
 Fujiwara no Michikane 68
 Fujiwara no Michinaga 68
 Fujiwara no Tokihira 70
Fukuoka 37
Fukuzawa Yukichi 148, 201, 245–7
funerals 61–2, 66, 209
 appeasement rites 69
 see also burial, voluntary
Furu-Koga 279, 281

Gall, E. J. 23
Gandhi, Mahatma 253, 264
Gauls 63
geishas see prostitutes
Gembun era 181
Genet, Jean 274
Genji clan *see* Minamoto clan and *Tale of Genji*
Genji Monogatari see Tale of Genji
Genroku era (1688–1704) 141, 147, 181

Genyosha see Society of the Dark Ocean
Germany 182, 205, 211, 225, 235
 suicide rates 17; women 46
 see also Prussia
ghosts 171–3
Gidarin-ji 115–16
Gide, A. 256
Gikei-ki (Minamoto no Yoshitsune) 85
gir (duty of gratitude) 154–6
Go-Daigo, Emperor 88, 218
Goethe, J. W. von 245, 247, 253–4, 256–7, 272
goro-e (Assembly in Honour of Souls) 71
Go-Toba, Emperor 88
Greece, ancient 3–5, 43, 183, 244, 273–5, 285
Guadalcanal, battle of 223
Guyana (1978) 91

Hachi no Miya 67
Hagakure, The 127, 131–2, 136–41, 161–2, 164, 183, 207, 212, 232, 275, 280
Hamada 214–15
Hamaguchi (Prime Minister) 220
hanging 64, 248–9, 268
haniwa (clay burial figures) 61–2
Hara, Lord 139
Haraguchi Tozo 269–71
harakiri see disembowelling (*seppuku*)
Hashino 139–40
Hegel, G. W. F. 6, 23, 57, 59, 75, 128, 251, 278
Heian era 72–3, 75–6, 109, 231, 241, 255, 264
 Heian Kyo (city) 55, 68–9, 75, 77–8, 112; *see also* Kyoto
Heike clan *see* Taira
Heishi clan *see* Taira
Heizei, Emperor 67
hell 52, 115, 172, 266–7
Heraclitus 13, 42, 98
Herodotus 61
Hibasu, Empress 62
Hibiya 212

Hiei, Mt 77
Hiraoka Kotaro 203
Hiro, Shinohara (author) 119
Hirohito, Emperor 227, 234–5, 264
  assassination attempt on 212
Hiroshima 234
Hitler, A. 235
hitobashira 54
Hizen clan 150
Hojo clan 88, 90
  Hojo Nakatoki 90–1
Hokkaido 211
Hölderlin 247, 249
homosexuality 127, 161–2, 183, 279–80
Honen 110, 114–15
  see also Pure Land sects
Hong Kong 221
Honjo, General 218
Horyuji temple 107
Hoshina clan 141
Hsuan Tsand 104
Hugo, V. 175, 258
Hui-Ko 108
Hungary 14
husbands 179–80
Huysmans, J. K. 244
Hyogo 94

I Am a Cat (Natsume Soski) 251
Ibsen 253
Ichigaya base 280
Ichigon Hodan 107
Ida, Colonel 236
Ihara Saikaku (playwright) 160–1, 169–70, 173, 183–7, 279
Ii clan 141
ikka shinju 48
Imai no Shiro 81–2
Imibe (guild) 53
immortality 8, 10, 41
  resurrection 56–7
Imperial Way (*Kodoha*) 217–18
India 11, 61, 67, 70, 74, 104, 115, 223, 253
Indonesia 221
infanticide 34

Inoue Junnosuke 214
Inukai Tsuyoki (Prime Minister) 216–17
in World War II
  suicides in; by civilians 224–5
Iphigenia 54
Ippen Shonin 108
Isaac 54, 62
Ise, temple of 192
Ishidomaru 113
Ishihara Shintaro (author) 16
Ishikawa Goemon 135
ishikozume see burial, voluntary
Islam 13, 63, 101
Itagaki Taisure 201
Italy 224
Iwate 34
Iwojima 225
  battle of 233
Izanagi (god) 51
Izanami (goddess) 43, 51
Izayoi and Seishin (Mokaumi) 183

Jacob, Max 257
Jains 99–100
Japan
  mortality statistics 19
  suicide: attitude to 2–3, 5, 10–11, 25–6, 41–2; ceremony of 2, 25–6, 85–6, 124, 130; and discontent with civilization 24; favoured locations 32–3, 249; by non-samurai 124–5, 173–9, 180, 253–5, 259–60
  suicide statistics 14, 17, 23–4, 28–9, 31–6, 250, 262: history of 23–4; by age 15, 34; compared to West 21; and murders 40; decline in around 1000 AD 71–4; of women 34; in eighteenth century 174; in World War II 224; postwar 14–16, 18–19, 265
  and West 193, 195, 202, 219, 221, 245–7, 246, 249, 252, 274: isolation in seventeenth century 125; arrival of foreigners in

seventeenth century 122; arrival of foreigners in nineteenth century 148
Japanese Air Force 225-7, 229, 239
Japanese Army 188-92, 194-5, 197, 199, 202-5, 211, 214-17, 234-5
   1882 Imperial Rescript: suicide 203, 217
   Law of National Mobilization (1938) 221
   political control by: coups and terrorism 218-19, 236; 1936 mutiny 218-20; effect on World War II surrender 225; in World War II 223-5, 234-7: demobilization of 239; suicide attacks 223, 225; *under* Meiji 215-16
   postwar restrictions on 264
   Self-Defence Force 277, 279-80
   see also Japanese Emperor
Japanese Emperor
   imperial myth 71, 191, 196-7, 213, 217-18, 238: in Meiji era 201-2; and Mishima 275-7; renunciation of divinity 264-5, 275-6; sacrifice of 53, 207
   practical position of 65: in Army 215, 221; assassination attempts on 212-13; in Heian era 75-7
   sacrifice of 234-5: *see also* individual emperors and eras
Japanese empire
   expansion of before World War II 193, 201, 203-6, 223
Japanese language 66-7
   proposal to ban 263
Japanese Navy 211, 214, 223, 225, 234
   naval air force 226-7
Jesuits 114, 124, 128-9
Jiao (god) 267
jibaku (self-destruction in war) 225-6
Jikisho (monk) 92

Jiroemon 91
Jiyuto (Freedom Party) 201
Jizo Bosatsu (bodhisattva) *see* Ksitigarbha
Jo, monk of 92
Job (prophet) 101
Jokyu era *see* Shokyu era
Jones, Rev Jm 91
joruri (ballads) 182
Judaism 13, 43, 70, 91, 226
   and voluntary sacrifice 54
Judas (apostle) 101
Jukai 32-3
Julius Caesar 3, 11, 63, 100
junshi see companionate suicide
Just, The (Camus) 144
justice 44
   as motive 5-6
Justinian 5
jusui ojo see drowning

Kabuki theatre 131, 143-4, 146, 174-5, 182-3, 274
Kacyapa 104
Kaempfer, Engelbert 133
Kafka 267, 269
Kagoshima town 194
kaizoebara (assisted *disembowelling (seppuku)*)
   see under suicide
Kamakura *bakufu* 2, 64, 86, 90, 180, 221
Kamakura (city) 79, 268: fall of 91-3, 219
kamikaze 194
   kamikaze pilots 225-33, 238-9: statistics 228-9
Kamo river 78
Kanadehon Chushingura (Chikamatsu) 143
Kanken 104
Kannon (bodhisattva) 110-11, 114, 156, 187, 267
kanshi see protest
Kant, I. 63, 226, 246
Kanto earthquake 255
karma 48, 86, 106, 109, 111, 241

Karuizawa 255, 257
Kasoya no Saburo Muneaki 91
Katsura, River 115
Katsura Taro 215
Katsushige, Lord 131–2
Kawabata Yasunari (author) 255, 283
Kawakami Hajime 261
Kaza matsuri (festival) 52
Kegon
 waterfall 249, 270
 school 108
Ketsumeidan see League of the Oath of Blood
Kido, Marquis 238
Kii peninsula 112, 114, 120
Kikuchi, Baron 217
King Lear 163
Kira Yoshinaga 141–6
Kita Ikki 216, 220
Kitamura Tokoku 247–9
Kitano sanctuary 71
Kiyomaro 67
Kiyomizu Temple 222
Kiyomori 78–9, 81, 83–4
Klein, Melanie 42
Kobe 152
Kobo Daishi *see* Kukai
Kochi 34
Kodama, General 204, 207
kofun jidai (Age of the Ancient Tombs) 60–1
Koga, Lt 216
Kojiki 51
Kokurukai see Association of the Black Dragon
Komoto, Colonel 220
Konishi Yukinaga 124
Konoe Fumimaro, Prince 222, 240–1
Korea 61
 Meiji invasion plans 193, 201, 203, 205, 215: annexation of (1910) 193, 210
Koreans 66, 255
Korean War 16
Koremori 116

Koromogawa 79
Koshoku ichidai onna (play) 161
Koshoku ichidai otoko (play) 161
Koskoku gonin onna (play) 160–1
Kotoku Shusui 212
Koya, Mt 104–5, 112
Kozaisho, Lady 82–3
Kropotkin, P. 254
Ksitigarbha (bodhisattva) 111
Kukai (Buddhist monk) 12, 104–6
Kumamoto 194–6, 280
Kumano sanctuary 112, 114, 187
Kuroda clan 141
Kurushima Tsuneki 211
Kusuhara, Lt-Cdr 211
Kusunoki Masashige 94, 97, 118, 189, 231
 widow of 94–5
Kusunoki Masasue 97
Kusunoki Masatsura 94
Kyoho era (1716–36) 181
Kyoto 208, 221
 Shimabara district 163
 University of 261
 see also Heian
Kyushu island 60, 69, 124, 193–4, 238

Lafargue, Paul and Laura 25
La Rochefoucauld, F. de 127
la Rochelle, Drieu 258
Lawrence, T. E. 284
'League of the Divine Wind' (*Shimpuren*) 194–5, 198, 280
'League of the Oath of Blood' (*Ketsumedan*) 214
Le Cid (Corneille) 155–6
Lévi-Strauss, C. 60, 143
Leyte, battle of 226, 233–4
Lhasa, Council of 109
liberty
 as motive 5–6
Life of an Amorous Man, The 169–70
Lillo, John (playwright) 175
love
 Confucian attitude to 155–6

as motive   57–60, 72–4, 153–87, 254–5, 276, 280–2: 1723 decree against *shinju*   180–2; Japanese and Christian attitudes   156–7, 167–8; *see also* adultery
Lucretia   101
Luther, M. *quoted*   47

Mabalacat   226
madness   4–5, 23–5, 80, 102–3, 172–3, 181, 282
Maeterlinck, M.   254
magic   68–71, 119
Mahasattva, Prince   107
Mahayana (Buddhist sect)   106, 109, 111, 114
Maitreya (Buddha)   104–5
Makarenko, A.   25
Malaysia   221
Mallarmé, S.   257
Manchuria, expansion into   193, 203, 210
  Manchurian Incident (1931)   220
Manichaeanism   13
Man'yoshu, The   57–9, 69, 73
Maoism   276
Mara (Buddhist god)   104
Marivaux, P. de   165
Marubashi Chuya   135
Marxism   25, 29, 31, 213, 254, 259–62, 267–8, 284
  see also Maoism
Masada   91, 226
Masaryk, T.   24, 29
Mashita, General   280
Matsudaira clan   144
  Lord of Sagami   137
  Matsudaira Hideyasu   140
Maupassant, H.   246
Mayakovsky, V.   260–1
Mazaki, General   218
Meiji, Emperor   146, 151, 207, 214, 224
  assassination attempt on   212
  death of   208
Meiji era (restoration)   17, 20, 54, 147–52, 150–1, 162, 188, 188–209, 245–52, 263
  1889 constitution   202, 213
  ideology of   95, 189–91
  oligarchs   189–90, 191, 193
  end of   215
Mexico   40
Midway, battle of   223
Mikawa province   52
miko (priestesses)   53, 60, 71
Mikuma (cruiser)   226
Mimana colony   61
Minamoto (Genji) clan   77–8, 81–3, 91, 112
  Minamoto no Tomonaga   78
  Minamoto no Yrimasa   80–1
  Minamoto no Yoritomo   85, 221
  Minamoto no Yoshitsune   79, 83, 85, 87–8
Minatogawa, battle of   94, 97
Minobe, Professor   190
Mishima Yukio   33, 100, 128, 161, 195, 219, 242–4, 271–86
  creates political faction   276–8
  death-wish of   275
  and success   272
  suicide of   281–5: Japanese reaction to   284–5
  Western influence on   275
Mitford, A. B.   151–2
Mitsushige   141
Miyakoji Bungonojo   182
Miyamoto Kenji   259–60
Miyekezaka   236
modesty
  as motive   55–6, 129
Mokauni (playwright)   183
monasticism   72, 75, 78–9, 113
Mongolia   210
  invasion of Japan (1274)   88
  invasion of Japan (1281)   88, 194, 227
Montesquieu, C. L. de Secondat   134
Mori, General   236
Mori Arinori   192
Mori Ogai (author)   253
Morinaga Shinno, Prince   88–9

Morita 279, 281, 284
Mukden 220
munenbara see vengeance
Murakami Yoshiteru 88–9
Murasaki Shikibu 74
  see also Tale of Genji
murder 40
  suicides after 211, 214
Muromachi era 180
Myoe Shonin 108

Nabeshima clan 141
  Nabeshima Naoshige 139
  Nabeshima Tsunashige, Prince 128
Nachi 112, 119–20
Nagai Kafu (author) 255
Nagano 233
Nagasaki 234
  lord of 92
Nagatsuka, Pilot Officer 230
Nagumo, Admiral 224
Nanking 240
Napoleon, Emperor 183
Nara era 68, 109, 154
narcissism 44–5, 55
National Association for the Service of the Empire (*Taisei sankai*) 221–2
nationalism 189–92, 203, 212–13, 216–17, 242
  patriotic leagues 210, 213–14: *see also* League of the Divine Wind; League of the Oath of Blood; Virtuous League of the Country of the Gods; *see also* Society of the Black Dragon; Society of the Cherry Tree; Society of the Dark Ocean; *see also* Society of the Shield
Natsume Soseki (author) 251–2
Nechaiev, S. 212
nembutsu 115, 116
Nero, Emperor 236
Nichiren sect 109
Nietzsche, F. W. 7, 10, 13, 24, 41, 44, 50, 97, 99, 166, 243–4, 259, 264, 273, 275–6, 283

Also Sprach Zarathustra 243, 250, 275, 278
  Will to Power, The 243
nihilism 99, 212–13, 243–62, 266, 271, 274, 277
Nihongi, The 51, 62
Niigara 34
Nikko forest 249
Nîmes, Council of 100
Nintoku, Emperor 55–7, 61
Nirvana 99
Nishida Zei 220
Nitobe (author) 87, 189
Noashige (person) 131–2
Nogi Maresuke, General 204–5, 207–10, 212–13, 237, 239, 243, 251, 253–4, 256, 258, 283
Nomi, Lord 62
non-violence 68
No theatre 111, 113, 171
Novalis (Leopold, F.) 244

Oda Nobunaga 125, 128
Oedipus
  complex 40–2, 42–3, 46, 154, 158
  myth 47–8, 53–4, 97, 269, 274, 285
  play (Sophocles) 176
Ogawa 279
Ogyu Sorai 145
oibara 127, 139
Oishi 141–3, 146
Okabe Hirakuze 232
Oka Masafumi 250
Okazaki (author) 14–15
Okinawa 224, 230
  battle of 223, 229, 233
Okudaira Tadamasa 141
Okuma Shigenobu, Marquis 201, 211
Onin era (1467–77) 123
Onin War 221
Onishi Takijiro, Vice-Admiral 226–7, 229, 231, 233, 237–8
opium 134
Origen 111

Orléans Council of 100
Orphism 9, 51
Osaka 124, 126, 143, 148, 160, 174–5, 178–9, 181, 204
  prostitution in 163
Osazaki, Prince 55–7
Oshio Heihachiro 148–204
Oshiyama, Lord 55
Osugi Sakae (anarchist) 255
Otomo no Tabito *quoted* 12
Ototachibana, Princess 55–6
oyaku shinju see under children and families

Parsva 100
Pasolini, P. 274
patriotic leagues 210, 213
Patriotic Party (*Aikokuto*) 242
Patriotism (Mishima) 274
Paul, St 102, 118, 167
Pavese, Cesare 268
Pearl Harbour 222–4, 234
Peking 220
Pelagia, St 101, 240
Peregrinus 100, 117
peripatetics 3
phenomenalism and emphasis on action 11–12, 47–8, 86–7, 95, 127, 146–7, 155, 159, 165, 213, 253–4, 273, 278
Philippines 221
  battle of the 226–7
Pindar 10, 13
Plato 1, 8–10, 44, 95, 119
  Platonism 3, 11, 13, 86
pleasure
  Japanese view of 52
Plutarch *quoted* 1–2, 282
poison 241, 258, 267
Poland
  suicide rate for women 46
political blackmail
  as motive 202, 214
political parties, foundation of 201
Port Arthur (1904) 204, 206–7, 210–11, 222, 252
Potalara, Mt 114

Potsdam Declaration 234
poverty 31–2, 265
prostitution 159–60, 162–4, 167–74, 176, 181, 185–6
  in theatre 182
protest (*kanshi*)
  as motive 128, 141–2
Proust, M. 267
proxy suicides 139–40
Prussia 191
  see also Germany
punishment (*tsumebara*)
  as motive 57, 130–1, 133–5, 133–7, 141, 144, 151–2: abolition of 150; decline of 68; witnesses to 151–2; *see also* self-punishment
Pure Land sects 11, 84, 110–12, 114, 116, 118, 261, 267
Pythagoras 9

Red Army Faction 283–4
religion 245, 263
  as motive 97–121
  see also Buddhism; Christianity; Shintoism
reproof
  as motive 211–12
resentment (*sunshi*)
  as motive 128
responsibility 38–9, 44–8, 128–9
Richelieu, Cardinal de 141
Rigaut, Jacques 267
Rimbaud, A. 268, 270
Risshisha 201
Robespierre, M. 213
Rolland, R. 254
romanticism 57–60, 74, 244, 246–9, 276, 282
Rome, ancient 1–5, 7–8, 11, 101–2, 134, 244
ronin 135, 141–4, 149, 162, 183
  see also Forty-Seven *ronin*
Rougemont, Denis de 156
Rousseau, J.-J. 28, 246
Runaway Horses (Mshima) 195–6
Russia 211–12, 217

and suicide statistics 25
  in World War II 233–4
  see also below and Port Arthur
Russo-Japanese War 193, 206–7, 210–11, 225, 251
  see also Port Arthur

Saburo Hyoei 91
sacrifice
  in Buddhism 100, 106–8, 110
  in Christianity 100
  to the dead 61: substitutes for 61–4
  of emperor 53, 207
  human 53–5, 61–2
  in Japanese animism 52–3
  as motive 29, 34, 212–14
  self-sacrifice see suicide
  in Shinto 52
Sadaneo (governor of Mutsu) 93
Sade, de 226, 274
Saga insurrection 201
Sago 213
Saigo Takamori 149, 193–4, 199–201, 204–5, 217, 246
Saigon 109
Saikaku see Ihara Saikaku
Saint-Lo (aircraft carrier) 227
Saionji Kinmochi, Prince 214–15
Saipan 224–6, 233–4
Saito, General 224
Sakaguchi Ango (author) 265–6, 276
Sakurakai see Society of the Cherry Tree
Sakura Sogoro 147
samsara see becoming *under* Buddhism
Samson 101
samurai 77–96, 123–4, 133–4, 205, 277, 280
  and death 80, 98, 137–40
  decline of 150–2, 188, 193–6, 266: final stand 200
  ethic see *bushido*
  in Meiji era 146, 148–50, 193
  statistics 194
  and Tokugawa peace 126, 136–8, 137, 163
Sanuki-no-san-i 117
Sartre, J.-P. 269
Sasaki Hachito 230–1
Sato Eisaku (Prime Minister) 282
satori (illumination) 12
Satsuma province 150, 189
  rebellion in 194–5, 203
School of Peers 253–4
Schopenhauer, A. 99, 249
Scythians 61
Sea of Fertility, The (Mishima) 278
Seifukuji 151
Seikanji (Edo) 164, 181
Seiwa, Emperor 71
Sekigahara, battle of (160) 124, 148, 150
sekigunha see Red Army Faction
sekinin jisatsu see responsibility 48
self-mutilation 165–6, 169
self-punishment
  as motive 39, 129–30, 248, 282
Seneca 1, 7
Sengakuji 142, 146
sengoku jidai see Age of Warring Kingdoms
seppuku see disembowelling
Setegaya 219
Settsu, lord of 92
Shakespeare, W. 164, 245
Shakyamuni (Buddha) 12
shame 39–40, 42, 48
  as motive 136–7
Shanghai
  'three brothers' incident 226
Shelley, P. B. 246
Shiga Naoya (author) 263
shikarare jisatsu 45
Shikegage 113
Shikido okagami (Fujimoto Kizan) 165–6
Shikoku 205
Shimabara 182
Shimane 34
Shimazaki Tosn (author) 246

Shimpuren see League of the Divine Wind
Shinagawa district   133
Shine'emon (person)   92
Shingon (Buddhist sect)   68
Shingon sect   12
Shingon sect of Japanese Buddhism   106
Shinju Okagami (Shokoken)   157–9, 183
shinju see love as motive
Shinju Ten no Amijima   175, 179
Shinju Yoigoshin (play)   153–5, 179
Shinran   110, 114–15
   see also Pure Land sects
Shinto   51–4, 72, 194, 204
   and asceticism   108
   blood taboo   130
   proposal to ban   263
   rituals and sacrifices   52–4, 61
Shirakaba (review)   253, 256, 263
Shoen Okagami (Saikaku)   160
Shohoken (author)   157–9, 183
Shokyu era (1219–22)   88
shooting   239–40
Showa Restoration movement   146, 190, 193, 200, 216
Siberia   203
sickness
   as motive   8
Siddhartha Gautama Buddha   92, 99–100, 104, 106, 108, 112, 119
sincerity   204, 219, 266
Sino-Japanese War (1894–5)   205, 211, 220–1, 226, 247
slavery   5–7, 9, 102–3
socialism   213
   and suicide   24–5
Society of the Black Dragon   211, 214
Society of the Cherry Tree (*Sakurakai*)   216
Society of the Dark Ocean   203, 211
Society of the Shield   276–80
Socrates   9–10, 100, 220
Soga Iruka   67
Sonezaki shinju (play)   173–6, 181

Sophocles   4, 143
sorcery   68
soul   98
Sound of Waves, The (Mishima)   273
Sparta   134
Spinoza   264
Spitz, R.   35
Stalin, J.   9–10, 200
starvation   101, 169–70, 205, 253
Stendhal   127
Stoicism   3, 7–8, 11, 244
Strindberg   253, 257
Sugawara no Michizane   69–71, 144, 171
Sugiyama Hajime, General   240–1
suicide
   in Ancident World   1–11, 80, 100
   historically conditioned   49–50
   'social suicide'   28
   typology of   27–9
   see also countries, methods, motives and types
Suinin, Emperor   62
Sun and Steel (Mishima)   275
sunshi see suicide of resentment
superego   39–42, 44
Susanoo (god)   43
suttee   61
Suzuki Kantaro, Admiral   233–4
Switzerland
   suicide rate for women   46
swords   80–1, 86, 131–3, 223
   banning of, among samurai   194–5

Tadanobu   87
Taiheiki   93
Taiho legal code   109
Taika ('Reform') era   66, 264
Taira clan   77, 82–3
   Taira-Minamoto struggle   77–8
Taira no Koremori, General   112–13
Taira no Munekiyo   78
Taisho restoration movement   190, 212, 255
Takahashi Kurosaemon   91
Takarabe Takeshi, Admiral   214

Takashige (person) 92
Takashimadaira (Tokyo) 32
Takatoki (regent) 91–2
Takemoto puppet theatre 174–5
Takeshita, Colonel 236
Taki Zenzaburo 151
Tale of Genji 67, 71–5, 179, 255
tamamushi zushi 107
Tamehisa 81
Tanaka, General 239–40
Tanizaki Jun'ichiro (author) 255
Tannhäuser 168
Taoism 126, 233
Tateyama, Mount 160
Tathagatas (some Buddhist élite) 104
Tel-Aviv airport massacre 283–4
Temple of the Golden Pavilion, The (Mishima) 274
Tempsi, Mount 70
Tendai sect 12, 106, 109
Tenno see Emperor 264
Tenno shugi (imperial cult) 217
Tenno shugi (imperial doctrine) 193
Terauchi Hisaichi, General 214
terrorism 210–17, 220, 277, 284
  moral justification of 213–14
Tertullian 101
theatre 174–9, 182–3, 283, 285
  see also Bunraku theatre; No theatre; Kabuki theatre; Takemoto puppet theatre
Theresa, St 102, 167
Thomas Aquinas, St 119
Tiberius, Emperor 7–8
time 12–13
Tissot, C.-J. 24
Togo Heihachiro, Admiral 225
Togo Shigenori (foreign minister) 234
Tojo Hideki, General 222, 224, 240–1
Tokinobu 90
tokkotai see kamikaze
Tokugawa clan 109, 124, 129, 148–50, 189, 194
  Tokugawa Hidetada 133
  Tokugawa Iemitsu 133, 140–1

Tokugawa Ieyasu 124–6, 133, 140
Tokugawa Tsunayoshi 142
Tokugawa (Edo) era 54, 124–50, 153–4, 161, 167–8, 171–2, 181–2, 190–1, 193, 218
  compared to Meiji era 192
  resistance to 197
Tokyo 146, 209, 218, 224, 238–9, 255, 279–80
  earthquake (1923) 53
  University 269, 271, 277
  Yoshiwara district 162, 181
  see also Edo
Toledo, Council of 100
Tolstoy, L. 245, 254, 261
Tono (servant) 81
torture 183
Tosa clan 150, 201
Toseiha faction 217
Toyama Mitsuru 214
Toyotomi Hideyoshi 125, 135
transcendence 10
  and Zen Buddhism 118
Traviata, La 167–8
Trotsky, L. 200
Troyes, Council of 100
tsumebara see punishment
Tsunetomo (author of Hagakure) 161–2, 164
'True Pure Land' sect 110

Ueda Akinari (author) 171
Uehara Yusaku, General 215
Ueno 163
Ugaki, Vice-Admiral 238
Ugetsu monogatari 171
Uji 81
ukiyo (illusion) 161, 164–7
Umezu Yoshijiro 234
Unahi, maid of 57–60, 69–70
Ur of the Chaldees 61
USA 210, 254
  suicide rate for women 46
  and World War II 222–6, 229, 239
Ushijima, General 224

USSR *see* Russia
Usugi clan   144
Utsonomiya factory   240

Vache, J.   267
Valéry, P.   128–9
Van Gogh, V.   28
Vatel (majordomo)   48
Vedantism   13
vendetta (*katakiuchi*)   141–4
vengeance (*munenbara*)   141–4
  for adultery   179
  of the dead   69–71
  as motive   128
Venice   163
Verdun, battle of   206
Verlaine, P.   257, 267
Vietnam   109
Villon, F.   186
'Virtuous League of the Country of the Gods' (*Shinshu gidan*)   212
Vishinsky, A.   200–1
Voltaire, F.-M. Arouet de   258
Vos, G. de   45

wakizashi   88
Wang Yang-Ming   148, 194, 199, 204, 217, 254
Waseda University   279
Werther   174, 182
Whitman, W.   254
widows
  in Japan   34–5
Wilde, Oscar   256
will   244, 249
  in Buddhism   100, 104
  in Christianity   47, 108
  and Japanese militarism   123–4, 203–4, 223, 227, 231, 235
  in Nietzsche   282, 285
William the Silent   199
Will to Power (Nietzsche)   243
women   139–40, 176, 248
  and adultery   179–80
  conditions in Japan   34–5, 46–7, 154–5
  sacrifice of   53–5

suicide rates   34, 46, 49
suicides of accompaniment   62, 82–3, 124, 153–4, 240, 257, 267–8: for love   57–60, 72–5, 82–3, 179–83
mothers   38–43, 48–9, 63, 118: suicides of   216; statistics of suicides   49
mothers-in-law   153–5
see also prostitution
Wordsworth, W.   246
work   5–6, 33, 242
  as solution to suicide problem   29–30
World War I   193
World War II   182, 220–1, 222–37, 255, 261
  casualties   224
  postwar suicides   241–2
  suicides in   233–4
  suicide statistics   16, 18, 262
  war crimes tribunal   241
  see also kamikaze and under Japanese Army

Yaksukuni jinja   224
Yakuo-bosatsu   109
yakuza   242, 276
Yamaga Soko   129–30
Yamagata Aritomo, General   200–1, 203–5, 210, 215–16, 222
Yamagishi, Lt   216
Yamamoto Isoroku, Admiral   223
Yamamoto Kichizaemon   131
Yamamoto Tsundekomo   141
Yamamoto Tsunemoro   138
Yamamoto Tsunetomo   131–2, 144
Yamashiro (prince imperial)   67
Yamato, plain of   60–1
Yamato Takeru no Mikoto   54–5, 196
Yanagita Kuno (author)   53
Yanami, Lord of Musashi   139–40
Yasuda Zenjiro   212
Yayoi period (to 250 AD)   60
Yodoya family   181
Yokawa   78

Yokohama earthquake (1923)   53
Yokoyam Yasutake   195
Yonai Mitsumasa   234
Yosano Akiko   206–7
Yoshida Shoin   204, 217
Yoshino mountains   88
Yoshitomo   78
youth   35–6, 241
Yudono, Mount   106
Yui Shosetsu   135

Yuryaku, Emperor (457–79)   133

Zarathustra *see* Nietzsche
Zen Buddhism   12–13, 86, 108–10, 118–19, 138, 186, 204, 232, 256, 261, 274
Zengakuren movement   277
Zola, E.   246, 256–7
Zoroastrianism   13